AN ETHIC FOR ENEMIES

AN ETHIC
FOR ENEMIES

Forgiveness in Politics

DONALD W. SHRIVER, JR.

OXFORD UNIVERSITY PRESS

New York   Oxford

Oxford University Press

Oxford   New York
Athens   Auckland   Bangkok   Bogata   Bombay   Buenos Aires
Calcutta   Cape Town   Dar es Salaam   Delhi   Florence   Hong Kong
Istanbul   Karachi   Kuala Lumpur   Madras   Madrid   Melbourne
Mexico City   Nairobi   Paris   Singapore   Taipei   Tokeyo   Toronto   Warsaw
and associated companies in
Berlin   Ibadan

Published by Oxford University Press, Inc.
198 Madison Avenue, New York, New York 10016

First issued as an Oxford University Press paperback, 1997.

Oxford is a registered trademark of Oxford University Press, Inc.

Library of Congress Cataloging-in-Publication Data
Shriver, Donald W.
An ethic for enemies : forgiveness in politics /
Donald W. Shriver, Jr.
p.   cm.   Includes bibliographical references and index.
ISBN 0-19-509105-1; ISBN 0-19-511916-9 (Pbk.)
1. Christianity and politics.
2. Forgiveness–Secular aspects–Christianity.
3. United States–Politics and government–20th century.
4. Civil society.
5. Political ethics.
I. Title.
BR115.P7S514   1995
172—dc20   94-14773

5 7 9 8 6 4

Printed in the United States of America
on acid-free paper

Dedicated to the Memory of

the One Hundred Million Humans Who Perished

in Wars of the Twentieth Century

Though Dead They Yet Speak

Acknowledgments

This book has been a long time gestating. It began in my experience as pastor of a small congregation in North Carolina, where I first confronted the problem of how groups of humans can combine moral judgment with enough forbearance and empathy to hold the group together. My interest in that problem expanded during my graduate work when I posed it in the context of a mental hospital, its broad tolerance for the antisocial behavior of its patients, and the limits it imposed on them for the sake of their healing and its institutional existence.

My suspicion that there is such a thing as forgiveness in politics was then roused, in the 1960s, by active participation in the civil rights movement and the coalitional politics of the North Carolina Democratic Party. In both of these settings I learned that group resentments against other groups often have deep roots in memories of a traumatic past and that the ability of former enemies to live in some degree of *civic*—and civil—relation to each other is a complicated, socially indispensable maneuver. Robert Frost's line, "To be social is to be forgiving," impressed me in all these relations as sober realism.

That realism dawned even more clearly on me during the years of the seventies and eighties, when I undertook the presidency of an ecumenical theological seminary whose variety of constituents and mixes of diverse opinion guaranteed regular eruptions of conflict that could only be contained when some of the participants took care to ask the questions that underlie this book: What moral wrongs, and what memories of the same, do we bring to our conflicts with other human beings? What difference does a process of listening to other people's experience of hurt make to the building of some new communal relation between them? And if the building of relationships is at the heart of *ethics*, how can that goal be served rather than frustrated by the moral judgments which hostile groups often make about each other?

Slowly, over these years, I have arrived at the belief that the concept of forgiveness, so customarily relegated to the realms of religion and personal ethics, belongs at the heart of reflection about how groups of humans can move to repair the damages that they have suffered from their past conflicts with each other. Precisely because it attends at once to moral truth, history, and the human benefits that flow from the conquest of enmity, *forgiveness* is a word for a multidimensional process that is eminently political. The purpose of this book is to explore that process as it unfolds in some of the great traumatic events of twentieth-century human affairs.

In the research and writing I found myself indebted to many a teacher and companion: to H. Richard Niebuhr, who taught me the meaning of ethics focused on mutualities of value and interests in the webs of history; to James Luther Adams, Robert Bellah, James Gustafson, Hans Hofmann, and Robert Rapoport, supervisors of my doctoral thesis on forgiveness, who encouraged me to take my own experience and convictions as seriously as those of others; to numerous academic colleagues at North Carolina State University, who for ten years demonstrated to me that one of the most political of institutions—the university—can become political in the best sense of the word if its leaders will practice among themselves the art of patient listening; to colleagues at Union Theological Seminary who not only, from time to time, forgave the sins of their president but who read or discussed this manuscript—especially George Landes, Robin Scroggs, Richard Norris, Larry Rasmussen, Kosuke Koyama, and James Cone; to Glen Stassen of Southern Baptist Theological Seminary; to Helmut Reihlen of Berlin, president of the Berlin-Brandenburg Synod of the Evangelical Church in Germany; to Eberhard Bethge of Bonn; to Lionel Shriver of Belfast for her careful preparation of the index; to my two able research assistants at Union, Roger Sharpe and Richard Knox; and to Cynthia Read for her equally careful work as my editor at Oxford University Press.

In her patient, searching conversations with me about the text and themes of this book, no person has been more helpful in its writing than my wife Peggy L. Shriver, whose acuity in things literary, theological, and political never fails to astonish me.

In addition I am indebted to colleagues in Great Britain who organized and participated in the Forgiveness and Politics Project of the British Council of Churches in the early 1980s, especially Martin Conway, the chairman, and Brian Frost, its tireless editor and organizer. Haddon Wilmer of Leeds University, another participant in the project, has been one of its intellectual pioneers; from him I have also learned much.

Finally I want to thank an array of political leaders, church leaders, and scholars in six universities in South Africa, with whom I discussed the principal themes of this book during three months of a visit to that country in early 1992. Although I have been careful to follow the advice of more than one of them—"We hope you stay in South Africa long enough *not* to write a book about us!"—they have, almost to a person, strengthened my belief that at some junctures of socially devised human evildoing, the only way to recover is the way of political forms of forgiveness. The viewpoint of this book is American; I want to know how Americans might understand and enact an ethic for their enemies. But for this effort the people of South Africa have much to teach us, as do the people of many another culture around the world. Among all the groups of people who have moved me to write this book, however, no one else has influenced me quite as much as a company of friends, fellow Christians, ministers, and academic colleagues in the community of African Americans. I am white, male, southern-born, and in many ways an American of privilege.

Over the decades, African Americans have been my teachers in matters of justice, forbearance, empathy, and the dream of a political order in America hospitable to all sorts and conditions of human beings. In their embodiment of that dream and their persistence in pursuing it, I count myself among their students. They will have to judge if I have been a good learner of what they have to teach us all.

New York   D. W. S.
May 1994

Contents

AN ETHIC FOR ENEMIES

Introduction

In the aftermath of the most destructive urban riot in American history, the man whose case ignited it all touched millions of Americans when he said: "People, I just want to say, you know, can we all get along? . . . I mean, we're all stuck here for a while. Let's try to work it out."[1]

In those simple words Rodney King was implicitly defining *politics*: how humans "get along" with each other in spite of their conflicts.

So defined, the political is one of our most necessary and most fragile human achievements. From a million years back, we have been a fractious species. Fighting comes easily to us. But cooperation had to come too, or else we might not have survived our own combativeness.

This is a book about how human enemies, some or all of whom have greatly harmed each other, can grope toward political association again; if they are not to be derailed from that goal, they will find themselves practicing a collective form of forgiveness.

How necessary, and how lacking, forgiveness is in the ordinary push and pull of human politics has many contemporary illustrations, but none more graphic and horrible than the civil war in the former Yugoslavia. The world cringes at a Serb's willingness to kill a Muslim in revenge for ancestors who fought the Battle of Kosovo in the year 1389; but in fact every nation has among its citizens those who have vast unresolved resentments against the descendants of some other group of citizens. The majority of us are apparently a long way from ceasing to hold the sins of the ancestors against their living children. Were the ancestors still living, we might be willing to refight our wars with them. In the early 1990s, one did not have to travel to Bosnia to find vivid examples of that truth in the life of the United States of America. As Euro-Americans prepared to celebrate the 500th anniversary of Columbus's voyages, a mixed chorus of domestic voices rose in protest: "Our ancestors had nothing to celebrate in that landing. Neither do we." It was one way of saying—if one were African American, Hispanic American, or Native American—that something more moral than Euroimperialism had better be at the base of a publicly shared memory capable of uniting the United States of America.

The critics of the Columbus Quincentennial did not deny that the European discovery of the New World was an historic event; but they insisted on remembering it
from the standpoint of those who suffered most from it. What "your" people did to
"my" people is a thought that haunts political argument here. In part the argument is
over what memories of the past are mandatory for everyone in a community to own
up to—if it is not to be a community forever divided by clashing assessments of the
crimes of ancestors.

I have written this book chiefly to address the frame of mind which resists dealing
with the leftover debris of national pasts that continue to clog the relationships of
diverse groups of humans around the world. The debris will never get cleaned up
and animosity will never drain away until forgiveness enters these relationships in
some political form. To dismiss this concern as a preoccupation with ancient history
is to miss all the evidence for the truth that William Faulkner put on the lips of one
of his characters: "The past is not dead and gone; it isn't even past."

Americans, in general, find this truth hard to comprehend, for ours is a culture
that disparages history in our drive to get on with the future. We tend to forget that
memory, one taproot of civic peoplehood, can also be a time bomb ready to explode
into political conflict.

A visit to Romania some ten years ago underscored for me the difficulty of achieving a sense of shared citizenship between groups of people with a long-slumbering
history of mutual hostility. As I casually mentioned to my Romanian Orthodox Church
companion the fact that I had German immigrant ancestors who came to Philadelphia in 1688, he commented that the Germans in western Romania were now mi-
grating back to the land of their ancestors in great numbers. "I think they should all
go back to Germany," he mused. "They have been here only 500 years." At first I
thought he was joking. Not so; "real" Romanians trace their ancestry back to the first
century C.E., when the Romans settled Dacia. For him a 2,000-year-old ethnic identity defined rights of membership in his political community. And if sheer ethnic
history were not enough to justify sending the Germans back "home," there were
plenty of sins of the Austro-Hungarian Empire to throw into the brew of reasons for
doing so.

At first blush a contemporary American is likely to dismiss these things as aspects
of the European provincialism and oppression that many of our immigrant ancestors
crossed the Atlantic to escape. We decry the current violence of neo-Nazis in Germany. We applaud the banner slogan of their German counterdemonstrators: "Yesterday, Jews; Today, Turks." We sigh with relief that we live in a country that for
long has been building one nation from many nations—*e pluribus unum*.

But then a Los Angeles riot and the poignant plea of a Rodney King bring that
comforting thought up short, reminding people like me that in 1688 African slaves
were also crossing the Atlantic. King's ancestors have been a part of American life
longer than have my German ancestors. His Hispanic American neighbors can boast
of forbears who inhabited the now American Southwest long before the "Pilgrim
Fathers." And there is a coterie of Los Angelenos who trace their yet older ancestry
back to tribes that Columbus mistook for Indians. Already in southern California these
folk form a majority of the population; sometime in the first half of the twenty-first
century, demographers tell us, they will compose a nonwhite majority of the people

of the United States. Like Langston Hughes, many of these contemporaries confess that "America has never been" for them. With Rodney King, many hope that "America will be"—an America in which neither ethnicity nor centuries of residence counts for citizenship and in which ancestral crimes no longer poison the civic relationships of their descendants.[2]

The world—with the United States— has a long journey to such a day. To arrive there, we must dig up buried memories that haunt our current politics, especially so long as we remain unconscious of their power. Southern-born as I am, like Faulkner, I have long understood that in political and military defeat a people may take a very long time to compose relations with a victorious enemy. Perhaps, among Americans, southerners were best equipped by their Civil War experience to help the people of this country to recover from national defeat in Vietnam. Real political recovery from catastrophic, unjust suffering involves some really new relationships with enemies and their descendants. Eventually, if they are not simply to go to war again with each other, former enemies must find a way of living together. Sometimes soldiers see this more clearly than their civilian supporters. On the last day of the American Civil War, Confederate General Robert E. Lee signed the surrender papers in the McLean House at Appomattox. Before Lee's departure, Grant introduced his staff. One of them was his military secretary, Ely Parker, a Seneca Indian. In a gracious gesture Lee remarked to him, "I'm glad to see one real American here." To this Parker replied as graciously—and with political acumen for what the war had been all about: "We are all Americans." Grant himself soon ordered his troops to cease their celebratory gun salutes: "The war is over, the rebels are our countrymen again, and the best sign of rejoicing after the victory will be to abstain from all demonstrations."[3]

In his own poignant way, Rodney King, too, was saying, "We are all Americans." Will the planet earth ever host a species who, by a great majority, will gladly say, "We are all humans?" When moralists and religious visionaries express that hope, they are often accused of being unpolitical idealists. But the human world of the twenty-first century is shaping up as a world in which peace among nations is a practical necessity, not merely an elusive, optional ideal. As he stood before the Lincoln Memorial in 1963 to deliver his "I Have a Dream" speech, Martin Luther King, Jr., was expressing something more than a pious hope for the future of the United States and the world. By 1963 he had already suffered the diatribes, the prisons, the rocks, and sundry other expressions of the politics of exclusion. But in that year, world reality was on the side of the politics of inclusion. It was not just visionary idealism that would impel King to write a sentence like: "We must either learn to live together as brothers, or we are all going to perish together as fools."[4] The world's nearest brush with nuclear war was hardly a year past as King insisted on his dream. The great devastations of the Vietnam War were in the making. Many Americans may have basked in a prosperity not yet under attack from worldwide economic competition, but the global village was already high on the horizon of King's vision. We were, all of us, on our way to *having* to learn to live with neighbors not of our choosing. As King said to an angry, rock-throwing white teenager in Louisville, "You're going to grow up in a world that we're going to live together in."[5]

Enmity and enemies are not likely to disappear from the human scene anytime in the future, but our politics had better take into new account the *access* the world's peoples have to each other for mutual good and evil. The Persian Gulf War of 1991, the 1992 civil war in the former Yugoslavia, and the 1993 bombing of New York's World Trade Center were reminders of that great new fearsome fact of the late twentieth century, which alerts all of us to our unprecedented self-interest in Rodney King's hope that we can "get along." We are certainly "all stuck here for a while." Whether we can stay together enough to keep from killing each other is an ominous question. It is fundamentally a political question. It is equally a fundamental question of ethics.

To be sure, from Los Angeles to Baghdad, a majority of us may still linger over the old question: Do "we" really have to live with "them"? Aware of their constituents' vulnerability to that question, politicians the world around know how to stir them to hostility that moves toward war, genocide, "ethnic cleansing." But politicians who know how little isolation *succeeds* in the modern world must sooner or later stir in their constituents another kind of political loyalty: sober acceptance of the fact that people do not have to *like* each other in order to become politically settled into ongoing relationships. Politics can be, ought to be about the business of learning to live with neighbors, some too different to be likable, who have too many interests in common with us to be dismissed from our civic company.

In sum, if the conflict-ridden and conflict-prone peoples of earth are to move away from a Hobbesian "war of all against all" into forms of politics that are not merely war by other means, we must do something about the memories and the continuing legacies of the harms we have inflicted on each other in the recent or remote past. That is the *empirical*, historical observation in which most of this book is rooted. A major "something" that we have to enact is a social, political form of forgiveness. That is the *moral* claim of the book. The factual-moral claim is: Absent forgiveness and its twin repentance, political humans remember the crimes of ancestors only to entertain the idea of repeating them. Factual and moral claims, I trust, will not drift far from each other in any of these pages.

A Complex and Multidimensional Concept: Some Definitions

No reader can be blamed for supposing that to speak of forgiveness *in politics* is to risk an oxymoron. What is more unforgiving than clashes of the powerful? What is politics about if not the amassing of power to overcome rivals? And, insofar as ethics enters political struggle at all, should we not restrict our ethical claims to such modest political virtues as tolerance, respect for law, and forms of justice that emerge tenuously from balances between centers of power? The burden of western political ethics has usually rested on this very fulcrum—*justice*. Seldom has any major political thinker considered forgiveness as an essential servant of justice or as indispensable in the initial formation of political associations.

One modern exception to this tradition in political philosophy was the late Hannah Arendt, who identified forgiveness as one of two human capacities that make possible genuine social change. For her, the other was our capacity to make new promises or covenants. Much liberal-democratic thinking of the past several centuries has assumed that humans "naturally" have this latter capacity of entering into new agreements with each other. Not every theorist has explained why enemies, in particular, may not exercise this capacity. Hardly any has supposed that one of the reasons is a politics-paralyzing refusal of forgiveness.

A kindred reason for the sense that forgiveness is a strange candidate for a central place in politics is its long-time exclusive association with the vocabulary of religion. The word *forgiveness* has a religious ring in the ears of most modern westerners in a way that *justice* decidedly does not. As we shall see, theologians themselves have been most responsible for this impression. Perhaps the greatest of modern politically oriented theologians was Reinhold Niebuhr, who followed western tradition in seeing justice as the political ethical virtue par excellence. When Christians talk about "love" and its highest expression, "forgiveness," in a political setting, said Niebuhr, they are likely to become sentimentalists, expecting too much of ordinary self-interested human beings. If we rise to ethical behavior at all in our politics, we come to justice. Love and forgiveness may motivate the religious citizen to seek justice in society, he conceded; but these high virtues finally transcend justice. They are "there" to aspire to idealistically, but they elude empirical, collaborative political form.

If forgiveness is to escape its religious captivity and enter the ranks of ordinary political virtues, it has to acquire more precise, dynamic, and politically contexted definition than it has usually enjoyed. Along the way in this study I seek to give it that definition through rehearsals of historical narrative. I resort to narrative because forgiveness is a morally complex concept, and it is in our stories that humans seem most likely to encompass and to communicate the complexities of our lives. In the stories we tell each other to "explain" our life experience, we often interweave events and perceptions that elude the nets of other forms of explanation. Certainly, when citizens try to tell each other what it means for them to belong together in one civic community, they are likely to resort to historical recollection: "Fourscore and seven years ago. . . ."

But to begin a volume that tries to avoid preoccupation with abstractions in deference to story, let me resort to a formal definition of forgiveness here for purposes of initial orientation.

Forgiveness begins with memory suffused with moral judgment. Popular use of the word *forgiveness* sometimes implies that to forgive is to forget, to abandon primary concern for the crimes of an enemy. Quite the reverse: "Remember and forgive" would be a more accurate slogan. Forgiveness begins with a remembering and a moral judgment of wrong, injustice, and injury. For this very reason, alleged wrongdoers are wary of being told that someone "forgives" them. Immediately they sense that they are being subjected to some moral assessment, and they may not consent to it. Absent a preliminary agreement between two or more parties that there is something from the past to *be* forgiven, forgiveness stalls at the starting gate. Especially between antagonistic groups of humans, consensus on the wrongs that each may have inflicted on the other may take a very long time. Logically forgiveness goes from wrong-sufferers to wrongdoers, but in human societies, and most of all in political conflict, it may have to go both ways.

That is one moral complexity in the transaction: making moral judgments of an enemy's behavior. If and when the two come to some agreement on that, they may turn attention to the related complexity of determining what restitution, compensation, or penalty should now be leveled against the offender. Forgiveness, in politics or any other human relation, does not require the abandonment of all versions of punishment of evildoers. But it does require the abandonment of *vengeance*, and this is its second constituent element. Forgiveness gets its real start under the double impetus of judgment and forbearance from revenge. Forbearance opens the door toward a future that will not repeat the old crimes. Unaccompanied by forbearance in this very beginning, moral judgment often fuels new enmity. Who are more ferocious in battle than the morally empowered? Who is more tempted to make sure that the enemy pays for its crimes many times over? Moral justifications have been great friends of vengeance from time immemorial.

The forbearance element in forgiveness is likely to surprise former enemies. "Do unto others what they have done unto you" seems the ordinary rule of give and take in human associations. But equally surprising may be a third element in the transaction that has great significance for the construction of new political relationships: empathy for the enemy's humanity. Empathy should be distinguished from sympathy. The moral stance of forgivers usually precludes sympathy with the enemies' cause and their methods of pursuing it. With that remarkable empathy which their common suffering enables soldiers on all sides sometimes to show for each other, Ulysses S. Grant at Appomattox wrote in his journal: "I felt . . . sad and depressed at the downfall of a foe who had fought so long and valiantly, and had suffered so much for a cause, though that cause was, I believe, one of the worst for which a people ever fought."[6] This combination of moral judgment upon wrong with empathy for wrongdoers may be rare in human affairs, but in fact acknowledgment of fellow humanity lays a groundwork for both the construction and the repair of any human community. It is *not* true that "to understand all is to forgive all." But it *is* true that understanding the humanity of enemies is another step toward entertaining the possibility of living with them as fellow human beings. Even in the midst of war, enemies need understanding of each other's humanity. For lack of it, some great military mistakes have been made: one thinks of Hitler's stereotypes of the English as a nation of shopkeepers and the Russians as racially unfit for war.

The analogy of political to interpersonal relations here is close. A political philosopher, Jeffrie G. Murphy, wrote recently: "I once heard a boy say, after learning that the class bully was in fact a victim of child abuse, 'That takes all the fun out of hating her.'" In this book we shall look at many instances in modern political affairs where empathy with an injuring enemy deprives the injured of this "fun."[7]

In its fourth dimension, genuine forgiveness aims at the renewal of a human relationship. Not merely an act of isolated moral high-mindedness, forgiveness aggressively seeks to repair the fractures of enmity. Therefore, forgivers are prepared to begin living with the enemy again on some level of positive mutual affirmation. In politics, that implies some form of *co-existence*. As Murphy and his co-author Hampton put it in their philosophically rich account of forgiveness: "[Forgivers] will not let the wrongdoing continue to intrude into . . . dealing with the wrongdoers in order that they can reestablish some kind of relationship—at the very least, the 'civil' relationship that prevails between strangers in a human community."[8] It is this civil relationship between strangers that will be the central concern of this book. We need not call the new relation *reconciliation*, a word best reserved, perhaps, for the end of a process that forgiveness begins. In the 1960s the word *co-existence* acquired a measure of hope in its use in the Cold War to indicate that the Soviets and the Americans could compete with each other without moving to destroy each other. Even Nikita Krushchev's famous remark, "We will bury you," was a threat of economic, not atomic, annihilation of the United States. Co-existence may be only the mildest of moves toward reconciliation and only the faintest anticipation of a genuine political connection. It may be little different from passive tolerance. But it is a move away from the past towards a new political future.

Forgiveness in a political context, then, is an act that joins moral truth, forbearance, empathy, and commitment to repair a fractured human relation. Such a combination calls for a collective turning from the past that neither ignores past evil nor excuses it, that neither overlooks justice nor reduces justice to revenge, that insists on the humanity of enemies even in their commission of dehumanizing deeds, and that values the justice that restores political community above the justice that destroys it. As such a multidimensional human action, forgiveness might be compared to a twisted four-strand cable, which over time intertwines with the enemy's responses to form the double bond of new politics. No one element in this cable carries the weight of the action; each assumes and depends upon the others. At any one time, one may have greater prominence in the negotiation, and all of them come up for repeated attention as the relationship grows more secure—e.g., forbearance can prompt a start toward confession of wrong, empathy can deepen that confession, as new political ties embody the purpose of the transaction. A forgiver does not need to dwell indefinitely on the enemy's past crimes unless evidence surfaces that the enemy no longer considers memory of those crimes important. Similarly, the forgiven does not need unending assurance that the other really does forbear, empathize, and intend a new relation, for along the way concrete evidences of all this have accumulated.

So defined, political forgiveness links realism to hope. It aims at delivering the human future from repetitions of the atrocities of the past. Given the scale of politically engineered atrocity in the twentieth century, nothing could be a more practical or more urgent gift to our neighbors of the twenty-first.

The Plan of the Book

Ours is the first century in which governments have acquired the power to kill the hundred million or so people who in fact have perished in war since 1900. The very fearsomeness of contemporary political relations should have an impact on how ethicists like myself write about politics. Urgency should compel us to resort here to communication that uses a wider lens on human affairs than is possible in the logical arguments of philosophy, the exposition of ethical theory, or the merely anecdotal vividness of illustration. Again, narrative—fictional and historical—seems to meet the requirements of urgency more nearly than any other method.

Thus, historians—rather than philosophers, social scientists, or theologians—have been my chief companions in this study. Adjunctive help I have borrowed from world literature, for poets and novelists sometimes recall us to the truth about human relationships more vividly than any of these scholars. But all have helped to discipline and illumine my thinking about forgiveness with stories that tell how humans behave toward each other and how they might behave.

The point of view in these pages is that of a citizen of the United States. That the politics of forgiveness has a place in every country's past and present I am certain; the daily news from Sarajevo, New Delhi, Belfast, and Johannesburg is enough to convince anyone of that. But the world is full of pundits who want to tell foreigners how to understand their problems, and I do not wish to be one of these. The twentieth century faces Americans with their own huge agenda of forgiveness in the form of many a lingering hostility in our internal and external political relations. I have chose to focus on three of them.

The first is our half-century of hostility toward Germany, followed by another half-century of mending this relation. The second is our torturous confrontation with Japan, fraught with cultural conflicts that make the case for forgiveness in Japanese-American relations more difficult and complicated than has been the case with Germany. Third, I focus on the legacies of what many Americans believe to be the most atrocious of all the collective sins that have littered our internal national history: the injustices visited politically upon African Americans. Astonishingly, I will claim, they have been our most important national teachers about the possibility that forgiveness can be a power for political change.

Recounting these three twentieth-century stories, from the standpoint of what they tell us about forgiveness in politics, is the heart of this volume. But just as every life story grows out of the stories of previous lives, the story preceding this one grows out of at least three ancient sources of American and European culture: the Greek, the Hebrew, and the Christian. As background account of how forgiveness entered (or failed to enter) the personal and political discourse of the West, I will sample the literary work of two Greek army veterans—Aeschylus and Thucydides—in the first part of Chapter 1; in the second part I will sample the writings of the Hebrew Bible, particularly one narrative there, the saga of Joseph, that portrays forgiveness in a very political setting.

Chapter 2 summarizes the major contributions of Christian churches and Christian thinkers to the subject, beginning with the New Testament, the internal life of the early church, and the expansion of the church into a multitude of connections with the political history of Europe. The puzzle I explore here is how, looming so large in the institutions and rhetoric of the churches, forgiveness had so minor a place in the principles of their express political ethics. Chapter 3 deepens this puzzle by posing a problem uniquely intense in a modern, pluralistic ethical culture: Can humans in our time agree on any ethical standards? If they cannot, forgiveness becomes an irrelevancy, as does the hope that society *has* an overriding, binding ethic. The minimal ethical agreement I propose for our late twentieth century is the affirmation of life itself and its negative—the repudiation of the massive death of which our political systems are now capable.

These materials are the background. In the next chapters I turn to the three cases with which modern Americans still have much to do: Germany, Japan, and African Americans. These chapters compose the bulk and the burden of the book. In conclusion, I try to indicate what these case studies imply for the future thinking and behavior of American political leaders and their constituents in the upcoming century.

The principal purpose of the whole study is to identify both the need and the actual presence of forgiveness in political history, and thus to encourage readers, as citizens, to consider the political wisdom inherent in this neglected virtue. Is forgiveness indispensable for turning political enmity into political neighborliness? To make sense of that too rarely asked question is the aim and hope of the book.

1

Revenge, the End of Politics, and Justice, the Beginning

Running from Switzerland to the Channel like a gangrenous wound across French and Belgian territory, the trenches determined the war of position and attrition, the brutal, mud-filled, murderous insanity known as the Western Front that was to last four more years. . . .

Men could not sustain a war of such magnitude and pain without hope—the hope that its very enormity would ensure that it could never happen again and the hope that when somehow it had been fought through to a resolution, the foundations of a better-ordered world would have been laid. . . . When every autumn people said it could not last through the winter, and when every spring there was still no end in sight, only the hope that out of it all some good would accrue to mankind kept men and nations fighting.[1]

Barbara Tuchman

It did happen again, and they called it World War II. Almost every observer of that first half of our century acknowledges, ruefully, that the seeds of the "second round" were sown in the Versailles Treaty, as clear an illustration of vengeful international politics as the century was to yield.

In the midst of that second round, in the year 1943, Edwin Muir, a Scot, wrote a poem about his near despair over the murderous "wheel" of history that corrupts one generation with the crimes of the last one.

". . . Loves and hates are thrust
Upon me by the acrimonious dead,
The buried thesis, long since rusted knife,
Revengeful dust. . . .
How can I here remake what there made me
And makes and remakes me still?
Set a new mark? Circumvent history?"[2]

The question has haunted morally reflective people for many centuries, and no ancient people wrestled with the question more soberly than did the Greeks, particularly the Athenian dramatic poets and at least one Athenian historian. The first pre-occupation of these Athenians, as the virtual inventors of European political philosophy, was their painful experience of the truth: nothing is more "natural" in human relations than revenge, and nothing is less political.

It seems right to begin this study of forgiveness in politics with this truth and to document it in two versions: first, the drama that Aeschylus wrote to portray the triumph of justice over revenge as the most primitive, and most necessary, step that any group of citizens can take if they mean to form a political association; and second, the next-generation history that Thucydides wrote to remind the Greeks that in fact, not just in poetry, revenge is one of the great destroyers of politics. Against the background of great evils done and great evils suffered in the relations of human groups to each other, they stand at a fork in the road: if they take the fork of revenge, they will never emerge from a political culture truly primitive. If they take the other fork, they may learn to call it "justice" and to distinguish it from the revenge with which it is sometimes confused.

Aeschylus: The Taming of Revenge by Institutions of Justice

In the early sixth century B.C.E., the "golden age" of Athens began in the mind and legal inventiveness of Solon, whom tradition credited with revising the code of Draco with its alleged[3] single punishment of death for every infraction of law. In his poetry, Solon set forth a vision of human community grounded not in the power of the stronger but in justice. He differed from the old tradition of Hesiod (ca. 750 B.C.E.) in that he saw injustice not as human crime inexorably punished by external divine powers but as inherent harm to the ability of humans to form and preserve political community among themselves. For Solon, says Werner Jaeger, a "transgression of justice is a disturbance of the social organism. A state thus punished is afflicted by party feuds and civil war," not by plagues and famines imposed by the gods. Humans had better impose some restraints upon themselves as they engage in the "universal battle for the good things of this world," or the good things themselves will perish. For Solon, "this is not a prophetic vision, it is a statesman's diagnosis of the facts."[4] Even so, Solon regarded the workings of justice in communal history as inexorable, because they were backed by divine powers. Justice is "the retribution of Zeus, which lets none escape. One man makes amends soon, another late; and if the guilty man escapes punishment, his innocent children and his descendants suffer in his stead." Shaky, then, were Draco and Solon's efforts to prevent insatiable intergenerational thirst for revenge. Over the century following, the political and moral problem of just and unjust punishment of wicked deeds would continue to occupy "the very core of the religious doctrine which . . . created Attic tragedy."[5]

Thirty-five years old when he was a participant in the Battle of Marathon (490 B.C.E.), the poet Aeschylus lived in the era when Athenian democracy was at its height and under severe external attack. He died (456 B.C.E.) a generation ahead of his city's great political mistake—the Peloponnesian War (431–404). In the years just before his death, he experienced renewed onslaughts of political turmoil in his native city. A. J. Podlecki summarizes this context:

At center stage of most of Aeschylus' dramas stands man as a political being, reflecting the playwright's concern and the time in which he lived. Aeschylus was born
under tyranny . . . grew up in the turbulent period when the Athenian democracy had
to prove itself against self-seeking politicians at home and invaders from abroad, and
himself took part in the city's first struggles against the Persians. He later watched
the political battle between liberals and conservatives, each fighting to turn Athens
into their idea of what it should be.[6]

Aeschylus's view of human nature, says Podlecki, was "city-centered and essentially
democratic," and his version of the Orestes legend, in three final plays, is preoccu-
pied with the theme of revenge in relation to the unity of the Athenian state.

In 462 the Athenian constitution was reformed along radical lines and the conservative Cimon exiled, not without the infliction of deep political wounds by the opposing factions and the actual shedding of blood. Aeschylus' Orestes trilogy of 458 reflects this atmosphere of citizen armed against citizen, "tribal war" in the poet's own
phrase; but, in the Aeschylean resolution, strife gives way to harmony, bloodshed to
peace, revolution to the rule of law. Old divinities such as the Furies are transformed
and given a constructive function in Athena's city, and they thus become its
Eumenides, or "Well-Wishers."[7]

Individual and collective acts of vengeance have dire political consequences: that
is the empirical certainty behind Aeschylus's third drama in *The Oresteia*, *The
Eumenides*.[8]

The beginning and end of the Orestes story were well known to the original Athenian audience of these dramas: In the shadows of remote history, two brothers,
Thyestes and Atreus, become enemies. Thyestes violates the wife of Atreus, who
exacts ingeniously cruel vengeance by killing Thyestes' two sons and then serving
them up to their father at a banquet. Agamemnon, the son of Atreus, unwittingly
prepares new vengeance upon his family when he sacrifices his daughter Iphigenia
to ensure the victory of the Greeks over the Trojans. In long-delayed revenge for this
murder of her daughter, Clytemnestra, the wife of Agamemnon, murders her husband. This provokes the son of the family, Orestes, to murder her in turn.

Eumenides opens at this stage of the story. The drama consists of an extended court
trial in which the god Apollo defends his client Orestes against the collective pros-
ecutor, "a grisly band of women," the Furies,[9] "who are quasi-symbols of conscience."[10] Silent throughout the drama, a jury of twelve Athenian citizens, all men,
are the audience before whom the trial is played out. At the end they are to decide
between Apollo's case for Orestes and the Furies' case against him. This jury is the
mythical prototype of the supreme court of Athens, the Areopagus. But there is a
thirteenth voter in the case—Athena, patron goddess of Athens, the city-state whose
civic perpetuation and welfare are actually the central concern of the drama. The issue
is this: What justice will take precedence in the civic life of Athens—just revenge
leading to just counterrevenge in escalations leading to civil war, or the justice that
condemns past murder in ways that inhibit its repetition?

In the preceding drama, *The Choephori*, the chorus had summarized the terror of
unending vengeance in these verses:

> . . . the law is sternly set—
> Blood-drips shed upon the ground
> Plead for other bloodshed yet;
> Loud the call of death doth sound,
> Calling guilt of olden time,
> A Fury, crowning crime with crime.[11]

Now gods and citizens are met to decide if there is any other way to deal with one crime than by committing another.

In the opening arguments of the trial, the Furies defend their priority rights as older than those of the Olympian gods, a claim whose force Apollo dismisses with an invitation to the Furies to flee Athens for some barbarian city where they can "prowl" and be at home.

> Go where men lay on men the doom of blood,
> Heads lopped from necks, eyes from their spheres plucked out,
> Hacked flesh, the flower of youthful seed crushed out,
> Feet hewn away and hands, and death beneath
> The smiting stone, low moans and piteous
> Of men impaled—Hark, hear ye what feast
> Ye hanker after. . . .[12]

Aeschylus is describing the warfare which he knew as a participant, a "feast" as gory as the one that Atreus had once prepared for Thyestes.

Following up his attack, Apollo observes to the Furies that they are strangely passive toward a wife's murder of her husband while pursuing relentlessly a son who has murdered his mother. Leaving aside the antique (and male-chauvinistic) casuistry about the relative rights of men, women, and children throughout the play,[13] the modern reader can detect here the ordinary relativities of the human judicial process: it nails some injustices and ignores others.

The human subject of these opening arguments then enters a plea of his own: I have undergone ritual cleansing at the shrine of Apollo, says Orestes; and, further, *time* is on the side of lessening my guilt "among my fellow men." The Furies scorn these arguments: neither ritual nor time can deal with guilt for matricide. Such guilt is eternal; and the Furies intend to carry Orestes off to Hell. Their jurisdiction transcends that of humans and their gods. They implement the relentless primitive law:

> Queens are we and mindful for our solemn vengeance.
>   Not by tear or prayer
> Shall a man avert it. In unhonored darkness,
>   Far from gods, we fare.[14]

At this point Athena, founder and protector of the Athenian state, enters the courtroom. And who are you? she asks the Furies. "We chase from home the murderers of men," they answer. "And where at last can he that slew make pause?" she asks. "Where this is law—" the Furies answer, *"all joy abandon here."*[15] With the air of authority, Athena then accuses the Furies of serving "the form of justice, not its deed," a distinction vital to the work of judges in all human courts of law. Athena asks the Furies to consent to her final authority in the case; and, out of reverence for her parent, Zeus, they so consent, modifying their alienation from gods in a nod toward monotheism. In turn, Athena concedes that the issue of blood guilt "gives pause" to "even me," but in "this my city's name" she will assume this burden of power. In wielding it she has to find a way between ignoring the Furies and the "dropping plague-spot of eternal ill" which their vengeance portends in the human world. "Thus stand we with a woe on either hand." As she turns to the institutionalizing of the Areopagus, she admonishes her human appointees that they, too, must walk this middle road.[16]

At this the Furies erupt in a hymnic lament: Athena overthrows Justice, whose advocates should be immune to "earthly lure" or other compromising human interests. Life itself will no longer be safe under a regimen open to such compromise. The lines are thus drawn between the theory that revenge serves the cause of human life and the theory that it serves life very poorly. With formal, deontological ethics of all times, the Furies side with the sacredness of principle. With utilitarians and advocates of the plural virtues of human society, Athena pleads for recognition of the diversity and multidimensionality of law in its service to the concrete goods of humans and their societies.

Apollo then introduces a dimension of divinity which Aeschylus will implement in his resolution of the crisis at the end of the drama: true authority can reverse itself. The very gods can change. "He that hath bound may loose: a cure there is."[17] The chains of fate can be broken; otherwise Fate rules a world where no power can intervene to set in motion benign counterpower.

Athena now delivers her closing argument and charge to the human jury: awe before the shrine of Justice is to be the rule in her city. But just vengeance upon lawbreakers will exclude unjust vengeance—that is, vengeance uncontrolled by regard for the integrity of the city. As the judges proceed to vote, all the main characters rehearse their arguments again, and Orestes reduces his argument to a poignant prayer: "O bright Apollo, what shall be the end?" Throughout, the two gods have pressed their answer: "Whatever the right way to end it, there has to be an end—to vengeance." Throughout the Furies have cried, "There is no just end to it for the guilty."

The ballots of the twelve judges are now counted, and as evidence of how seriously Aeschylus takes the Furies' case, the vote is 6 to 6. At this, Athena casts her deciding vote on behalf of Orestes, who immediately exclaims:

> . . . now shall Grecian lips say this,
> *The man is Argive once again.* . . .[18]

He has been restored to membership in his civic community. But there is a larger hope which he now can entertain for that community: that its "chieftains" will turn from the way of vengeance to the ways of building and keeping the peace of "Argive land." Let the chiefs, even after death, Furylike, haunt those who destroy the *peace* of the Greek city states. Not only the personal crime of murder but the social-political crime of war between the city-states now has official constrainers: vengeance is subject to law and legal institution, and the logic that allows both scope and limit for vengeance shifts from the sacredness of pure principle to the sacredness of civic society among the Greeks. In service to that society, the Greeks are to be always ready to unite in war against the barbarians. No universal human ethic dawns here, nor these thirty-two years after Marathon was there likely to be such a dawn. But it is an Athenian solution to an ageless question: *Once broken, how can any society be put back together?*

Athena turns, in the end, to answer the question by finding a new place for the Furies in the scheme of Athenian society. "With balanced vote" *their* "cause had issue fair"—half of the Athenian jury had sided with them. The just weight of their claims on wrongdoers needs recognition and location, which Athena now accords them in the underground of the Areopagus. There they can receive the honor due to punitive Justice; but there their wildness can be tamed to the service of judgments about the actual good of the body politic. They now are invited to live "deep in the heart" of the land.[19] In a profound, political sense, they are civilized.

Ironically, mysteriously, even mystically, the Furies now have their name changed—they become the Eumenides, the Well-Wishers. Their overt function changes, too—they become the goddesses of fertility in the earth and in human families. The Furies find their transition sudden and strange, in common, doubtless, with the original audience of the play. So, in an extended sermon, Athena speaks persuasively of the attraction the Furies should feel for becoming honored members of the world's best civil society—Athens! Once a part of it, you can lend your energies to the taming of the "war-god's spirit" that burns hotly in some young Athenians, "keen for fight" against "their country and their kin."[20] Where once you excelled in stirring up animosity, excel now in "fair mercy, gratitude, and grace as fair"—a radical shift of orientation that seems to take leave of vengeance.

In this double message to the Furies, something new emerges while something old remains in their role among the Athenians. Blessing can be combined with retribution if the purposes of retribution are not chiefly to satisfy abstract justice but to correct a concrete evil in a civil society. The Furies are at last converted from the service of justice in the abstract to justice as the bringer of good to a community. In terms that will later preoccupy philosophical ethics from Plato and Aristotle to Immanuel Kant and John Stuart Mill, justice is for the conferring of *good* as well as the upholding of *right*. In a previous chorus, the Furies had proclaimed that righteousness would in fact bring reward to humans, but never before had they taken it upon themselves to be agents of the rewarding.[21] Now revenge has been subjected to a principle of blessing, for Athena has converted even the powers of Hell to the service of "my town's prosperity."[22] Having done so, she adverts again to the continuing function of the Avengers—it will still be possible for humans to follow "the downward path" into the Furies' underground clutch; but now, in their "present power for righteousness," these former agents of curse have become agents of socially shared blessedness.[23]

As the drama draws to its close, Athena, as philosopher of the democratic order, rejoices out loud in her own persuasive powers, reflecting those of father Zeus, "king of parley," who uses language as the medium of political exchange rather than raw power. Only in that medium is democracy truly safeguarded. And the Furies, now Eumenides, chant their agreement with Athena in a summation of the play's message to its Athenian audiences:

> And nevermore these walls within
> Shall echo fierce sedition's din
> Unslaked with blood and crime;
> The thirsty dust shall nevermore
> Suck up the darkly streaming gore
> Of civic broils, shed out in wrath
> And vengeance, crying death for death!
> But man with man and state with state
> Shall vow *The pledge of common hate*
> *And common friendship, that for man*
> *Hath oft made blessing out of ban,*
> *Be ours unto all time.*[24]

From now on, it will be "common friendship" among Athenians, implying "common hate" for the external enemies of the city. Hate for evil and love for good in human relationships have provoked much logic twisting in the play. How the Eumenides will both subdue and loosen their fury remains as ambiguous in theory as it would continue to be in the practice of Athenian politicians, citizens, lawyers, and priests. As for the backlash of hate for barbarians, that ambiguity does not touch the spirit of this play. Enough, Aeschylus seems to say, that fractious local politics should become less saturated with blood and more with rhetorical deliberation. Turn our hates toward the barbarian: he is our real enemy now.

In an apparent coda, touching for us who read these dramas for something less awesome than the wisdom of gods, human beings have the last word. Athena leads the Eumenides offstage down to the undercroft of Mars Hill. The only humans besides Orestes to speak in the drama, a chorus of Athenian women and children now celebrate the procession. For them too, not only for men and the male-bonded citizens of Athens, have the issues of the drama been played out. Like the end of some modern productions of Richard Wagner's *Götterdämmerung*, a company of real human beings rises up on stage. In a play whose message has centered on the antagonism of justice and mercy, an aged Aeschylus expresses his love for Athens by giving to the women and children of Athens the final word. From the unending shower of the arrows of revenge, who has deserved more protection than they?

Thucydides: The Triumph of Fury in War

Born a few years before Aeschylus's death, Thucydides lived through the times of Athens' greatest cultural achievements and its most appalling political disaster: the Peloponnesian War. Some critics believe that his principal work, *History of the Peloponnesian War*, "was composed as a prose tragedy under the spell of the great dramatists"—Aeschylus, Euripides, and Sophocles.[25] As a companion piece to their dramatic myths of civic origin, Thucydides' *History* undergirds the symbols of high Greek culture with the grim facts of its actual political life.

As he tells it, no incident in the war with Sparta was more saturated with vengeance than the sequel to the revolution of the city-state of Corcyra—modern Corfu. Unlike Aeschylus before and Plato and Aristotle after, Thucydides tried to resist the theologizing and moralizing of political conflict. But in the Corcyra debacle he was as appalled as Aeschylus about the breakdown of political community under the trampings of revenge. He is sure that vengefulness poorly serves the cause of state power inside and outside of its boundaries. Again and again in his account of the miseries of the Peloponnesian War, he demonstrates that unreasoning vengeance, like the war aim of unconditional surrender, can tear up the internal unity of states, lengthen war between them, and exhaust the resources of all parties to the conflict. Political power is his chief interest—how it comes about, what politicians do with it, how they lose it. But he knows that external political power depends on the mundane internal strengths of a society—food, clothing, public collaborations of all sorts.[26] Revenge, asleep in the depths of every civic order, wakes up in time of war. And it can destroy state power. Like the twentieth-century novelist William Golding, as he reflected on the era of World War II, Thucydides would adduce the Athenian-Spartan collision at Corcyra as proof of the conclusion that "anyone who moved through those years without understanding that man produces evil as a bee produces honey, must have been blind or wrong in the head."[27]

In the incident that precedes the Corcyraean tragedy, Thucydides describes the fate of the city of Plataea, whose leaders had the misfortune of siding with Athens over against the Spartans and their Theban allies. Sparta subdues Plataea, and the Thebans, with their own reasons for wanting revenge on the Plataeans, persuade the Spartans to take it for them. The Spartans oblige, executing the Plataean men, enslaving the women, and turning Plataea over to the Thebans, who raze it to the ground. The Spartan attitude toward the whole affair, says Thucydides, "was mainly adopted to please the Thebans, who were thought to be useful in the war at that moment raging. Such was the end of Plataea, in the ninety-third year after she became the ally of Athens."[28]

As the grim politics of power unfolds, leaders on all sides resort to elaborate rhetorical justifications of their actions, and the air is especially heavy with talk about justice. But the rhetoric mostly masks the interests of the strong. Unlike the arguments of gods and humans on Aeschylus's stage, this is the actual cynical civic speech of wartime. As Jaeger observes:

> Thucydides' work provides many illustrations of the problem provided by party-shibboleths—the problem of the relation between ideology and fact in politics. The Spartans, as champions of Liberty and Justice, are bound to play up their role by uttering streams of sanctimonious moral sentiment, which usually harmonizes with their own interest so neatly that they need not ask themselves where one ends and the other begins. The position of the Athenians is more difficult; so they are forced to appeal to National Honor. Cynical as that appeal may seem, it is often a good deal more sympathetic than the cant uttered by the "Liberators."[29]

The lesson for Thucydides is that, in time of war, few laws of justice govern collective human thirst for retaliation against enemies—and no dependable rewards are likely for allies, either. Violence feeds on revenge; revenge, on violence. The Corcyraean revolt provides a long, misery-laden illustration of this vicious cycle.

First of all, the Corcyraeans fall into civil war among themselves over the question of alliance with Sparta or Athens. Conspiracy and counterconspiracy escalate to assassination and counterassassination. With the Athenian fleet standing offshore, a reign of terror sweeps the little port city. For seven days,

> the Corcyraeans were engaged in butchering those of their fellow citizens whom they regarded as their enemies: and although the crime imputed was that of attempting to put down the democracy, some were slain also for private hatred, others by their debtors because of monies owed to them. Death thus raged in every shape; and, as usually happens at such times, there was no length to which violence did not go; sons were killed by their fathers, and suppliants dragged from the altar or slain upon it; while some were even walled up in the temple of Dionysius and died there.
>
> So bloody was the march of the revolution, and the impression which it made was the greater as it was one of the first to occur. Later on, one may say, the whole Hellenic world was convulsed.[30]

Thucydides means to describe the working of political power with a cool empirical eye, but here he plainly lets down his guard against moralizing. Revenge is the great corrupter of politics, even the politics of war: observers of war in the former Yugoslavia in 1993 will know how up to date on this point is Thucydides. In one long searing paragraph he describes the dissolution of Corcyraean society:

> ... In peace and prosperity states and individuals have better sentiments, because they do not find themselves suddenly confronted with imperious necessities; but war takes away the easy supply of daily wants, and so proves a rough master, that brings most men's characters to a level with their fortunes. Revolution thus ran its course from city to city, and the places which it arrived at last, from having heard what had been done before, carried to a still greater excess the refinements of their inventions, as manifested in the cunning of their enterprises and the atrocity of their reprisals. Words had to change their ordinary meaning and to take that which was now given them. ... Reckless audacity came to be considered the courage of a loyal ally; prudent hesitation, specious cowardice; moderation was held to be a cloak for unmanliness; ability to see all sides of a question inaptness to act on any. Frantic violence became the attribute of manliness; cautious plotting, a justifiable means of self-defence. The advocate of extreme measures was always trustworthy; his opponent a man to be suspected. To succeed in a plot was to have a shrewd head, to divine a plot still shrewder; but to try to provide against having to do either was to break up your party and to be afraid of your adversaries. In fine, to forestall an intended criminal, or to suggest the idea of a crime where it was wanting, was equally commended, until even blood became a weaker tie than party, from the superior readiness of those united by the latter to dare everything without reserve; for such associations had not in view the blessings derivable from established institutions but were formed by ambition for their overthrow; and the confidence of their members in each other rested less on any religious sanction than upon complicity in crime. The fair proposals of an adversary were met with jealous precautions by the stronger of the two, and not with a generous confidence. Revenge also was held of more account than self-preservation. Oaths of reconciliation, being only proffered on either side to meet an immediate difficulty, only held good so long as no other weapon was at hand; but when opportunity offered, he who first ventured to seize it and to take his enemy off guard, thought this perfidious vengeance sweeter than an open one, since, considerations of safety apart, success by trickery won him the palm of superior intelligence. ... The leaders in the

cities, each provided with the fairest professions, on the one side with the cry of political equality of the people, on the other of a moderate aristocracy, sought prizes for themselves in those public interests which they pretended to cherish, and, recoiling from no means in their struggles for ascendancy, engaged in the direst excesses; in their acts of vengeance they went to even greater lengths, not stopping at what justice or the good of the state demanded, but making the party caprice of the moment their only standard, and invoking with equal readiness the condemnation of an unjust verdict or the authority of the strong arm to glut the animosities of the hour. Thus religion was in honor with neither party; but the use of fair phrases to arrive at guilty ends was in high reputation. Meanwhile the moderate part of the citizens perished between the two, either for not joining in the quarrel, or because envy would not suffer them to escape.[31]

Thus was society "divided into camps in which no man trusted his fellow," wherein "there was neither promise to be depended upon, nor oath that could command respect; but all parties dwelling rather in their calculation upon the hopelessness of a permanent state of things, were more intent upon self-defence than capable of confidence."[32]

Like most Greek philosophers and almost all political conservatives, Thucydides cherished a "permanent state of things," a known and institutionalized social order, ruled by reason, moderation, and compromise between interests for the sake of a larger social good. Most of all he feared anarchy, and twenty years of the Peloponnesian War taught him to do so, as the tides of vengeance swept city after city into its blind depths. Corcyra was the beginning of this flood. Surely, said the historian, all parties in that city had their just reasons for complaining against each other. The rulers were "insolent" toward the common people and excessive in their grasping after wealth. The commoners were envious and willing to go to any length to remedy their poverty. "Ungovernable passions," stirred in all and brought all to ruin. Society and human life cannot continue without some subjection to general law and social good, he reflected summarily.

> Indeed men too often take upon themselves in the prosecution of their revenge to set the example of doing away with those general laws to which all alike can look for salvation in adversity, instead of allowing them to subsist against the day of danger when their aid may be required.[33]

In passages like these, Thucydides is as moral in his reading of history as any disciple of Solon, Aeschylus, or Plato. The "general law" of relations between states may be close to the lawless sway of naked power[34]; but as for the foundations of political community inside a state, he was sure that there were other more benign general laws. One such law was surely this: *Revenge destroys political community*. Thucydides' conservative temper made him sympathetic with the "moderate aristocracy" side of Athenian politics. But he was democrat enough to believe that humans of roughly equal virtue often differ in political opinion, and that they cannot pursue the practical meaning of their differences without a certain trust in each other, translated into the confidence that neither seeks to destroy the other. Such trust, verging on humility about the virtue of all parties to a political conflict, embodies one strand of democratic wisdom. On grounds of such shared confidence, political argument can go its vocal way as humans engage in conflict without the fear that sheer destruction threatens them in every moment of the civic dialogue. With typical Athenian balance, Thucydides insisted that social institutions owe respect to individuals and that individuals owe respect to each other through institutions.

In short, Thucydides would have sympathized with Thomas Hobbes's fear of "war of all against all," for he had seen such war. But he could not have sympathized with liberal eighteenth-century philosophers like John Locke, who reduced social relations to optional contracts between individuals. Social-political order preserves some of those relations, so that life itself, and many a contract, can be preserved. Whether through institutions or under the voluntary constraint of moral realism, a certain nonviolent loyalty among citizens must precede conflict between them, else the barriers to civil war have dissolved. However much interstate relations may resemble a jungle, there can be no existence in that jungle, either, without some minimal obligations which people feel toward each other. Even in the midst of a war, collaborations necessary for the prosecution of war have their analogy in the mutualities of interest that should eventually bring an end to war. Above all, for both of these army veterans—Aeschylus and Thucydides—the rampages of human revenge have to be contained. Willingness to subjugate the memory of past injury to the hope of future blessing must prevail. Otherwise humanity itself will not prevail, nor the politics meant to protect it.

Cain, Joseph, and Their Kin: A Saga of Restorative Justice

Whatever else they mean, the ancient myths of a culture express some truths about contemporary human life which, through such stories, heighten our present awareness of ourselves and our empirical histories. Classic Greek drama, the Bhagavad Gita, and the Book of Genesis have this capacity in common: they alert us to truths that may be ordinary enough, but only after the myths themselves have made them so.

Ordinary, in fact, is the truth that something went wrong in the world before any one of us arrived in it or had time to think about the nature of that wrong. Whether in families that impose the faults of a previous generation upon their children or in political communities that do the same, we never have the luxury of a truly fresh choice of the battlefield of our own struggle with evil. This is what Christian theologians chiefly mean by *original sin*, a term that Aeschylus would probably have understood as implying not a single event in some prehistory but an event truly historical in the sense that every generation both inherits and repeats it.[35] Politicians ancient and modern have their own versions of the sobering realism of Edwin Muir: the stones of the past weigh down the present; the burden of history is one of the chains of office, and every new set of leaders adds something to that weight. Nobody ever completely cleans up the "mess in Washington," campaign promises to the contrary. We may call it truth or truism, but in our most reflective moments we are bound to acknowledge that, in indefinite regress, wrong arrived before we did.[36]

As the first book of a five-book account of the origins of the Hebrew people, the Book of Genesis is as political a work as the dramas and histories of the later Greeks.

Misled by the different theological premises of the two cultures, readers of the Bible in our day are often little aware of its political undertow. But when the Hebrews first told the stories of Genesis to each other, they were as aware of the politics of community formation as was any Greek audience viewing an Aeschylus play.

The opening chapters of Genesis, as it happens, are as concerned with the problem of murder and vengeance in human society as were the great Greek dramatists. Hardly has the human race begun with protoparents Adam and Eve than the authors turn to the story of the "first murder" of one of their sons, Abel, by another, Cain. In this story appears the first use of the word *vengeance* in the Hebrew Bible. Superficial acquaintance with the text (Gen. 4:1–16) leaves many readers with the impression that God the Creator avenges the murder of Abel by banishing Cain from contact with other humans—enforcing this regimen with "the mark of Cain," a signal on his forehead to warn others away from him. But the story has a more profound relation to social justice and forgiveness than this impression allows. The law codes of the Hebrew Bible mandate "an eye for an eye, a tooth for a tooth," but with the understood qualifier, only an eye for an eye, thus putting a limit upon human impulses toward measureless revenge (Ex. 21:24). But these same codes mandated capital punishment, making it all the more remarkable that, in exact retaliation for the murder of his brother, God does not impose death upon this "first" murderer. Instead, assuming that his fellow humans will speedily seek the death of Cain, God puts a mark on his forehead in order to *warn off* any human neighbor who dares to take vengeance into his or her hands. The penalty for not respecting the mark of Cain is a "sevenfold" outbreak of divine vengeance, suggesting the theological paradox that God will outdistance any human display of vengeance with depths of vengeance that only divinity commands, so intent is this divinity on shortcutting any future rampage of human vengeance (Gen. 4:15).

Meantime, in the story, Cain's punishment fits his crime: having banished his brother from the company of the living, Cain must endure living with no permanent human company. "You shall be a vagrant and a wanderer on earth." (4:12). Sheer isolation, however, is not the fate of Cain, the story goes on to say. He marries, has children, and responds to his banishment from agriculture by "building a city."[37] He has not totally abandoned a human community, nor it, him.

With all of its antique subtlety and inconsistency, the myth of Cain and Abel is an early resonance of two conflicting themes in the Hebrew Bible as a whole: (1) If there is to be just vengeance on earth, God alone is to be trusted to effect it, both against Israel for its sins and against her national enemies. In texts that would be quoted in the Christian New Testament, the Book of Deuteronomy has Moses hearing the divine word,

> Vengeance is mine, and recompense. . . . I will take vengeance on my adversaries and will requite those who hate me. . . . (Dt. 32:35, 41)[38]

Neither human power nor human goodness can effect proper vengeance against human evil, according to this theology. But there is a second theme forecast even in the primitive tones of the Cain myth: (2) If God alone is the custodian of vengeance, God alone is custodian of forgiveness, too. The social results of a certain modicum of forgiveness already suffuse the story—Cain is to enjoy a distant relation to God and his fellow humans; he is not condemned to solitary confinement. This punishment is initiated and secured by divine prerogative, against the proclivities of human society and its usually misguided tactics of revenge.

How to combine vengeance and forgiveness remains a great mystery here. The writers of the Hebrew Bible are sure that no human has the power to combine them. In almost the entirety of the thirty-nine books of the Hebrew Bible, vengeance and forgiveness, exercised in combination or apart, fall under divine prerogative. The hope that they may be thus combinable stirs up one of the great, recurring theological agonies of the whole tradition. Notable in this tradition is the relegation of the issue to the exclusive jurisdiction of divinity.[39] Occasional vengeful action may be commanded of politicians, priests, and prophets in the history of Israel; but of forgiveness as a social-political rule we hear very little in the Hebrew Bible.

Early in these scriptures, there is a notable exception. It is the story of Joseph and his brothers. Created by an unknown artist, perhaps in the era of Solomon, the tenth century B.C.E., the story was probably told to explain how the family of the patriarch Jacob—son of Isaac, grandson of Abraham—moved from the land of Canaan to the land of Egypt, where, four hundred years later, the family would become the nation of Israel under the leadership of Moses. It is a family story told to explain a political transition "from the tribal orientation of the patriarchal traditions to the people orientation of the Exodus traditions."[40] If it was indeed written in the time of David and Solomon, its author must have been as conscious of political tension among the scarcely united twelve tribes of Israel as all of the Greek dramatists were of similar tensions in and among the city states. In the Hebrew case, too, a civil war would soon be breaking out, splitting the tribes into two kingdoms. No narrative could be more political or more practical. Great crimes and great reconciliations lie behind the formation of the people, Israel. Without the reconciliation after the crime, Israel might not have existed: this is the point of the Joseph story.

Occupying almost a third of the Book of Genesis, the Joseph legend is remarkable for the sparse occurrence of the word *God*. With one exception,[41] only the human actors use theological terms, and they do that rarely. Divine Providence works here, but in very worldly disguise.[42] It is a story to test the claim that religiously contexted narratives can be as empirically pertinent to human political life as their most secular counterparts.

Like *Eumenides*, the Joseph story is a chapter in a previous history of rivalry, domination, trickery, and alienation in a family. Guile, greed, and malice run in this family. They have run consistently in the life of the father, Jacob.[43] It is not the story of a model family but rather of how human community can survive some of the worst possible assaults against it.

The plot is familiar: Seventeen-year-old Joseph—who, along with his younger brother Benjamin, is a son of Rachel—is the apple of his father's eye. He accepts his favored status eagerly and naively. Bursting with adolescent innocence and pride, he shares with his ten half brothers his dream of having them "bow down to him" in a grand reversal of the rights of the eldest and the youngest. For many years the half brothers' hatred of him has been gathering: ". . . when his brothers saw that their father loved him more than all his brothers, they hated him, and could not speak peaceably to him" (37:4). Now to the excesses of paternal preferential love there is added the contempt of older brothers for a younger one: "So they hated him yet more for his dreams and for his words" (37:8). On next sight of Joseph, a majority of them promptly devise his murder; but two (Reuben and Judah) urge other strategies, one of them remembering the curse of blood guilt that lay on Cain's forehead and urging a self-interest that will serve them all better than revenge: "What profit is it if we slay our brother and conceal his blood?" (37:26). A caravan of slave traders comes down the road, and off goes Joseph to Egypt sold by his brothers into slavery.[44]

There, almost immediately, as his dreams had predicted, "he became a successful man" (39:2). After a bout of adversity, he becomes more successful yet. "In crisis situations, in despair and poverty, in power at all levels, [Joseph] is the image of a well-disciplined leader, an ideal administrator of a powerful office."[45] His experience of suffering and his access to power have apparently matured him, and now he enjoys the full fruits of maturity: wealth, family, influence. The dreams are coming true, and his good fortune in the present gives him good reason to forget the rancors and pains of the past. He names his first child Manasseh, "Making-to-Forget." "'For,' he said, 'God has made me forget all my hardship and all my father's house'"(41:51).

But he has not really forgotten any of the painful past. The stage is set for an agonizing reconciliation with "all my father's house," but set, too, for an interplay of retributive and restorative justice that is the Bible's earliest clue to what a human act of forgiveness looks like.

Having remained in Egypt for twenty-two years, Joseph is now thirty-nine years old and the officer in charge of Egypt's efforts to cope with a worldwide famine which has devastated Canaan, too. So the elder brothers come, seeking grain for their starving kin. When they make their appeal for help to Joseph himself, they do not recognize him and will not do so until the end of the story. Here at the first meeting they encounter a hostility in Joseph which the tellers of the legend expect their hearers to understand without commentary. With guile Joseph accuses the brothers of coming to Egypt as spies (42:9). It is his first in a long series of moves designed to throw the brothers into anxiety and fear for their lives. He is using the tricks of power to punish them, raising great question as to whether this is the story of an "ideal administrator." It may rather be the story of a man who, remembering those who most sinned against him in his youth, flirts with the temptations of revenge.[46]

One of the brothers remains innocent and precious in his memory—Benjamin, who has been left behind by the ten brothers on the chance that he might suffer harm in Egypt. Although they have attempted to cover their tracks with lies to Jacob about the fate of Joseph, they might not be able to do so with Benjamin. Whether simply from wanting to see his full brother again or to deepen the half brothers' anxiety, Joseph demands that they bring Benjamin to Egypt. Immediately they sense awful retribution in the wind. Speaking the Hebrew language which, they think, Joseph does not understand, they rehearse with each other the old haunting guilt: "In truth we are guilty concerning our brother [Joseph]. . . . So now there comes a reckoning for his blood" (42:21–22). Overcome by a mixture of memories and emotions, the still unrecognized brother bolts from the room in tears.

Mistrust in this family runs long and deep. Joseph insists that one of his brothers, Simeon, be jailed as security for the return of the others with Benjamin. But astonishing good fortune accompanies them: to full sacks of grain Joseph has ordered added the money they paid for the grain. He surprises them with gifts that both display his power and play with their fears. Afraid and mistrustful rather than grateful, the brothers are overcome by a sense of fateful retribution: "At this their hearts failed them" (42:28). The apparent generosity of the great Egyptian official must be a mask of malice. Not largesse but more trickery must hide here; no wonder they delay a return to Egypt as long as the new supply of grain holds out. Caught finally between hunger and a father's resistance to sending his youngest son to Egypt, the brothers persuade the old man with a pledge from Reuben that Jacob can kill Reuben's own two sons if Benjamin perishes in Egypt. The excesses of blood revenge stalk the story as truly as in any Greek tragedy.

Laden with the defenses of double money and luxurious gifts, they go off again, bent on appeasing the anger of the man in charge in Egypt. He meets them with an invitation to dinner, which throws them once again into paroxysms of paranoia: "It is because of the money, which was replaced in our sacks the first time, that we are brought in, so that he may seek occasion against us and fall upon us, to make slaves of us" (43:18)—a retribution that exactly fitted their crime of old. At the ensuing banquet, their defense against disaster is an attempt to restore the commercial relation. To do so, they must clear up the strange matter of the money in the sacks. We have brought it all back to you, they tell him, and more for another purchase. He replies to them nonchalantly, in a mixture of religious piety, fact, and guile: "Rest assured, do not be afraid; your God and God of your father must have put treasure in our sacks for you; I received your money" (43:23). Then he releases Simeon from jail; and the feast goes on, segregated by Egyptian and Hebrew tables, "because the Egyptians might not eat bread with the Hebrews, for that is an abomination to the Egyptians" (43:32). The comaraderie of the occasion flourishes, however, above uneasy currents of plots and suspicions which only Joseph comprehends.

Joseph lays one more deception in the brothers' way. They are back on the road with the grain, and a silver cup turns up in Benjamin's sack. Back they go under police guard to make account to Joseph, their provider. Now the old threads of rancor, retribution, guilt, and fragile hope for the future gather together in an amalgam which will yield an astonishing reconciliation on all sides of the shattered family: In a long, eloquent plea for the life and freedom of Benjamin, Judah rehearses the story of how the heart of old Jacob will break with grief if this second son of Rachel should perish. Newly out of jail, Simeon also pleads that he be permitted to "remain instead of the lad as a slave to my lord; and let the lad go back with his brothers" (44:33). As Coats comments, Joseph has now driven the tension between himself and the brothers "to its most excruciating peak. . . . Compassion for Benjamin and Jacob replaces hostility and deceit. But the change occurs as if in response to a call for the future, not as an uncovering of character [among the brothers] already effective in the past. The change is thus not the work of any one figure in the scene. To the contrary, the change transcends the people who thought they controlled the crucial event," including Joseph himself.[47] Floodgates of affection, compassion, and grief now open in Joseph.

Joseph could not control himself before all those who stood by him; and he cried: "Make every one go out from me." So no [Egyptian] stayed with him when Joseph made himself known to his brothers. And he wept aloud, so that the Egyptians heard it, and the household of Pharaoh heard it. And Joseph said to his brothers, "I am Joseph; is my father still alive?" But his brothers could not answer him, for they were dismayed at his presence. So Joseph said to his brothers, "Come near to me, I pray you." And they came near. And he said, "I am your brother, Joseph, whom you sold into Egypt. And now do not be distressed, or angry with yourselves, because you sold me here; for God sent me before you to preserve life. . . ." And he kissed all his brothers and wept upon them; and after that his brothers talked with him [45:1–5,15].

Undertows of fear, suspicion, and guilt will tug at this reconciliation down to the very end of the story. In this dramatic moment all the dimensions of forgiveness between humans have at last emerged: painful, judgmental truth; forbearance of revenge; empathy and compassion; and a new solidarity between enemies. But if these are the requirements of a genuine act of human forgiveness, the story seems to say, their convergence can be difficult, long delayed, and forever imperfect. To this point in the Joseph story, no one has used the word *forgive*, and the word in fact will not appear until the very end.

The old wound in family unity, now some twenty-five years old, has apparently been healed. Joseph, with Pharaoh's concurrence, invites the whole family of Jacob to "sojourn" in Egypt and to occupy grazing land in Goshen. Old Jacob has seventeen years in which to enjoy the restoration of his family. On his deathbed he blesses his sons and grandsons in a poem (49:1–27), which mixes images of future tribal fortunes with assessments of the diverse characters of the brothers and their respective descendants. So Jacob, who once lived in Canaan, through Joseph and a great reconciliation, dies in Egypt in the expectation that the family will return to Canaan. There, in fact, he wants his bones buried (47:30). A new nation has begun, but it could not begin until something decisive was done about evils that threatened the unity of a family apparently bent on destroying itself. That decisive something was a long-drawn-out process of forgiveness.

That word[48] finally appears in the very end of the story in a coda that recapitulates the long trek from crime to fear of revenge to the difficulties that humans experience in believing that another human is capable of real forgiveness. Seventeen years of restored relations with Joseph (he is now about 60 years old) are insufficient to quiet the undertow of the brothers' fears. Perhaps Joseph has been lenient only out of respect for his father? "It may be that Joseph will hate us and pay us back for all the evil which we did to him." So they concoct a story, as was their life habit: Before he died, Jacob had requested them to "say to Joseph, Forgive, I pray you, the transgression of your brothers and their sin . . ." (50:17). As part of a fabrication, forgiveness for them is a bare, almost speculative possibility. For them, the law of revenge stands always ready in human affairs to swallow up this unlikely contender, forgiveness. Two radically different expectations of the future of human communities have been in collision here, and the tug of the old expectation dies hard.

At this Joseph weeps again: For how long will they continue to suffer from that awful past? And when will they open their eyes fully to the mysterious good at work in the midst of all this evil? "Fear not, for am I in the place of God? As for you, you meant evil against me; but God meant it for good, to bring it about that many people should be kept alive, as they are today. So do not fear; I will provide for you and your little ones" (50:15–21).[49] It is an exact rehearsal of his speeches to them seventeen years before: The cruelty of the original crime has not been canceled, nor has it merely been subject to damage control. Rough-hewn human purposes have all been overruled here in the divine purpose to establish a new human community in spite of famines, murders, and assorted betrayals. "It is in the potential for the future, not in the treachery of the past that God's agency in the event can be seen."[50] In a story almost wholly concerned with sin and reconciliation on the level of one human family, this is the one salient theological element. The author of the story believes that the existence of his society has depended, from the first, on divine power and intention *made real in the tortured but successful attempt of Joseph and his brothers to knit up their broken relations in a genuine act of forgiveness*. The message here is clearer than it would be in *Eumenides*, but it is much the same message: Cities, nations exist because they have managed to name the evils of their past, to name the agents of evil, yet to maintain some community among evildoers—since, in a story as candid about human nature as the Joseph story, responsibility for evil is widely distributed. So too is the benefit of the reconciliation: women and children are safe in Athens now because the Furies of vengeance have been tamed into the Eumenides of blessing, and the "little ones" of Israel have a future because their fathers stumbled at last into peace with each other in spite of themselves.

From beginning to end the Joseph story is dominated by the realism of human conflict and the equal realism of what it takes to turn conflict from tragedy to "blessing." The ingredients of blessedness, in the saga of the Hebrew people, were "down to earth" in a literal sense: land, peoplehood, abundance, and the promise of descendants dominated their hopes for the future; above all, the purposes of God in the world centered on the *preservation of life*. "God sent me before you to preserve life . . . to preserve for you a remnant on earth, to keep alive for you many survivors . . ." (45:5,7). The religious message of the story is that human life matters to its Creator, who means to preserve it against these creatures' tendencies towards self-destruction. As future chapters of the Book of Exodus will make clear, law, morals, regulation, and political structure have as their overriding purpose the "blessing" of the world. They are not ends in themselves, just as the forgiveness of evildoers is not an end in itself but a means toward the blessedness of renewed community. There is something profoundly "utilitarian" in the spirit and substance of theology and morality here, but the utilitarianism has its home in the life of a society in whose good its members find their individual good. In this respect, in their mutual concern for the integrity of their communities, the Greeks and the Hebrews were equally political in the core of their ethics and theology. But at least in the Joseph story the Hebrew had the clearer grasp of what forgiveness is and how it can serve the life and combat the death of human relationship. Forgiveness, as a human event, means the commitment of members of a society to each other, because, in spite of evil, "only in that relationship does life make sense," or continue in ways worth the living.[51]

"Who Can Forgive Sins but God Alone?"

The scarcity of attention to forgiveness between human beings in the Hebrew Bible is a surprise to careful readers of the Joseph saga. So eloquent, realistic, and dramatic a story would have resulted, one might think, in a host of echoes in the law, political events, and prophetic ethics in the later history of Israel. That later history suggests that the old story of family reconciliation proved to be an idle, wishful tale, a precedent honored chiefly in its defiance. Civil war split ten of the tribes from two, and neither within nor between the two little countries did anyone speak often of forgiveness as a solution to the problem of human alienation. The "ideal administrator," Joseph, found few imitators in this history, as kings, princes, and foreign enemies went about their business of achieving and protecting power. The myth of Cain and Abel was regularly reenacted; the story of Joseph apparently found few serious imitators.

Instead, with mounting intensity, the theological-ethical question to which the religious leaders of Israel regularly returned was whether and how the God of Israel might be the forgiver of human sin. As the author of laws under which humans prosper in relation to each other, God is the one who, first of all, is offended by their offenses. Thus, in a notorious incident of politically implemented sin, David's theft of the wife of Uriah (II Sam. 11) found its classic liturgical memorial in a prayer attributed to David as repentant man of power:

> Against thee, thee only, have I sinned,
> and done that which is evil in thy sight,
> so that thou art justified in thy sentence
> and blameless in thy judgment [Ps. 51:4].

Only a profound sense of divine involvement in human affairs could have produced such a prayer and its traditional association with the sins of David, Israel's favorite king. On the surface, to say that David's adultery with Bathsheba was sin against God and God "only" is to reduce to trivial importance the multiple damages done to human beings in the incident. But the narrative associated with the later psalm (II Sam. 11–12) does not permit such an interpretation: there a child dies, a king suffers public humiliation at the hands of a prophet, and the future of his kingship suffers too. The point of Psalm 51 is that the God of Israel takes its sin more seriously than it does. As with the Greeks and many other religious traditions, God and the gods are protectors of the moral order, springing into actions of judgment and punishment when it suffers violation. But in the Hebrew case, the sense of personal affront to the divine is stronger; the one God of Israel is never on vacation from attentiveness to its sins.

So in Israel, perhaps with more consistency and urgency than in any other contemporary culture, great theological agony grew up around the question: What will God do about all this human evil that only God *can* do? What will God do to change the "inward being" (Psalm 51:6) of humans? Institutions of law, religion, and government do restrain human sin partially; but only a "new creation" will really cure humans of the guilt, corruptions, and continuing infections of their evildoing. Time enough, the Hebrew Bible seems to imply, to speak of forgiveness between human beings once one can speak with confidence about the forgiveness of God. *Divine* forgiveness alone will produce an interior renovation of humanity sufficient to renovate relations between humans. Once God has "written the law" upon the inner selves of humans, they will have no need of outer instruction and outer institutions of law. In the day that this high hope for a new, divine initiative comes to pass,

> ... no longer shall each person teach their neighbor ... saying, "Know the Lord," for they shall all know me, from the least of them to the greatest, says the Lord, for I will forgive their iniquity, and I will remember their sin no more [Jer. 31:35].

Great blessing will follow in the society that "knows the Lord" in this transformative event, whose promise in this famous vision of Jeremiah encompasses earthly benefits to Israel akin to those envisioned in the Joseph story—land, agricultural abundance, peace, and right relationship among citizens.

> I will bring them back to this place, and I will make them dwell in safety. And they shall be my people, and I will be their God. I will give them one heart and one way, that they may fear me for ever, for their own good and the good of their children after them [Jer. 32:37–39]).

The spirit and substance of the hope here in Jeremiah is consistent with the same in the Joseph saga. Both presuppose the coming of a powerful, transforming renewal of the human, whose true beginning is the forgiveness of sins. But Jeremiah speaks of this event as wholly the work of the Divine. The author of the Joseph story assumes that something of this renewal was available in the present, thanks to the mysterious initiatives of God and the ability of humans themselves to play a part in the drama of reconciliation. Tension and distance between the two points of view are not resolved in the Hebrew Bible.

One group of heirs to its tradition, however, would lessen the tension and shorten the distance between divine and human forgiveness: the Christians. What they believed about the connection of the two would republish and expand the Joseph story in ways that will occupy us below in a second introductory chapter.[52]

Interlude: Reflections on Revenge, Justice, and Forgiveness

For the sake of its own preservation, society cannot permit revenge to go its unhindered way; on that principle these ancient texts agree. But they also agree that some form of punitive, institutionalized social response to wrongdoing is equally indispensable to the social fabric. As the narratives of this chapter imply, revenge "in due measure" has no easy formula—which is one reason we have courts as well as laws.

What measure of punitive response is "due" a wrongdoer at the hands of a wrong-sufferer, whether the latter is an individual or a society? There is a spectrum of possible answers, most of them acknowledged as potentials of human behavior in these narratives. A summary of the potentials may be useful for characterizing ways in which an "ethic of just vengeance" might be distinguished from an ethic of unjust vengeance. The list below begins and ends with lawless responses to wrongdoing. The in-between responses are the diverse candidates for defining just vengeance.

Terror is the response of amoral, autocratic powers to actions of others that they oppose. The motto of terrorism is, "For damage to one of our eyes, we put out all the eyes we wish." The gate opens here to measureless revenge.

Vindictiveness is a first cousin to terror. Its motto is, "Two eyes for one, or a few more for good measure." Within slight hailing distance of some restraint, the vindictive nod, at least, to the idea of proportion.

Retaliation can be defined as response in kind, "eye for eye, tooth for tooth, and no more." The word carries this literal meaning, and its synonym should probably be "retribution." A special difficulty of this concept in practice is the elusiveness of exact retribution, as when the original offenders are absent, dead, or otherwise inaccessible.

Punishment is a word best reserved to a wide array of social disciplines, some of which only remotely fit the offense. The motto of the punisher is, "For your hurt, we hurt in return, but not necessarily in kind. Above all we must reassert the standards which you have defied; our punishment must not defy them either." (The latter is the claim urged by those who believe that no society should institutionalize capital punishment.)

Restitution, or restorative justice, moves by the motto, "Restore what was lost." From cookies taken from the jar to lives squandered in a bombing raid, there is something just indeed about the imperative: "Put it all back." But empirical finitude and tragedy haunt both retaliatory and restorative justice here: Often "it" is gone forever, so that cries for justice have only the recourses already described. Yet some forms of restitution can diminish tragedy, while retaliation may add to it.

Protest is the barest of responses in the spectrum and is the recourse of those who have no other motto than "Let us live with the loss, but let us at least *name* its injustice out loud." One may have to admit that there are wrongs that no human court can properly punish or rectify. But to leave that fact unremarked is to abandon the cause of justice itself.

Passivity, like terror, belongs to this moral-political spectrum only as a boundary. Terrorist power and its passive objects have *anomie* in common—that is, lawlessness. Terror is the anomie of the powerful, passivity that of the powerless. The one defines just punishment as it wills, the other lives with the motto "There is no escape."

Each of these terms has implications for a society's norms for the just use of power in its institutions. To what degree is retaliatory justice as essential to social well-being as restorative justice? In a book that begins to explore this vexed question in its ancient formulation by the Greeks, Susan Jacoby advocates the wisdom that societies persist in a "balance between compassionate and retributive impulses." Once they are committed to such balance, "individuals and societies turn their attention to the question of what forms of retribution, and which forms of forgiveness, afford *the opportunity of an existence that encompasses both justice and love.*" It would comport better with the setting of these "impulses" in concrete social relations if Jacoby had said *a social existence that encompasses both a just love and a loving justice.* This more relational way of putting it is consistent with Jacoby's own conclusion that "true justice partakes of both qualities," for:

> The entire modern argument over the relation between revenge and justice turns on [the] question of the equilibrium between memory and hope. With moral and legal balance firmly in mind as a social goal, the formula of "justice, not revenge" has the same absurd ring as "justice, not forgiveness."[53]

Unfortunately, in the ears of many modern people, "justice, not forgiveness" sounds sensible enough, while "justice, not revenge" does sound absurd.

Perhaps the conclusion of the complex matter has to be that concrete determinations of just retaliation are hard enough, but once restorative justice enters its claim, the determination is harder yet. Aeschylus paid tribute to the complexity of punitive justice when he imagined that even the gods argue over its meaning. The author of the Joseph saga made the same point by describing a long-drawn-out process in which punishment for crime and promise of reconciliation vied for prominence in the resulting "justice." *Simple* justice is elusive in these narratives. Their summary theme is that forgiveness thrives in the tension between justice-as-punishment and justice-as-restoration. To take both sides seriously is to ponder how "due retribution" can play a restorative role in the future relation of wrongdoers and wrong-sufferers, and how forgiveness makes room for punishment while making wider room yet for the repair of damages and renewal of relation between enemies.

Another way of expressing the wisdom here is to concede that justice is a search as well as a single event. The characters in the stories rehearsed in this chapter often display great dogmatic certainty about the just thing to do in their fractured societies. Their failure to see social justice as requiring *deliberation* among all concerned parties sometimes ensures the triumph of injustice. Courts of law; mandates that compel enemies into direct communication with each other; and other processes of negotiation that require time, energy, and vulnerability to learning on all sides—such processes facilitate the discovery of genuine justice and the experience of real forgiveness. Neither is an instantaneous given.

In his film on the conflict between Robespierre and Danton, the Polish director Andrzej Wajda seems to say that in the conflicts of human politics "there are some points to be made on both sides, and suggests that compassion, some tolerance, some warm human doubt and not frigid, bloody certainty are the best ways" to face such conflict. Nothing but exhaustion and cruelty can come when citizens and their leaders "play at being Gods,"[54] which means pretending to know what is "best" when disputed definitions of the best are the heart of the public debate. Once a local North Carolina judge put this wisdom very clearly in a public address: "Justice is a search. Our forebears cut off the hands of thieves, and we realize that this was unjust. . . . We shouldn't define justice too closely, for then our searching would cease, and we would cease."[55]

Aeschylus, Thucydides, and the author of the Joseph saga all portrayed that search as a long one. Bloody conflicts continued to erupt in their own times. They did not expect the search to end soon.

2

Forgiveness in Politics
in Christian Tradition

People associate not only to transform themselves, but also to change the social
world in which they live. Associations . . . are a sword as well as a shield.[1]
Robert Cover

One of the signs of the new twentieth-century dialogue between Jews and Christians
is the use, increasingly common, of the term *Hebrew Bible* as substitute for the traditional Christian term *Old Testament*. In the first century of the Christian movement,
its Bible was the Hebrew Bible, and most Christians today consider that collection
of thirty-nine books to have an authority wholly akin to that of the twenty-seven books
added to compose the "New Testament." The latter phrase was almost certainly derived from Jeremiah: God's promise of a new covenant, which, Christians believed,
was effected in Jesus of Nazareth.

Into the great range of issues among scholars and contemporary adherents of these
two great religions, we need not enter here. But it is proper to record my impression,
strengthened by the work of numerous modern Jewish and Christian scholars, that
the *ethical teachings* of Jesus recorded in the New Testament are, on the whole, not
only consistent with those of the Hebrew Bible but are dominated by the biblical
teachings of the synagogues in which Jesus himself was brought up. In the records
they made of the teachings of Jesus, early Christians accentuated the authority of the
teacher but not the originality of what he taught. He may have "taught them as one
who had authority, and not as their scribes" (Matt. 7:29). But in numerous ways he
did teach what the scribes taught; indeed, on many occasions he called scribes, Pharisees, and his own followers back to the ancient authority of Moses and the prophets.
Like the Hebrew prophets themselves, Jesus could easily be termed an ethical conservative in that he revered the Mosaic tradition and called upon all his hearers to
test contemporary "tradition" against that older one.[2] This, in itself, would be enough
reason for Christians early and late to take the Hebrew scriptural tradition, by whatever name, as authoritative.

Jesus, the "Discoverer" of Social Forgiveness?

Modern secular Jewish political philosopher that she was, the late Hannah Arendt was not inclined to treat either of these religious scriptures as authoritative for her understanding of human political reality. But in her account of how human societies govern themselves, cohere, and change, she used two terms that are profusely present, respectively, in the Hebrew and Christian Bibles: *promise* and *forgiveness*. Her reading of the empirical truth of human politics, in this double connection, is a vital contribution to the way in which modern Jews, Christians, and their secular neighbors might discuss the issues central to this study: How do societies get over the evils in their pasts, and how do they change for the better?

Arendt's summary answer to this pair of questions was striking:

> . . . the remedy against the irreversibility and unpredictability of the process started by [human] acting does not arise out of another and possibly higher faculty, but is one of the potentialities of action itself. The possible redemption from the predicament of irreversibility—of being unable to undo what one has done though one did not, and could not, have known what he was doing—is the faculty of forgiving. The remedy for unpredictability, for the chaotic uncertainty of the future, is contained in the faculty to make and keep promises. The two faculties belong together in so far as one of them, forgiving, serves to undo the deeds of the past, whose "sins" hang like Damocles' sword over every new generation; and the other, binding oneself through promises, serves to set up in the ocean of uncertainty, which the future is by definition, islands of security without which not even continuity, let alone durability of any kind, would be possible in relationships. . . .[3]

The language of human promises, of course, is the language of contracts and covenants. Americans are familiar with the idea that governments begin in agreements and commitments between human beings, voluntarily, in a fresh start of which we are all alleged, by the liberal theory, to be capable. This theory has a natural ally and extension in the notion that, in their freedom, humans can change their behavior, commit to new relationships, and turn from certain pasts toward different social futures. From here the theory easily slides into the everyday moralism in which humans assure each other: "If we should do it, if we want to do it, we can do it."

Both the Hebrew and Christian Bibles are ambiguous about human moral capacity. Deuteronomy 30:14 assures the people of Israel that the divine word for governing their life is "in your mouth and in your heart, so that you can do it." Yet Jeremiah and many another prophet are not so optimistic: only a "new heart" will render sinful humans capable of right behavior, a Spirit-empowered reformation of human character. A similar ambiguity meets the reader of the New Testament, especially in the contrast between the teachings of Jesus and those of Paul. Jesus seems much more inclined to say to his listeners, "You can do it. . . . " Yet the *you* in many of his teachings is plural, addressed to a company of followers who are expected to encourage each other in the new life, disciplined by love of God and neighbor. You can do it, but you are not to try to do it alone.

In short, as repair of broken social relations, forgiveness has to be learned in a community: that seems basic to the ethical teachings of Jesus. Hannah Arendt saw this clearly and credited him and his imitators in the early Christian movement with the "discovery" of the indispensable role of forgiveness in processes of social change. Sensitive to the resistance in her fellow social scientists (and in herself) to accepting religious reasons for any assertions of scientific fact, she went out of her way to point out that religious people, too, can be the source of perfectly valid truths about human society:

> The discoverer of the role of forgiveness in the realm of human affairs was Jesus of Nazareth. The fact that he made this discovery in a religious context and articulated it in religious language is no reason to take it any less seriously in a strictly secular sense. It has been in the nature of the tradition of political thought . . . to be highly selective and to exclude from articulate conceptualization a great variety of authentic political experiences, among which we need not be surprised to find some of an elementary nature. Certain aspects of the teaching of Jesus of Nazareth which are not primarily related to the Christian religious message but sprang from experiences in the small and closely knit community of his followers, bent on challenging the public authorities in Israel, certainly belong among them, even though they have been neglected because of their allegedly exclusively religious nature. . . .
>
> It is decisive in our context that Jesus maintains against the "scribes and pharisees" first that it is not true that only God has the power to forgive, and second that this power does not derive from God . . . but on the contrary must be mobilized by men toward each other before they can hope to be forgiven by God also.[4]

The religious mind, at least that shaped by the Bible, must balk at the notion that any human power "does not derive from God"—but there is considerable room in the debates of theologians over the differences between ordinary human ethics, knowable and doable by all, and "special" ethics accessible only to the inspired believer. Biblical texts abound for fortifying one side or another of this classic debate, but the point here is that, even if Jesus was not the "discoverer" of the place of forgiveness in human affairs, it came into new prominence in his teachings, and it acquired very practical, prudential connotations. Among the practicalities was what forgiveness does to ensure the continued existence of a fractured human community.

Arendt was surely right in seeing the community of Jesus' followers, the young church, as the testing ground, the laboratory, so to speak, for demonstrating the truth of this "discovery."[5] Emphasis on spiritual reformation of the human "heart" has impelled many interpreters of the Christian message, ancient and modern, to equate the faith with the most intense moral individualism. Such interpretations move further and further away from any basic religious concern for horizontal human social relationships, and these versions of Christianity add to its reputation for not having much to do with society at large or even with this world in contrast to the next. Recent scholarship has undermined this supposed individualism of Jesus' teachings, however, by pointing to several levels of their setting in the economic, social, and political reality of the time. A sketch of that context is in order.

The Political Context of Jesus' Ministry

Some recent scholars see Jesus' ministry as intending a "Jewish revitalization movement" leading to nothing less than the transformation of the whole nation.[6] Others note that on occasion he called whole towns to repent, and that his sense of collective accountability focused on the witness of his disciples in the local village.[7] The Gospels record mixed success in Jesus' pursuit of such aims, and many scholars note that in calling of twelve disciples and in his habit of teaching wider groups of followers he was creating an alternative community, a "contrast society" that would exist in the midst of the wider society as "leaven in the lump" and "salt of the earth" (Matt. 5:13–16). By this account, Jesus intended to leave behind neither a withdrawn sect nor some new powerful institution but a group of people whose lifestyle already embodied and reflected the present "reigning of God"[8] in anticipation of its ultimate coming at the end of history. Here enters the notion of the Christian movement as an "eschatological community," not waiting passively for the end of the world but actively anticipating what the human world looks like when its relationships are being shaped by the reforming Spirit of God.

Like many a narrative in the Hebrew Bible, the Gospel stories are full of political references: Roman occupiers, Jewish kings, powerful high priests—all of them seeking to control a society none of whose members knew anything about "separation of church and state." Indeed, in spite of the politically "tamed" final versions of some of the Gospel narratives,[9] Jesus' challenges to powerful politicians and institutions come through clearly in many passages. Richard Horsley is surely right to characterize Jesus as a leader who did not engage other leaders only "from a distance."

> He consistently criticized and resisted the oppressive established political-economic-religious order of his own society. Moreover, he aggressively intervened to mitigate or undo the effects of institutionalized violence, whether in particular acts of forgiveness or exorcism or in the general opening of the kingdom of God to the poor. Jesus opposed violence, but not from a distance. He rather entered actively into the situation of violence, and even exacerbated the conflict.[10]

He certainly exacerbated it in his early controversy with his neighbors in Nazareth (Lk. 4:28–30), in his open challenges to "that fox" King Herod (Lk. 13:32), in his unmistakable (perhaps satirical) public challenge to popular images of "kingship" when he rode into Jerusalem on a donkey, and immediately after in his assault on the "robbers" and their commerce in the Jerusalem Temple (Matt. 21:1–13).

None of this makes Jesus a political revolutionary in the ordinary sense, but it does make him revolutionary in an extraordinary sense: before he stood before Pilate, he had taught his disciples that the humane form of *power* was *servanthood,* not the domination seen in the world's "kings who lord it over their subjects." (Lk. 22:24–27). The next day he stood trial before such a "king," Pilate, and Christians ever after remembered that trial as a confrontation, nonviolent from Jesus' side, between the two definitions of humane power. John Howard Yoder sees in the event something more momentous than a theoretical conflict over definitions.

Jesus chose not only to stumble over diversities of definition but to be crucified on them. He refused to concede that the men in power represent an ideal, a logically proper, or even an empirically acceptable definition of what it means to be political. He did not say (as some sectarian pacifists, or some pietists might) "you can have your politics and I shall do something else more important"; he said, "your definition of *polis*, of the social, or the wholeness of man in his socialness is perverted."[11]

One can, with some twentieth-century theologians, dismiss the implications here as typically "religious" and therefore "unrealistic." Who expects the politically powerful to give up their urge to domineer or their self-glorification? One answer seems to be that Jesus did. His expectation had in it as much ethical realism as that of Aeschylus and Thucydides when they expected the Greek city-states to give up revenge. If they did not, they were flying in the face of their own real collective self-interest. They were not yet being truly, prudently political.

Religious people, including Christians, have not always posed their quarrel with antagonistic cultures, institutions, and leaders in terms of human self-interest. Authoritative principle, dogmatic presupposition, and religious arrogance have marked their side of the antagonism; and, even if recommended in some humbler spirit, the teachings of Jesus in the New Testament sometimes come across to modern readers as an example of a "rigorism" that demands self-sacrifice and reaches after the impossible. All this adds up to ethics for the few. But this version of Jesus' teachings omits two notes struck frequently in the Gospel story: First, that "the time is at hand" for humans to see the power of God at work in their midst; second, that there is enough moral capacity in ordinary men and women to act accordingly. Everything that John the Baptist tells his followers to do lies quite within their power: sharing of food and clothing, no cheating in business, "no bullying, no blackmail" in soldiering (Lk. 3:10–14). The context of these ethics is what God is doing and what humans can do.

> Jesus . . . made clear in his message and his actions that the reign of God already was breaking in full of promise and effectiveness, that it was becoming visible symbolically in his own deeds, healings, assurance of forgiveness of sin, turning toward the poor, the disregarded, and the oppressed. The rule of God is already now a discernible reality and places on his hearers the urgent appeal to conduct themselves accordingly.[12]

The teachings are instructions to act on; "none is an impossible action; each is a practical way of deliverance out of the vicious cycles" of wrong answered by wrong.

Jesus did not convince contemporary Roman and Temple leaders to reform their behavior after the patterns of the Sermon on the Mount, but he did convince a band of followers to take him and his teachings seriously enough to form themselves into an ongoing association, a new, concrete social reality, the church. The forming of this church (a gathering whose Greek name, *ekklesia,* meant "called out") was implicit in his decision to "call" twelve disciples. "The realism of Jesus' proclamation included its power to create its own sociological base; without this he would have been no threat" to the religious and political establishment. Loose as it was, his *organization* frightened religious and secular politicians alike.[13] Later sociologists would call it a "social" organization as opposed to a "political" one, on the assumption that to be political is to be on the track of accumulating power. More historically, one might say that Jesus was one of the early inventors of a society that could not be defined or subsumed under the umbrella of the state. In the church, the society of Jesus could, without plotting to overthrow the state, refuse to take its primary guidance for human behavior from the state. In this sense it was indeed an alternative society, an alternative sphere for working out relations of leadership, power, and human connection, modeled not on Roman culture but on Hebrew culture reaffirmed and augmented by Jesus himself. In this sense Jesus was not just a moralist or spiritual teacher but "the bearer of a new possibility of human, social, and therefore political relationships." His execution therefore ought to be seen as "the punishment of a man who threatens society by creating a new kind of community leading a radically new kind of life."[14]

Forgiveness as Community Building in the New Testament

Teachings and activities related to forgiveness occur in at least five settings in the Gospels. In each setting Jesus apparently went out of his way to affirm that forgiveness is the doorway through which a diversity of humans—many of them alienated by social custom from each other—can come together to form a new community. The five settings were (1) healings, (2) prayer, (3) eating, (4) public enemies, and (5) discipline inside the new community.

Healings

Early in the Gospel narratives occurs an incident of healing with intimate, dramatic pertinence to both the theology and the politics implicit in Jesus' offer of forgiveness to distressed persons (Mk. 2:1–12). The social setting is the small town of Capernaum where Jesus is "at home" teaching in a crowded room. Four men open the roof above his head and lower their paralyzed friend into the room. In Jesus' view, the four become partners in the healing: "When Jesus saw their faith, he said to the paralyzed man, 'My son, your sins are forgiven.'" For the moment, no healing ensues, but rather a strenuous argument with "some lawyers sitting there" who "thought to themselves, 'Why does the fellow talk like that? This is blasphemy! Who but God alone can forgive sins?'" It was the orthodox view. Also orthodox was the expectation that the business of securing the forgiveness of God belonged in the Jerusalem temple, not on the streets of a Galilean town. Jesus, intuiting this orthodoxy in the lawyers, announces his intention to validate his right to forgive with a demonstration of his power to heal. To the paralytic he says, "Stand up, take your bed, and go home."[15] In addition to freeing him from a psychosomatic connection between sin and sickness, Jesus thus freed the man from depending on a remote religious institution for forgiveness. A localizing of the process took place here. As Richard Horsley puts it:

> By pointing to the forgiveness of God as directly available, Jesus was exposing the religious means by which the social restrictions on the people were maintained.

Thus, instead of the people continuing to blame themselves for their suffering, they were freed for a resumption of a productive, cooperative life in their communities.[16]

(There was plenty of blame to share for suffering at all levels of the society, Horsley assumes, but the freedom here consisted partly in Jesus' refusal to accept the jurisdiction of powerful religious and political institutions over the definition and the cure of the paralytic's situation.[17])

The linkage of forgiveness and physical healing is nowhere in the Gospels more dramatic than in this incident. Jesus was apparently careful on some other occasions to dispel the old theology that blamed illness on personal faults.[18] The striking impression of the incident on its witnesses is expressed in the Matthew version as their "awe at the sight" and their praise to God "for granting such authority to men." The plural here would be significant to Hannah Arendt: Was Jesus demonstrating his uniqueness as a forgiver of other people's sins, or was he demonstrating, in Arendt's phrase, "one of the potentialities of [human] action itself"? Whether all humans have that potential is a question left in abeyance in the New Testament, but it is certain that Jesus had no intention of arrogating the power to forgive to himself alone. To the contrary, early and late, he insisted that his followers had access to that power and should regularly use it. Who among the followers might have *special* access to it would become a momentous question of church history to come.

Prayer

Without entering into recent scholarly argument over whether or not the words of the so-called Lord's Prayer came directly from the lips of Jesus, one has to observe that the forgiveness-petition in the famous prayer, along with the intimate address to God as *abba,* has little or no parallel in classic Jewish prayer. Concerning the forgiveness-petition, the author of Matthew thought it important to append an underscoring commentary: "For if you forgive others the wrongs they have done, your heavenly Father will also forgive you"—but if you do not, God will not (Matt. 6:14–15). The two texts of the prayer support just this rigor. Not only is God no longer the sole source of forgiveness, but humans who pray are forbidden to petition for divine forgiveness without their own forgiveness in hand.

> Forgive us our debts,
> As we also have forgiven our debtors. (Matt. 6:12)

> Forgive us our sins, for we ourselves forgive every one who is indebted to us. (Luke 11:4)[19]

Nothing in the tenses of the Greek verbs here permits the reading (which some writers of the New Testament epistles found more comfortable theologically), "Forgive us so that we will have the power to forgive." The connection seems blatantly reversed: "We dare not ask You to forgive unless we are already forgiving."[20] With this radical, unorthodox point, if no other, Jesus introduces something new to the religious tradition into which he was born.

Eating

To the most casual observer of the ministry of Jesus of Nazareth, two of his regular activities seemed to define the intentions of that ministry: healing and *commensality*, John D. Crossan's term for those social gatherings around tables which included such a variety of ordinary people that everyone could see in their eating together the breaking of many a social taboo. Crossan explores this theme with the help of modern anthropology:

> In all societies, both simple and complex, eating is the primary way of initiating and maintaining human relationships. . . . Once the anthropologist finds out where, when, and with whom the food is eaten, just about everything else can be inferred about the relations among the society's members.[21]

Crossan believes that, in the meals that Jesus shared with disciples, other friends, strangers, "sinners," some of the religious elite, and an utter miscellany of people from the villages of Galilee, one sees "the heart of the original Jesus movement, a shared egalitarianism of spiritual and material resources."

The act of sitting down to eat is a human gesture of consent to human company; where barriers of social custom or a history of hostile relations have stood in the way of such consent, the mere joint presence of the alienated, now around the same table consuming the same food, can be a powerful symbol of the beginning of negotiation on its way to reconciliation. This is *companionship* in the original Latin sense. As another of Crossan's anthropological authorities puts it: "Eating is a behavior which symbolizes feelings and relationships, mediates social status and power, and expresses the boundaries of group identity."[22]

If the mealtime events recorded in the Gospels were remembered with accuracy, they were often occasions on which social boundaries were *broken* and then *redrawn inclusively* by the chief guest. Prominent in the Gospels is the accusation against Jesus by religious leaders that he "eats with tax-gatherers and sinners."[23] This accusation appears soon after the healing of the paralytic—accentuating the expansion of "healing" from physical to social dimensions. A tax gatherer, Levi, accepts Jesus' invitation to become a disciple; to demonstrate that, he invites Jesus to a meal in his home. At table for the occasion, in the version of Mark 2:15, were "many bad characters." Reproached for these table associations, Jesus replies: "It is not the healthy who need a doctor, but the sick; I have not come to invite virtuous people, but to call sinners to repentance."[24]

The most numerous incidents relating to food as a matrix for forgiveness and the gathering of an inclusive human community occur in Luke. A famous incident comes late in the story—in Jesus' aggressive self-invitation to the home of Jericho's rich "superintendent of taxes," Zacchaeus, who undergoes a dramatic repentance manifested in acts of restorative justice: he vows to return ill-gotten gains "four times over" (Luke 19:1–10). Three other meals in Luke, however, take place in the homes of Pharisees, suggesting that Jesus did not exclude so-called virtuous people from his companionship. On one such occasion, he replies to their continuing suspicion of him with a sharp judgment against their hypocrisy (11:37 ff.). On another (7:36–50), an "immoral" woman lavishes gratitude on him, and in reply to his host's shock Jesus explains that the woman has come because she already senses in Jesus the promise of forgiveness. The third occasion (Luke 14:1–24) takes place in the home of a leading Pharisee and on a Sabbath. In blatant disregard of religious and social custom, he heals a man sick with dropsy, lectures the guests on the folly of their attempts to advance their social standing by clambering for seats close to the host, and finally advises the host that in fact he has invited the wrong set of guests to his banquet! These present are your relatives, friends, "rich neighbors." They will repay you with their own hospitality and favors in kind. Try a guest list of folk who have nothing to give you in return: "When you give a party, ask the poor, the crippled, the lame, and the blind; and so find happiness" (14:12–14, NEB). He is describing the "radical equalitarianism" that seems to have infused the early Jesus movement.[25]

Against the background of all this eating and drinking, it is not surprising that the early Christian church should have seized upon a *mealtime* as the single best symbolic way to remember Jesus and the human community that was forming around him in the last days of his ministry. Without entering here into two thousand years of debate among Christians as to what this meal—the Last Supper, the Communion, the Eucharist, the Mass—meant originally,[26] one can only be struck by the many connections throughout these stories between the physical presence of alienated people, the offer of forgiveness around a table, and the simple act of eating together there.

Public Enemies

The presence of "enemies" on some perimeter of Jesus' ministry is obvious in his dealings with those who were enemies in various degrees—the collaborator Zacchaeus, the pharisaic and other establishment mediators between the Jewish tradition and their own Roman enemies, and a few of those latter enemies themselves, such as a Roman soldier or two. Some trace of forgiveness was offered in some of these relations, but only implicitly. The focus of his attention was plainly the mass of people born, like him, in a rural village and largely shut out from access to the great, sometimes menacing powers headquartered in Jerusalem. Concerning an offer of forgiveness by Jesus to these latter for their great sins against justice and mercy for the poor, we hear very little in the Gospel stories.

There is one famous exception to this rule, an exception that has puzzled, tantalized, and inspired innumerable readers of the Gospel of Luke down through the centuries: "Father, forgive them, for they know not what they do" (Luke 23:34). Modern manuscript study leads most scholars to regard these words as a late addition to the text of Luke, who sometimes went out of his way to portray Jesus as no enemy of Rome. The words are apparently addressed to the Roman soldiers who have just crucified him but who are in no position to "know what they are doing." One might conclude here that ignorance of the full scope of one's complicity with evil makes forgiveness easier for the forgiver, as Hannah Arendt concludes. Taken as written, however, the words are a striking combination of an intercessory plea for divine forgiveness with a human offer of forgiveness to fellow humans in the most public of settings. Here was a radical conformity to the words attributed to Jesus in Mark 11:25 in echo of the teachings on prayer: "Whenever you stand praying, forgive, if you have anything against *anyone,* so that your Father also who is in heaven may forgive you and your trespasses." Here was forgiveness thrown into the teeth of political violence: "anyone," indeed.

Did the early Christians remember these words or merely attribute them to the dying Jesus? No sure answer to the question is likely. The same question can be raised about the most literal imitation of the words, in the most parallel of situations, in Luke's account of the first martyr of the early church: Stephen, who in the midst of being stoned to death, is said to have utter the words, "Lord do not hold this sin against them" (Acts 7:60). The impact of this scene upon one of its witnesses—the Pharisee Saul of Tarsus—becomes in Luke's eyes a key event in his eventual conversion. For modern interpretations, perhaps the most important conclusion to draw is that, very early in its development, the new Christian community associated forgiveness with the whole career of Jesus right down to his death; that Stephen's manner of death was believed to be in close imitation of that of his "Lord"; and that the imminent development of a theology of *divine* forgiveness effected through Jesus' crucifixion—especially in the writings of Paul—may have overshadowed the place of human forgiveness in the minds of many future generations of Christians. We know that the literature of the four Gospels, written forty to seventy years after the death of Jesus, originated in the attempts of various Christian communities to transmit recollections of Jesus orally, and that much of this oral tradition must have shaped ways of behaving in these communities long before it was reduced to writing. The Stephen tradition would be one example, but the more general examples are those places in the Gospels which have Jesus spelling out instructions for the conduct of the future community's life, including the discipline of its members under the rule of forgiveness and repentance. The earlier writings of the New Testament Epistles contain similar, parallel accounts of the central importance of such a rule in the norms of the new community. Between the remembered teachings of Jesus and the disciplines of that community there would be some remarkable continuities.

Community Discipline

Many times in his teachings Jesus had stressed the initiative to be taken by a disciple who, either as offender or offended, experiences an alienation from a fellow disciple. Prompt pursuit of reconciliation takes precedence over formal religious worship (Matt. 5:24) and, even prior to the express repentance of an offender, one may expressly offer forgiveness to him or her (cf. Mark 11:25). The initiatives and the processes here are the responsibilities not only of individuals but may compel the involvement of the whole local community of disciples. Two passages are enough to underscore this involvement.

The first is Matthew 18:12–25, where the author has Jesus prefacing and summarizing instructions about community discipline with parables: in one, a man with a flock of one hundred sheep goes in search of one sheep that has "strayed." Members of the community must be as diligent in seeking to recover to full membership one of their number who has strayed. Jesus calls for a strenuous, sustained, three-stage effort potentially involving the whole membership:

If your brother commits a sin, go and take the matter up with him, strictly between yourselves, and if he listens to you, you have won your brother over. If he will not listen, take one or two others with you, so that all facts may be duly established on the evidence of two or three witnesses. If he refuses to listen to them, report the matter to the congregation; and if he will not listen even to the congregation, you must then treat him as you would a pagan or a tax-gatherer. [Matt. 18:15–17 NEB.]

For a Gospel allegedly written by a reformed tax gatherer, this was an ironic, sobering note: none of the Gospel references to "tax gatherers and sinners" suggests that one could stay in one's exploitative tollbooth or be unrepentant about real sins and still become a faithful member of the Christian community. Like every community, religious or secular, this one had boundaries to maintain. Some behaviors were grounds for exclusion, however inclusive might be the invitation to become a member in the first place. But as the instruction here makes clear, exclusion is an extreme measure, never to be resorted to hastily and always fraught with the anguish of the community. Furthermore, initiative and readiness to forgive must be the repeatable rule. "How often," inquires Simon Peter, "am I to forgive my brother if he goes on wronging me? As many as seven times?" Jesus' reply, in effect, is: "As often as he repents, without limit." And he then tells a parable that illuminates the import of the earlier teachings on forgiveness and prayer in Matthew 6:14–15.[27] A king forgives a servant an enormous debt, and the servant forthwith refuses to follow suit in relation to a small debt owed him by a peer. When the king hears about it, he revokes his original generosity and condemns the debtor to the merciless care of jailers and torturers (Matt. 18:23–35). That's the way it is in the "Kingdom of heaven," says Jesus: divine forgiveness and human forgiveness belong together; accept the one and you are bound to practice the other—or else.

The rigor of this rule was not lost on many members of the Christian churches of the first generation, if two surviving letters of Paul are any indication—that is, First and Second Corinthians. These letters reflect the apostle's intimate acquaintance with a congregation where "he settled down for eighteen months" (Acts 18:11) as its pastor. Pastoral concerns over conflict suffuse this correspondence. From many a recorded detail, we know that the church at Corinth bore all the marks of cultural variety endemic to a crossroads Greek city. The letters portray the Gentile Christian community as rife with disputes over theology, partisan loyalty to rival leaders, spiritual snobbery, gross sexual immorality, ritual food taboos, quarrels over wages for church leaders, drunkenness and gluttony during observances of the Lord's Supper, and various forms of contempt of richer members for poorer.[28]

In conformity with Matthew 18:15–20, Paul advises the congregation how it should respond to this array of fractious offenses against its integrity. He distinguishes between two levels of offenses. On the one hand there are those ordinary defects of human social behavior that, while not excusable, are duly subject to forgiveness if given diligent personal and collective attention: "quarreling, jealousy, anger, selfishness, slander, gossip, conceit, and disorder" (II Cor. 12:20–21). On the other hand is behavior that, inside the Christian alternative society, must be considered criminal and grounds for expulsion from the community.

. . . you must have nothing to do with any so-called Christian who leads a loose life, or is grasping, or idolatrous, a slanderer, a drunkard, or a swindler. You should not even eat with any such person. What business of mine is it to judge outsiders? God is their judge. You are judges within the fellowship. Root out the evil-doer from your community. [I Cor. 5:9–13, NEB.]

But uprooting even the most notorious offender against elemental church standards was an ultimate, not a peremptory step. Toward both classes of deviants Paul urged "patience and kindness" (I Cor. 13:4) in a process of discipline that matches the spirit and many of the details of Jesus' instructions in Matthew 18:15–20. Collective discipline, rooted in the pastoral hope that members could develop "the same care for one another" (I Cor. 12:25), seeks ways to reform and restore even the most serious offenders. But the process could also lead to expulsion. In either event, the Corinthian correspondence offers a picture of a group of strong-willed people struggling with definitions of moral norms, moral authority, their obligation to preserve their relations with each other, and the fit of all this with Paul's certainty that in the good news of Jesus and the power of the Spirit, they have the capacity not only to judge but also to forgive each other's undoubted sins.

One can summarize this intracongregational ethic as a process of restorative justice with room in it for punitive justice. The severest of the punishments—expulsion—fits the characteristic which the offenses principally share: they all tear at the fabric of community cohesion. Moral norm is not abstractly revered here; norms serve the upbuilding of the com-panionship. Not even the norm of "love" in I Corinthians 13 or the norm of forgiveness-as-repairer-of-brokenness is understood by Paul as apart from the concrete life of the little society. Forgiveness thus becomes the sober, patient virtue of people who know that the fewer offenses there are to forgive, the better—but who also know that the supreme end served by that process is the renewal of a social relationship. Here the early Christian community is a long way from institutionalizing its repair of relations in formal rules and offices that one day would be called the sacrament of penance. Authority to forgive rests, as Jesus seems to have intended, in a body of people.

From afar Paul records his alternating anxiety and pleasure in the Corinthian church's dealing with one particular scandalous offender. The congregation has practiced both severe judgment and long-suffering forbearance toward this person—both pastoral empathy and express intention to win the person back to his place at the supper table. When Paul receives news of the completion of this painful process, he celebrates. As their former pastor, he knows the rifts and hostilities that have threatened to destroy the bonds of community (*koinonia*[29]) of that body of Christians. He has left them to deal with their most recent fracture in ways to which, he hopes, he has helped accustom them. In his total Corinthian correspondence—probably at least four letters—he pays tribute to an astonishing set of interconnections in this local congregation, not only between the elements of forgiveness but also among the human beings who are learning to participate in each other's sorrows, joys, and very lives. The process is at once personal, interpersonal, and collective; it is concerned with moral discipline in intimate relation to social healing. Anyone who could write this way knows what forgiveness is as a local, vigorous, long-suffering communal practice:

... if any one has caused pain, he has caused it not to me, but in some measure—not to put it too severely—to you all. For such a one this punishment by the majority is enough; so you should rather turn to forgive and comfort him, or he may be over-whelmed by excessive sorrow. So I beg you to reaffirm your love for him. For this is why I wrote, that I might test you and know whether you are obedient in everything. Any one whom you forgive, I also forgive. What I have forgiven, if I have forgiven anything, has been for your sake in the presence of Christ. . . . [II Cor. 2:5–10]

The language, the event, and the effects recorded here are not far from those of an-other story: that of Joseph and his brothers. But now the potential receiver of for-giveness is anyone who chooses to join the congregation gathered in the name of Jesus.

Did Early Christians Believe that Forgiveness Belonged in the Public Sphere?

We have seen that divine forgiveness enjoyed a high place in the theology of the Hebrew Bible, alongside fitfully present interhuman forgiveness. The latter came to new prominence in the ministry of Jesus, and that prominence was reflected in the development of the ethics and life of the early church. The new prominence does not mean that "forgiveness" is the most important word in the vocabulary of New Tes-tament ethics or that forgiveness, divine or human, is the essence of the New Testa-ment faith. In the sermons of Acts, as in the writings of Paul, the new, transformed life of the Christian goes by many names—salvation, justification, life in the Spirit. In this transformation, forgiveness has an indispensable place, but it is not the um-brella word for all things true and celebrated in the new faith and its churches.

The theme of horizontal forgiveness does take its place in the churches in what seems an authentic echo of Jesus' own examples and teachings: that is the major conclusion to be drawn here. Left hanging is the question of what pertinence, if any, the early Christians discerned for their communal life in its relation to the wider, secular society. We have noted that on a few occasions Jesus and someone in the early church extended words of forgiveness to their persecutors, but for the most part Jesus directed his teachings on the subject chiefly to his disciples, and they, in turn, undertook to practice forgiveness chiefly inside the ranks of the church. There it func-tioned as one theme, among many others, defining the ethical profile of the church as an alternative society.

To the extent that they are serious about offering such an alternative, however, religious communities new and old have the enduring problem of walking the line between protecting themselves from the corrupt surrounding society and their own missionary efforts to get the society to change its ways. They are a "sword" as well as a "shield," in Robert Cover's images. The desire for social change will always be the more insistent the more the religion has a bent toward inclusiveness. Early Chris-tianity had that inclusive bent in common with one side of contemporary Judaism, notes John Crossan. Christians are apt to forget that in its openness to sharing its faith with interested Gentiles, inclusivist Judaism could have gone on to convert them in numbers that would have rivaled or eclipsed the church. As it turned out, exclusivist Judaism grew in the wake of the destruction of the Jerusalem Temple by the Romans in 70 C.E., while Christianity was becoming attractive largely to Gentiles.

But "success" and "failure" are ambiguous concepts for religion. Crossan sees the tension between the exclusive and the inclusive social boundary as a basic human dilemma, at its most intense, perhaps, in religious communities. "To be human is to balance particularity and universality. . . . You can lose your soul at either end of the spectrum, and one can and should ask with equal legitimacy: did [inclusivist] Judaism give too little in failing to convert the Roman Empire? did Christianity give too much in succeeding?"[30] On the Christian side, generations of critics of Christianity as the future established religion of Europe would emphatically answer yes.

It is only one example of what the church may have given up, but the example is a crucial one for the rest of this book: did forgiveness get lost to the public ethics that the church was eventually to commend to secular society? Given the distinctive importance of forgiveness in the internal life of the early church, its theologians and others might have been expected to give some attention to its place in their ethical expectations for public life, once the church became respectable and established in that life. But in the history about to unfold, it was not to be.

Only a cursory survey of that history is possible or desirable here, but as postlude to the biblical narratives just recalled and prelude to a leap into the twentieth-century pertinence of the subject, let us look at the fitful presence of forgiveness in this history of western political ethics on that side of the history influenced for a millennium by the theology, ethics, institutions, and power of the Christian church. What happened to forgiveness as a potential ingredient of public life in these centuries? There are several plausible summary answers in as many stages of church history.

Appearances and Disappearances of Forgiveness in the "Christian" Political Order

The Augustinian Beginning

In *The City of God*, the first great treatise on the relation of the Christian religion to the public life of the Roman Empire, Augustine of Hippo set out to defend the Christian movement from the accusation that it was responsible for the Empire's weakness in face of the barbarian invasion of Rome in 410 C.E. The critics fastened not only on a theological argument—that Rome fell because Constantine had deserted the old Roman gods—but on a political one—that the ethics of Christianity were incompatible with the building of a strong political order.

It tells us something about outsiders' perceptions of the major claims of the new "establishment" religion that one of them, Volusianus, pointed up his critique by picking on two passages from the New Testament that were directly related to the theme of forgiveness: "Do not repay injury with injury" (Rom. 12:17) and "if a man strikes thee on thy right cheek, turn the other . . ." (Matt. 6:39).[31] Volusianus was in strong political company. In his virulent rejection of the Constantinian religious settlement, during Augustine's own childhood, the Emperor Julian ("the Apostate") poured contempt upon Christianity as an escapist religion that excused its adherents from "the iron law of retribution." In a satirical portrait of Jesus, Julian has him appearing before Constantine with an offer "to make him clean" from guilt for crime "if only he will smite his head and beat his breast." In fact, observes Julian, Constantine did not escape the gods of vengeance during the rest of his career. "Pity, love, and forgiveness in lieu of justice" are no basis for a political commonwealth.[32]

Justice, on the other hand, was such a basis; and Augustine insisted that, while the early Romans practiced something of that political virtue, the late Romans had not done so; indeed, Christian ethics had much to teach the latter about "true justice."

> [Rome] was never a true republic, because in it true justice was never practiced. . . . However, according to some definitions that are nearer the truth, it was a commonwealth of a sort, and it was better governed by the earlier Romans than by those who came later. But true justice is not to be found save in that commonwealth, if we may so call it, whose Founder and Ruler is Jesus Christ—for, no one can deny that this is the weal of the people. . . . True justice reigns in that state of which Holy Scripture says: "Glorious things are said of thee, O City of God."[33]

In this passage and numerous others, Augustine set the stage for many a political debate to come in western civilization. How much overlap could there be between the ethics of the two "commonwealths"? Did the one, the City of God, have any reason to expect the other, the Earthly City, to imitate Christian virtue? Is the Earthly City all that important for the life of Christians, who counted themselves already members of that City whose real embodiment was in another, heavenly world? Augustine's answers to these questions were rich with suggestiveness but weak in clarity. There was such ambiguity in his approach to the relations of the Two Cities that his writings would in the future authorize many a monk to abandon active membership in secular society while permitting ordinary Christians to live with provisional comfort in that society, knowing that it was temporary anyway. When Augustine discovered in some Roman history traces of a version of justice that made room for forgiveness, he readily credited the phenomenon to the providential rule of God, who was fully in charge of the world long before Christians appeared on the scene.[34] If in service to "true justice" a Roman general relented on the retaliatory principle, *vae victis*, the God of the Jews and the Christians was responsible. Indeed, on grounds of this theology, Augustine can accord to various political orders an array of wisdom, justice, and other virtues which stand on their own secular integrity, sufficient for ensuring a certain prosperity to the Earthly City but set apart from the more exalted virtues of the City of God.[35] The latter virtues belong to a churchly sphere which, in the future thinking of medieval theologians, would be a "second story" of the human habitat, the gateway to the Heavenly City. The connections and the separations of the two cities vie for prominence here, yet on balance Augustine was content to leave the relationship pervasively ambiguous. A hundred years into the Constantinian era, he felt no obligation to spell out a comprehensive theological ethic for the conduct of secular politics.

But as a bishop of the church, he felt the keenest obligation to concentrate on its earthly spiritual prosperity. As Etienne Gilson concludes, "The transcendent importance of the building of the City of God relegated the temporal order to a place . . . clearly secondary."[36] The primacy of building the church involved the politics of *that* very human body, however, and no event in Augustine's career better illustrated his role as a manipulator of episcopal power than the famous Donatist controversy, at whose heart were the old questions of Matthew 18:21 and I Corinthians 5:13: How often should a Christian forgive another's offense, and are there offenses that justify "rooting out the evildoer from your community"?

The offense on which the Donatists focused was the apostasy of some Christians during the Julian persecutions. If any infidelity merited exclusion from the ranks of the church, this one did. On this ground Donatist bishops and their followers formed their own church organization in growing contempt for the inclusivist latitude of Augustine's claim that until the end of history the human church would remain a "mixed body" of the truly faithful and the truly unfaithful. God would separate the two eventually, and meantime all had to practice repentance for sins great and small, for

> Our very righteousness, too, though true in so far as it has respect to the true good, is yet in this life of such a kind that it consists rather in the remission of sins than in the perfection of virtues. Witness the prayer of the whole city of God in its pilgrim state, for it cries to God by the mouth of all its members, "Forgive us our trespasses as we forgive those who trespass against us."[37]

The Donatists drew an earthly line between forgivable and unforgivable sins. "Puritan and exclusivist in spirit, the Donatist church . . . regarded itself as the one body of Christians in the Roman world which had maintained the spirit and tradition of the martyr-church of old."[38] Between the two ethical temperaments lay a great gulf, and many years of patient attempts by Augustine to bridge it came to grief, especially as zeal for a pure church led some Donatists into violence against orthodox church property and members. This conduct pushed Augustine to consider a painful form of the Donatists' own moral passion for purity: How much schism could even the "mixed" church tolerate? And what immoral behavior had to be controlled whether or not it was forgivable?

Unable to persuade them to join the ranks of a church that defined itself as a company of forgiven forgivers, Augustine drew his own lines against the Donatist churches by resorting to the secular political custodians of violence—the Roman police power. With its help, the Donatists were crushed. After all, they had, on occasion, themselves resorted to violence against the property and persons of the orthodox. "Even the heavenly city . . . avails itself of the peace of earth," Augustine had written, but he had insisted that resort to the rough instruments of such peace must not involve Christian "scrupling about diversities in the manners, laws, and institutions whereby earthly peace is secured" in the church or in the civil community. Now scruples had been invoked: Caesar had been called in, not only to protect the authority of Christ but to uphold the authority of some Christian officials over others. Doubtless, in Augustine's mind, the move met some of the criteria for a "just war," whose formulation became one of his major concrete contributions to the political ethics of the coming medieval church. Wars—just and unjust—were already ripping the Empire apart in Augustine's own lifetime, but in asking for the help of the state's coercive power to settle a question of law and order in the church, he seemed to contradict the spirit of his own theory of the church's mystical unity in its members' love of God. It was a contradiction heavy with import for the next millennium of church-state relations, and equally heavy with the difficulty of proving that there was any difference in practice between forgiveness in secular and in church politics. For the next thousand years, only with great ambiguity could Augustine's disciples make good on his clear distinction between the two cities as the difference between the love of power and the power of love: "In the one, the princes and nations it subdues are ruled by the love of ruling; in the other, the princes and subjects serve one another in love, the latter obeying, while the former take thought for all."[39]

The Sacramental Captivity of Forgiveness, 500–1500 C.E.

No one among early Christians had set out to establish a new political order, but they did form a social body—the church—with many of the features of a political order.

> To join it was to become part of a separately organized, centripetal community, which not only had its own leaders and officers, its own characteristic rites in baptism and eucharist, its own calendar of observances and celebrations, its own properties and finances, but also maintained a continuing hostility towards the religious foundations of Roman society. . . . Even in its more "liberal" movements, therefore, the church tended to appear in the cities of the Roman world as that most knotty of problems for any political or cultural order: an alternative society.[40]

When, in Augustine's own lifetime, the Emperor Theodosius declared Christianity the only legal religion in the empire, he officially abolished that alternative society, which was, for a thousand years, to survive chiefly in monastic movements. Among other momentous implications for church-state relations in the coming millennium, the two now acquired a common interest in the great theological-political question of who belonged and who did not among the ranks of faithful Christians.

Of the two, the church had wrestled longer with the question. Critics of Augustine's resort to the "secular arm" for settling the Donatist controversy could always claim that he defied ancient biblical norms for the church's dealings with its own theological and moral deviants. But Donatism added momentum to the development of two orthodox institutional norms: the centering of authority to forgive in the office of the bishop and formal procedures defining an acceptable process of repentance. In the centuries-long debates on these two institutions, the questions of what sins were forgivable and who possessed authority to forgive regularly interlocked. In general, the debates and ecclesiastical decisions would move the church toward the leniency parties and away from the rigorists. If properly repented of, almost any sin could be forgiven, even apostasy. The when, how, and by whom of the process became steadily more subject to precise institutionalization, first in the bishop, eventually in the parish priest, and finally in the canonical discipline of the sacrament of penance.

One casualty of this development was the long-standing tradition, growing out of literal adherence to Matthew 18:15–17, of confession and repentance as requiring the public attention of whole congregations and the local bishop. Now the process moved out of the congregation into the confidentiality of the priest-penitent relation.[41] It was a momentous change, especially for any explanation of how the notion of forgiveness in European culture acquired its reputation as a personal, private, religious, and anything but political transaction. In its eventual authoritative formulation of the discipline of penance in the year 1215, the Fourth Lateran Council laid down a mandatory pattern which secured the jurisdiction of the church over individual conscience while securing individual access to the earthly church and thence to the hope of heavenly salvation.

> The contrite, or at least attrite, sinner made a secret confession of his major sins and of their attendant circumstances to the priest in the confessional, where the priest could not see and might not even recognize him. The priest was bound to the strictest secrecy; to divulge information granted in the confessional meant lifelong imprisonment in a monastery doing penance. When the confession was completed, the priest by virtue of the power of the keys absolved the sinner from the eternal guilt of his sin, thus without further ado freeing him from the terrors of punishment in hell.[42]

Furthermore, at least once a year,

> Every single individual within the jurisdiction of the Church who was at all concerned over his salvation must henceforth submit an oral record of his sins to his priest and undergo punishment therefor. The Church had attained a point of prestige where it felt that with one stroke of the pen it could subject the consciences of western European Christendom to its supervision and control.[43]

Thus, over a period of some eight hundred years, the forgiveness of sins in western Christianity became a very private affair linked to very public church claims to power. As various incidents in the history of the medieval church demonstrate, the sacrament of penance could now be put to political use in ways that had to do with forgiveness more as a political weapon than as a power for political reconciliation. The most famous dramatic incident—coming at the time when a reforming pope was consolidating papal jurisdiction over all clergy and the definitions of their powers— was the standoff between Pope Gregory VII and the Holy Roman Emperor Henry IV of Germany. To enforce his authority to ordain bishops in Germany, Gregory excommunicated Henry, canceled his legitimacy as a ruler, released all his subjects from fealty toward him, and barred them, too, from access to the sacraments. Expecting to seal these decisions in Germany in a council composed of his allies, Gregory was about to cross the Alps when a shrewd Henry crossed first, found his papal enemy cooped up in the castle at Canossa, and there—outside its walls in the snow—did penance for three barefooted days.

History would rightly remember the incident as irony piled on irony: Gregory achieved the symbolic humiliation of a great politician, but the latter had saved his power by following the penitential rules, thus turning the weapon thrown at him back upon his enemy. In fact, Henry lived to see his right to participate in the investiture of bishops reaffirmed and to see Gregory die, exiled from Rome, in flight from Henry's armies. The humiliation, like the manipulation of the sacrament of penance in the service of power, went both ways. The incident is fraught with warning for those who would leap too quickly to the invocation of the concept of forgiveness in political conflict. As a weapon for the increase of power over an enemy, forgiveness is corrupted. As an ingredient of just peacemaking between two sides of a wrong-filled political relationship, it is something else, as will be demonstrated at length later in this book.

Before leaving this cursory survey of how forgiveness went into a decided medieval captivity in the sacrament of penace, one should not forget that both church and secular powers of that era, under the canopy of an allegedly Christian civilization, made certain attempts to express some version of forgiveness in terms of public norms and public policy. Faced with the disintegration of political connections in Europe after the collapse of the western Roman Empire, the church had an interest in holding the forces of social chaos at bay. In all the early medieval centuries, "the emerging feudalism was dividing Europe into a multitude of political entities which combined with the wars and the bad state of the roads, piracy, and banditry to render an inclusive Christian fellowship extraordinarily difficult."[44] In such a deteriorating ethos, cycles of vengeance and countervengeance were rampant; and feudal lords themselves had reason to fear that, uncontrolled, vengeance could destroy them all.

The most ambitious church attempt to control this escalating feudal violence orginated in the late tenth century in southern France in a church ordinance called the Peace of God (*Pax Dei*). At first, it aspired to rule out all violence whatsoever under threat of ecclesiastical sanction. Then various classes of innocent victims of war were singled out for special protection. How much they needed protection is vividly illustrated by the surviving text of an oath that some knights were induced to take:

> I will not invade in any way churches, or the crypts of churches, unless it be to seize malefactors who have broken the peace or committed homicide; I will not assault clerks or monks not bearing secular arms. I will carry off neither ox nor cow nor any other beast of burden. I will do nothing to cause men to lose their possessions on account of their lord's war, and I will not beat them to make them give up property. From the first day of May until All Souls' Day I will seize neither horse nor mare nor foal from the pastures. I will neither destroy nor burn houses, nor root up nor cut down the vines under pretext of war.[45]

In such documents we learn about the ordinary sins of local medieval warfare which the *Pax Dei* was designed to curb. Protection of noncombatants was one of the principles of Augustine's doctrine of the just war; therefore, as the danger to them became increasingly great, church officials soon devised a more comprehensive set of rules for the protection of whole populations during certain times of the year—the Truce of God, which forbade "private warfare during the period from 'vespers on Wednesday to sunrise on Monday.'" From there the truce was extended to seasons of plowing, sowing, and planting.[46] In the same eleventh century, the pious Holy Roman Emperor Henry III "proclaimed the Day of Indulgence, using it to announce forgiveness to his foes and to urge his subjects to follow his example."[47] Capping the whole effort, a pope in the next century sought to prohibit all wars whatsoever, again backing up the rule with the church's most comprehensive spiritual threat, excommunication. "Obviously this was not adopted," says one historian dryly, but it did "exercise some restraint upon the disorders of the times."[48]

Just as obviously, the lords exercised—to some degree—certain rudiments of for-giveness—acknowledgment of wrong, forbearance from vengeance, and empathy for some of their enemies. In these public ways, then, the church and secular elite of medieval Europe did try to promote a version of forgiveness in politics, and—how-ever idealistic the *Pax Dei* and the Truce of God may have been—Latourette ob-serves that "the sense of being part of Christendom, of membership in a family of nations, laid the foundations for a body of law designed to govern the relations among princes."[49] The very assent of some lords to these principles suggests their tangible interest in protection from the uncontrollable plagues of war. As the disasters of the coming fourteenth century would demonstrate, starting wars was easier than stop-ping them, and at some point a cry for peace—and a modicum of preference for liv-ing with one's enemies over dying with them—drowns out the clamor for continued "just" redress of grievances. Medieval Europe furnished as many demonstrations of this truth as did the era of Thucydides.

Its perennial wars also planted roots of interethnic vengefulness, which would live and thrive into the twentieth century. As summarized memorably by Barbara Tuchman, the most devastating century of the age—the fourteenth—laid the ground for hostili-ties that would fracture the peoples of Europe for the next five hundred years. The great disaster earned the name, the Hundred Years' War, the "longest war" in Euro-pean history. Neither the power of the church nor kings, neither the Peace nor the Truce of God, neither the sufferings of commoners nor the devastation of fiefdoms, finally called a halt to that war. Sheer exhaustion ended it. When it was over,

> . . . perhaps few were aware of it. After so many truces and renewals, who could have realized that the end had come? . . . The Hundred Years' War, like the crisis of the church in the same period, broke apart medieval unity. The brotherhood of chivalry was severed, just as the internationalism of the universities, under the combined ef-fect of war and schism, could not survive. Between England and France the war left a legacy of mutual antagonism that was to last until necessity required alliance on the eve of 1914.[50]

In that same fourteenth century grew the roots of the conflict which, in 1993, was tearing apart the peoples of Yugoslavia. Their war, as this is written, was grinding to an end in the same exhaustion: "Resentment has grown beyond easy soothing, re-morse beyond the point of repentance and grief beyond sensible forgiveness. The war will burn out when its fuels are depleted."[51]

Sleeping but never dead: the Furies, "the acrimonious dead, the buried thesis, long since rusted knife, revengeful dust."[52]

Reformation Reformulations

Martin Luther. Williston Walker describes the spiritual temper of early-sixteenth-century Europe as offering "weighty evidence that the church's entire sacramental system, above all the central sacrament of penance,was experienced by the faithful as more oppressive than liberating, not least because the spiritual benefits offered by the church were so often bound up with money matters and political purposes."[53]

The *assurance* of divine forgiveness of personal sin was the heart of the Protestant Reformation, and Martin Luther's quest for that assurance set a pattern that would define the "evangelical" experience for millions of Christians down to the present. In Luther's rediscovery of the Gospel of forgiveness, God takes all the the necessary steps; everything ecclesiastical fades to the background, including the social-disciplinary side of the sacrament of penance, so that, if the new Lutheran pastor hears a parishioner's confession, it is for purposes of consolation, not moral discipline. The old custom now has a new meaning: neither by exhaustive confession nor by priestly absolution do sinners achieve assurance of their salvation. The Word of God, carried by its preaching and the Spirit, is fully sufficient, the only true source of eternal consolation in time and for eternity.[54]

As he experienced a new understanding of the church as a congregation of forgiven sinners, Luther stumbled onto implications of the experience for church-state relations. Never intending any profound change in the medieval political order, he lived to see his theology of the spiritual "liberty of the Christian man" turned to purposes of political revolution against governments that had protected Luther himself from death as a heretic. Like all medievalists, Luther could not imagine a "separation of church and state" which—as did the sectarians—simply consigned the two to insulated compartments in society. Even when he spoke of "two kingdoms," he was as sure as Augustine had been that both belonged to an overarching Kingdom of God. Indeed, like the Calvinists after him, Luther was so confident of God's providential presence in all of reality that he urged Christians to abandon the idea of monastic holiness and to throw themselves into the service of God in their own "callings" in society. Not free to change the social location of those callings, they were free to do their Christian duty without special instruction or coercion from the church, which had no more wisdom to offer about shoemaking than it had for telling a soldier how to fight or a king how to govern. "As [a Christian] cannot derive the laws of medical procedure from the gospel when he deals with a case of typhus, so he cannot deduce from the commandment of love the specific laws to be enacted in a commonwealth containing criminals."[55]

Luther was sure that God ordained institutions other than the church for the containment of human sin. Foremost among these was the state, which had a duty to control the behavior of criminals as much as the church had a duty to preach the grace of God even to criminals. The old question of love's relation to justice now acquired an ethical theory and an institutional form that verged on paradox. "Love" has no more place in secular politics than punitive justice has place in the church, concluded Luther.

There are two kingdoms, one the Kingdom of God, the other the kingdom of the world. . . . God's kingdom is a kingdom of grace and mercy . . . but the kingdom of the world is a kingdom of wrath and severity. . . . Now he who would confuse these two kingdoms—as our false fanatics do—would put wrath into God's kingdom and mercy into the world's kingdom; and that is the same as putting the devil in heaven and God in hell.[56]

For Luther, comments H. Richard Niebuhr, government is an instrument of wrath to protect citizens from the wrathful. It is one thing to be personally merciful toward the thief who steals your purse; it is another to let the thief loose in the community. It is a great sin "to want to be holy or to exercise mercy where mercy is destructive. As God does 'strange' work—that is, a work not apparently merciful but wrathful— in natural and historical calamities, so He requires the obedient Christian to do 'strange' work that hides mercy of which it is the instrument."[57]

Mercy—or love—may seem hidden in the exercise of political power; but some Lutheran scholars point out that the Christian magistrate, in Luther's view, was bound to the rule of love in government as well as in the church, so that the theory might be called "dialectic" rather than "dualistic." Lutherans of later generations tended to dissolve the distinction. Among some of them, says Klaus Nürnberger, "the dualist misunderstanding took root and caused a lot of harm"—most notoriously among twentieth century Lutheran Germans who mustered quotations from Luther in active and passive support of Nazism.[58]

In short, the dualities—or dialectics—here were in great danger of falling into dualisms and mysteries of paradox that only God could comprehend. In contrast to the medievalists with their theories of hierarchy, Luther put God in unmediated charge of a rebellious world and then drove deeper the wedge between the faith of believers and the merely outward world of human social law, institution, and custom; between personal Christian ethics and Christian responsibility in secular organizations; and above all—for purposes of this study—between the duties of forgiving mercy and those of punitive justice. For Luther, God could see how all this fitted together; among some of his followers, the theory seemed to license numerous splits between the sacred and the secular, leaving some Lutheran politicians free to protect the social order with the sword while trusting in the forgiveness of God to maintain their personal spiritual integrity. Solidly at home in the personal and churchly realms, the Lutheran reformation left forgiveness more insulated than ever from legitimate political expression. It remained in captivity in the church and a stranger to politics.[59]

Calvinism. Even in its church captivity, however, the discipline and comfort of the forgiveness-and-repentance process had always emerged from a real social relationship. Rather than justifying its reputation for making "every person his or her own priest," original Protestantism restored the comforts and disciplines of penance to the congregation, and this was to be as characteristic of Calvinism as of Lutheranism. Ever since it abandoned a congregational context for penance, observes a contemporary Catholic scholar, the moral theology of that church for centuries has tended to define "sin" as the act of an individual.

> . . . and more often in the context of his eternal fate than in the context of the social well-being of others.
>   This stress on the individual, with a view to his confession, is one reason why the Church's moral tradition has found it difficult to handle the idea of collective responsibility on a large scale. . . . It is an approach to "social justice" in which the influence of confession has led to a concentration on individuals and a reluctance to "exonerate" them by recognizing a more social meaning to sin and an element of sinfulness in institutions, or, indeed, in social circumstances . . . [T]he Church's individualistic

moral tradition has experienced considerable difficulty in adapting its thinking to such issues of macro-ethics, as well as to the moral implication of increased democratic participation in public politics and decisions, and to the new phenomenon of what might be called responsibility spread thin. . . .[60]

When Catholic scholars acknowledge this weakness in the ethical effects of the traditional sacrament of penance, however, it behooves Protestant scholars to remember that the narrow confines of the confessional can still be the fulcrum of some significant leverage on an individual penitent's relation to some large, momentous societywide evils. As Thomas Tentler reminds us, no one illustrates this potential more dramatically than Bartolomé de Las Casas, a contemporary of Luther and Calvin, who was converted in the confessional from being an exploiter of enslaved native Mexicans to being "an apostle of Indian liberation."

> The refusal of a Dominican to hear Bartolomé's confession because he held unfree Indians was an important event in this dramatic story. While Bishop of Chiapa, in 1546, Las Casas wrote a manual for confessors to be used by priests in his diocese. It deals with only one subject: the strictest and more absolute requirement of restitution by all who enjoy ill-gotten gain by conquest. To Las Casas it is an extremely populous category of sinners; and he is uncompromising as he defends the rights and obligations of confessors to demand full restitution as a condition of absolution. He even spells out procedures for drawing up and notarizing contracts by which penitents surrender the lands and persons they hold contrary to God's law. . . . The means Las Casas chooses are the most rigid application of the disciplinary weapons of sacramental confession.[61]

Here was the sacrament of penance turned to quite a different political use than the battles of popes and emperors: an attack on an institution, slavery, whose evils were to corrupt the "new world" society from its very beginning. That Las Casas and some of his priestly peers failed to convince either their church or their governments to abolish slavery should not obscure the potential of the old institution of penance for putting pressure, through individuals, upon secular institutions.

Of all the church movements of the sixteenth and seventeenth centuries that tried to address questions of "responsibility spread thin" and to press for the reform of all institutions whatsover, none was more zealous than that of the Calvinists. With no Lutheran ambivalence, they abolished penance as a formal institution and located it once again in the life of the congregation. Calvin conceived religion and politics as related neither in the "two-level" medieval Catholic hierarchical scheme nor in the "two-kingdom" paradoxes of Lutheranism. Calvin's God was sovereign over the whole of reality, and the unceasing divine activity in the whole world implied not passive acceptance by believers but engagement in the same whole world in obedience to the divine will. In this vision, between the realm of the church and the realm of the state there were no qualitative differences of ethical norm or ethical responsibility. "The good of the whole community," as Ernst Troeltsch put it, was the constant theme of Calvinist ethics,[62] which forever called its adherents—whether government officials, ordinary citizens, or church leaders—to the same criticism and reform of sin-beset but redeemable human institutions.

Quarrels with both this vision and its flawed enactment by Calvinists would flourish in centuries to come. They flourish yet. But there is substantial agreement among historians with the judgment of Sheldon S. Wolin that Calvin "stemmed the flight from civility" in Protestantism, in the sense that he reintroduced the Christian individual to a vocation for civic reform over against forces as religious as monasticism and as secular as feudal wars, all of which tempted the faithful to retreat from politics. Calvin did this, says Wolin, chiefly by producing "a political theory of church government";[63] his followers, in turn, produced a religious theory of the state.[64]

Calvin's new polity of the church mandated ingredients of member participation that the medieval order lacked: real power for lay people in representative structures of governance, ministers subject to "peer review" but not hierarchical control, educational occasions in which all congregation members were asked to participate, and the obligation of the church to discipline its own members for sins spiritual or social through the deliberation of the congregation or its elders, without interference by secular authorities. Membership in Calvinist churches was thus a kind of exercise in citizenship, to which was added the expectation that the secular community was equally an arena for the exercise of both personal and church stewardship of the public welfare. For Calvin, says Wolin, "government existed to promote values that were not necessarily Christian even though they might be given a Christian coloration; they were thus values necessary for order, and, as such, a precondition for human existence."[65] Here the "world" was neither a mere vestibule to the Kingdom of God as the medievalists envisioned it; nor the rough shadow side of that Kingdom as in Luther; it was "the theater of God's glory." Any part of it might become glorious when rightly and vigorously reformed.

The reform of moral and political order in Geneva became the inspiration for Calvinist movements to attempt reform of whole countries. Little success attended their efforts in France, much in Scotland and Holland, some in England, and—in ambiguous ways—much in the young United States. In these attempts they acquired a larger reputation for conflict initiation than for peacemaking—or for public forgiveness. But their instinct for public and ecclesiastical order required some mastery of the arts of political coalition. This political feat was all the more necessary once the other side of the Calvinist spirit—personal conscience, conversion, and access to the study of Scripture—had guaranteed eruptions of conflicting opinion in church and civic settings. The combination of freedom and community resonated throughout this vision, requiring of its adherents active participation in the resolution of the conflicts that were bound to arise between the two poles. The enduring contribution of the movement, perhaps, lay precisely here—in its insistence on vigorous collective deliberation, inside the church and in the public square, over the nature of common goods. Calvinism provided its adherents with ethical warrants for risking the plunge into public life. Armed with a stout theology, they often entered the public arena on a high horse of rigid moral principle, but in the rough and tumble of democratic debate, it sent them out of that arena as pedestrians.

Political realism, therefore, required Calvinists, in spite of their reputation as stern legalists, to master skills of political fence mending while exercising their undoubted capacities for generating debate, conflict, and even violence. On the side of seeking reconciliation with antagonists, in fact, Calvin himself set some impressive examples.

It was he who proposed an ecumenical peace with the Lutherans of Germany on grounds of a common faith and a tolerance for theological diversity, and it was he who insisted on defining the Christian church as a worldwide community that transcended national cultures. In a famous letter to Thomas Cranmer of Canterbury in 1552, he professed his willingness to "cross ten seas for this business" of restoring the unity of the divided Christian churches.[66] The most impressive example, however, was his consent to return to Geneva as leader of its reformation in 1541, after having been dismissed from that position in 1538 by city officials. Calvin knew how political enmity could wreck a church or a city, and he himself could be a formidable political antagonist, but he knew that politics consists of collaborations between people who do not yet like each other but who have a common duty to live together and to search together for the interests that they have in common.

In all of this history, Calvin and Calvinists developed little explicit emphasis on forgiveness as a public virtue. But there was nothing dualistic in their ethical prescriptions for public life. In theory and often in practice, they proceeded to reform the distribution of power and responsibility in the church with a degree of appreciation for the subtle connections of power, consent, and moral principle that moved across the frontier between church and government with hardly a skipped step. Theirs was a political religion from the start, with "no abrupt transition," as Wolin says, from questions of power to restraints on power to a "life of civility" based on an array of analogies from religious to secular society. They had no hesitation, for example, in comparing the role of the pastor in the church to the role of the magistrate in government.[67] Each had role and power to influence the other but also to limit the other—because neither could rightly claim to be *the* representative of the divine will, and neither could alone represent the total interests of the society. The divine judgment and forgiveness that Christians shared around the communion table had unique depths of spirit and truth; but the duty to repent of sin and to offer forgiveness to the repentant could not in principle be confined to the church pew. In this insistence Calvin sustained his training as a humanist, seeing the life of Christians in the context of their kinship to humanity as a whole. For him, "the imperative to help others does not depend on Christian faith—and so cannot be restricted to Christian communities. It is a universal imperative: 'since God has united [people] in the bonds of mutual society, hence they must mutually perform good offices for each other.'" God has created humans to share one "flesh"—a common physical dependence upon each other—and in that flesh they share a common divine image. All of these affirmations make it "possible to live and work in the fallen world on different and more hopeful terms than the cynical view of the worldly," as one modern student of Calvinism has put it.[68]

The inability of fractious Puritan politicians in the English Civil War to compose their differences enough to avoid the dictatorship of Cromwell stands as proof that they found it hard to practice the prudential versions of forgiveness in politics that have since, in liberal democratic theory, gone under the names of tolerance, compromise, conciliation, and "the spirit of liberty that is not too sure it is right." Moral rigor lives uneasily besides these virtues of democratic process. When, on grounds of their particular moral principles, Calvinists broke apart, they illustrated the dangers of clashing moral stances for political negotiableness. When, in deference to their like propensity for continuing argument and learning in debate, they heeded Cromwell's very Calvinist principle, "Think that you may be wrong!" When they did so, they made a turn towards forgiveness in politics, if only in their willingness to keep on arguing.[69]

The Crisis for All Formulations of Forgiveness: The Enlightenment Perspective

We can terminate this excursion into church history here, for this sketch is enough to justify these several introductory conclusions: that secular observers like Hannah Arendt are not mistaken in finding a distinctive, prominent place for forgiveness in the teachings of the New Testament; that, in spite of its important if not central place in the ethics of the New Testament church, forgiveness seldom if ever attained an impressive place in the ethics that the church sought to commend to its secular host society; that the medieval institution of penance solidified this tendency, not only in the secrecy and individualization of the confessional but in its ordinary confinement of "sin" to the sphere of personal conduct; and that the Protestant Reformation, while making a strong attempt to resocialize the idea of forgiveness and repentance as a function of a church congregation, continued to stress the power of divine over human forgiveness.

These conclusions alone are enough to explain why, to this day, the notion of "forgiveness in politics" evokes a mystified response from many contemporary religious people, not to speak of the nonreligious who have always associated forgiveness exclusively with the language and the substance of religion.

Such conclusions are also enough to suggest that any twentieth-century reconsideration of this subject must treat it as an issue on the modern frontier of both religious and political ethics. The past provides us with much valuable prologue to this exploration, but the past, as here sketched, barely began the plowing of new ground. Some fresh thinking about forgiveness is required of the late twentieth century if the concept is at last to take on serious political meaning. In the chapters to follow, I seek to forward just this exploration in the context of some of the devastating political evils of our own time.

Before attempting this, however, there is one more historical era that any twentieth-century ethical study has to take into account: The so-called Enlightenment of eighteenth-century Europe, an era whose impact on the ethical beliefs and theories of Europeans and Americans has been so colossal that many religious and philosophical writers about ethics begin their reflections with its intellectual legacy. Indeed, the legacy is so powerful in contemporary western thinking about religion, ethics, and politics that the long books of these writers sometimes come down to footnotes on what the Enlightenment did to *undo* the possibility of credible modern talk about ethics for a society.

In sum, the philosophers of this eighteenth-century movement progressively peeled away the religious cover of moral reasoning and then the social cover as well, leaving, as sole custodian of moral knowledge and agency, the lone individual. The thinkers who bracket this century-long development and who best illustrate the great divide between both medieval and Reformation thinking about ethics and modern western ethical culture are John Locke (1632–1704) and Immanuel Kant (1724–1804).

Born into a Puritan household, Locke lived through three drastic changes of English government. His work in one of those governments enabled him to observe at close hand some abrasive relations between religion and politics. He brought to his practical work in government (as secretary of the Colonial Council of Trade) the two sides of his Puritan upbringing: personal accountability to God and social responsibility to the human neighbor. In common with the Puritans and their medieval forbears, Locke assumed that both individuals and societies had access to sure moral knowledge in the Natural Law. "The *State of Nature* has a Law of Nature to govern it, which obliges every one: And Reason, which is that Law, teaches all Mankind, who will but consult it, that being all *equal and independent*, no one ought to harm another in his Life, Health, Liberty or Possessions."[70]

The ancestry of the American Declaration of Independence was here, of course; and it would be in the young United States that Lockian doctrine would enjoy its greatest continuing influence. Crucial in this synthesis of religious, moral, and political principle was the access of all humans to enough knowledge about "public good" for them to join in deliberation about it as citizens—an expectation solidly rooted in Calvinism. Responsible to God and to the moral authority of natural law, citizens are to hold all government to the test of higher authority.

> . . . the Law of Nature stands as an eternal Rule to all Men, *Legislators* as well as others, the *Rules* that they make for other Men's Actions, must . . . be conformable to the Law of Nature, i.e. to the Will of God, of which that is a Declaration; and the *fundamental Law of Nature being the Preservation of Mankind,* no human Sanction can be good or valid against it.[71]

Locke's serene confidence in the identity of natural law with the will of God marked him as a true Puritan; but seventeenth-century politics had taught him the danger of assuming that churches had any moral vocation for directing the business of governments. In describing the insulation of the two, he took a long step away from the spirit of Calvinism: "[E]ach of them [must] contain itself within its own Bounds, the one attending to the worldly Welfare of the Commonwealth, the other to the Salvation of Souls."[72] Religion and government must be protected against each other, a view that James Madison would one day heartily applaud. Between the two, after all, stood the bond of the natural law, which guides the moral conscience of the magistrate as well as that of the parson. Locke will not equip the conscience of the one with rules different from those for the other; and in this he remained Calvinist. But the strict separation of church and state in the theory harked back to Lutheranism; this accent would become a door to the insulation of politics from religion through which legions of liberal democrats would march in two centuries to come.

One contemporary student of Locke summarized his outlook as a "combination of level-headed common sense with a deep religious sentiment."[73] Locke was sure that belief in God was the linchpin that holds the human world together. "Those are not at all to be tolerated who deny the Being of a God. Promises, Covenants, and Oaths, which are the bonds of Humane Society, can have no hold upon an Atheist. The taking away of God, tho but even in thought, dissolves all."[74]

But in the natural law there lurked an invitation to "thought" to separate the knowledge of the public good from belief in God. Already in his suspicion of church incursion into politics was a lever for prying the two completely loose. And already in the ordinary rancorous conflicts of parliamentary debates almost any observer could ask if there really was any "common sense"—i.e., natural law—shared by all these minds, interests, and power struggles of citizens.

The next step, obviously, was to undermine Natural Law and human reason's direct access to it; in the near future, David Hume and Immanuel Kant would take just this step. In the process, they uncoupled piety, personal moral consciousness, and ethics-for-society in ways remote from fifteen hundred years of Christian tradition.

In an astute summation of the spirit and substance of Kant's complex, awesome philosophic achievement, T. M. Greene wrote:

> The eighteenth century . . . was distinguished for its uncritical individualism, its lack of historical imagination, and its exaggerated reliance upon reason as the cure of human ills and the guide to all truth. These are but aspects of a single attitude toward life, and Kant shows himself to be a true child of the Enlightenment in his willing acceptance of this attitude. He gives voice to the individualism of the period in his doctrine of man's moral autonomy and freedom. Believing that man should recognize no authority in heaven or on earth superior to his own conscience, Kant requires him to make his own moral and religious decisions and work out his own salvation. Historical events and personages may yield man an occasional clue; certain institutions may afford him a modicum of social support; and even revelation, were its authority beyond cavil, might hasten his discovery of the eternal verities; yet all these aids are no more than adventitious, and the strong man will avoid reliance upon them, trusting, so far as possible, in himself alone. For, irrespective of racial heritage, social environment, or personal traits, the inner voice of reason is always his surest guide; and the fact that his own conscience commands him to be perfect bespeaks a corresponding ability to obey its behest through his own efforts.[75]

Kant reasoned his way to belief in God, but that God, comments Greene, "is certainly, by all religious standards, related to the world and man in no vital way."[76] Kant's rational, responsible individual is not related to other individuals, either, in a "vital way," if by *vital* is meant the necessary, justified, inevitable influence of one person on the inmost reasoning of another. Furthermore, for Kant the capability of the individual to reason and act morally is so unassailable that there is everything to blame and nothing to excuse—or forgive—in immoral behavior. Indeed, Kant's logic strikes a double blow against the idea of forgiveness as a moral virtue: he slips the reflective moral self into a cocoon immune to concern for what other people think, and he refuses any outside help for the achievement of moral knowledge or moral agency. In an ordinary sense of the word, his rational, free individual has no need of *grace.* When one neither reasons nor acts morally, the defect is in the person; the only cure for the defect is an effort of self-correction. The possible help of forgiveness from so much as one other person, for repairing a morally damaged relationship, is quite unnecessary. Indeed it is *immoral* to expect from outside of the self either human or divine help for the correction of one's past mistakes. The problem of guilt disappears here as an irrelevancy: humans do not need alleviation from their guilt but from repeating the same deed the next time. Anyone who salutes the maxim, "I ought, therefore I can," will have no nerve to ask for forgiveness when—able to know what ought to have been done—he or she did not do it.[77]

The precipitates of all these old arguments are alive and vigorous in the contemporary political culture of the West; they are the stuff of many a long treatise that attempts to answer the "demand for ethics"[78] in various persons and sectors of twentieth-century society. Kant's exquisite, profound individualism remains little known to most Americans, but the ideas, even the words, of John Locke's qualified individualism have found a home in American culture, as almost every commentator on it feels bound to mention.[79] Locke was heir to questions which the medieval and Calvinist precedents had furnished him. He provided some fresh, tenuous answers to them, only to be followed by Kant and other moral individualists who worried less and less about the moral "glue" that may be required to hold any society together. Can a conflict-prone society, proud of its personal freedoms, persist when individual consciences have no agreement on what the "common good" *is*? Can the common good be discovered in any amount of public debate if some or all of the participants refuse to assent to any authoritative interpretation of moral norms? Lacking such norms and interpretation, does society, in the end, resort for its coherence to the coercions of the strongest? At least on the level of the battle of ideas, was Hobbes right to see society as always a potential "war of all against all"?

Americans, in particular, tend heartily to acknowledge that democracy has as its keynote a whole skein of separations: religion from government, the personal from the political and institutional, ethics from law, ethics from politics. What holds it all together? In all consistent conformity with the trap of such a culture, the answers are likely to begin with the disclaimer, "In my personal opinion. . . ." Nothing now is right or wrong but personal thinking makes it so. Accordingly, a yet deeper crisis awaits those who blithely affirm this view: What if one begins to doubt the truth of one's personal opinions? What guide remains when thinking no longer makes it so?

The individual crisis is matched and overshadowed by the social. Suppose that a Ronald Dworkin is descriptively right in asserting that the "central doctrine" of so-called liberal democratic society is "the thesis that questions about the good life for man . . . are to be regarded from the public standpoint as systematically unsettleable."[80] Accept that thesis and there may be no bases from which citizens and their leaders can deliberate with each other or even mount a meaningful argument about what might be the measure of a good or a bad policy, law, candidate for office, or posture for one's nation in international affairs. Here disappears the philosophical-ethical consensus necessary for civic talk and with it the pertinence of talk about the moral tragedies of human history, morally encased memory, and morally empowered, social forms of forgiveness—in politics or any other human relation.

Before turning to candidates for just such talk in the political conflicts of our own century, the question has to be further attended to: How, in a culture that seems so bereft of agreements on the moral base of human life, can humans locked in any degree of antagonism presume to make moral judgments of each other? Against the background of all the history sketched in these first pages, the question has an ominous, modern ring to it. It would be presumptuous indeed to suppose that a book, or the next chapter in this one, will move to convincing new, high ground for "systematically settling" this cluster of questions. The Dworkin dilemma is too real for any one of us to think that we can tell others how to move decisively beyond it. But move we must: if anything is clear about many a circumstance of the twentieth century, it is that we cannot treat some questions of human social obligation as morally relativistic, whether the society is as small as a family or as large as the gobal human community. Our favorite ancestors—Joseph, Jesus, Augustine, Aquinas, Luther, Calvin, Locke, Kant, and the like—may have occupied high moral ground that we can only envy. We cannot recover exactly their ground for our stand in our circumstances. Where might we find a solid, if modest and partial, ground that humans might occupy for the restoration of some moral consensus about our present and future relations with each other? That is the question to which I feel bound to give some answer in the next chapter.

3

Political Ethics as Moral Memory

We cannot always get what we want, but if we lose the ability to think of wanting other things beside what we are given, then the game is lost forever. . . . To act morally in politics is to consider the results of one's actions.[1]

Bernard Crick

A Hasidic story speaks of an isolated kingdom where the grain harvest one year turns poisonous. Everyone who eats it will become mad. Yet there is no other food available. Finally, the king turns to a trusted counsellor. "We must all eat, or we will die," he said. "But you, try to eat less. Preserve enough sanity to enable you to remind us, through the long dark period ahead, that we are mad. Tell us. Again and again. The time will come when we are sane again."[2]

Albert Friedlander

How can one forgive those who make it impossible for us to forget—so far as we dare to forget—because they on their side are determined to behave as though they no longer know what there is to forgive and forget?[3]

Manes Sperber

In his introductory essay to Kant's *Religion Within the Limits of Reason Alone*, John Silber calls attention to Ivan Karamazov, in whom Feodor Dostoevsky personified Kantian abstract moral individualism and subjected it to subtle rejection.[4] In *The Brothers Karamazov*, Ivan and Alyosha discuss the ancient nagging question: What can any one of us do about the atrocious evils that some of us perpetrate? Or the assorted evils that all of us sometimes condone? We can *protest* against them, Ivan answers; and in the final analysis that is what, above all and always, we must do, never settling for any form of erasure, atonement, retribution, or future "harmony" that makes evil into something to forget or something to serve some final triumph of good on earth, in heaven, or in hell. For atrocities like the landowner's torture of an eight-year-old child for causing a minor injury to his dog,

> How are you going to atone for them? Is it possible? But what do I care for avenging them? What do I care for a hell for oppressors? What good can hell do, since those children have already been tortured? And what becomes of harmony, if there is hell?

I want to forgive. I want to embrace. I don't want more suffering. And if the sufferings of children go to swell the sum of sufferings which was necessary to pay for truth, then I protest that the truth is not worth such a price. I don't want the mother to embrace the oppressor who threw her son to the dogs! She dare not forgive him! Let her forgive him for herself, if she will, let her forgive the torturer for the immeasurable suffering of her mother's heart. But the suffering of her tortured child she has no right to forgive; she dare not forgive the torturer, even if the child were to forgive him! And if that is so, if they dare not forgive, what becomes of harmony? Is there in the whole world a being who would have the right to forgive and could forgive? I don't want harmony. For love of humanity I don't want it. I would rather be left with unavenged suffering. I would rather remain with my unavenged suffering and unsatisfied indignation, *even if I were wrong.* Besides, too high a price is asked for harmony; it's beyond our means to pay so much to enter on it. And so I hasten to give back my entrance ticket, and if I am an honest man I am bound to give it back as soon as possible. And that I am doing. It's not God that I don't accept, Aloysha, only I most respectfully return to Him the ticket.[5]

The *passion* in this moral outburst is quite foreign to Kant, but the truly un-Kantian detail is the "even if I were wrong." Ivan retreats from formal rationality to a pure, willed protest against particular evils to whose very existence he can never be reconciled. The slim hard center of his moral self is a will pitted against unjust sufferings inflicted by humans upon their fellows which no revenge and no forgiveness can ever alleviate. Ivan has stolen from Kant a true categorical imperative but infused it with memories from history that give this imperative concrete moral content from its beginning. By cutting short sophisticated reasoning and facing the facts of human cruelty head-on, Ivan frees himself from rational, social, and religious supports of moral judgment with a clarity that will long influence the world's readers in ways that Kant's dense prose is unlikely ever to do.[6]

The Politics of Death and Life

Ethical theorists like such "cases," for in such stories moral issues stand out simply and clearly. Behind the story, of course, lay the social-political structures of nineteenth-century Russian life, which granted to aristocrats a certain freedom to exploit serfs. Ivan does not ask whether, when it comes to either moral judgment or forgiveness, the whole social system should be targeted.

There is a parallel, contemporary incident that does just that. It belongs alongside Ivan's passionate protest against cruelty to a single child. In 1903 Dostoyevsky's contemporary, Leo Tolstoy, received a very political American visitor, William Jennings Bryan. Knowing Tolstoy's pacifism, Bryan asked him the typical test question: What should one do if a criminal is about to kill a child? Tolstoy, who recorded the conversation, replied that in all of his seventy-five years he had never

> encountered that fantastic brigand, who, before my eyes, desired to kill or violate a child, but that perpetually I did and do see not one but millions of brigands using violence toward children and women and men and old people and all the labourers in

the name of the recognized right of violence over one's fellows. When I said this my kind interlocutor, with his naturally quick perception, not giving me time to finish, laughed, and recognized that my argument was satisfactory.[7]

Tolstoy would die, seven years later, in that vestibule to the twentieth century where the new technological war-making capacities of governments had only begun to fill with the weaponry and organization that would have fueled his pacifism with yet more passion had he been seer enough to know what was coming. Mass death in political conflict had already furnished one theme of his greatest novel, however; and he was surely aware that the nineteenth century so far held the historic numerical record for deaths in war. The approximate four-century statistics, largely for Europe, were as follows:

Soldiers and Civilians Killed	
1500s	1,600,000
1600s	6,100,000
1700s	7,000,000
1800s	19,400,000

The total is some 34 million. But there was yet to be a total that would put this in the shade: deaths from warfare in the first ninety years of the twentieth century would come to *107,800,000* in all. Walter Wink's comment on this appalling contemporary record comes right out of an Ivanesque instinct for moral horror unmediated by sophisticated theory: Choose any likely total of human deaths from human violence in all the centuries in which strong governments have existed on this planet (since 3000 B.C.E.) and it has to be true that *"more people have been killed in war in our century than in all the preceding five thousand years combined.* And yet there are still Christian ethicists soberly pondering the question of justifying wars!"[8]

The most realistic among those ethicists have always bracketed their theories of "just" war with the qualifier that wars always wreak injustice. Further, the theory has always aimed at restraining governments from starting wars (always as a "last resort") and at limiting the damage to enemy life and property to that necessary to bring the war to an end. A late-twentieth-century focus on the nicely balanced seven- to tenfold principles of a just war, however, easily and conveniently diverts the attention of citizens and their leaders from certain arguably more fundamental facts that afflict the theory with the *feel* of moral triviality. *There has been so colossal an accumulation of injustice in the conduct of twentieth-century wars, and the weapons for inflicting future injustices are so ready at hand, that only a very brazen moralist will think serenely of commending the "just war" theory to the political thinking of the twenty-first century.*

To say this is to make a first primitive reply to the "demand for ethics" in the political sphere of modern human affairs. It is also to allow for the possibility that, unless and until we moderns attend collectively to the reduction of massive violence among our own kind, we may not have the right to spin out elaborate moral codes for the conduct of politics.[9] The proposition sounds rather simple-minded: unless our immediate successors on this planet attend to our unprecedented capacity for mass violence—for collective defiance of the original first public *social* command, "Thou shalt not murder"—we risk preoccupation with the "lesser things of the law." It is one thing to begin a list of human rights with the classic Jeffersonian "life, liberty, and the pursuit of happiness"; but it is another to acknowledge that, two centuries after the American Declaration of Independence, human enjoyment of liberty and happiness is now dependent on the capacity of governments to restrain their (and our general human) potential for killing each other.[10]

A positive way to propose this beginning for a modern political ethic is to insist that the first "law" of politics is the preservation of human life, and that offenses against this law have been so pervasive, so notorious, and so atrocious in our time that none of us can be blamed for ethical narrow-mindedness if we keep on insisting that Tolstoy was right about the overriding importance of *globalizing* the moral protest of Ivan Karamazov against all the "morality" that justifies organized, massive, lethal cruelty.

The insistence that political ethics, now and in the future, must *begin* with life and remain life-centered might also have the ring of superficiality if this beginning were not already so entrenched in the very moral traditions that have occupied us in these pages thus far. The Greeks' fear of vengeance in politics was fear of unending organized murder. Joseph assured his murder-prone brothers that the preservation of their and their descendants' lives was the master motive of all his dealings with them. Behind the Joseph story lay the Hebrew memory of a liberation from Egyptian slavery—which, itself, was a kind of living death. The persistence of a Hebrew people, generation to generation into indefinite perpetuity, is the ground-swelling hope undergirding most Jewish theology and ethics then and now. Not by chance do Jews propose their classic toast, "To life!" Even the insistence of the early Christians, with Augustine, that the Creator had granted them life in this world as a preparation for "eternal" life in another, was an assertion of an astonishing divine premium on human existence. Protestantism, with its insistence on a "this-worldly" ethic of perpetual response to the grace of God, reasserted the potential value of every scrap of human existence. And when John Locke and Thomas Jefferson started their most general listing of the "rights" that for political justice must predate all governments, "life" again headed the list. It stands high in the 1948 *Universal Declaration of Human Rights* of the United Nations, adopted by forty-eight of the fifty-six members of that organization in the wake of World War II. And when, in November 1993, South Africans promulgated their first-ever draft of a constitutional Bill of Rights, "Every person shall have the right to life" was its first article.[11]

The cry for ethics in the late twentieth century is a cry for life. One can soften the apparent narrowness—and shrillness—of this first axiom for a political ethic by adding the reminder that human life does not consist of existence alone. Were this book attempting an outline of a comprehensive political ethic, it would be natural at this point to explore at length what a "politics of life" might be. Indeed, we humans go to war with each other in the name of certain values that, we say, justify the risking of our lives. Rightly, justly considered, the question of what is worth the risking of *enemy* lives belongs fully in this moral calculus. On all sides in a pluralistic global culture, of course, the identity of these life-and-death values is in great dispute—and that dispute is not likely to end with the twenty-first century unless our leaders manage to make it the last century of human life on this planet. Making the world safe from war and for *this* controversy might be as certain a goal for politics as our century is likely to have to offer to the upcoming one. *We can afford to dabble in ethical relativism only if we are not relativistic about the value of human life itself.* Our cry for a life-preserving political culture is in part a cry for the political safeguarding of the varieties of human culture. The indispensable moral agreement that we must have, therefore, in face of our moral and other disagreements, is that we be safe in our disagreeing. At stake here is a nonnegotiable moral definition of politics itself, set out clearly by Sir Bernard Crick when he wrote that the task of the political leader is to "hold divided societies together without destroying diversity," for, he said, "Politics involves genuine relationships with people who are genuinely other people, not tasks set for our redemption or objects of our philanthropy. They may be genuinely repulsive to us, but if we have to depend on them, then we have to learn to live with them."[12]

The certainty that "we have to depend on them" has grown apace in our earthly time, and it can only grow in time to come. Our experiences of "genuine otherness" of world neighbors will likewise multiply. We are not likely to give up our arguments over matters as tangible as who gets to use up the petroleum or as overarching as whose religion is the right one. Such argument, we know, right down into the early years of the 1990s, has already cost thousands of lives, sowing the seeds of resentment—in the wake of the Persian Gulf War of 1991, for example—that one day may again produce the evil fruit of wars of revenge. One pragmatic counsel, in the face of these depressing facts, is to count on the human capacity for forgetting. But humans do not easily forget their own suffering or that of other humans with whom they identify. And memory of the suffering of one's "own" has no apparent statute of limitations: the Battle of Kosovo in the year 1389 remains vivid and powerful in the minds of ordinary Serbian soldiers in 1993. Constantly watered with intergenerational resentment, the memory of past horrors prepares the ground for their repetition in the future.

Cherishing hope for revenge is one way sufferers of atrocity cope with their memories. But there is another way: the facing of still-rankling past evils with first regard for the truth of what actually happened; with resistance to the lures of revenge; with empathy—and no excusing—for all the agents and sufferers of the evil; and with real intent on the part of the sufferers to resume life alongside the evildoers or their political successors. That is the moral courage of forgiveness.

Our teachers here have to be the sufferers themselves, the victims of colossal evil or those with the most right to represent them. It is one thing to read the data on the slaughter of 6 million Jews by the Nazis; it is another to listen to survivors of that atrocity or to their children. For such sufferers, not to be listened to is a second assault on their dignity. More politically: when the story of their suffering gets shoved aside in public political discourse, a barrier has been erected to their reentry to the body politic. Some members of that body remain capable of reenacting the atrocities, and many of them are more comfortable following the pleasant advice of Christina Rossetti: "Better by far that you should forget and smile/Than that you should remember and be sad."[13] Not so, say the surviving victims: our civic vocation in your midst is to remember on behalf of those you prefer to forget, and to make it difficult for you to do so.

Convincing one's civic neighbors that particular evils should be remembered and remembered again is a task deeply threatened by a relativistic moral culture which auctions off the great moral questions, so to speak, to individual bidders. Was this or that event really *evil*? Who is to say what evil is greater than another? Does any particular alleged evil have prior claim on our collective memory? At stake here is the intellectual issue of whether there are any moral reasons for reading and writing history. When a culture abandons the notion that there are nonnegotiable moral reasons for studying history and "justifies" that abandonment with its own moral relativism, it readily comes to agree with Henry Ford that "history is bunk." Consistent, radical moral individualism is the enemy of all but idiosyncratic moral assessment of the past. Unfortunately, whether we say so explicitly or not, many of us Americans internalize just that individualism; we are naively puzzled by neighbors for whom our remembering of *their* history is the test of whether we intend to be their neighbors. It may also be the test of our active intention to join them in political work to build a different future for them and ourselves.

In sum, if we believe that the preservation of our neighbor's life is the first rule of politics, we might contribute to a new politics of life by accurately recollecting what the politics of death did to them or their ancestors. This painful study of pain-filled history is the beginning of forgiveness in politics. To begin to forgive one's political enemies past and present is, first of all, to identify what there is to forgive, and to identify it in utmost possible detail. Three "exercises" in that sort of historical study—which I commend especially to fellow Americans—constitute most of the rest of this book. But to engage in such exercise one must be willing to learn history from the viewpoints of those who were its agents and its sufferers. The latter, in particular, deserve to be listened to. As an introduction to the elaborate exercises to come, consider the following.

Remembering History Morally

The first is fiction, sieved out of its author's own experience of the blood and mud of the German side of World War I. Most critics think that the 1928 novel *All Quiet on the Western Front* was the best fiction to emerge from that war. Its "hero," soon to die in the trenches, visits an army hospital.

> A man cannot realize that above such shattered bodies there are still human faces in which life goes its daily round. And this is only one hospital, one single station; there are hundreds of thousands in Germany, hundreds of thousands in France, hundreds of thousands in Russia. How senseless is everything that can be written, done, or thought when such things are possible. It must be all lies and of account when the culture of a thousand years could not prevent this stream of blood being poured out, these torture-chambers in their hundreds of thousands. A hospital alone shows what war is.
>
> I am young. I am twenty years old; yet I know nothing of life but despair, death, fear, and fatuous superficiality cast over an abyss of sorrow. I see how peoples are set against one another, and in silence, unknowingly, foolishly, obediently, innocently slay one another. I see that the keenest brains of the world invent weapons and words

to make it yet more refined and enduring. And all men of my age, here and over there, throughout the whole world see these things; all my generation is experiencing these things with me. What would our fathers do if we suddenly stood up and came before them and proffered our account? What do they expect of us if a time ever comes when the war is over? Through the years our business has been killing—it was our first calling in life. Our knowledge of life is limited to death. What will happen afterwards? And what shall come out of us?[14]

Written before the collapse of the Weimar Republic, Remarque's moving portrayal of "what war is" clashed with other ways of remembering that "Great War" among his fellow Germans. Adolf Hitler would stir those other ways into the collective passion that became the "second round."

The people who endured that round began telling their stories before it was over. One was Iulia de Beausobre, a Russian emigre who gave a series of lectures in England in 1940 under the title *Creative Suffering*. She had left the Soviet Union and would escape direct experience of the horror of the Nazi invasion of 1941. But she spoke for her English audience, already at war, when she said:

> . . . suffering seems quite lately to have acquired a sweep, a vigour, a variety, and a precision that it lacked in former times, so that most people are today aware of an astonishing extent of suffering going on all around them. . . . And since knowledge is always, even with the least imaginative of us, a kind of participation, we can all be said to take part, if only dimly and at second hand, in a great deal of suffering. But there are countries, and Russia is one of them, where first-hand knowledge of suffering has become universal, where every man, woman, and not infrequently many a child, is directly confronted with the thing itself, with suffering as a fact of personal experience.[15]

Russia was indeed "one of them." Iulia de Beausobre's fellow Russians were about to suffer a catastrophe greater than any that could be remembered in 1940. I was asked in 1984 by a group of them, "How many Americans died in World War II?," I replied, "Three hundred thousand." "Ah," they responded, "it's nothing compared with our country." It was not nothing; but, beside their memory of the war, with its 20 million dead, American suffering seemed almost trivial.

Can we truly empathize with each other's suffering? For the sake of achieving political community after its fracture, we must hope so. But the tension between first- and secondhand experience of evil cannot be dissolved, and the firsthand sufferers are the first to insist on the difference.

Few in our time have insisted on it more than the Jewish survivors of the Nazi attempt to exterminate Jews and Judaism—and few are more insistent on the claim: "We tell you about it for your sake and not only our own." The faith of Jews has always claimed that the survival of the Jewish people, like their destruction, has significance for the whole of human history.

Among the tellers of the Holocaust story since 1945, Romania-born Elie Wiesel has promoted the claim with special intensity and precision. In 1991 he said to an American interviewer:

[The Holocaust] is immeasurable and incomparable. It's a unique event. It must remain a unique event. Never before have such plans been conceived. Never before have so many people killed so many people in a systematic, cynical, calculated way. The link is memory. I mean, I had always hoped that if we remember, our memory would shield other people as well.

Later in the interview Wiesel was not so hopeful: "Why haven't we succeeded—we who have been victims of hate—in transforming that hate into a warning? Why haven't we—that bothers me—into a warning, into a kind of alarm, saying, 'Look, look, hate means Auschwitz'?"[16]

Wiesel himself has created for the post-1945 world a body of literature that, with rare eloquence, has sounded the alarm. He is rightly perplexed at the fact that not just any way of remembering human atrocities of the past will protect the future against their repetition. In his own and many other examples of Holocaust literature, a Jewish moral perspective underpins the narratives. That perspective suffuses the following excerpt from Primo Levi, an Italian Jew who survived Auschwitz, which was liberated by a patrol of young Russian soldiers on January 27, 1945:

They did not greet us, nor did they smile; they seemed oppressed not only by compassion but by a confused restraint, which sealed their lips and bound their eyes to the funeral scene. It was that shame we knew so well, the shame that drowned us after the selections [by the camp guards of inmates to live or die], and every time we had to watch, or submit to, some outrage: the shame the Germans did not know, that the just man experiences at another man's crime; the feeling of guilt that such a crime should exist, that it should have been introduced irrevocably into the world of things that exist, and that his will for good should have proved too weak or null, and should not have availed in defence.

So for us even the hour of liberty rang out grave and muffled, and filled our souls with joy and yet with a painful sense of pudency, so that we should have liked to wash our consciences and our memories clean from the foulness that lay upon them; and also with anguish, because we felt that this should never happen, that now nothing could ever happen good and pure enough to rub out our past, and that the scars of the outrage would remain within us for ever, and in the memories of those who saw it, and in the places where it occurred, and in the stories we should tell of it. Because, and this is the awful privilege of our generation and of my people, no one better than us has ever been able to grasp the incurable nature of the offence, that spreads like a contagion. It is foolish to think that human justice can eradicate it. It is an inexhaustible fount of evil; it breaks the body and the spirit of the submerged, it stifles them and renders them abject; it returns as ignominy upon the oppressors, it perpetuates itself as hatred among the survivors, and swarms around in a thousand ways, against the very will of all, as a thirst for revenge, as a moral capitulation, as denial, as weariness, as renunciation.[17]

The black hole of the Nazi death camps came close to swallowing up every trace of moral dignity and moral power among inmates and SS guards alike: it left no one as innocent as Ivan Karamazov tried to be, for it uncovered the possibility that there is nothing good and strong enough in human being to resist the evil in human being. Left with his own shreds of undamaged moral awareness, Levi still fears the revenge, the forgetfulness, the final triumph of evil—its victim's imitation of it.

Can Nations Remember, Repent, and Forgive?

The ability of assorted individuals to remember and forgive does not translate easily into the claim that forgiveness is pertinent to the collective realities of political life. But when the individual is a highly placed political leader, the interchange between person and collective can be significant indeed. In 1977 Anwar Sadat, the president of Egypt, paid his unprecedented visit to Jerusalem in a quest for peace between his country and Israel. His hosts took him to Yad Vashem, the museum memorializing the 6 million Jewish victims of Nazism. Afterwards, Sadat said that he had never realized the scope of Hitler's war against the Jews. "I had always thought it was exaggerated for mere propaganda. But seeing the portrayals and exhibits strengthened my determination to achieve peace for those who suffered the tragedy. I saw with my own eyes how Israelis, and Jews the world over, must feel. They are victims not of war alone but also of politics and hatred."[18]

A political leader who speaks publicly of how his mind has changed is beginning to teach his constituents to change too. Such a leader fulfills both sides of Edmund Burke's famous definition of what democratic representatives should represent: not only the interests of constituents to the whole body politic but the interests of the whole to the constituents. It could not have been easy for Anwar Sadat to speak publicly of Egypt's need to move toward peace with Israel. He was to pay for his courage with his life. But such leaders generate the glimmer of forgiveness in politics.

Can whole nations repent? Forgive? Engage in processes that eventuate in collective repentance and forgiveness? Rather than arguing theoretically for an answer of "yes" to these crucial questions, the rest of this book will examine at length the history of three twentieth-century enmities that have profoundly shaped the lives of every living American: our wars with Germany and Japan and our centuries-old internal struggle for just relations between African Americans and the country as a whole.

In turning to careful historical study of these three cases of American participation in the politics of death, I narrow the principal method of the rest of this study in two dimensions:

1. I mean to resist the temptation to study political-ethical questions from a global standpoint that encompasses concern for what forgiveness or repentance might be in the history of peoples only remotely related to the history of my own country. There is much to be gained from careful study of countries, cultures, and conflicts other than those to which one's own national history is connected.[19] But the risk in this overview approach is that of becoming so occupied with the affairs of other countries as to tread lightly over the affairs of one's own. Forgiveness in politics is a relatively new, fragile subject of investigation. Further, it overflows with such complex and sensitive issues of collective history in every part of the globe that it is surely presumptuous to pretend that one American has any right to tell any other people how they experience or might experience forgiveness in their politics. The presumption diminishes when one is determined to speak as an American chiefly to fellow Americans and, indirectly, to those whom America on occasion has deemed its enemies. It is one of the rights and obligations of democratic citizenship thus to speak, or so I will assume in the rest of this book.

2. But this restriction of purview to one's own national history still involves a very wide potential focus. The events and relationships in American history that are candidates for this investigation are many. Among those who have been, in one sense or another, the collective enemies of some American government are the Tories of our Revolution, the Native Americans of our Indian Wars, the inheritors of both sides' memories of our Civil War, plus Mexican, Cuban, Filipino, Chinese, Vietnamese, Central American, and Iraqi peoples who, over the past century and a half, have diverse reasons to consider themselves our former or present enemies. Fractures galore yawn between the United States and many of these historic antagonists or their descendants. Our national agenda includes much homework yet to be done in lingering relation to these antagonisms.

But the rule I have here chosen to follow comes down to this: if, at the end of this century, we Americans could learn what it means to inject forgiveness into the tortured relations of this country to Japan and Germany, and if we could do the same in relation to the greatest of all atrocities in United States history—slavery and its legacies—some of us might acquire the wisdom to think responsibly about a myriad of other enmities external or internal to our history. The argument for a certain case-study thoroughness in these matters, as opposed to a survey, is strong here. Better to wrestle with a limited number of large, central, tough histories than to presume to speak to and for a great number of them.

There are two case omissions here, however, that demand something like a word of apology. One is that of Native Americans. Within the past decade their historic quarrels with their treatment at the hands of European expansionists have reached an unprecedented level of national concern. If my biography and my education had equipped me to be a scholarly partner in these growing concerns, Native America might have occupied a chapter in these pages. The work that needs to be done on forgiveness in the long history of this often tragic relationship, I must leave to others. Those others, I am glad to observe, are at work in growing numbers.

I tender a somewhat different apology for my omission of that one relationship which ranks with my chosen three in its centrality to twentieth-century American history: the relation of the United States to the Soviet Union. The basic reason for this omission is the astonishing collapse of the political structures of the USSR in 1991 and the current confusion of many Americans and their political leaders about how we are to assess our behavior in the so-called Cold War. We are not ready, I am not ready, to sort out the dense mixture of good and evil that has suffused the enmities of that "war." Suffice it to note that as national societies we two prepared to undertake an atrocity that, even by twentieth-century standards, would have set a new, geometrically more awesome record in the politics of death. But we have somehow refrained from carrying out that uniquely modern potential for committing the unforgivable sin. Had we not refrained, I would probably not be here to write this book, nor would you be there reading it.

Protecting the next generation's right to live and work, to write and to read, is the simple moral core of forgiveness in politics. The next three chapters concentrate at length on three large historical opportunities for Americans to learn this beginning to global human existence.

4

Vengeance and Forbearance: Germans and Americans

For the Church and for the individual believer there can only be a complete breach with guilt and a new beginning which is granted through the forgiveness of sin, but in the historical life of nations there can always be only the gradual process of healing. . . . The only question is whether the wounds of this past guilt are in fact healed, and at this point, even within the history of the internal and external political struggle of the nations, there is something in the nature of forgiveness. . . . It is recognized that what is past cannot be restored by any human might, and that the wheel of history cannot be turned back. Not all the wounds inflicted can be healed, but what matters is that there shall be no more wounds. . . . This forgiveness within history can come only when the wound of guilt is healed, when violence has become justice, lawlessness has become order, and war has become peace.[1]

Dietrich Bonhoeffer

Thou shalt not be a victim. Thou shalt not be a perpetrator. Above all, thou shalt not be a bystander.[2]

Yehuda Bauer

With what right can we by our forgiveness allow this crime to blossom out again one day or by the refusal of our forgiveness allow hatred to harden and spread itself? And then time and oblivion, those two curses, come and cut this Gordion knot in the public conscience.[3]

Vercors

The world is not likely to forget Adolf Hitler and his works. Now that he lies almost fifty years in the past, what influence, if any, should twelve years of Nazism exert upon the relation of other nations to Germany and its people?

There are answers to the question which the assumptions of this study require. These answers must rest upon the following.

If the crimes of Nazism were unique, remembering them accurately is a unique moral responsibility of politicians, educators, and citizens of the world, beginning with Germans themselves.

If the crimes of a government cannot be totally divorced from the responsibilities of its citizens, questions of collective shared guilt cannot be excluded from political philosophy and political ethics.

If one group of humans has, as its responsibility, the acknowledgment and correction of errors of its predecessors, their contemporary neighbors have the right to ask if, in fact, the acknowledgment and correction are genuine, active, and promising of permanent change.

Further: if political history in one nation develops in part from its relations to other nations, then they are mutually implicated in each other's virtues and vices, and the net of collective responsibility requires acknowledgment and correction on all sides.

Finally, if one of the enduring problems of political relations is their repair in the face of evils inflicted by one side or another, other requirements for that repair come up for deliberation: what sort of "justice," what restorations of damage, what degree of possibility that people once bent on killing each other can enter into some new form of positive political community?

Germans and Americans: 1914–45

Americans born in the first and second quarters of the twentieth century will naturally think of their relation to Germany as a first illustration of the pertinence of all these concerns. The first fifty years of the century were, in many respects, an "anti-German" era for most Americans. We can date our first patriotic entry into world-scale warfare at 1917, our most self-protecting reversion to isolationism at 1920, our most grudging national awareness of our entanglement with a world economic system in our experience of the Depression of the 1930s, and our permanent commitment to world power politics at our entry into World War II. In all of these momentous events, German-American hostility was central and the occasion of unprecedented organized destruction of human lives worldwide.

With our blithe national habit of trying to get on with a future unencumbered by a past, a post-1950 generation of Americans may find it curious that anyone born twenty years before should, in 1994, think it important to dwell on that painful past of German-American relations. We have seen many examples in this study of "revengeful dust" waiting in the deep basements of national memories to stir itself into a dust devil of renewed violence; but Americans like to think that they are immune to such antiquarian politics. We will have reason to wonder whether this comfortable American pragmatic forgetfulness is self-delusion as we survey the historic cases of the next three chapters.

The twentieth-century case of the United States and Germany is a proper beginning to any exploration of repaired relations between modern enemies because in so many respects the enmity resembles a family quarrel, with all the ambivalences thereof. As a psychological term, *ambivalence* means a conflict of opposite personal feelings, but the word can also tag those mixtures of symbolically reinforced attitudes in a political culture which are rooted in a great density of positive and negative experiences of a whole people.

For over a century, the ambivalence of Americans toward Germans has had at least three sources: the tide of immigrants from Germany who crossed the Atlantic to join a young culture that insisted on their becoming "Americans" as rapidly as possible; a huge American cultural debt to Germany, especially in art, philosophy, theology, and science, that would often meet with American suspicion of high theory and exotic pedantry; and a shared tradition of hard work and technical proficiency, which would confront a like American suspicion of aristocracy and German aptitude for democratic government.

Between 1820 and 1920, some 5.5 million Germans left home for America, outnumbering English immigrants (though not the total from the British Isles as a whole).[4] Most of the biographies of these immigrants followed the American pattern of progressive distancing from ties with the old country. For the twentieth-century version of the story, no famous American better illustrates the ambivalences of being born into the two cultures than young Reinhold Niebuhr (1892–1971). Niebuhr's father, Gustav, left Germany in 1881, at age 18, pushed by his distaste for patriarchal family life and the threat of the military draft. A young seminary graduate when the Great War broke out in 1914, Reinhold spent much energy during the war years establishing his public identity as a American, supporting the Allied side of the war, campaigning for a change in the German name and dominant language used by his church denomination, and supporting President Woodrow Wilson in his internationalist idealism, which finally helped induce the American government to enter the war.[5] Though publicly critical of the failure of many of his fellow German-Americans to assume the active duties of citizenship, he tried to walk a line between idealizing and rejecting either national culture. "I have been pained as much by the unwarranted criticisms that some Germans have made of everything American as I have been hurt by the slanders against my father's country on the part of so many Americans," he wrote to one of his critics in 1916.[6]

In the months after the United States' entry into the war, however, Niebuhr's ambivalence about the conflict yielded to bursts of patriotism close to that of millions of other Americans of 1917–18. In the summer of 1918 he wrote to the Sunday school teachers of his denomination that "American entrance into the war has given the conflict a new meaning. What began as a crime is ending as a crusade and for the first time in the history of the world we have the inspiring spectacle of a nation making every sacrifice of blood and treasure for aims which do not include territorial ambitions or plans for imperial aggrandizement."[7]

That same spring he persuaded his congregation to spend $5 for the purchase of an American flag, and two months after the war's end they voted to eliminate the German language from their worship.[8] By the beginning of the 1930s, Niebuhr was becoming famous for views on religion and politics in which he struck a far more ambiguous stance about the virtues of his or any other nation in its wars, and in fact he did not wait that long to be provoked into a revision of this patriotic idealism. The failure of Wilson to protect a defeated Germany from the vengeful features of the Versailles Treaty sobered him and moved him toward a period of pacifism in the 1920s. But it was his 1921 visit to the devastated Ruhr, recently occupied by the French in their attempt to commandeer reparations, that shocked him the most. Starving children, divided families, economic chaos, and tangible hatred were everywhere. "The Ruhr cities are the closest thing to hell I have ever seen," he wrote in his diary. "I never knew that you could see hatred with the naked eye, but in the Ruhr one is under the illusion that this is possible. The atmosphere is charged with it."[9] Soon after, in a report to his denominational paper, he writes one of his earliest suggestions that forgiveness may have a place in international affairs. Vengeance, at least, is not working in Germany: "The only hope of Germany is America," for only England and America "are not animated by motives of revenge. But England is practically powerless because America has withdrawn from European affairs and has left the continent to the tender mercies of French chauvinism." Europe needs to "learn to overcome its hate and learn the divine art of forgiveness" from America.[10] This, too, was an idealism about his country that he would one day scale down in attacks on the "chauvinism" of Americans, too. His public reports to his church on his Ruhr visit, however, do not dwell on the postwar suffering of the Ruhr, as if for the moment empathy for the enemy's widows and children can be reserved for his diary. In these years he is still the inheritor of Americans' disposition to think that, if the world is to be saved, they may have to do it.

That disposition, stirred by Woodrow Wilson, evaporated from American public life in the 1920s, and in the next ten years Niebuhr's own amalgam of German and American loyalties underwent severe refinements. Once again George Washington's ancient warning to his fellow citizens against "entangling alliances" dominated the political mood of Americans. Few protested the decision of the U.S. Senate not to join the League of Nations; and, in the meantime, the struggles of leaders of the Weimar Republic to introduce Germans to democracy generated little sustained curiosity or support on this side of the Atlantic. By newspaper, radio, and film, Americans came quickly in the early thirties to believe that the "war to save democracy" had brought no democratic result. Quite the opposite: long before they took power in 1933, Adolf Hitler and the Nazis were exemplifying anew what German immigrants to America had been fleeing. Finally, preoccupation with the Depression added powerful reason for public hope that the United States, this time around, could keep out of Europe's treacherous international affairs and its even more treacherous wars. Their classic isolationism renewed, Americans and their politicians left Europe to the Europeans.

Democracy at War: A Note on "Just War" Ethics, 1941–45

Suddenly in late 1941 isolationism collapsed. With Pearl Harbor and Hitler's declaration of war against the United States, the country was plunged into the "second round" for which its own disdain of world politics could be held partly responsible. This time it would be war on a truly world scale.

The aftermath of World War II in American-German relations is my principal concern here. But a note on wartime relations between the two peoples is a necessary prelude to a more extensive survey of the postwar history.

A common observation about World War II is that in its course humans invented "total war." We Americans like to give credit for the invention to Germany, whose aircraft enabled Fascist forces to bomb the village of Guernica in the Spanish Civil War and its own air force to destroy large parts of Rotterdam in the opening year of World War II. Historians remind Americans, however, that their ancestors took a giant step toward total war in the military strategies of Generals Lee, Grant, and Sherman. The logic of total war fits the facts of a modern industrial economy: civilians produce the equipment necessary for the military side of the combat. For practical purposes they are among the combatants and therefore legitimate targets of military action. "Just war" theorists in and out of political power in this era were not at a loss to accommodate this fact: it is still possible, they urged, to discriminate between war-producing targets and other more strictly civilian ones. But World War II provided massive illustrations of the easy practical erosion of this theory in face of the technology, the mass suffering, and the political passions generated in modern war. As the destructive power of the technology grew, its precision declined, with the resulting need of later military leaders to invent terms like "collateral damage." Early in the war, especially in their bombing of London, the Germans justly or unjustly acquired a reputation for caring little for civilian deaths; thus they helped prepare democratic politicians, strategists, and citizens alike for the proposal that the enemy was a whole national people. Defeating them, of course, not killing all of them, was still the aim of the war. But so long as the war lasted, discrimination between civilian and military targets became, even when possible, less and less a tactical priority.

In the vast multiple "theaters" of the war, however, the various Allies could report to each other that this enemy waged different sorts of warfare on different fronts: Germans fighting French, English, or American armies displayed conformities with the rules of just war that suggested a respect for these opponents as equals. Germans fighting in Russia had other views of the enemy: there, Nazi hatred of Communists and Nazi racist definitions of Slavic peoples combined to turn the German war against the USSR into an attempt at the annihilation of a society. "No pity for Ivan" was the instruction given German troops by their officers on the Russian front.[11] The combined tolls of deaths and crippling injuries on both sides[12] alone tell a story of unparalleled twentieth-century desertion of every shred of just war ethics. Both sides learned the arts of indiscriminate destruction, and modern-day Russians remember their experience of World War II correctly when they say that they fought the Germans on a different scale than the rest of the Allies ever fought them. On their side, German survivors of the war would rightly remember that they had more to fear from the vengeance of Russian troops than from their other enemies. Unlike the British and the Americans, both sides of the Russian front came to experience the horrors of invasions which became wars between peoples.

Modern wars approach their climax in the rise of collective passion for victory at any cost to the enemy. Inside Germany, even in 1993, the bitterest, longest-lasting memories of living survivors of the war center on those escalations of the British-American air war that visited indiscriminate destruction upon German cities.[13] Hamburg and Dresden are the famous examples, each of them consumed in a technical result of massive bombing—the fire storm—which not even the military clearly foresaw.[14] Someone has observed that democracies are slow to stir to the anger that fits them for entry into a war; but once stirred, democracies go to war with zeal. They go with moral conviction that sweeps ambiguity and doubt away. As the European war of 1944–45 approached its end, public feelings in Britain and America mixed hope, satisfaction, and composure in response to Allied killings of 100,000 people in one night of bombing: hope that the more the Germans suffered, the sooner they would quit; satisfaction that now the Germans were getting what they deserved; and composure that, however innocent some victims of such bombings might be, people all over the world had been paying a similar price for six years. Only much later, especially because of a novel by Kurt Vonnegut,[15] were many Americans to wonder if the obliteration bombing of a nonmilitary target, the museum city of Dresden, was a matter for composure. (Later, too, the researches of the United States Air Force on the psychological results of the bombings on the German population would discover that the hope for thus hastening their capitulation was misplaced. Civilians under rains of bombs apparently grit their teeth and strengthen their resolve to go on fighting the enemy. Londoners already knew that.)

If racism entered into the way Germans fought different enemies with different degrees of ferocity, it entered as well in the difference with which Americans fought Germans and Japanese enemies in this war—a contrast on which the next chapter will focus at length. For the moment it is worth observing that the feelings with which Americans entered, fought, and ended the second round of war with Germany in this century, exhibited both kinship and contrast with feelings of an earlier generation of Americans in 1917. Then, led by their Presbyterian president, they went to war on a high tide of nationalistic idealism; now, they went with grim determination to get rid of an evil, Nazism, about which they knew more now than the former generation had known about Imperial Germany. Then, they were nervous about the loyalties of German Americans in their own ranks and attacked some of them with hysterical fear; now, they knew—partly through the testimony of refugees from Nazism, newly arrived in America in the thirties—that delivering Germany and all Europe from the scourge of Nazism made this a "good war" for German Americans too. Then, they had ended their short participation in the war only to be told by the Allied victors that they, not the Americans, knew how to deal with the defeated Germans; now, they were aware that political isolationism would not work ever again and that this time Americans had better insist on having some of their own way in the settlements of the peace.

What would that way be? Looking back on the years 1945–50, Americans and Germans of the 1990s have reason to remember the answers which their leaders of that generation managed to give. Now, several decades later, one can say that they shifted German-American relations away from the fatal lockstep of two successive wars into a new chapter of remarkably growing political reconciliation and collaboration. The story of that shift ought to be central to any contemporary review of the possibility of forgiveness in the tortured relations of nations.

Vengeance versus Truth, Reparation versus Restoration: 1945–60

Like many Europeans, Americans born in the first half of this century grew up with an undertow of expectation that every twenty years or so the western world would go to war. The change in designation from the "Great War" to "World War I" sig-

punitive justice against enemy crimes and not their own but their right to distinguish the most guilty from the less guilty in the enemy's political system. In the deliberations, the identity of the "more or less guilty" remained as a huge residual category.

By 1945 modern totalitarianism had made these distinctions difficult indeed. Take the Nazi theory of *Führer-Prinzip* at its literal ideological word, and one had to concede that the whole of Germany was simply following the orders of its dictator. One had to invoke concepts of individual moral responsibility to oppose this theory, but could one invoke them against an entire population? Here is one of those instances in moral deliberation about politics where moral theories and political facts collide, intermingle, and condition each other with perplexities that seem peculiarly characteristic of twentieth-century national and international affairs. In their situation of "responsibility spread thin," were Germans obligated to obey all the orders of their government? Lutheranism had prepared some to think so, but aside from that ambiguous religious background the Nazi government forcefully commanded them to think so. In fact, all political systems require of their members a readiness to follow orders in the name of the coherence of the society, and only an extreme moral individualism—such as, ironically, Americans often applaud—requires a citizen to be ready to disobey almost any government-backed order. True to his own upbringing in Prussia, Immanuel Kant was sure that moral education would ready children to be obedient to law as well as moral principle, and, while not as popular in America as in Germany, obedience had its place in the acclaimed virtues of family life in both countries. So, too, the excuse "I was only following orders." That defense would one day get new prominence during the American war in Vietnam, in the case of William Calley.

But the Allies had fought the war in alleged defense of a polity that asserted individual rights and responsibilities, and the Nuremberg judges were ready to impose the concept as their part in a legal assault on Nazism. More than a Hitler had to be responsible for the atrocities. How many more? It was one thing to celebrate those few heroic individuals and groups who gave or risked their lives in opposition to the Nazis, but between them and the top of the government hierarchy were millions in the bureaucracy, the military, and the general citizenry who carried out the orders and were thereby instruments of the atrocities in ways that the interconnections of people in a modern industrial society make uniquely possible. Now that Hitler was dead, who should be held either morally or legally "guilty?" The moral answer, "almost everyone," was not judicable. Yet, given the slippery slope from leaders to lieutenants to willing followers to mute protesting bystanders, the facts as well as principles of moral responsibility lend plausibility to the notion that there is no innocence for most citizens of modern countries that commit "crimes against humanity." Many German parents of children growing up in the postwar era would find themselves asked the question implicit in this moral slant on the ethics of citizenship: "What did you do in the Nazi time?"

But legal institutions, national or international, have little ability to ask such a question of all the inhabitants of any country. However necessary were the symbolic retributions handed out by the Nuremberg court against leading Nazis, its judges had to peer down the slope toward other candidates for "justice" who were too numerous for courtrooms or jails, too ambiguously "criminal" for confident prosecution, or too necessary to the immediate rehabilitation of a devastated society to be prudently re-moved from it.[21] This last necessity frequently appears as evidence of moral "cyni-cism" in the treatment of agents of political evil: the victors know whom to "for-give" by knowing whom they need to run the industry, the government, the spy system, and the new alliances of their former enemies. The moral argument here again rests on balances between punitive, restorative, and distributive justice in a nation's dealings with its enemies: changing the future *behavior* of enemies, not only punish-ing them for past behavior, may be a justice best not only for them but for the victor nation too. In this, an ethic of good intermixes with an ethic of right, especially if "right" is defined in a way that calls for the righting of relations in such a way that good increases on all sides.

Allied attempts to make distinctions of guilt in Germany took other less ambigu-ous, more political and pragmatic forms than Nuremberg. Prominent local Nazi leaders were banned from holding office in the new government. Persons with a record for resistance to the Nazis were installed in their places. Trade unions, schoolteachers, and media owners found themselves instructed in organization and free speech in a liberal democracy. And, when the leaders of newly formed political parties went to work to write a new *Grundgesetz* or constitutional law for Germany, all varieties of political parties were legitimated except those "aiming to overthrow democratic society." One such party was banned in 1952 by the new government of the Federal Republic.

That new government, following the precedents of the Allied occupation, contin-ued the prosecution of former Nazis for various crimes. By 1970 some 12,900 per-sons had been prosecuted; 5,200 had been imprisoned, 76 of these for life.[22] That this process should have continued over the first twenty years of the legal system of the Federal Republic is remarkable, especially to American eyes accustomed to stat-utes of limitation and "swift justice." Many German families in the nineties, how-ever, remember the denazification trials as much too swift, as clumsy attempts to mete out judgments *wie am Fliessband*—like an assembly line. Justice in many of these twilight cases must have been very rough—as when citizens with little sympa-thy for the Nazis had tried to use posts of responsibility in industry to mollify the suffering of slave labor there.[23]

If we are to concede that the new German government broke new ground in its efforts to extirpate former Nazis from public life, we must also acknowledge that, in this instance if anywhere in human history, justice falls limp before monster-sized evil. No justice could be prompt, complete, or comprehensive enough to match these crimes. We are told that in 1970 about half of the 15,000 active judges and other magistrates in West Germany held office in the Nazi era. Did the Christian Democratic Party and its Chancellor Konrad Adenauer fail in their commitment to remove such officials, or would such removal have been a crippling blow to institutions neces-sary for the pursuit of justice itself in any society? One can make a strong case for an unending, even if forever incomplete, search for such still surviving agents of a disas-trous past. Not only Israelis but some Germans make the same political-pragmatic argument, as German historian Eberhardt Jackel did in 1985: "Whether these and other [magistrates] were personally guilty is not the point. It was bad for German democracy, and it set a bad example to the younger generation, that people with *any* kind of Nazi record should have been given such posts."[24] One trouble with this claim is the *any*. The slope from active to passive collaboration with their regime faces citizens everywhere; while moral conscience as well as political fact may both testify to the guilt of the passive collaborators, law cannot place all of them in the dock. For subsequent prosecution of Nazis, lines between the more and the less responsible had to be drawn if legal punitive justice was to stop short of sweeping most of the population into its net. The drawing of such lines will always be an act of power as well as a perception of past fact. The resulting justice will always display some arbitrariness and much ambiguity; to some extent it will be the justice of the victors.

In face of this inevitability, a second trouble with the argument is that "bad for democracy" cuts both ways. That every citizen participates in some degree of guilt for the crimes of the society matches the oldest democratic thought in the Judeo-Christian tradition: the equal propensity of all humans to sin. Reinhold Niebuhr used to say that the universality of sin is the only concept in this tradition that is empirically verifiable. To be sure, some actions of governments may be so far removed from ordinary citizens' influence that it will be absurd to connect their generic capacity for wrongdoing with those actions. But empirically considered, there is always a range of political actions that have the tacit and passive support of citizens, else they would never have become political actions—as Adolf Hitler himself recognized when he counted on the support of the German *Volk* as a whole for the success of his policies over against many a German legal institution.

In this misty world of responsibility-spread-thick-and-thin, the relativities and the realities of shared political guilt have their cloudy being. In their different but kindred ways, Americans and Germans share a culture that permits individuals to divorce themselves from what their governments do. As Ardagh comments, from his long and close acquaintance with modern Germany, personal and public norms of behavior exhibit a decided split among Germans ancient and modern. Persons "he" cares for personally, says Ardagh, the average German "will defend, whether innocent or not; those he does not know he will leave to their fate," expecting official public agencies to determine that fate.[25]

Contemporary Germans may wonder at the right of an American or English citizen to call this split "an abiding flaw on the German social character," but a generational difference may be evolving in Germany on the point. A poll taken in 1977 asked a sample of the public: "Did the German population have any practical means of influencing Nazi policy, for instance over the concentration camps?" Four percent of Germans over sixty years of age answered yes and 86 percent no, while 16 percent of those under forty-five years of age answered yes and 53 percent no.[26] In most American eyes, so small an intergenerational change is disturbing, though both answers suggest some impact of thirty years of experience in a democracy, which has perhaps taught younger people about the influence of citizens on government. Retrospective assessments of human responsibility are inherently risky, and Germans of all ages might be inclined to say to Americans: "You never lived in a modern dictatorship. You can oppose it and die, but you cannot influence it." To this many non-Germans, not just Americans, are likely to reply: "But you are responsible for cooperating with it as little as possible. Those who failed to do so deserve to be punished." The reply gets a nod from a growing majority of Germans since 1945, but they continue to accompany that nod with their own national debate about how "clean" a clean break can be with the past and present legacies of an evil history. Reflecting on a 1985 interview with Richard von Weizsäcker, president of the Federal Republic, James M. Markham summarized the "paradox" of the largely successful German attempt to build a democracy while these remnants of the Nazi past still haunted the present:

> If [the president] succeeds in leaving a political legacy to Germany, it may be in reconciling emerging generations to paradox. It is a paradox—one that younger Germans have trouble embracing—that the most tolerant and successful democracy in German history was built by men and women who emerged from the moral ruins of Nazism. Few were free of some kind of complicity with the past, and many were spiritually lamed, but these burdens did not condemn the democracy they erected. The president does not boast about this transition, and in his Bundestag speech [of May 8, 1985] he phrased it with characteristic restraint: "There was no 'zero hour,' but we had the opportunity to make a fresh start. We have used this opportunity as well as we could."

But they could have done more: that is the moral-empirical truth about citizenship everywhere, as von Weizsäcker added at the conclusion of the interview:

> When one looks into history 40 or 50 years later it is better as a young person to judge someone for having behaved wrongly if one has also experienced such a situation. The tendency to believe that people then were evil but today they are good is very widespread. And this tendency, naturally, is not good.[27]

A decade later, as Germans wrestle with the apparent resurgence of racist xenophobia in their public life, even the young are experiencing the intransigence of some political evils. At the end of this chapter we will return to von Weizsäcker's May 8, 1985 speech and to the provocative event that was its context, the visit of an American president to a military cemetery in the German village of Bitburg. In that event, too, the old evils were passionately remembered again on all sides. For the moment I suggest, on behalf of Americans, that one of the gifts of postwar Germany to the world may be its example of wrestling with the necessity and the enduring problems of breaking with an evil political past not only in broad, symbolic ways but in terms of concrete assignments of guilt and punishment to some of the perpetrators of the evil. However ambiguous and selective, such measures are therapeutic additions to law, political precedent, and citizen education. A summary of certain other moments in this postwar wrestling over questions of personal and collective guilt is in order. Americans ought not to forget any of them.

Confessing a Nation's Guilt on Its Behalf: The Churches

In a moving recollection of his own wartime experience as a prisoner of war in Glasgow, Jürgen Moltmann narrates how in September 1945 the British authorities compelled all Germans in the camp to view photographs of Bergen-Belsen and Auschwitz. Their first reaction was unbelief and certainty that the pictures were propaganda. The second reaction was fatalistic: "Everyone did his duty, even if the Devil was giving the orders. . . . Everything was destiny." But there was a third:

> . . . the horror at the crimes of Bergen-Belsen and Auschwitz bored its way deeper and deeper into one's soul. I became ill and wanted, more than anything else, to die. . . . How could one belong to a nation on which such a burden of guilt lay? Should not one renounce it and make a fresh start somewhere else? I remember the cold fury that welled up in me. In 1944 my generation was driven to the fronts which were already annihilated, just to die there so that Hitler and his fellows could live a few months longer; still more, just so that the terrible murder in Bergen-Belsen and Auschwitz could continue.

But finally, at the end of October 1945, a word came to the Glasgow camp which started Moltmann and some of his fellows on a road back to claiming their German identity again: the brief "Confession of Guilt" adopted and published by the Council of the Evangelical Church in Germany, October 18–19, in Stuttgart. At first, with many others in the camp, Moltmann felt that the confession was an insult:

> "Through us [said the Declaration], infinite suffering has been inflicted on many peoples and countries." In my own captive soul, too, the truth of these words was slow to dawn, until I sensed the liberation to which this confession of guilt led me— a liberation from the suppression of guilt, and from an obtuse belief in destiny; a liberation from the armour of insensibility and defiance in which we had encased ourselves; a liberation which set us free to achieve self-respect and to assume responsibility for crimes and failures to act. It is true! A person who thus admits his guilt and complicity renders himself defenceless, assailable and vulnerable. He stands there, muddied and weighed down. Everyone can point at him and despise him. But he becomes free from alienation and the determination of his actions by others; he comes to himself, and steps into the light of a truth which makes him free and brings him into a new comradeship with the victims—readiness for reconciliation. How can one look the victims in the eye? The victims always have a better memory than the wrongdoers and those who run with the pack. For that reason there is never an end to the admission of guilt; the Stuttgart Confession of Guilt remains topical. It gave me the courage to return to the "solidarity of guilt" and to the "community of suffering" of my nation, and no longer want to escape.[28]

The Stuttgart Declaration. In retrospect after forty years of public German reckoning with the Nazi past, the Stuttgart document seems notoriously brief (some 300 words in its English translation) and even more notoriously general in its lack of specification of the crimes of the Nazi era. The authors included some (Martin Niemöller, Hans Lilje, Wilhelm Niesel), who had gone to prison for their open opposition to Hitler, and a future president of the Federal Republic (Gustav Heinemann). The text spends three sentences in confession, and the rest is given over to recalling how many of the authors had opposed Nazism from their pulpits, to the hope that now "violence and revenge . . . may be controlled" toward Germany, and to joy in a reconnection with delegates from the other European churches who had asked for the Stuttgart meeting and an expression of the German church's stance in relation to the recent disastrous past.

A mild confession it was, but the Stuttgart Declaration raised a storm of protest, not only from politicians and journalists but from other prominent German church leaders. Among the latter was Helmut Thielicke, who in a Good Friday sermon the next spring enumerated the unjust policies of the occupying Allied powers and called attention to the guilt of other nations for some of the excesses of Nazism. "I can no longer listen to the public confessions of guilt by the Church," he said, "among whose first members I count myself, without this other aspect also being publicly stated." Even leaders of the surviving Confessing Church, at the beginning of 1947, expressed their "fear . . . that the Church would lose credit with the German people unless it now speaks of the 'injustices committed by the other side' too." Such thinking, says Werner Krusche, as he quotes these testimonies of the time, illustrated a German characteristic which Karl Barth identified as "loving to reply . . . to every political accusation with a counter-accusation as soon as possible." So, says Krusche, "a good year after Stuttgart, a confession of guilt had surreptitiously developed into an accusation of guilt against others; those who had been accusing themselves had turned into plaintiffs."[29] One of the signers, Gustav Heinemann, who had paid tribute to the Declaration as the "turning-point and pivot of his political outlook," said sadly: "This confession was not, all things considered, taken to heart by our congregations and our nation. . . . Thus on the whole, our experience of *hubris* and catastrophe, judgment and grace, did not provide an opportunity to turn over a new leaf and think again."[30]

Debate about the significance of the Stuttgart Declaration was to continue for a long time among German church leaders. Was it a document with an "alibi function" or a "successful tactical move" in the direction of more telling confessions of guilt to come?[31] In his assessment written a quarter-century later, Eberhard Bethge scores the document for its "tone of self-justification" and most of all for its avoidance of *naming* the sins of the church in the Nazi era: "In the place where solid responsibility for concrete specifics should have been formulated, there elbow in categories of general human weakness."[32] As one of the ecumenical leaders who had urged the German church to hold the Stuttgart meeting, Church of England Bishop G. K. A. Bell said to the gathering on its last day, "We have now to recognize the cause of this suffering." That meant digging into the facts of recent history, and not many Germans, including church leaders, were yet ready to do so. "Something approaching a national amnesia gripped the country" in 1945[33]; and, from the standpoint of popular unreadiness to speak of anyone's "guilt" for Nazism, the Stuttgart Declaration may well be judged as a "successful tactic." But from the perspective of realists like Bethge and Heinemann, the Declaration was a retreat from political responsibility in a way that one side of classic Lutheranism had made only too tempting to many Germans. Stuttgart, said Hans Lilje, "is not a political declaration, but an ecclesiastical one. It was never intended for the world in general." Indeed, said Bishop Maharens, it was "a confession before God and not before man" at all, for it is not "the task of our church to clarify questions of political development and international law." With fine Lutheran precision, the church leaders of Schleswig-Holstein stated: "From this point it is clear that no political guilt is being established here. The apportioning of such guilt is a political and historical judgment. . . . On the contrary, what we have here is a strictly religious confession of guilt before God, which is unassailable as such." Reverting to a notion of guilt and forgiveness as a matter between the individual soul and God, Stuttgart thus declared "political sin" an oxymoron. This theology was the fundamental problem, concluded Bethge. "The guilt of the church must be perceived, analyzed, and named, not in terms of generalities and principles, but as historically concrete." Painful the analysis may be, but the church has moral reason to study history and its part in history. Concretely, the very theory of an "unpolitical" church was one of the reasons why the Nazis could glide to power with so little protest from the church in 1933. Practicing the analysis that he recommends, Bethge notes that this is just the theory that suits the purposes of a totalitarian government. "Depoliticization is the politics of the unpolitical," who thereby permit the totalitarians to take power over every sector of society. "The unpolitical is the culprit in the catastrophe of a total politicization."[34] Leaving the political world to itself means isolating it from religious criticism—from the "Lordship of Christ," in church language. But a church that so depoliticizes itself makes its authoritative Christ into the "Christ of the authorities."[35] General statements about "courage and weakness" are all very essential to ethics, said Bethge, "but unfortunately dangerous," too. "Dangerous, because they block confession" and justify racist politicians who tell the church it has no right to criticize racist political policy.[36]

At best, from this point of view, the Stuttgart Declaration was an "intermezzo," a step away from publicly pretended innocence that was not yet a step into publicly confessed guilt. It left the task of specifying the guilt of Germany's Christians to other occasions.

The Darmstadt Declaration. A break with this tradition had begun implicitly in the Barmen Declaration of the Confessing Church in 1934, which had affirmed, in language rather unprecedented for the Lutheran side of the Evangelical Church's tradition, "God's powerful claim on our whole life." In context it was a rejection of the central claim of Nazism: the supremacy of Adolf Hitler *über Alles*.[37] Barmen had taken aim at Hitler's *Führerprinzip*, but it had said nothing about his racism and anti-Semitism. Sensitive to the abstract generality of both "confessions," leaders of the Confessing Church met in 1947 in Darmstadt to start the process of naming the sins of Nazism, Germany, its citizens, and its Christians. Under the leadership of H. J. Iwand, the body leveled four specific charges against the political-ecclesiastical culture of Germany: (1) its "dream of a special German mission to the world," which "set our nation on the throne of God"; (2) denial of the democratic right of revolution against "absolute dictatorship" and with this denial an upholding of authoritarian hierarchy and patriarchy; (3) the formation of a "front of good against evil," such as was implemented in the war against the Soviet Union; and (4) a failure "to make the business of the poor and deprived the business of Christianity," as Germany was prodded now to do by the challenge of Marxism. These were brave words in many church circles in the Germany of 1947, and they remained disputed words inside and outside of the churches. Darmstadt was not an official statement of the Evangelical Church in Germany (the EKD), however; and it fell far short of the detailed identification of the crimes of the Nazi era that many of its victims were demanding of Germans at large.

Notably missing here was any mention of anti-Semitism and the Holocaust, not to speak of the other predations of the German armies in Poland, the Soviet Union, and most of Europe. Not until 1950, in fact, did a local (territorial) synod of the Evangelical Church finally put on the public record the words: "We declare that through negligence and silence before the God of mercy, we have shared in the guilt for the crime which was committed by men of our nation against the Jews." Synod President Gustav Heinemann, a layman, in a closing address to the synod, recollected October 1945 and said that Stuttgart "had on this occasion been defined in real terms at last."[38]

If there is wisdom for the world to read in this history of painful attempts by the German church to deal with a painful history, it is that in order to do even rhetorical justice to the truth about some enormous evils of the past, human persons and groups require considerable *time*. Yet this in itself is a great, dangerous fact, for (as Martin Luther King was to say in a classic document of the American civil rights movement), time alone does not change anything in a human society; indeed, especially for purposes of social memory, time can be the great eroder, the friend of forgetfulness, the silent route of escape from human remembering or human rectification of colossal past wrong. Especially in Germany from 1950 to 1965, the coming of the Cold War meant the shift of German political attention and alliance to a new war with Communism. The new alliance with their former western enemies and the new eastward-directed hostility dampened and almost drowned the beginnings of church and public readiness to face the truth about old hostilities. Once again, echoing official rhetoric of the thirties, a German government in 1950 enlisted Christian symbols to stir public resistance to the dangers of Communist atheism.[39]

As in war itself, it is hard for citizens and governments to remember their past sins against enemies while fighting new battles with those enemies. Those who attempt such projects risk the label of traitor, as did the group of church leaders around Niemoeller, Heinemann, and Barth in the years 1950–75. In some American church circles such German church people were thought to be "dupes" of the Communists. On their side, as they went about their business of trying to create openings in the Iron Curtain, these leaders were refusing to regard the Soviets as devilish or the North Atlantic Treaty Organization as angelic. Important interests were at stake on both sides, they conceded, but this new phase of the seventy-five year war was as much a contest of power as of virtue against vice.

The Churches and Ostpolitik. In spite of the contrary domestic political winds of the era, various groups of Christians in Germany did succeed, in the years before 1970, in maintaining the "confessional" momentum begun at Stuttgart. In particular, a series of unofficial gatherings of theologians and lay people began to address the tangle of leftover hostilities that originated in the German invasion of Poland in September 1939.

Like the Sudetenland of post-1918 Czechoslovakia, the border areas between Poland and Germany had long been in dispute when the Nazi regime annexed them as *Lebensraum* for Germans in 1939. For centuries some 9½ million people of German descent had lived in these areas.[40] As the war came to its furious end in 1945, old and new German residents of these border areas fled westward by the million before the Russian armies, joining the eventual staggering total of 13 to 14 million refugees who flooded into West Germany from the East between 1945 and 1961 and increasing that country's population by 20 percent. "[I]t was the greatest migratory movement of modern times. . . . All in all, in 1944–46 about 8 million Germans were on the move westward, many of them on foot, struggling along weary and underfed, clutching a few precious belongings. Over a million are estimated to have died en route."[41] The sight of their leave-taking must have stirred up many a wave of bitter, retributory feeling among eastern populations delivered at last from their Nazi occupiers.

The short-range problem of war-devastated West Germany was how to cope with this influx of impoverished people. From the beginning of the process, western governments, including the new government of the Federal Republic, granted the refugees citizenship rights. Then, in 1952, the Federal Republic enacted an "equalizations of burdens law" (*Lastenausgleichsgesetz*), whose provisions Americans in particular should find astonishing: Germans who had been fortunate enough to survive the war with all or most of their property intact were required to cede half of its value, over the next thirty years, to those who had fled from the East, suffered war damages, or emigrated to escape Nazism in the 1930s. By 1982, DM 121 billion had been thus redistributed, or about $75 billion.[42] As an example of distributive and compensatory justice, this was a remarkable national policy. But it represented only half of equally large financial restitutions that the Federal Republic made in the same period to people in all the Nazi-occupied nations who could prove that their occupiers had robbed them or inflicted gross suffering upon them. Included in these measures of the fifties was a DM 3 billion payment to Israel, plus hundreds of millions more in compensation to individual Jews who had survived the Holocaust.[43] Through 1986, the Bonn government settled some 4½ million such personal claims for a total of some $40 billion.[44] The several compensation (*Ruckerstattung*) laws of this latter decade laid down provisions that by the year 2000, according to a 1988 government document, international payments in excess of DM 100 billion, or some $70 billion, would have been made.

That document, published by the Bonn Information Office, began by noting that the German language has a less fiscally tinged synonym for *compensation*—*Wiedergutmachung*—a morally ambitious word that means literally "making good again." The document ends with contrasting moral sobriety: "No matter how large the sum, no amount of money will ever suffice to compensate for National Socialist persecution. . . . But in dealing with the legacy of the Hitler regime, the Federal Republic of Germany has established a precedent, namely that of legislating and carrying out a comprehensive system of restitution for injustice. . . ."[45]

Implied here is the acknowledgment that some political crimes transcend economics. The politics of German reconciliation with its former enemies required more than these restitutionary shares in the growing West German "economic miracle." Inside and outside the new borders of the Federal Republic, hostilities abounded that no money payments could diminish. Inside, West Germans harbored vast stores of renewed resentment of Soviet, Polish, and other eastern peoples arriving among the ranks of the East German refugees. Some had been ejected from places they had inhabited for generations, and many hoped to return home again. Many new West German neighbors hoped the same—early signs of a problem that would erupt anew in the 1990s. In the fifties, the political challenge of getting its citizens to accept the new neighbors and new borders as permanent must have been daunting to the new government.

Quietly and slowly, the churches began to help—first in small gatherings of exiles to work "at conquering their feelings of hatred and vengefulness" against former eastern neighbors; then in larger gatherings whose leaders, in 1950, issued an "Exiles Charter" which declared their "intent to renounce revenge and violence."[46] Little evident in these meetings was the refugees' readiness to renounce their right to return to the East. Their hope of doing so fueled both backward-looking politicians in West Germany, determined to repossess the eastern lands, and the new Communist leaders of Poland, who sought to unite Poles in a continuing fear of "the avenging Germans."[47] In the fifties, the coming of normal relations between West Germany and the People's Republic of Poland seemed far in the future.

In the ensuing fifteen years, however, largely under church leadership, the ground for a new "eastern policy" slowly cleared. An elite group of scientists, theologians, and lawyers met in Tübingen in 1961–62 and publicly called for the recognition of the new Oder-Neisse frontier of Poland, the diplomatic recognition of Poland itself, and the abandonment of any expectation by Germans that they would return to their old Polish homes. The prestige of the authors of the Tübingen Memorandum guaranteed it serious attention and great opposition in the West German public as a whole. In response to the furor inside Evangelical Church circles, Dr. Ludwig Raiser, lay president of the EKD and professor of constitutional law at Tübingen, led the church to write another memorandum "On the position of the exiles and the relationship of the German people to their eastern neighbors." This document too prompted a furor inside the church; but, comments Martin Stöhr, it contributed to politics what politicians themselves could not for the moment contribute: "space in which to conduct an honest discussion, with an eye to the future, of a suppressed complex relating to the war which Germany had lost . . . and to act in an innovative fashion in politics."[48] To the collapse of Communist governments in 1989, the churches would make a similar contribution.

One cost of this witness to the church in 1962 was the loss of some members, who rehearsed the old dualistic protest that the church should confine itself to pastoral comfort of those who suffer from political conflicts—that it should not dare to shape the political attitudes of its members or to suggest new policies to governments. Resonance for this theory went back at least to the sixteenth century, of course. Americans likewise knew the theory well. In fact the "Eastern Memorandum" constituted a real departure from the old Lutheran theory, as Martin Stöhr implicitly recognizes when he wrote in 1988:

> The Eastern Memorandum . . . reminded its readers that now (in 1965) there were Poles living in the former German eastern territories who in their turn had been driven out even earlier. Should they be turned into the street again? Was the vicious circle of power not to be broken at last? Could it be forgotten that not Poland but Germany began the war? That, therefore, not only Poles must bear the burdens of suffering, but also Germans? . . .
>
> Pastoral and political thinking frequently diverge. . . . Those, however, who only operate on a pastoral level without touching on the taboos of political realities, produce new repressions and blockades of a mental and political nature. The poisoning of the present and above all of the future by the past must be interrupted.[49]

Notable here is the assertion that sometimes the political judgments of theologians may be based on a more profound *empirical* understanding of political reality than the dualisms of some theological and some secular theorists permit them to perceive. Historic resentments, expressed little in public deliberation, can build up to outbreaks of public anger that destroy deliberation and fuel new violence. Not only to quell anger but also to give new opportunity for *expressing* it is surely one public responsibility of religious bodies who want to make an eventual contribution to civic peace. Equally evident here is the empirical impossibility of separating the "personal" and the "political" aspects of human suffering on all sides of this painful, long-drawn-out controversy in the recent history of Germany. To touch the one was to touch the other, as the authors of all the documents summarized here learned in this period— if they had not already learned it in their experience of the 1930s.

In short, in the Eastern Memorandum of 1965, "after twenty years, the Stuttgart Confession ha[d] been translated into concrete terms as regards Poland."[50] Fifteen years of wrestling by a minority of church and other German leaders with this complex of "eastern" questions now opened new space for the action of political leaders themselves.

Among those expressing gratitude for the Memorandum was Willy Brandt, Socialist Democrat and Mayor of West Berlin, who became vice chancellor and foreign minister of the Federal Republic in 1966. Upon becoming chancellor in 1969, he formulated his well-known *Ostpolitik*. The "east" included, first of all, the German Democratic Republic. Germans west and east, said Brandt in a demonstration of great prepositional acumen, "must first learn how to live alongside each other and then, eventually, how to live with each other."[51] Then, finally, came diplomatic recognition of the People's Republic of Poland in a treaty ratified by the German parliament in 1972 and accompanied by words of acknowledgment from other political leaders of the churches' role in these changes.[52]

Two remarkable events followed ratification, both related to new *symbols* by which historically hostile societies creep toward new realism and new ways of remembering their respective painful experiences of the past. One was a series of meetings between Polish and German teachers and historians for the purpose of revising the school textbooks of the two countries so that the story of their twentieth-century relations would be interpreted to each other's young people in mutually acceptable accounts. The other was a visit by Chancellor Brandt to Warsaw in December 1970 for the formal treaty signing, during which he visited that city's memorial to the Warsaw ghetto uprising of 1943. In an apparently spontaneous upsurge of feeling, he fell on his knees before the monument as if to express repentance for Nazi crimes against the Jews. Brandt had been in exile in Scandinavia during the entire Nazi era, and he was thus among those Germans who could most easily have avoided a sense of personal guilt for the atrocities of Warsaw and Auschwitz. But now he was chancellor of the Federal Republic, and his action had inherent representative power. Not all Jews or Germans liked the representation: did the chancellor think that he could repent on behalf of a whole nation? In the face of the colossal crime to be remembered, what good does one such act do? But Brandt's admirers outnumbered his critics on both sides of the now-stabilized Oder-Neisse line. "Long as the road to reconciliation still is," said Martin Stöhr in 1988, "the process of alienation and violence was longer."[53]

Even after his resignation from the office of chancellor, Willy Brandt was translating that view into public, international political speech. In 1990 he remained, said a *New York Times* reporter, the "only German who is genuinely popular" in Poland. In March of that year, a few months after the fall of the Berlin Wall, Brandt visited Frankfurt-an-der-Oder as he was campaigning for his party in East Germany and took the occasion to cross the bridge into Poland. Before a cheering crowd of 10,000, he said in English: "I came to tell our Polish friends that I belong to the overwhelming majority of Germans who think they must not return to the past. We have to live with the borders as they are and do everything possible to make borders more transparent." The restoration of these borders in 1945, he said, was not perfectly just, but "we have to say that terrible injustice occurred before. At one point Europe must pull out of this devil's circle of injustice, injustice, and new injustice." Germans on the west side of the Oder, observed the reporter, seem now to "accept the loss" of their homes on the other side even though the trade that moves both ways across the bridge continues to fuel German hostility "to Poles in general."[54]

Brandt did not destroy the "devil's circle," but he broke it in some crucial places. When he had assumed the chancellorship in 1969, he had exclaimed, "I will not be Chancellor of a conquered Germany, but of a liberated Germany!" In his brief tenure in the office he pursued a form of liberation rare in politics: liberation from denials of the past and from cheap forms of political reconciliation. He took impressive steps toward restorative justice. At his death on October 8, 1992, an American news commentator rightly said: "He laid the foundation of the end of the Cold War." With good fortune not often granted the visionary political leader, he lived to see his vision realized.[55]

The United States and Germany: Forty Years after World War II

Germans' struggle with the stern disciplines of historical guilt as well as their effort to confront their recent past without becoming imprisoned in it is instructive not only for Germans. Like other nations, they have a long way to go toward recovery from that past and toward a genuine form of reconciliation with their twentieth-century enemies. One thinks especially of the people of the former Soviet Union, with whom exchanges of confession and forgiveness have been modest or nonexistent for half of the century of continued German and American antagonism toward "the Communist world." Seldom in these years have the political gestures of German or American church or governmental leaders taken public account of the losses sustained in the Nazi invasion of the USSR, which exceeded by far the numerical losses of every other country in the war.[56] The road to reconciliation remains long and many-sided in this history. Nonetheless, the German experience of traveling that road, with halting and never unanimous public consensus, is full of instruction for the citizens and leaders of other countries in the world, not the least the United States. That is reason enough for the discursus above into the internal German struggle since 1945.

Americans have a weak record for apologizing to other peoples for what the United States has done to them; and this fact claims additional attention in the next two chapters of this book. To close this chapter, few events could better summarize and symbolize the scope, limit, and dynamics of the vengeful and the forgiving elements in the political relations of the United States and Germany than their respective observances of the fortieth anniversary of the end of World War II. Concerning this anniversary, history is likely to note a particular incident that demonstrates the ambiguities and conflicting interests conditioning the attempt of any pair of nations to remember the pains of great, costly conflicts between them. This incident will always have the name Bitburg Cemetery. No event in recent years has displayed more clearly the difficulties that modern western societies encounter among their political leaders, their journalists, their religious leaders, and their citizens in public grappling with the concept of forgiveness in international affairs. What forgiveness means and what it does not mean stood silhouetted in this incident. The flurry of rhetoric on both sides of the Atlantic around the crisis of "Bitburg" rightly deserves careful study by all who include or exclude the word *forgiveness* from the lexicon of political speech. Because in this event Americans tended to use the word often and carelessly, it is particularly instructive for our side of the century-long hostility between the United States and Germany.

Bitburg: Remembering, Forgetting, Forgiving

Anniversaries are times set aside in human social schedules for remembering and symbolizing the importance of certain past events. Politically understood, they are occasions when societies, institutions, and persons acknowledge their present values in terms of the history in which they are rooted. There is not much rationality in anniversaries. For future-oriented pragmatists, they are rather useless.

But humans are the creatures who remember a past and anticipate a future with the aid of rituals. Without anniversaries, societies as well as individuals might lose touch with their identities. One might even coin this rule for political societies: By their anniversaries shall you know them. Political anniversaries are many-sided occasions. The inheritors of political memory are diverse in what they recollect, what their interest in recollection is, and what future use they want to make of the past. So political anniversaries have this in common with family anniversaries: they bring diverse experiences of the past to the fore, and diverse emotions too. As James E. Young perceptively wrote in reflecting on the Bitburg event:

> . . . [A]n inescapable partnership grows between a people and its monuments. It is precisely at this point, however, that a critical approach to memorials might rescue us from a complicity that allows our *icons* of remembrance to harden into *idols* of remembrance. For memorialization occurs not merely within these icons, but between the events and icons, and then again between the icons and ourselves. By recalling this movement between events, icons, and ourselves, we accept more than a ritual responsibility for the images that lie enshrined in our monuments. It is not to Holocaust monuments as such that we turn for remembrance, but to ourselves within the reflective space they both occupy and open up. In effect, there can be no self-critical monuments, only critical viewers.[57]

One might even suppose that this "ceremonial" side of politics has little to do with "real" politics—that is, with clashes of power and interest. The ceremonies of politics often conceal these clashes or paper them over with high ideological public talk. Like the speeches that legislators give before they vote, such ceremonies are easily seen as window-dressing and hardly constitute an occasion for front-page news.

If German-American relations of the entire postwar period offer one dramatic exception to this skeptical account of political anniversaries, it is the furor surrounding the proposed visit of an American president to a small Rhineland town in West Germany in the week of May 8, 1985, to mark the fortieth anniversary of the formal end of World War II in Europe. The event generated more passion, rancor, and publicity than any participant anticipated. Most of all, it induced a wide cross section of leaders and constituents in both countries to ask openly, and for days on end, a pair of questions rare in modern public dialogue: What *is* "forgiveness in politics?" What is it *not*?

In fact there has been no other occasion in the lifetime of this author when so much *journalistic* attention has been devoted explicitly to this question. The reason is easy to fathom: significant attention was given it by a multitude of heads of state, their immediate associates, artists, writers, theologians, historians, and a cross section of citizenry up and down the social scale in both the United States and Germany. For the understanding of the scope, limit, and possibility of forgiveness in modern politics, the Bitburg Cemetery controversy will long be pivotal. As Chancellor Helmut Kohl was to say, in an understatement, during the tortured finale of the event, "It is not often that the link between the past, present, and future of our country reaches us as vividly as during these hours at Bitburg."[58]

The background of the incident was as follows. Excluded from the June 6, 1984, ceremony marking the fortieth anniversary of the Normandy invasion, the German chancellor visited President Ronald Reagan the following November and expressed a strong desire that the president visit Germany in May, 1985, as a sign of reconciliation between the two countries in the intervening decades. Over the next four months, the Reagan White House would vacillate publicly about the proposal, moving from a January 28 announcement of its acceptance, to a February 14 plan to avoid a presidential visit to Germany on May 8, to a March reversion to accept a visit on that date.

Then, at a news conference on March 21, Mr. Reagan made an announcement that set off the first of two explosions which were to escalate the event into six weeks of political agony for him and his advisers. Against the advice of some, he said, he had decided not to visit the site of a concentration camp in Germany, because he felt "very strongly" about not "reawakening the memories" of wartime. Secondly, on April 11, the White House announced that the president would instead lay a wreath in the German military cemetery at Bitburg, 25 kilometers east of the Luxembourg border, as a gesture of reconciliation between the two former enemies.

The choice of Bitburg had behind it a twenty-five-year annual precedent of joint American-French-German ceremonies in the same location in memory of "the victims of Nazism and the two world wars."[59] In addition, a large NATO-American Air Force base in the city had enjoyed cordial relations with the population of the town for many years.

A flood of protest greeted this April 11 announcement. One day later the White

House conceded that the cemetery visit was under review, and by April 16 it announced a reversal of the decision not to visit a concentration camp. The president would go to Bergen-Belsen.[60]

By now various American groups had researched the history of the Kolmeshöhe cemetery enough to discover that among the graves of the 2,000 German soldiers there were some forty-nine members of the elite Waffen SS. The presence of these forty-nine[61] bodies soon became the symbolic heart of the protests about to erupt from many directions among Americans high and low.

American war veteran and Jewish groups were among the first to protest. They were joined, by April 18, by 53 U.S. senators who signed a letter urging the president not to go to Bitburg. Simultaneously a similar letter was being written in the U.S. House of Representatives. Then, also on the 18th, Mr. Reagan answered extensive questions about the visit from a group of editors and broadcasters meeting with him in the White House. Was it really the right place for a gesture toward reconciliation? In answer, the president explained at length that he was seeking to imitate the precedent of Chancellor Kohl and President Mitterand when they met at a Verdun Cemetery, in June 1984, to symbolize the cessation of hundreds of years of war between France and Germany. He then admitted that as far back as November Chancellor Kohl had in fact suggested that Dachau be included in the visits of May 1985. The White House had demurred. A camp visit, he said, would "run the risk of appearing as if I was trying to say to the Germans, 'Look what you did,' and all of this when most of the people of Germany today weren't alive or were very small children when this was happening." Furthermore, German and Japanese leaders have visited the American cemetery at Arlington; why should an American not be willing to visit Bitburg?

So "you're still going?" asked one of the journalists. The answer that came from the president was to catalyze yet more protests and swell them to astonishing public proportions in the course of the next twenty days:

> I think that it would be very hurtful [if I did not go] and all it would do is leave me looking as if I caved in in the face of some unfavorable attention. I think that there's nothing wrong with visiting that cemetery where those young men are victims of Nazism also, even though they were fighting in the German uniform, drafted into service to carry out the hateful wishes of the Nazis. They were victims, just as surely as the victims of the concentration camps.[62]

In the eyes of millions of Americans who were to read this in the next few days, the "great communicator" had committed a facile moral mistake.

As his luck would have it, Mr. Reagan was about to grant to a truly great communicator a national forum for saying so. The place was the White House; the occasion, the award to Elie Wiesel, recent winner of the Nobel Peace Prize, of the Congressional Gold Medal of Achievement, highest honor that Congress can bestow upon an American citizen. The week had been full of debate in the press over Bitburg, and at week's end Wiesel told reporters the details of how he had agonized over whether to accept the award from such a president, in such a place, in the wake of such circumstances. He had conferred with colleagues in the U.S. Holocaust Memorial Council (of which he was chairman), with members of the Congress, and with leaders of

Jewish organizations. All of them agreed that the president's views on "victims" were outrageous. Most of them advised Wiesel to accept the medal anyway. Among the council members, he said, "There were many tears, a lot of anger. People said, 'What is happening?' People were very passionate."[63] Rising at 4 A.M. on the day of the award, Wiesel rewrote the last quarter of his acceptance speech. Even up to the last moment, he said, he was unsure of whether he should appear, especially in light of the last-minute attempt by the White House liaison officer for Jewish affairs to limit the acceptance speech to three minutes and to "bar any direct criticism of Mr. Reagan." Going over this officer's head to the White House chief of staff, Wiesel got the assurance that he would speak as freely as he wished.[64]

In this explosive situation, the speeches of both president and medalist demonstrated careful crafting. Reagan reviewed the agony of the Holocaust, "a time when exodus was refused." Our national pledge, he said, is "more than 'Never again.'" It is also "Never forget." But remembering is consistent with reconciliation, he observed.

> Today, there is a spirit of reconciliation between the peoples of the allied nations and the peoples of Germany and even between the soldiers who fought each other on the battlefields of Europe. . . . As the people of Europe rebuilt their shattered lands, the survivors rebuilt their shattered lives, and they did so despite searing pain. And we who are their fellow citizens have taken up their memories and tried to learn from them what we must do.
>
> No one has taught us more than Elie Wiesel.

Wiesel was sure that the occasion required some more teaching: about proper relations between truth, memory, distinctions in moral guilt, and the politics of reconciliation. His speech began with a tribute to the common spirit and common goals which he shared with the president. "We were never on two sides. . . . We were always on the side of justice, always on the side of memory, against the SS and against what they represent." Then, straining at the limits of words, Wiesel recollected that today, April 19, was the anniversary of the 1943 Warsaw ghetto uprising, ignored and left to its destruction by the Allied powers, who aided every underground movement in the war except the Jewish one. And then, drawing on his own experience of the camps as a boy of thirteen, he said:

> Mr. President, I have seen children, I have seen them being thrown in the flames alive. Words, they die on my lips. So I have learned, I have learned, I have learned the fragility of the human condition. . . .
>
> But I have also learned that suffering confers no privileges. It all depends on what one does with it. And this is why survivors . . . have tried to teach their contemporaries how to build on ruins, how to proclaim faith to a generation that has seen it shamed and mutilated. And I believe, we believe, that memory is the answer, perhaps the only answer.

Finally, remembering in some detail the friendship which the Reagan administration had demonstrated to Israel and to Jews in the Soviet Union, Wiesel came to the revised last quarter of his speech.

Mr. President, I wouldn't be the person I am, and you wouldn't respect me for what I am, if I were not to tell you also of the sadness that is in my heart for what has happened during the last week. And I am sure that you, too, are sad for the same reasons.

What can I do? I belong to a traumatized generation. And to us, as to you, symbols are important. And furthermore, following our ancient tradition, and we are speaking about Jewish heritage, our tradition commands us to "speak truth to power". . . .

I am convinced . . . that you were not aware of the presence of SS graves in the Bitburg cemetery. Of course you didn't know. But now we all are aware.

May I, Mr. President, if it's possible at all, implore you to do something else, to find another way, another site? That place, Mr. President, is not your place. Your place is with the victims of the SS.

Oh, we know there are political and strategic reasons, but this issue, as all issues related to that awesome event, transcends politics and diplomacy.

The issue here is not politics, but good and evil. And we must never confuse them. . . .

. . . Mr. President, I know and I understand, we all do, that you seek reconciliation. And so do I, so do we. And I too wish to attain true reconciliation with the German people. I do not believe in collective guilt, nor in collective responsibility. Only the killers were guilty. Their sons and daughters are not.

And I believe, Mr. President, that we can and we must work together with them and with all people. And we must work to bring peace and understanding to a tormented world that, as you know, is still awaiting redemption.[65]

The president was said to be deeply moved by these words, addressed so directly to himself. But the policy remained immovable: he was going to Bitburg.

Meantime, across the Atlantic, the American furor had already found a reverse, negative echo in the public utterances of German politicians and commentators. At the chancellery of the Federal Republic, there was little doubt about what the American president should do: he should go to both Bergen-Belsen and to Bitburg. In a televised interview in Bonn, Chancellor Kohl said that he was "gratified that the American president, 40 years after the war, is ready to make this gesture of reconciliation." He conceded that Germans "ought to be very reserved" toward the current American debate; but that, even as he too joined Jews and others in revulsion against "the Nazi barbarity," he had to oppose the concept of "collective guilt" of all Germans, past and present, for that barbarity. "Collective shame," however, was another matter. He could share in that, he implied. A confirmation of these feelings in the chancellor, one speculates, might have gotten expressed by a proposal that the president and he visit some graves of members of the German *resistance* movement of the thirties and forties. So far as the record shows, no person in Bonn or Washington made such a proposal.[66]

Less measured, more hostile German reactions to the American debate found a high-level, second-echelon voice this same day in Alois Mertes, minister of state in the German Foreign Office and parliamentary representative of Bitburg since 1972. The controversy was generating "bitterness" among Germans, he said, and could alienate young Germans from America, even threaten the NATO alliance. The resolution of 53 U.S. senators, he hoped, "does not represent the feelings of the American people"—a hope that was bound to sound odd in the ears of Americans who assume that senators are often, if not always, their representatives and that Bundestag members saw their work similarly. Indeed, Mertes presumed to speak frankly on behalf of his home district:

> I find it an insult to the President to rate his visit to the Kolmeshöhe Cemetery in Bitburg as anything but a noble gesture toward the German people, whose guest he is and who in the last 30 years as close allies of the United States have built a democratic state in the free part of Germany. . . .
>
> For my constituents, who have such good ties to Americans, the declarations of the Senators are not understandable. The bitterness is growing.
>
> We Germans are aware that the genocide against the European Jews was not an event of war. It was a terrible crime that happened in the name of Germany.

Ignoring the fact that, for the Nazi government, World War II was very much a war against Jews, Mertes went on to underscore the issue that rankled Germans the most: they were repelled by the notions of "collective guilt and race liability" on the part of people born after the end of the war, precisely because "race liability" (*Sippenhaftung*) was a term that the Nazis had used against the Jews. Germans cannot reject that hated badge without rejecting it on the lips of Americans.[67]

In sheer volume of outrage, however, the American reaction to Bitburg overrode the German. Over the next two weeks, the rallies, news columns, editorials, remonstrances from Jewish and Christian leaders, telegrams from labor unions, and protests from veterans' organizations flooded the White House. On April 21 in Philadelphia an assembly of Holocaust survivors gathered with family members from around the world. There in front of the Liberty Bell they paid tribute to the role of the United States in making their and Israel's survival possible, but their attention was focused on Bitburg, especially by two speakers, Elie Wiesel and Menachem Z. Rosensaft, chairman of the International Network of Children of Jewish Holocaust Survivors. Wiesel was terse and foreboding: "This is the beginning [of] . . . the rehabilitation of the SS. To go to that place" means "that in a few years it would be acceptable to honor the SS, and we find that unacceptable. We believe in reconciliation with all people except the killers." Rosensaft, born at Bergen-Belsen soon after it was liberated, was more blunt in placing absolute blame on the president: his refusal to cancel the Bitburg visit was "a calculated, deliberate insult to the memory of the victims of the Holocaust. . . . For heaven's sake, let him find another cemetery. There must be at least one in all of Germany which does not contain SS men."[68]

It was clear in these and other angry speeches by Jewish Americans that the SS was the heart of the issue. One positive gain of the week, from their side, had to be some increase in the American public's knowledge of the nature of this particular band of troops in the Nazi military. Called a "Guard Unit" (*Schutzstaffel*) and headed by Heinrich Himmler from 1929, the SS was an elite organization. All of its members swore special allegiance to Hitler. Its military arm, the Waffen SS, were all volunteers until 1943. Its various divisions had specialized assignments: In 1939 its "Death's Head Division" organized some 6,500 concentration camp guards to run the death camps, to round up partisans for execution, to murder Jews in the mass (as at Babi Yar in Russia), and to carry out other atrocities such as the massacre of all 642 inhabitants of the French village of Oradour-sur-Glane as a punishment for having harbored people in the Resistance. Most of the SS soldiers buried in Bitburg has been members of the division that carried out the massacre at Oradour, but the SS crime most vividly remembered by some American veterans of the war was its murder of 64 unarmed Canadian and British prisoners of war in June 1944.[69]

Try as his staff did to claim that the Bitburg visit paid the president's respect to Germany's war dead generally, critics insisted that the merest breath of respect for the bodies of these particular 49 troops, even a floral wreath, was a moral outrage, a crossing of the line from association with relative evil to association with absolute evil. Perhaps there was some earthly moral limbo to which the troops of German armies could be assigned, but the SS was in the lowest reaches of the Nazi hell, and they should be left there.

As the day of the visit approached, reporters went to Germany to test public reactions there. True to the predictions, they found some signs that surviving veterans of the SS did feel "rehabilitated" by the president's refusal to shun the bodies of their fallen comrades. "Long the pariahs of West Germany society . . . this year they are returning reporters' telephone calls, and talking, quietly, assuredly over beer, in the bars of the Nesselwang hotels." There for an anniversary convention, veterans of the Death's Head Division said that the Bitburg event "made them feel better about their role in history" because it showed (in the words of Johan Rosenberg) that "we were soldiers just like the others. I never committed a war crime, and I don't know anyone who did." As for the notion that in 1943 young men were conscripted into the Waffen SS, "That is nonsense," said Rosenberg. "Kids were proud to get in, it was an honor." And one of his colleagues, Gerd Höfer, confided to the reporter that "my proudest moment as an SS man was when I stood guard outside [Hitler's] hotel room in Leipzig in 1941."[70]

In the meantime Chancellor Kohl marked the liberation of Bergen-Belsen by delivering "one of the most forthright and unflinching [speeches] a West German leader has made about the Hitler era." Without alluding to the coming visit of an American president to the same site, Kohl remembered the death of Anne Frank here and the slaughter of 50,000 Russian prisoners of war in the area. He announced the government's decision to set up an archive for the study of Jewish history in Germany. We acknowledge two important facts, he said: "Reconciliation with the survivors and descendents of the victims is only possible if we accept our history as it really was, if we Germans acknowledge our shame and our historical responsibility, and if we perceive the need to act against any efforts at undermining human freedom and dignity."[71] But we also acknowledge that West Germany's forty-year reintegration with the West "was only possible because those nations—and not least the former concentration camp inmates and relatives of victims—reached out their hands to us in reconciliation." Left unsaid in the Kohl speech was the fact that the forthcoming ceremony at Bitburg was making it harder for victims and their relatives, for the moment, to reach out their hands to Germans or to an American president.

Finally, after two long weeks of high-intensity political debate, Ronald Reagan went to Bitburg for gestures as brief as his advisers could devise. Standing silently before a monument far from the SS graves, he laid the wreath down and left to deliver a speech at the nearby U.S. Air Force base. As he introduced Reagan, Chancellor Kohl welcomed him to Germany, remarking on the vivid linking of "past, present, and future" in this event. "I thank you, Mr. President, both on behalf of the whole German people and I thank you very personally as friend for visiting the graves with me."

In his ensuing speech the American president addressed the wide spectrum of issues that had come knotted together in this complex international occasion. He spoke of the breaking out of "old wounds" in what should have been "a time of healing." He paid tribute to the presence of American and German officers from World War II, noted that one soldier buried in Bitburg was not quite sixteen years old, told the story of three American soldiers who during the battle of the Bulge found shelter in a German home with four German soldiers at the dinner table, expressed his awareness that "the crimes of the SS must rank among the most heinous in human history," distinguished again between the "willing" followers of the dictator and the forced conscripts, again disowned "collective guilt" in the name of the God who alone "can look into the human heart," and tendered his hope that today "we can let our pain drive us to greater efforts to heal humanity's suffering." Perhaps the most eloquent moment in the speech was his extension of John F. Kennedy's famous "I am a Berliner" to include all sufferers from tyranny, especially those in areas under Communist control. "I, too, am a potential victim of totalitarianism." But the two central themes in the speech were those that had tortured three weeks of acrid public debate in two countries: (1) "Many of you are worried that reconciliation means forgetting. I promise you, we will never forget." (2) "Too often in the past, each war only planted the seeds of the next. We celebrate today the reconciliation between our two nations that has liberated us from that cycle of destruction."[72]

How do the two fit together? Whatever the answer, an impressive chorus of voices, back in the United States on May 5, was proclaiming that neither Germany nor the United States had found in Bitburg the symbol that expressed the fit. Bill Bradley, U.S. senator from New Jersey, rang changes on the president's and the White House's obliviousness of history, and Theodore Brooks, past leader of the Jewish War Veterans of the United States, painted the event in stark, absolute moral colors: "I cannot reconcile and I cannot forgive and I cannot forget the crimes which they [the dead of Bitburg] have perpetrated on the human race. I regret that this day has come to pass when the president of the United States honors an enemy."

But a less absolutely moral, more nuanced, and soberly political word came from the man who had first made the incident front page news: Elie Wiesel. Forgiveness between Germans and Americans, he suggested, was not the only issue here. A large American constituency now had a forgiveness problem with their president: "In the long run, I'm sure that the wounds will heal. After all, he is the President and we must deal with his policies, with his staff, with his Administration. But the wounds are there and the wounds are deep. I felt excluded, rejected, almost unnecessary, when I watched the Bitburg visit."[73]

How do the deep wounds of a human community, worldwide, get healed? It was an old question, but seldom in recent American history had it been posed so painfully, deliberated so publicly, or left so many reflective citizens so perplexed about the answer.

Resolved and Unresolved: Issues in the Debate

Without doubt the Bitburg controversy raged more hotly among Americans than among Germans. The controversy stirred levels of public dialogue, journalistic commentary, and open conflict around basic issues of political morality rare in any political event. Just as a key claim of protesters concerned the priority of social memory of an evil past, so the furor itself deserves to be remembered for the depth and eventual integrity of public reflection generated in its torturous course.

A review of the issues can be attempted here, with an eye to relating them to the dominant themes of this book. Polls taken soon after the event in the United States strongly suggested that the American public was evenly split on Mr. Reagan's Bitburg visit. A CBS-*New York Times* multiregion sample of 692 adults tallied 41 percent in favor, 41 percent against.[74] Some rather alarming facts turned up in the results. Citizens on the two sides of the debate betrayed little understanding of each other's arguments; this in spite of hundreds of television hours and thousands of column inches in newspapers devoted to the event. "A total of 30 percent of those favoring the visit said they did not know why others opposed it, and 44 percent of those against the trip said they did not know why others favored it." This is a disturbing finding for the cause of democracy: One political reason for public deliberation about any conflictful issue is the achievement of deeper mutual appreciation of diverse interests. Those interests have to be verbalized before they can become part of official *redefinition* of the public interest. Similarly disturbing—and a form of the opaque reception of some critics in the ears of the others—were signs of anti-Semitism in some of the respondents. "Sixty percent of those who supported the cemetery visit and 18 percent of those who opposed it, said they agreed that 'Jewish leaders in the United States protested too much over his visit.'" But, said the pollsters, a majority of the American proponents of the visit showed some sympathy for the Jewish protest: "I can understand the Jewish outcry because of the atrocities," said a 56-year-old World War II veteran from Texas. But only 9 percent of the 41 percent who opposed the visit gave the Waffen SS killing of Jews as an explanation of why the Bitburg cemetery was so despicable to Jews.[75]

If a simultaneous, less scientific sampling of German citizens on the streets of Bitburg by journalists is any index, the anti-Semitic response was more pronounced there. Marvin Kalb reported these comments from a May 6 visit to the city:

[A native of Bitburg in his twenties]: "We Germans and Americans had been cooperating very well until the Jews began to make trouble."

"Imagine the nerve of a Jew [Elie Wiesel] lecturing President Reagan. I saw him on television, making trouble the way they all do."

[An elderly woman who complained that Reagan had spent only eight minutes at the cemetery]: "You know why the visit had to be cut back? Because of the Jews."

"If they don't like it here, the Jews, let them go away. We were better off without them in Germany." [There are only 28,000 in Germany now, Kalb reminded him.] "Too many," he replied.

In Bitburg, a largely Catholic town which voted against Hitler in 1933, comments Kalb, "The Jews are seen as a group separate from Germans and Americans—an indigestible lump, a foreign body."[76]

What is the moral service of just such a "foreign body" in the human body politic? That is a first issue of this remarkable public debate.

The Service of Victims to Political Truth. An often neglected but utterly obvious truth of human experience is that those who suffer evil not only remember it longest but have most reason to insist that others remember it. Illustrations abound in American history; illustrations will multiply in the final chapters below. On a world level, the Jewish community is a special illustration in several dimensions. By religious conviction, many of its members have often refused to be simply "digested" by any national culture. By dint of their twentieth-century losses to Nazi genocide, they have reason to claim that this particular atrocity was unique in human history. Finally, American Jews constitute the largest body of contemporary Jews in any country in the world. Their virtually unanimous protest against the visit—20 out of 21 Jews in the CBS-*New York Times* poll—says something basic about the Jewish people worldwide: Their twentieth-century identity, for better or for worse, has been fundamentally shaken and reestablished around the trauma of the Nazi Holocaust.

What is the service of such a people *to* the political life of any country in which they find themselves? The Bitburg event furnished a dramatic, not-to-be-forgotten answer to this question. They can be agents for keeping a society reminded of past evils which a majority of its members easily forget because neither they nor their families and friends were touched intimately by those evils. Who are the more likely and trustworthy agents of such a service to the democratic public interest than just such a group? Theirs is an "epistemic privilege," for they are the authorities on what they have suffered[77].

But it is a privilege that entails a burden to be shared as soon as possible with other citizens. When not taken up by them under a common obligation to remember, the witness of victims fails in its purpose of persuading others to count the cause of victims as their own, too. Lacking this persuasion, the victims are left alone to continue their witness under the double burden of suspecting that they are the only ones with an interest in remembering. They can never be sure that their repetition of their witness will not be received with new resistance and hostility on the part of others—as was the case with a number of Germans and Americans during the Bitburg incident; they can never breathe a sigh of relief that others are now sharing in the task of jogging the society's memory. When others regularly take that share in their books and public utterances—or when, for example, the society establishes a Holocaust Memorial Museum—something of that burden is being publicly lifted.

Impatience with, and resistance to, such a contribution among one's civic neighbors are likely to persist, which should put victims and their descendants on the alert against public forgetfulness—as many a Jewish American was alerted during the Bitburg incident. A natural impulse in most humans says of great evils, "I couldn't do it," or "It couldn't happen to us." Here the analogy between personal and public remembering is close. In a review (published the week of the Bitburg visit) of Eberhard Jaeckel's *Hitler in History,* Professor Fritz Stern ended with a quotation from

Nietzsche: "'I have done that,' says my memory. 'I cannot have done that,' says my pride, and remains inexorable. Eventually memory yields." And "the worst distortion," comments Stern, "is willed amnesia, whether for the sake of self-exculpation or some sort of convenient reconciliation."[78]

The Holocaust taught Jews the grim lesson that every human in this and the next century had better learn: that what political power has done to any group of people it can do to any other. As Dennis B. Klein wrote one year after Bitburg:

> The Nazi mobilization of state resources against a people reminds us that much that we value . . . can be deployed as much to violate the sanctity of human life as to protect and enrich it. Our concern today about the capacity of any state to destroy is in part attributable to our first confrontation with the Holocaust, our struggle to understand it and the absorption of that experience into the fabric of our culture.

Klein's comment grows out of surveys in 1986 of two midwestern American states and of Germany, both indicating that a large percentage of citizens in both locales are (in the words of one young member of the Bundestag) "sick and tired of having to remember" the Nazi crime against the Jews. Hopefully enough, 61 percent of Germans under the age of 25 said that they "wanted to know more about the Nazi era."[79] Most human minds grow weary of negatives. They can absorb only so much repetition of truths that are unwelcome from the beginning. And this psychological reaction suggests that the victims of any vast suffering should worry over the tactics as well as the morality of their public protests against forgetfulness. This public inclination calls them to greater alertness to the difficulty (and therefore the greater urgency) of their democratic moral vocation for public remembering. In the Bitburg event, American Jews exercised that vocation with passion, consistency, and organization.

That they could do so organizationally touches one of the facts on which anti-Semitism feeds in American society as it seeks to claim that Jews have more influence on the media, the government, and public opinion generally than their numbers warrant. Such a view violates American tradition, which at its best has never assumed that the justice of a cause is to be measured by the size of its constituency or that a minority of *one* has no right to organize an association of fellow citizens to advance a cause. If in fact the American Jewish community is very well organized for its self-protection, the Bitburg event only underscores the importance of such organization for the advancement of public truth and justice. Armenian Americans have long complained that the world has almost forgotten the genocidal murder of at least 1½ million Armenians by the Turkish government in 1915. Hitler himself is recorded as asking his cohorts rhetorically in 1939, "Who, after all, speaks today of the annihilation of the Armenians?"[80] Indeed, if it were not for the existence and public witness of the Armenian Orthodox Church in America, fewer Americans would probably remember that massacre. African Americans have long looked to their churches for just such a public function in relation to their own history of oppression. The general political-sociological truth is that in complex democratic societies, effective public memory requires effective organization. From the American civil rights movement in the 1960s, many groups of Americans learned this lesson well enough to become organized for the promotion of a great assortment of causes—women's rights, reproductive choice, environmental protection, corporate social responsibility, justice for gay and lesbian citizens.

Jews have known this strategy of minority survival from many centuries ago, often under regimes anything but democratic. Christianity shared the same strategy in its earliest history as a minority in an imperial state. It remains one of the open secrets of how morality finds protection in a democratic order: certain people, who perceive the morality of the affair deep in their historical bones, testify to peoples who do not perceive it—to their peril. To victims belong the civic-moral task which academic historians, in their own vocations, pursue in their insistence upon the discovery and the preservation of truth about the human past. Robert Penn Warren expressed it as the vocation of poets, too, in a cryptic reference to his own "compulsion to try to convert what now is *was/* Back into what was *is*."[81]

Above all living peoples, Jews have the most reason to warn the world that the "was" of the Holocaust becomes the "is" of new threat to humanity whenever public memory of such evil grows dim. Whenever we let particular historic evils slip into forgetfulness, we lay ourselves open to a future in which we will no longer "understand what evil means."[82]

In this context, the Bitburg event can now be assessed in 1994 as a political blessing. William Safire put it precisely and eloquently when, on May 6, 1985, he wrote:

> Ronald Reagan, a month ago, had no real grasp of the moral priorities of the Holocaust or the fear of forgetfulness that prevents forgiveness. His journey of understanding— his own "painful walk into the past"—opened the minds of millions to the costs of reconciliation in a way no other process could have accomplished. In driving home the lessons of history, his incredible series of blunders turned out to be a blessing. . . .
>
> In seeking at first to sidestep the smoldering resentments, the President brought on a firestorm 40 years after a Holocaust, which in turn forced a forgetful world through a most necessary grief.[83]

Political Responsibility: Agents, Collaborators, Bystanders. The moral and political mistakes of the Reagan administration, in the course of the Bitburg event, were legion. A first link in the chain of error came in late March 1985, when the president turned aside from the suggestion that his forthcoming visit to Germany should include a visit to the Dachau concentration camp. No, he said, that evil place is a part of the past to which most Germans have no personal connections. "Very few" Germans today were alive during World War II, and none "were adults and participating in any way" in that war.

It was a factual error that demonstrated how unprepared this president was to frame or to reflect on questions of moral responsibility in historical and political contexts. Any demographer could have told him that an even 50 percent of contemporary Germans were alive in 1945, and a sizable portion of that half had vivid memories of the Nazi era. Moreover, he misjudged the impacts of the postwar education of younger Germans if he thought that they had no vivid even if second-hand impressions of that time or that he would offend older and younger Germans by joining the majority of them in being sure that the Nazi experience never disappeared from the history books. Many young people in the Federal Republic of 1994 may feel tired of learning about the Nazi past of their country, but the educating reminders of that past are tangible in their upbringing. In Berlin they can see the carefully preserved ruin of the Gestapo prison on Prinz Albrechtstrasse, where members of the German Resistance Movement (including Bonhoeffer) were interrogated. The museum memorials at Dachau attract 6 million domestic and foreign visitors a year, and public comparisons between the "neo-Nazis" of 1992 and their predecessors of the thirties have to be well understood by young Germans who come, by the hundred thousand, to demonstrate against ancient and modern versions of this political scourge. Older Germans, and especially their political leaders, understandably want to draw a *Schlussstrich*, a bottom line, that closes accounts on the past, but questions about collective responsibility *for* the past have not yet vanished from internal or external German affairs, as the Bitburg event amply demonstrated. The twin question, of course, concerns collective responsibility *to* the future.

Difficult questions of public truth-telling, guilt, and responsibility received rough, sometimes facile treatment in the Bitburg incident. Like the word *forgiveness* in western political talk, religion and legal institutions combined here to confine the word *guilt* to individuals. Time and again journalists, scholars, and politicians, American and German, disdained the concept of "collective guilt" spread from generation to future generation. Various participants in this dialogue, however, were less hesitant about speaking of various levels of "responsibility" for a past in which they themselves were implicated in differing degrees. The Nuremberg trials and the continuing war crimes investigations of the Federal Republic have assumed that the great criminals of the Nazi era had to be brought to justice and that most former Nazi Party members had to be excluded from political office. But this very distinction clearly recognized greater and lesser degrees of active collaboration with the evils of a regime which, in spite of its evil, probably did some political good. These observations land us again on the misty flats of collective political life, in which governments and citizens are in a constant, shifting matrix of reciprocal influence for good and for evil. The question of moral distinctions between the greater and the lesser sinners here is fundamentally and *empirically* clouded by the facts of life in a political community.

Such facts, down through the years since 1945, have led some older Germans to revert to the excuse "we were only obeying orders" of a dictator who was the only leader licensed to give the orders. In late April 1985 the Christian Democratic Party's floor leader in the Bundestag, Alfred Dregger, blamed all the evil of the Nazi era on Adolf Hitler. Ronald Reagan's reference to "one man's totalitarian dictatorship" in his Bitburg speech was not far from the same scapegoating. From here to Johan Rosenberg of the Death's Head Division of the SS ("I never committed a war crime, and I don't know anyone who did") is merely a steady slide down the slope into amoral political ethics and equally amoral forgetfulness.

The arguments and counterarguments of guilt and innocence here are rooted in conflicting perceptions of political reality and conflicting definitions of moral responsibility. The two, in fact, interact: if I divide my responsibilities between what I can personally control and what I consent to let others—e.g., a government or a church—control, then I can be liable for guilt in the one and claim innocence in the other. Am I obliged to *monitor* the orders handed me by others? Can I be a moral citizen with-

out doing so? The Bitburger who criticized Elie Wiesel for daring to criticize a president in public echoed a very old pattern of German political culture, just as Wiesel
was acting on a very solid American tradition of civil liberty and a very ancient
Hebrew prophetic tradition of the right to "speak truth to power." Neither the Bitburger
nor Wiesel supposed that he was free to ignore government or to exempt himself
from responsibility to others in the structures of a political process. It is just here that
the empirical and the moral meet in political life: citizens *should* not be free to ignore
the rest of the community, and only with great difficulty *can* they do so.

At the very least this combination of empirical and normative perspectives yields
the likelihood that in every collective action of a body of people all of its members
have some degree of responsibility, even if it is a responsibility exercised in passivity. In part the confusions of terms in the Bitburg debate grew out of a certain fuzzing
of distinction between the "for" and the "to." During his tenure, Helmut Kohl often
proclaimed himself Germany's "first postwar chancellor," born in 1930 and a mere
teenager at the end of the war. His predecessor, Helmut Schmidt, was twelve years
older and a *Wehrmacht* lieutenant decorated with the Iron Cross. Does that distinction of age and participation in the war lead to a distinction of moral guilt between
two such leaders? Perhaps so, but one might suppose that any experienced democratic politician might close the difference between the two with a sober principle
like, "Some are always more responsible than others, but we all are responsible."[84]

As it happened, only one in-office senior German leader spoke out of conscious,
detailed fidelity to that principle during the fortieth anniversary of the war's end, in
a speech to be reviewed carefully below. Here it can suffice to observe that the flight
from acknowledging responsibility for the sins of a body politic—whether by officials or ordinary citizens—is fraught with the twin dangers of deception about who
commits the sins and with whom they are committed. Especially in a modern state,
political crimes are social deeds; those who are quick to say "I had no part in it" must
bear the burden of proving it.

During those spring weeks of 1985, both Helmut Kohl and Ronald Reagan seemed
to learn something about responsibility to the past: to remember it and to remember,
when necessary, with "shame." If he had occasionally seemed to ask Americans and
the world to draw the *Schluss-strich* and to forget the past, Kohl's Bitburg-related
speeches kept stressing that no German political leader must ever forget, or ask his
people to forget, the Nazi past. "Our shame" and "our . . . responsibility" for "our
history as it really was"—that is what we must accept, said he at Bergen-Belsen.
Mr. Kohl's specifications of the evils of the Nazi past had tended to be sketchy; he
was in haste to get on to the new future. The Bitburg event made it clear that such
haste is best made slowly.

Every citizen, as well as every leader, enters a political community as an heir to its
past. Each has a right to be proud of some of it and an obligation to be ashamed of
some of it, even if it is centuries in the past. All have this obligation as humans who
wisely admit to themselves and others that they did not have control of the beginnings of their lives; that circumstance preceded their response to circumstance; that
they responded under veils of ignorance and partial awareness which are the lot of
all humans; that they learned to be the more responsible as they listened to their neighbors, acted with them, and viewed the results of those actions; and that, while they

had no choice about counting themselves part of a collectivity, neither are they ever to deny their part in its choices. Ongoing loyalty to that collectivity, in fact, demands that they shoulder their implication in its past record of both virtue and vice.

"Looking Truth in the Eye": Representative Repentance as a Political Vocation. Published six months after the end of World War II in Europe, the Stuttgart Declaration of church leaders stirred up "a storm of indignation and calumny" among many Germans,[85] even though it was a brief document offering few details of what its authors meant by their "solidarity of guilt" with those who perpetrated the Nazi disaster. As we have seen, some prominent church leaders, notably Helmut Thielicke, criticized the issuing of the document as an invitation to Germany's triumphant enemies and their churches to turn up the volume of their own accusations against a defeated Germany, thus avoiding having to face questions about their own guilt for the beginning and the course of World War II.

As Jürgen Moltmann realized in his Glasgow prison camp, such fear betrayed a profound misunderstanding of the effects of "confession of sin" in ordinary human relationships. Whether in interpersonal relationships or in public life, the confession "I was/we were wrong" lessens the compulsions of wronged parties to keep on insisting, "Yes, you were wrong." Further, as almost every minister knows from her or his dealings with church members, nothing opens the doors of confession so readily as the ability of their leaders to come first with the declaration: "I was wrong."

In this respect, the sociologist Max Weber was only partly right when, in his famous lecture "Politics as Vocation," delivered soon after the end of World War I to a Munich University audience, he cautioned that:

> A nation forgives if its interests have been damaged, but no nation forgives if its honor has been offended, especially by a bigoted self-righteousness. Every new document that comes to light after decades revives the undignified lamentations, the hatred and scorn, instead of allowing the war at its end to be buried, at least morally.

He then went on to warn politicians against "politically sterile questions of past guilt, which are not to be settled politically" and which merely express "the hope of the defeated to trade in advantages through confessions of guilt."[86] These words doubtless reflected German fears, including Weber's own, of what was about to be meted out to them at the coming end of the war. The Versailles Treaty would soon be justly accused of reflecting Allied self-righteousness, especially in its famous "war guilt" clause. Weber feared what accusations of guilt could do to a population not even sure it had lost the war, and he obviously knew something about unending cycles of international "hatred and scorn."

But he missed something very important about the "vocation" of the politician when he cautioned the profession to focus its leadership on "the future and the responsibility towards the future." Politicians also have a responsibility for accurately identifying the past, including the past that the enemies of their people are the first to call evil. The failure of Weber's brilliant essay even to touch on this aspect of *Politik als Beruf* is all the more regrettable in light of the grand climax of the essay, with its moral tribute to the vocation as requiring, above all, "trained relentlessness in viewing the realities of life, and the ability to face such realities and to measure up to them inwardly."[87]

Had he allowed room for the politician's ability to be publicly relentless about an evil national past, Weber could have been anticipating the behavior of Richard Freiherr von Weizsäcker, president of the Federal Republic of Germany, in a speech to its Bundestag on May 8, 1985. The speech achieved international acclaim almost overnight. It was dubbed by an editorial in the *New York Times* as "the week's only memorable presidential speech" and that "from an unlikely quarter." A year later, Anthony Lewis of the *Times* quoted from it at length and called it "one of the great speeches of our time."[88]

What impressed the world about this speech was its lengthy, unflinching, excuseless enumeration of Nazi crimes and many degrees of association with those crimes by millions of Germans in the years 1933–45. "It was believed to be the first time a senior West German leader had publicly challenged the widely heard justification that ordinary Germans were unaware of the Holocaust" and much else about the aims of the Nazi regime.[89] In fact, the speech was even more than a public confession of German sins. In eloquent, straightforward prose, von Weizsäcker comprehensively identified, and identified with, the sufferings of Germans during the war. He reviewed the new structures of power that came to eastern Europe with the coming of the Soviets and Communist governments there. He paid tribute to the vast national postwar accommodation of millions of refugees from the East. He empathized with the plight and adjustments of those refugees; and in an astonishing passage he went from empathy for the suffering of refugees in Germany to confess his inability truly to understand the suffering or the readiness for reconciliation among some of the still-living victims of the war:

> We cannot commemorate the 8th of May without making ourselves aware how much conquest of self the readiness for reconciliation demanded of our former enemies. Can we really identify with the relatives of those who were sacrificed in the Warsaw Ghetto or the massacre of Lidice?
>
> Yet how difficult it must also have been for a citizen of Rotterdam or London to support the reconstruction of our country, from which came the bombs that had fallen on his city only a short time before. For this there had to be a gradual growth of certainty that Germans would not once again attempt to correct a defeat with force.
>
> Among ourselves, the most difficult thing was asked of those driven from their homeland. Long after the 8th of May they encountered bitter suffering and severe injustice. We natives often lack the imagination, and also the open heart, to meet their difficult fate with understanding. . . .
>
> [This] enforced migration of millions of Germans to the West was followed by millions of Poles, and they in turn by millions of Russians. They are all people who were not asked, people who have suffered injustice, people who were defenceless objects of political events and for whom no compensation for injustice, and no disputation of claims, can make good what has been done to them.[90]

The evils we have to remember, implied von Weizsäcker, are too vast for the reparations that the government has in fact made to some of these groups of people, so that not even in this moment of a forty-year-old "reform" of our political behavior can we say that now we are safely beyond the clutch of the Nazi legacy. We can only hope to move beyond it if we remember it with utmost accuracy and in painful detail.

The body of the speech was a rehearsal of just those details. In a brief introduction, von Weizsäcker reviewed the mood of Germans on May 8, 1945: "Our fate lay in the hands of our enemies. Wouldn't they now make us pay many times over for what we had done to them?" The precedents of the 1920s gave Germans every reason to suppose so. Instead, he went on to say, we now know that our enemies have delivered *us* from "National Socialist tyranny," and looking back we must remember that this tyranny led to the war, not the faults of our enemies, whatever they may be.[91]

Then follows a catalogue of the groups of people singled out by the Nazi regime for murder, torture, and extermination:

> in particular the six million Jews who were murdered . . . the unthinkable number of citizens of the Soviet Union and Poland . . . our own countrymen who lost their lives . . . the murdered Sinti and Roma [Gypsies] . . . the homosexuals . . . the mentally ill . . . the hostages . . . the Resistance in all countries . . . the German resistance . . . [and all those] who accepted death rather than humble their consciences . . .

It all added up to

> the unimaginably vast army of the dead . . . a mountain
>   of human suffering:
>
> suffering for the dead,
> suffering through wounding and crippling,
> suffering through inhuman enforced sterilization,
> suffering in nights of bombing,
> suffering through flight and expulsion, through oppression and plunder,
>   through forced labour, through injustice and torture through hunger and
>   need,
> suffering through fear of imprisonment and death,
> suffering through the loss of all that one had mistakenly believed in and for
>   which one had worked.

The "one" of the last line of this litany must have included the president himself, who was a second lieutenant of nineteen in the German army which invaded Poland on September 1, 1939. Wounded twice on the Russian front, he survived the war to sit at Nuremberg as defending attorney alongside his father, Ernst von Weizsäcker, chief state secretary in the Nazi Foreign Office from 1938 through 1943. But there is little trace of personal confession in the May 8 speech. The president's biography was well known to the "hushed Parliament"[92] listening to this speech. The likes of it would hush any parliament in the world.

Concluding his litany with a tribute to the women of "our countries," including Germany, who bore so much of the wartime and postwar suffering, von Weizsäcker moved on to affirm the widespread responsibility of Germans high and low for most of these crimes. First and foremost, he said, was our widely shared knowledge that something awful was happening to our Jewish neighbors. To implement his "unfathomable hatred" of these, "our fellow men, Hitler had never kept it from the public, but rather made the entire nation the tool of this hatred." It was a crime without historical precedent. Though much of the gruesome operation was in fact "shielded from the eyes of the public," it was still true that:

> . . . every German could witness what Jewish fellow citizens had to suffer, from cold indifference through veiled intolerance to open hatred.
>
> Who could remain innocent after the burning of the synagogues, the looting, the stigmatizing with the Jewish star, the withdrawal of rights, the unceasing violations of human worth?
>
> Whoever opened his eyes and ears, whoever wanted to inform himself, could not escape knowing that deportation trains were rolling. The imagination of men is insufficient to encompass the means and the scale of the annihilation. But in reality the crime itself was compounded by the attempts of all too many people—in my generation as well, we who were young and who had no part in the planning and execution of the events—not to take note of what was happening.

In the next page of his text von Weizsäcker carefully distinguishes between the guilt of members of his generation and the guilt of other generations. "No feeling person expects [young Germans now] to wear a hair shirt merely because they are Germans. Yet their forefathers have bequeathed them a heavy legacy," and "all of us, whether guilty or not, whether old or young, must accept the past." We must accept it by remembering it and never forgetting it.

> . . . whoever closes his eyes to the past becomes blind to the present. Whoever does not wish to remember inhumanity becomes susceptible to the dangers of new infection.
>
> The Jewish people remember and will always remember. As human beings, we seek reconciliation. Precisely for this reason we must understand that there can be no reconciliation without memory. The experience of millions of deaths is a part of the inner life of every Jew in the world, not only because men cannot forget such an atrocity, but also because memory is a part of Jewish belief.

Before concluding this long address, von Weizsäcker noted the gains for democracy, industrial development, and the modern "densely woven social net" sustaining all German citizens. But from these expressions of pride in the progress of forty years—ordinary enough in the public rhetoric of German and all other politicians—he turns to a renewed litany of reminders of the connectedness of memory and genuine change in his society:

> We have no real cause for arrogance and self-righteousness. But we should remember the development of these forty years thankfully, when we employ our own historical memory as a guideline for our behavior in the present, and for the unsolved problems that await us.
>
> —When we remember that during the Third Reich mentally ill people were killed, we will understand the care given to psychologically ill citizens as our proper responsibility.
>
> —When we remember how those persecuted for their race, their religion and their politics, who were threatened with certain death, often stood before the closed bor-

ders of other states, we will not shut the door on those who today are truly persecuted and seek protection among us.

—When we ponder the persecution of the free spirit under dictatorship, we will guard the freedom of every thought and every criticism, however much it may be directed against ourselves.

—Whoever judges the circumstances in the Near East may ponder the fate that Germans prepared for their Jewish fellow men and that triggered the founding of the State of Israel, under conditions which even today oppress and endanger the people in that region.

—When we think what our Eastern neighbors had to suffer in the war, we will better understand that compensation, detente and friendly relations with these countries remains the central task of German foreign policy.

And, in an echo of *Ostpolitik,* the president saluted Mikhail Gorbachev's hope for friendship with the Germans (expressed in his simultaneous commemoration of May 8)[93] and voiced his own hope that Germans, west and east, might one day become "one people and one nation again."

At the very end, von Weizsäcker addressed young Germans. They may wonder, he said, why, "in recent months" (i.e., in the furor over Bitburg), "such lively disagreements about the past have arisen forty years after the end of the war." Why now, rather than earlier? The biblical narrative of the Exodus suggests the reason, he answered: "Forty years were required for a complete change of the generation of fathers held responsible at that time." The subsequent history in the Book of Judges, he added, tells us that forgetfulness afflicted subsequent generations of the people, and when it did, "peace was at an end." To forget the dark times is to cut off a nation's chances for a "new and good future."

Finally, in the blend of realism and sobriety that infuses the entire speech, von Weizsäcker cautions young Germans against hostaging themselves to dreams of "Utopian salvation" and to "moral arrogance."

> We older people do not owe youth the fulfillment of dreams, but rather integrity. . . .
> We learn from our own history what man is capable of. Therefore we must not imagine that we have become, as human beings, different and better. There can be no finally achieved moral perfection—neither for any individual nor for any country! As human beings we have learned, as human beings we remain endangered. Yet we always have the strength to overcome dangers afresh.
> Hitler ceaselessly endeavoured to stir up prejudices, enmities and hatred.
> Our request to young people is this: Do not allow yourselves to be driven into enmity and hatred
>
> > against other people
> > against Russians and Americans
> > against Jews or Turks
> > against radicals or conservatives
> > against black or white . . .
>
> See that we too, as democratic politicians, take this advice to heart, and provide us with an example.

> Let us honour freedom.
> Let us work for peace.
> Let us uphold the law.
> Let us serve our inner standards of justice.

Let us, on the present 8th of May, look the truth in the eye as well as we are able.

Like public media in many parts of the world that week in 1985, I have quoted this speech at length because few utterances of national leaders in the twentieth century have undertaken, with equal, stunning courage, to put together in one body of public words confession of their nation's sins; painfully accurate identification of the same; wide-spreading empathy for the victims of those sins; restraint and forbearance toward those among the nation's enemies who duplicated or collaborated in the sinning; much tribute to justice and no concession to revenge; and, above all, the hope that through right remembering of history, a people can rightly turn themselves politically toward reconciliation among themselves and with their former enemies.

If, as an American, I join millions of others in the world to express grateful astonishment for such a speech, I do so because there are moments in the history of nations when what leaders *say* to their public constitutes "political action" in its most constructive form. Abraham Lincoln was an American master of this truth; and as historian Garry Wills has recently written, Lincoln in his Gettysburg address coined words that virtually redefined the United States as united now in a "new birth" of equality as well as freedom.[94] Put in its tragic historical context, Lincoln's later, brief Second Inaugural Address is a similar stunning example of this high art of turning the attention of a people away from inexpressible suffering toward its moral meaning and the road to repair of deeply fractured collective relations.

Like Lincoln, von Weizsäcker sought to tame the legacies of "malice" and hatred in the wake of war, legacies that he knew still to be alive after forty years. Not once in the Bundestag speech did he use the word *forgiveness*, and it would have violated the spirit of the whole utterance if he had added the gratuitous note, "On these grounds, I hope, the nations of the world will forgive Germany." Asked once, four years later, if forgiveness has any place in politics, he expressed some doubt: we must face the evils of the past and try to achieve justice in the present; but it would be pretentious, he said, to think that we can ask forgiveness for the sins of nations.[95] Yet his May 8 speech touches almost all the requirements that are to be met by offending parties if genuine forgiveness is to be extended to them by the offended: acceptance of moral judgment; grateful acknowledgment that forbearance rather than revenge is being tendered from the other side; shared empathy for the hurts that have been inflicted; and the turn in principle, policy, and behavior toward a new reconciliation with the offended. If the von Weizsäcker speech is not a demonstration of the relevance of forgiveness to politics, it is nonetheless a powerful example of the relevance of public *repentance* to politics. In this respect it is an authentic beginning of the process by which nations plant their feet firmly on the road to reconciliation.

The Leader as Confessor. The Bitburg event as a whole sharpens issues that are only implicit in some early pages of this study:

If nothing can be done to change the past, what does it really mean to speak of forgiving it?

Is it morally acceptable to speak of forgiving *wrongs,* or should the language of the matter always refer to the forgiveness of *wrongdoers,* in various degree, as they are accepted again into a human community?

Ought we, must we in any sense speak of collective guilt?

All of these questions will be worth exploring in the two following chapters. Concerning the final question, it is important to remind ourselves again of the reason why secular moral philosophers since Kant have found forgiveness a "rather unfashionable subject"[96] especially in relation to political ethics: they accept the captivity of forgiveness to issues of individual, personal resentment, banishing from legitimacy the notion of third-party guilt and responsibility along with "third-party forgiveness." The third party, in Joram Haber's term, is anyone who was not "personally related" to a victim or an agent of the offense.[97] Dryden, notes Haber, was right to say, "Forgiveness to the injured doth belong," but perhaps the rule should be qualified by "in the first instance." The rule does not take much account of the shared injuries of social life or shared responsibilities for the confession and cure of injuries. Haber betrays the individualistic captivity of modern moral philosophy when he excludes from participation in forgiveness one not personally related to victims. As a corollary he also excludes, as irrelevant to the discussion, John Donne's famous moral-empirical claim, "No man is an island."[98] To treat that claim as significant for defining forgiveness is to "tribalize" the concept, says Haber; for forgiveness, says he (with most of western theology and philosophy) belongs in the realm of two-person transactions. On basis of this exclusion, I cannot rightly "resent" Nazi anti-semitism, for I am not a Jew. Neither can Russian Yuri Yevteshenko rightly identify himself with the victims of Babi Yar or make sense of the notion that an assault on the humanity of Jews is an assault on humanity as such. Quite different anthropologies are in collision here: Behind the individualization of an act of forgiveness lies the individualization of human victimization, guilt, and responsibility, a model of human society that ignores the ripples that flow out from initial victims to their literal kin to their political kin and thence to their moral kin. In point of fact, victimization and guilt have partners of greater and lesser degrees; and it is arbitrary to say in turn that such partnerships are candidates for neither forgiveness nor responsibility. Such arbitrariness flies in the face of the sociality of selves and the tragic as well as the redeeming consequences of that sociality.

In short, only in a context of perceived interconnectedness between participants in great traumatic political injustice can one go on to assert the symbolic, representative role of politicians in the enactment of a political form of forgiveness. An indefinite but real network of victims and agents calls for that role. Whether leaders accuse an enemy of crime, confess to crimes of their own people, or hold out hopes for a future reconciliation, they do all of this on behalf of one collective in addressing another. To deny this representative, symbolic role to politicians is to impoverish their service to a society's dealing with its past wrongs and its present corrective responsibility to the future.

Here one ought to note the tension, even inconsistency, in the distinctions an astute German leader made in his internationally applauded speech of May 8: if it was true that "Hitler . . . made the entire nation the tool of his hatred," why can von Weizsäcker

be so sure, six paragraphs later, that "guilt, like innocence, is not collective but individual"? The Nuremburg trials came to grief over the drawing of lines between the
notoriously guilty, the moderately guilty, and the only slightly guilty. In his treatment of "responsibility," the German president displays both the courage and the
realism of knowing that some political crimes can only be committed by a set of
willing collaborators, and no one of them is uniquely culpable. In his confession of
the passive collaboration of all Germans in the Nazi crimes against the Jews, he really
does sweep up his whole generation in guilt, being careful to say that this does not
mean that coming generations of Germans inherit that guilt. They do inherit a responsibility to (1) remember that particular past and (2) to use that past as a negative
measure of what they are responsible for not repeating in their present. Collective
responsibility is an apt concept here, combining as it does both recollection of the
past and commitment to act in new ways toward the future. From the power of evil
in their past, as Hannah Arendt says, the present and even the growing-old generations need to be released, and that is what forgiveness in politics is all about. Indeed,
collective responsibility, if it is not quite the reverse of collective guilt, seems to
combine the two sides of Arendt's prescription for genuine social change: release
from the past (through memory, confession, and a willingness of the offended to go
on living with the offenders) and new joint commitment to a future different from
the past.

On the matter of widening the network of responsibility rather than striving to
narrow it, religion has its own contribution to make to political culture. The witness
of some German church leaders of this era is a reminder of this fact. In their certainty
that all humans are sinners lay one secret—grounded in the Hebrew-Christian tradition—of humility in politics or any other human project. If over the centuries the
tradition let notions of sin and forgiveness drain off from politics into the commerce
of the individual soul with itself and God, it retained its potential for reminding adherents that "none is righteous, no, not one."[99] Unfortunately for the activation of
this potential in the political arena, many Christians both German and American must
report that their personal prayer and corporate worship usually keep confessions of
personal sins relatively insulated from the political entanglements of those sins.

It was the singular contribution of some German theologians, beginning with
Barmen, to start to break through this insulation in the face of the entrenched resistance of their own church constituents. No one better exemplified this contribution
than Dietrich Bonhoeffer. If anyone among German church leaders need have felt
no guilt about his conduct toward the Nazi menace, it was he. First among theologians publicly to condemn the Nazis in 1933[100] and among the last to die as members
of the German Resistance, Bonhoeffer could have claimed immunity from citizen-
guilt for Nazism just as could have Willy Brandt, who lived in Norway for all twelve
years of the Nazi regime. Yet it was Brandt who fell to his knees before the Warsaw
ghetto monument; and it was Bonhoeffer who in the summer of 1944 composed a
poem about a sleepless night in prison, "Night Thoughts in Tegel," in which he spoke
for himself and his fellow prisoners about their mixed guilt and innocence in relation to those who had imprisoned them. The fears of a Primo Levi about the fragility
of his own moral integrity suffuse the poem:

We accuse those who plunged us into sin,
Who made us share the guilt,
Who made us the witnesses of injustice,
In order to despise their accomplices.
Our eyes had to see folly,
In order to bind us in deep guilt;
Then they stopped our mouths,
And we were as dumb as dogs.
We learned to lie easily,
To be at the disposal of open injustice;
If the defenceless was abused,
Then our eyes remained cold.

[The poem turns into prayer:]

We saw the lie raise its head,
And we did not honour the truth.
We saw the brethren in direst need,
And feared only our own death.

We come before thee as men,
As confessors of our sins.[101]

One could respond critically to this poem that the "saints" seem to be those who are most conscious of their own sins, but it is an unwarranted deprecation of the political and personal realism of Bonhoeffer to accuse him of a spiritually exotic exercise of exaggerated responsibility for the political sins of his time. *In fact* every German of the thirties did have some such sins to confess, just as Americans all have some sins to confess in regard to the racism that will be the subject of the next two chapters.

The validity of von Weizsäcker's use of the confessional "we" is even more justified, of course. But again, his May 8 speech is notable for its lack of direct allusions to his life under the Nazis. In the speech he is going about the serious political task of speaking to and for a nation, a task that the authors of the Stuttgart Declaration did not presume to undertake when they spoke on behalf of their church. He had long been a leading postwar figure in that church, and it is interesting to speculate on what he learned therein about secular politics as well as ecclesiastical politics. Suffice it to note that in his fortieth anniversary speech he consciously occupies the role of the representative, in-office political leader who has a unique responsibility, not to be delegated, for speaking on behalf of citizens' truths that they may not like to hear. Here the constitutional system of the Federal Republic of Germany confers a particular freedom and a particular power upon its president. What it gives him, few ambitious politicians cherish: mostly ceremonial power. He heads the nation symbolically, while the power struggles, compromises, and electoral maneuverings of parliamentary politics go their necessary democratic way under the leadership of a chancellor. The president of the United States, of course, combines both roles, making the office very powerful indeed but facing the occupant with delicate choices about the political uses of ceremony. It is commonplace to observe that presidents, governors, and mayors in the United States are always campaigning for the next election; therefore they are always tempted to tell citizens what will help get them re-elected. "Speaking truth to power" is a necessary, sometimes frightening responsibility of the democratic citizen, but "speaking truth to citizens" is often as frightening to incumbent politicians, who like to claim bravely that they speak for the people's interests but who are more timid about giving voice to their sins.

Initially von Weizsäcker's speech received more applause internationally than domestically.[102] Later, when they observed how much gratitude their president incurred abroad for a speech directed chiefly toward his own nation, Germans' discomfort diminished. It turns out that *one way to convince others that you are making a clean break with the past is to recall it clearly and publicly.* Weizsäcker did so as representative of *two* German generations: his own and the present one. In this role he spoke for a collectivity, as is the privilege and burden of every institutional leader. The power of the speech stemmed in no small measure from this confluence of power, position, and history in the person who spoke it. It would have been one thing for an academic lecturer, a church pastor, or a city editor to have uttered that speech; it was another when the head of a state uttered it, implicitly on behalf of a people. Peoples of the world, not least Americans, are fortunate when their leaders re-present a shameful past and hail a different future with such intellectual and moral integrity.

Postscript: 1995 and Beyond

A long, tortured history has been sketched here. Americans in 1994 no longer share the same nationalism that sent their young people to fight the Germans in 1917. They no longer celebrate the isolationism of 1920–40, or the compulsion to pull up the cultural roots that now link Americans to every continent on earth. Moreover, as newspapers and television remind us daily, what happens politically inside other countries has now become relevant to us in ways few Americans of the 1900–40 era could have imagined.

On their side, Germans have come a long way, too. They have moved, by stops and starts, from denial to memory of their Nazi past; from absorption in their own wartime suffering to appreciation of the greater suffering imposed by Nazi Germany on others; from formal regret for the atrocities of Nazism to material restitutions to survivors; and from traditional cultural contempt for democratic government to the construction of such a government that has endured now for forty-five years.

None of these developments commanded the applause of every German, but over two generations majority support for them has certainly grown. The eruption of neo-Nazi violence against foreigners in the nineties should not obscure the significance of the new institutional barriers to the spread of that violence to proportions resembling the violence of the thirties. Some 300 neo-Nazi radicals achieved worldwide publicity in November 1992, when they threw garbage at President von Weizsäcker in the midst of a rally of 300,000 citizens gathered to protest xenophobia. But the 300,000 were more important than the 300.

No more convincing a witness to this judgment is likely to be found than Margot David, a seventy-two-year-old Jewish American from Chicago, who in March 1993 returned to her native Dresden for her first visit since she left with her family in the late thirties in flight from the Nazis. Said she to a reporter: "In 1933 there were no 300,000 people with candles in their hands going out on the street and protesting [against Nazism]. The skinheads today are a minority; then, anti-Semitism was government policy."[103]

Since 1990, the challenge of internal political reconciliation confronts now-reunited Germans. Americans have something to learn from their postunification struggles, but we had better remember, out of our own Civil War experience, that the German trek toward reconciliation has miles to go before the hostilities of World War II really sleep. This likelihood was vividly evoked in a recent incident in Germany which will serve to end this chapter with the reminder that politics, like forgiveness itself, is not dualistically divisible into personal and collective realities, any more than it is dualistically insulated between the past and the present.

British airmen are central to the incident. As allies of the Americans they were flying in an American plane over Pforzheim on March 17, 1945, three weeks after over 4,000 of its people had been killed in an Allied incendiary raid. Forced to bail out of their damaged aircraft, they parachuted into the village of Huchenfeld, in the district of Pforzheim. On the orders of the chief local official, a Nazi, Hitler Youth executed the five men on the spot.

Forty-four years passed. Nobody in Huchenfeld ever talked openly about the March 1945 incident. Then, in 1989, a 72-year-old retired Catholic priest, Curt-Jürgen Heinemann-Grüder, discovered "the village's hidden secret," and began to speak publicly about it. "Cowardice, just like fanaticism," he said, is a sin. "These are all our sins, and we seek forgiveness." It was only a micropolitical memory—a bit of village-level lore, one more incident in western abandonment of the rules of just war. But the incident proved to be the occasion of a local reflection of the substance and example set four years before by the president of the Federal Republic.

In the spring of 1992, the story came to the attention of a London newspaper reporter; that was how an Englishwoman, age 74, finally learned how her husband had died.[104] Meantime, the retired priest and others in Huchenfeld had begun a local campaign for money to erect a bronze plaque in memory of the five murdered airmen. It was, testified Pastor Horst Zorn,

> a "difficult process of persuasion, to get people in their hearts to face up to the past." The 1,700 marks needed for the tablet were painstakingly raised from villagers themselves, against much opposition, abusive phone calls, and talk of a mass walkout from the church. "One senior member of the [town] council threatened that the tablet would not stay up for long," said Father Zorn. "But the more we learnt of the brutal attacks against foreigners going on in Germany, of the new boldness of the neo-Nazis, the more we believed in what we were doing."

Present for the dedication of the tablet in November, 1992 was 74-year-old Marjorie Taylor. Around the list of five names on the tablet were woven the words in German: "In Memory of the British airmen killed on 17/18 March 1945 on Nazi orders. . . . Father Forgive. Let the Living Be Warned." Present also was Mayor Joachim Becker of Pforzheim, who earlier in the year had protested the monument being erected in London to "Bomber" (a.k.a. "Butcher") Harris and who also opposed the campaign for the Huchenfeld tablet. "But the fact that a widow of one of the mur-

dered RAF crew had been discovered, and was invited to the church service of reconciliation, appeared to change much for Mr. Becker." He showed up, along with an
aging man who sobbed out the confession to a deacon, "I was one of the Hitler Youths
who shot that night. I killed them." He did not have the strength, he said, to meet
Mrs. Taylor. She, in turn, said to the reporter: "I feel this whole business has been
harder for the Germans than for me. I hope to come back one day when they are not
so upset, and say thank you."

As a brief statement of the political purpose of forgiveness in politics and as a sign
of its never quite complete process, her words were just right: "I hope to come back."
Perhaps 1995 would be soon enough.

5

Enmity and Empathy: Japan and the United States

This was indeed Japan. A wall with windows no larger than gunports, windows to keep an eye on those coming in, not to look out upon the wide world.[1]

Shusaku Endo

Experience can be changed retrospectively. By changing our interpretive concepts now, we modify what we learned earlier. Thus we expose the possibility of experimenting with alternative histories. . . . Personal histories and national histories need to be rewritten continuously as a base for the retrospective learning of new self-conceptions.[2]

Michael D. Cohen and James G. March

War will not let us forget it.[3]

Roger L. Shinn

Pain can sear the human memory in two crippling ways: with forgetfulness of the past or imprisonment in it. The mind that insulates the traumatic past from conscious memory plants a live bomb in the depths of the psyche—it takes no great grasp of psychiatry to know that. But the mind that fixes on pain risks getting trapped in it. Too horrible to remember, too horrible to forget: down either path lies little health for the human sufferers of great evil.[4]

The survivors of battlefields throughout history have known the struggle with these unhealthy choices, but neither their forgetting of their stories nor the compulsive retelling of them serves the next generation. That generation will probably resent the retelling more than the forgetting; like young Germans of the nineties, they are likely to be impatient with the insistence of a Wiesel or a von Weizsäcker on the uncompromising, never flagging remembrance of evils past. Understandably, the young tire of that insistence: "We have our own problems, our own challenges; we have to get on with our own future, however instructive you may think your past is."

Who is more likely to speak thus than young Americans? To this complaint, the survivors of old evil have one very pragmatic reply: "The evils you face have some of their roots in the past. Our past in your present threatens your future." This argument is basic to the themes of this book, which returns to it often. But a second, philosophic reply amounts to an assault on the self-confidence of an upcoming generation. An older one is likely to be shy about resorting to it: "If we were capable of such great evil, so also are you."

In the dramatized version of the life of Françoise Fenelon, a French Jewish prisoner in Auschwitz, a Nazi woman officer commits a brutal act against one of the prisoners, who confides her agony to Fenelon: "How can anyone do such a thing? It's so inhuman." "Oh, no," replies Fenelon despairingly, "She is as human as ourselves. In her we learn something about ourselves, and it is not good news."

Resistance to this grim thought may be one of the ways in which we protect our ability to stare evil briefly in the face without losing hope for ourselves. In fact, an older generation risks losing the attention of the younger if it tells the story of the evil past with such passionate focus on its horror that the story never suggests how it too could have been *different*. In order to suggest that, historians, social scientists, and ethicists must write about the past with studied attention to the human *agency* that makes human history. One generation best serves the next when it discerns, if only in retrospect, how it was responsible in diverse degrees for the goods and evils of its own time. Certain survivors of the Nazi camps showed an astonishing level of this moral sensitivity when, after their liberation, they confided their own sense of guilt at having survived. Did they owe it to their fellow sufferers to have shared their death? Did they make too many compromises with the camp system in order to survive?

Human history results from numerous conditions that humans themselves cannot control, but the very assumption that evil is worth mourning depends upon our belief that at some point it is worth opposing. This is the importance of the confession of relatively good German citizens like Bonhoeffer, who could confess that they "saw the lie and did not honour the truth," and like von Weizsäcker, who could warn that "as human beings we remain endangered." The young will hear their share of lies. They too will be tempted to dishonor the truth. Their vulnerability to great evil can only increase if they believe themselves immune to it.

The moral philosophy of the matter conflicts head-on with the writing of political history that stresses "conditions" and "power interests" so uniformly that readers have no room for imagining how things should and could have been different. In the spate of letters and articles that appeared in American newspapers around the fiftieth anniversary of the Japanese attack on Pearl Harbor, for example, the authors of *The Coming War With Japan* complain that it is trivial to remember the surprise of that attack while making light of the clash of national interests which was building up in the Pacific between the United States and Japan. Japan needed oil and the United States embargoed that oil; each had economic and political aspirations in the Pacific. "Both nations had reasons to fear the intentions of the other, but why should American fears of Japan take moral precedence over Japanese fears of America?" This is an apt question, of the kind rightly asked by Reinhold Niebuhr and other critics of the moral pretensions of great national powers. But the fatalistic corollary these authors want to draw means the death of questions about moral claims by both nations: "The Japanese did what they had to do; we did what we had to do. By demonizing the Japanese in the Pacific war, we avoid the crucial issue of why the war happened and the more immediate question of whether or not the same forces are at work again."[5]

In his account of the disastrous Athenian attack on Syracuse toward the end of the Peloponnesian war, Thucydides describes the fate of the Athenian prisoners who perished as slaves in the mines: "Having done what men could, they did what men must"—they died. The Greeks had their own respect for "fate," but in Thucydides' reading of history, humans make mistakes that wisdom can avoid. Unless history, or a single human life, is a compound of "could" and "must," there is little point to writing books about "coming war" or past war; for, after all, "must" governs all. On this point there will forever be blunt disagreement between philosophies of history: it is one thing to accentuate the conditions of the *must* against the alternatives of the *could* in human existence, but it is another to opt for the one in exclusion of the other. Moralists would be deemed mindless idealists by their intellectual colleagues if they neglected to attend to the conditions that push our behaviors in one or another direction; but equally mindless—that is, untrue—is the contrary assumption that human beings never *push back*. Democratic ideologues may carry their favorite value of "freedom" to absurd lengths; but, along with theologians and historians themselves, they have in common a fundamental stake in the notion of the responsible self. That notion includes the possibility of seeing human collectivities and their leaders as "response-able" too. If we do not hold fast to that notion, the hopes of an older generation, as embodied in books, are futile.[6]

Remembering the Pacific War

Of the two replies to the younger generation about the uses of remembered evil, the more persuasive will probably always be "the same forces are at work,"—as Friedman and LeBard warn about U.S.-Japan relations in 1991. Assuming, in conflict with the view of these authors, that moral forces are to be included in any review of such relations, on which of these forces might one focus in any remembering of the Pacific war of 1941–45?

The options are several: the morality of national interest in conflict with other national interests, the morality of war itself as an instrument of those interests, the tendencies of great and aspiring powers to imperialism, and the relation of all these issues to the rights and wrongs of national struggles to accumulate and preserve wealth. But the issue of the Pacific War that may merit the most continuing attention of Americans is the one which we can easily forget yet have most reason to consider a candidate for repentance and forgiveness: *racism*.

More than geography distinguished the war that Americans fought against Germans from their war against the Japanese. Like World War I (when the Japanese, in fact, were among the Allies), the American war against Germany in 1941–45 was a cultural family affair. Whatever the ambivalences of older immigrants toward first- and second-generation German Americans in 1917, by 1939 many Americans, including politicians, were accustomed to making distinctions between the "Nazi beasts" and the German people. The Nazis, in turn, with their own stereotypes and contempt for their various enemies, put the French, British, and Americans in a category roughly equal to themselves, reserving a special depth of contempt for the "Slavic races" and a unique lower depth of hatred for Jews. During World War II, the American public heard little about the "Huns" of the previous war; and the successes of the German armies (e.g., in North Africa under General Erwin Rommel) met with the respect for military genius traditional in western culture. That common culture functioned at the end of the war, as we have seen, to recement a great variety of relationships between Germans and Americans. Ronald Reagan's speech at Bitburg included a story that was a vivid if sentimental token of the religious side of that culture: three American joining four German soldiers around a domestic Christmas table during the Battle of the Bulge. One of those four, a son of the household, remembered the event, said Reagan, as a moment when all seven "battle-weary soldiers" were "boys again, some from America, some from Germany, all far from home."[7] They were fellow humans in tragic violent conflict with each other. The image is morally attractive. The historical ties of Germans and Americans made the image available to both sides before, during, and after the war. It was quite otherwise between the Americans and the Japanese.

Like a high mountain chain, an immense set of barriers separated the two peoples: language, the widest of oceans, religion, and the brevity (less than ninety years) of their modern economic-political contacts. On both sides of this barrier, ignorance, misinformation, and stereotypes abounded. Equally abundant and powerful was the ideological weapon the Nazis had reserved for only some of their enemies—racism.

The fact that both sides made overt, consistent, and progressively more intensive use of this weapon is easily forgotten by descendants of both populations who fought this war. In his painfully detailed, morally centered history of this aspect of the Pacific war, John W. Dower has furnished for second- and third-generation memories on both sides a singularly powerful antidote to this amnesia. Historians may be divided on the academic worth of Dower's project—the isolation of a single moral issue in a complex event for a study of its ubiquitous influence.[8] But if they fear the power of racism between and within both their countries, contemporary Americans and Japanese ought to welcome any such study. Dower's book is painful moral education, a work that groups of Americans and Japanese citizens in the 1990s would do well to read and discuss together.

Racism has been defined as "prejudice plus power." On the prejudice side, it is conceptual dehumanization of the other; on the power side, it is putting the concept to work institutionally. Racists place themselves at the top of a hierarchy on whose middle and lower levels live lesser grades of humanity. At some point down the sliding scale, some "other" may lose human identity altogether. In time of war, the slide down can be rapid. Indeed, it may be impossible for any wartime population to maintain an image and consciousness of the enemy as fully human—for, under that image, the enemy is psychologically more difficult to kill. Added to the preconception of inferiority, an actual record of atrocious wartime conduct further mobilizes morality against enemies. Killing them not only assumes the alleged neutrality of killing animals but becomes a necessary and good deed. American response to the Pearl Harbor attack consisted of just this combination: a famous newspaper cartoon, published three days after the attack, showed a muscular American sailor boarding his ship with a bag tagged, "War Without Mercy on a Treacherous Foe."[9] A moral atrocity—a surprise attack, against the (European) rules of war—had begun the war, opening the door for *moral* revenge. As other atrocities were committed by the Japanese, the case for vengeance in kind grew steadily in the eyes of most Americans.

Mutual Dehumanization of the Enemy

It would be convenient to leave to faithful historians like Dower the task of detailing those evils in political history which provoke the moral question: How can we recover from them? Forgiveness is a form of recovery, but in order to make the case for what it can mean in human politics, one must keep recurring to the historic facts which make forgiveness morally serious and morally problematic. It is not enough for ethicists like me to tell readers, "Go read the history." One owes the reader and the subject some rehearsals of that history, even if it can be given only in fragments. American and Japanese people will need such rehearsals for many a year into the twenty-first century if they are to recover from the sins of their ancestors.

Dower is clear that, on the American side, racism in 1941 had an old history, of which Japanese propagandists would take full advantage.[10] From Aristotle to Cortez to George Custer, white Europeans looked down on people of other skin colors, and this ancient tradition was ready and waiting to be mobilized in American responses to the attack on Pearl Harbor. The immediate reactions were replete with racist rhetoric and not just nationalist anger at an invasion.

> As *Time* magazine reported it in the opening paragraphs of its coverage, "Over the U.S. and its history there was a great unanswered question: What would the people, the 132,000,000, say in the face of the mightiest event of their time? What they said— tens of thousands of them—was: "Why, the yellow bastards!" Such immediate evocations of the "yellow" enemy were utterly commonplace. Even the urbane *New Yorker* magazine responded to the attack on Hawaii with a short story in which the Japanese emerged as "yellow monkeys" in a barroom conversation. There was, however, a curious twist to this generally racist response, reflecting the long-standing assumption that the Japanese were too unimaginative and servile to plan and execute such a stunning military maneuver on their own. Germany, it was widely and erroneously believed, must have put them up to this. In a logical world, such secondhand treachery should have made the Germans doubly treacherous. It did not. The Japanese attack remained the arch symbol of the stab in the back, just as the Japanese soldier soon came to be seen as more barbarous and diabolical than his German counterpart.[11]

The "monkey" image of the Japanese was to dominate American cartoon art throughout the war, aided by a panoply of propaganda in the press, cinema, radio, political speeches, and newsreels, all of which contributed to the subhuman image of the enemy and facilitated the resolve of America to exterminate Japan's soldiers and—eventually—as many of its people as necessary for its defeat.[12]

Thus began, on both sides, an unceasing stream of interpretations of the enemy, filled with enough truth to be convincing and enough distortion to leave little room for the thought: "The enemy are as human as we." Dower describes at length the production, under War Department auspices, of the film, *Know Your Enemy—Japan*, directed by Frank Capra, now considered one of the "masterpiece" propaganda films of the era. Capra's angle on the Japanese was to permit them to interpret themselves though their own literature, history, government, and newsreels. In spite of this gesture toward empathy, Capra found little support in the War Department, which insisted that the script must not "portray the Japanese as ordinary humans victimized by their leaders, and as late as February 1945 the Pentagon was still blue-penciling scripts on the ground that the passages in question would evoke 'too much sympathy for the Jap [sic] people.'"[13] As of that date, the great fire-bombing raids on Tokyo and other cities of Japan were only weeks away.

On both sides, popular images of the enemy had been forming long before the war in accumulations of resentments over actual conflicts of national interests. To shape its propaganda, each side had only to draw its population's attention selectively to historic facts. From the American side could be recollected the long-time feudal "backwardness" of the Japanese, sealed by their long self-enforced isolation from the West since 1598; their resistance to Christian missions; their forced "opening" by Commodore Perry in 1853; the growth of militarism and antidemocratic spirit from the 1880s; and, for fifty years prior to 1941, imperial ambitions that led successively to invasions of Russia, Korea, Manchuria, and China. From the Japanese side, resentment had long seethed against the imperial ambitions of the West, realized in Southeast Asia's dozen European and American colonies; the denial to Japan of the right to imitate the white colonizer; a like denial in international treaties of equal naval power in the Pacific; and, particularly galling, the refusal of the League of Nations, to pass at Japan's request a declaration of equality among the races of the world—a refusal that the United States brazenly underscored in its extension of long-standing anti-Asian immigration and naturalization policies in the new law of 1924.

So the historical fuel for racist stereotyping was virtually inexhaustible. Dower summarizes the overall mutual effort to degrade the enemy in the following paragraph growing out of his careful study of popular and government media of the era:

> [The] portraits of the enemy reveal that stereotypes operated several ways. . . . First, they followed predictable patterns of contrariness, in which each side portrayed the other as its polar opposite: as darkness opposed to its own radiant light. Second, the positive self-images of one side were singled out for ridicule and condemnation by the other. Self-stereotypes fed hostile stereotypes: the [Japanese] group became the herd, for example, while the [American] individualist became the egoist. Third, and scarcely acknowledged during the war years, a submerged strata of common values developed in the very midst of the polemics each side employed against the enemy. Each raised the banner of liberation, morality, and peace. Whatever their actual deeds may have been, moreover, they condemned atrocities, exploitation, and theories of racial supremacy. Fourth, policies and practices that became fixated on exterminating the enemy—and verged, for some participants, on the genocidal—followed a stereotyping peculiar to enemies and "others" in general, rather than to the Japanese foe or Western foe in particular. This facilitated the quick abatement of hatred once the war had ended—while also facilitating the transferral of the hateful stereotypes to newly perceived enemies. Much of the rhetoric of World War Two proved readily adaptable to the cold war.[14]

Dower goes on to say that, unfortunately for them, by early 1945 the official, sustained insistence of the Japanese on "the unique and peculiar qualities of the Yamato race" and the "one spirit" of their people helped bring on the disaster the Americans were to visit upon their homeland. The Allies "agreed that Japan was 'unique'—albeit unique in peculiarly uncivilized and atrocious ways. On neither side did the propagandists offer much recognition of common traits, comparable acts, or compatible aspirations."[15]

The possibility of empathy with enemies in war seems remote from the experience of most humans who actually fight the battles. The possibility is remote enough in other, less violent contests between national populations—a truth to be remembered in the 1990s as the United States, Germany, and Japan compete economically. Nonetheless, empathy for the enemy before, during, or after the violence of war is an essential ingredient of the healing of enmity. It has an integral relation to forgiveness as we have so far defined it. In its systematic erosion of tendencies to empathize, racism is a peculiarly vicious enemy of forgiveness in politics or justice in any human relation. To empathize with enemies is to weaken one's readiness to kill them. That is why governments at war will always look with suspicion on interpretations of the enemy that link their characteristics to those of "our own kind."

These psychosocial phenomena are the more powerful influences on the actual conduct of warfare when fed by true and false accounts of an enemy's wartime atrocities. Americans went to war with Germany in 1941 with a grim commitment to stamp out Nazism, but hatred for Nazism reached its climax only after the publication of photographs of the death camps at the war's end. Hatred for the Japanese capacity for atrocity, however, had abundant exposure long before 1941. In the four years preceding Pearl Harbor, Americans would best remember the rape of Nanjing, where Japanese armies murdered, tortured, and raped tens of thousands of civilians in an orgy that fastened the badge of "bestiality" on the character of the Japanese generally in the minds of their western enemies.[16] "In America, in particular," observe two English authors writing in 1991, "revulsion at Japanese behavior produced significant and damaging results by underpinning the 'moral embargo' that by the autumn of 1938 had effectively stopped sales of American aircraft to Japan" and was to stop the sale of much else.[17]

War itself is atrocious human behavior; every side in a war commits atrocities in the eyes of its enemy. Yet, in their battles in the Pacific, both Americans and Japanese justified, enlarged, and glorified the death of enemies in ways that went far beyond military necessity. It is impossible to exclude rampant racism from the causes of these excesses. From the war with Germany there were no stories of "souvenir" bones of dead enemies sent home to family, not to speak of gold being dug from enemy teeth while the dying enemy was still alive.[18] We who read such stories have fifty years of distance from them; our horror grows more remote because of our limited ability to imagine soldiers slaughtering each other with machine guns, flame throwers, and bayonets inside volcano caves where sulfur fumes blend with gunpowder and flesh-rot to throw the odor of death over an entire rocky island. Moral horror pushes these images into the recesses of second-hand memory, where empathy for soldiers on both sides of the war may be for most of us an unaffordable emotional expense. But at almost any expense, morally speaking, we should join Dower's project of remembering the power of racism at work on both sides of these paroxysms of violence.

In these various ways, the "patterns of a race war" become like a palimpsest that continually reveals unexpected and hitherto obscured layers of experience. Centuries-old fragments of language and imagery are pulled to the surface. Harsh words are seen to be inseparable from the harshest of all acts: war and killing. What passes for empirical observation is revealed to be permeated with myth, prejudice, and wishful

thinking. A category as seemingly tight as "race" is shown to overflow into categories pertaining to "others" in general.[19]

In short, racism, as a set of cultural lenses once focused on actual enemy atrocity,
is a formula for the release of immeasurable collective vengeance. In the modern
era, nations have at their disposal instruments of vengeance of unprecedented ferocity. World War II was full of such ferocity, and in justice to salient fact, Americans—
as they remember Nanjing, Bataan, the Japanese prisoner-of-war camps, and the
massacre of Manila—will always have reason to believe that, when it comes to atrocity, "the Japanese started it." Their armies did indeed start certain kinds of mass cruelty whose duplicate in the West could only be found on the Russian front and in the
Nazi death camps. Documentation of these events is abundant, these fifty years later,[20]
however little they have as yet entered the schoolbooks of modern Japan. Those
schoolbooks, instead, are likely to contain their own salient references to what Americans did, before the war was over, to qualify as agents of atrocity against Japan.

What Americans did we consider in more detail below. For the moment it is important, again in deference to the history, to identify and distinguish between the
natures, numbers, and circumstantial justifications of atrocities on both sides without pretending that both sides were always equally atrocious. Their respective cultures *shaped* their vulnerability to this or that excess of violence; their interests in
winning the war shaped it as well, as did their differing perceptions of each other's
readiness to die for their respective causes. Important here is the moral and historical integrity that seeks to remember and distinguish evils as they actually were. The
shooting of Japanese sailors adrift in their lifeboats remains a blot on the American
reputation for adherence to the rules of "just war," but the murder of civilians in
Nanjing and the exploitation of Korean women as prostitutes for the Japanese armies
were evils as great or greater. If humans are to retain any ability to push against the
circumstances of war, we must attribute to them the capacity to choose lesser over
greater evils there, too. Allied armies in World War II came close on many occasions to abandoning the rules of just war altogether; but it little serves moral memory
or moral hope if we simply conclude that in a modern war there can be no such thing
as ethical discrimination in the treatment of enemies. We dare not jettison every element of the just war ethic. The severest test of the possibility of such an ethic may
always be connected to the darkest deed of World War II—in the Nazi death camps.
The story of Pierre Durand from Buchenwald remains fearfully pertinent: at the trial
of Klaus Barbie of Lyon, Durand testified that on the day of the camp's liberation,
"We, the inmates, took 220 German prisoners. But we locked them up and delivered
them to the American Army intact, and they were all assassins. That was the difference between them and us."[21]

In short, both sides in the Pacific war were sure about their differences from their
enemies and their superiority to them. In this they participated in ironic commonality. Doubtless effective military actions require combatants to be equipped with beliefs
about good and evil. The scraps of morality that soldiers take with them to the field,
however, have the doubled-edged potential to serve up dense mixtures of good and
evil simultaneously; this old truth is eminently worth installing in a culture's memory.

Most important of all—and most rare—is accurate memory of how each side experienced its conflict with the ancestors of the other.

Achieving International Empathy

War wounds every side's capacities for empathy, although many war veterans can speak humanely of a former enemy in ways that their civilian contemporaries find hard to imitate. American soldiers found it easier to empathize with their German counterparts than with the Japanese. Beliefs, events, and the gross military will to win connived in the Pacific to distance the ordinary American soldier from any strong sense of commonality with his Japanese enemy. The very fact that so many defenders of islands like Saipan and Iwo Jima were committed to die rather than surrender prepared the Americans to collaborate with that commitment: "Kill them all" was the rule and not the exception in the Pacific war, and here lay one of the tragedies of cultural conflict in the war. With little respect for the European tradition of laying down one's arms in the face of hopeless odds, Japanese officers taught their troops contempt for anyone who surrendered. The notorious cruelties (in western eyes) of their prisoner-of-war camps were consistent (in Japanese eyes) with this contempt. The commander of one Japanese regiment, for example, gave the following instructions to camp administrators:

> It is necessary that subordinates be trained so that in the future they will be capable of dominating white men and putting them to work. . . . You must have sufficient self-respect to place yourselves on a higher level and use them as Canton coolies. In giving orders, use bugles, whistles or Japanese words of command and make them move smartly. . . . There are some forces which, out of a feeling of compassion for the prisoners, give them too much rest. . . . Why should we waste compassion on a crafty enemy who has killed and wounded thousands of our comrades? . . . These men should be made to realise the feelings of their dead comrades.

At one of the camps for building the Burma-Siam railway, new Allied prisoners were "welcomed" with the announcement: "You are the remnants of a decadent white race and fragments of a rabble army. This railway will go through even if your bodies are to be used as sleepers."[22]

Americans entered the war believing that such blatant racism emerged from depths of immorality beyond anything they had ever been taught. Before any American, including this writer, leaps to so sure a conclusion, however, he or she will find it instructive to take an old book of the forties off the shelf and to read in it:

> You've got to rid yourself of squeamish feelings about killing these men who are your enemies. You may not hate these men now—but they hate you and killing them is the only means of defeating what they would kill you to accomplish. It is the only way to avoid being killed for what you stand for. You won't forget the acts of aggression committed by the enemy which started this war. You won't forget *why* you're fighting and killing. . . . The American way of living is a precious thing to you.

This is one of the final paragraphs of the pamphlet handed all newly drafted members of the U.S. Army from the fall of 1944 well into 1946.[23] It is standard wisdom in the troop training of almost all armies that civilian draftees must have some of their lifelong moral inhibitions broken down; they must be taught to hate. Standard also is the knowledge among most combat veterans that hate seldom rises to a fever pitch so surely as when some combat "buddy" gets killed or wounded. In this, American and Japanese soldiers were tragically akin.

To be sure, the moral judgment side of forgiveness may coexist uneasily with empathy, for the latter seems to require a certain temporary suspension of moral judgment for the sake of standing in, or standing under, the situation of the other. This is the justification of attempts, such as Ronald Reagan's at Bitburg, to say that the enemy was "as human as ourselves." Nonetheless, empathy toward evildoers must combine with moral judgment, or it collapses into excuse. Thus the rhetorical ventures of politicians into empathy with wartime enemies past or present is very hazardous; their understanding can be misunderstood, as when racism understood seems to imply racism excused. As a rule, empathy can only avoid the trap of sympathy when it is accompanied by moral judgment on one's own side of the affair.

While expecting political leaders to practice moral clarity in public rhetoric, the democratic humanist will ask politicians to portray the enemy empathetically, too—if not in the heat of battle, then afterwards. As an antidote to racism, wartime or postwar empathy is not a final antidote, but it can weaken the virulence of the disease. If only as a token exhibit of this norm, Americans like me should look again at the course of the Pacific war and acknowledge those human characteristics in the Japanese people and their army which, if not admirable in our own final, finite, retrospective moral analysis, were nonetheless humanly real and understandable. Authors like Dower and the Harrieses repay American reading from this point of view. They offer us a sober opportunity to remove the racist lenses through which most Americans of the war era peered at Japan.

Only a sample of these data is appropriate here, but even a sample captures some of the humanity on the other side of this vicious chapter in the history of the two countries. In the 1990s it is time, for example, that we Americans remembered:

> The long-standing resentment of Japanese people of the inferior status accorded them and other Asians in U.S. immigration policies during seventy years prior to 1941.
>
> The Japanese experience of being asked to imitate western democracy and technology while being told that they had nothing comparable to contribute to the West.
>
> Their dilemma of aspiring to become a modern technically advanced power in the absence of natural resources that undergird such power, a condition that southern Americans may best appreciate in their memories of the American Civil War.
>
> The "island mentality" of a people who, doubly isolated by choice and geography from countries in their own vicinity, are as used to the isolationist view of themselves as were Americans for at least a century after their Declaration of Independence.
>
> The capacity of the Japanese spirit for hard, disciplined, productive work, unappreciated among Americans in the prewar production of "cheap Japanese imports" appearing on the shelves of stores in the 1930s.
>
> The like, culturally ingrained capacity of this people to cooperate among themselves under leadership that calls on them to sacrifice for a national good. (That capacity was to aid in the transformation of Japan's politics, in relatively few postwar years, into western-

style democracy under the virtually dictatorial authority of an American general who used that authority in Japan in ways that Americans would have mightily resisted had it been used on themselves.)

And then there was the human character of the Japanese soldier, more difficult for Americans to empathize with, because the effects of that character were so lethal to so many Americans:

His patriotism, focused on loyalty to his emperor, a display of "love of country" that could well cause reflective Americans to inquire about the proper limits of that virtue.

His capacity for long marches on rations shorter than an American soldier usually tolerates, for endurance of hardship in jungles and islands as unlike the Japanese landscape as they were unlike the American, and for continuing to pull triggers and toss grenades when near death from starvation, disease, and wounds.

His assent to the tradition that there is a cause worth dying for, namely the honor of Japan, and his refusal, with awesome regularity, to save his life in face of "hopeless" odds, in hopes of joining the good spirits, the *kami*, of the imperial shrine of Yasukuni, more sacred by far than any Arlington plot to Americans.

A devotion to his cause that admitted of so little wavering that he accepted suicidal missions and other conditions of certain death as the price of his identity as a soldier, with the result that twenty-five years after the end of the war, some of his companions were still living in the jungles of southeast Asia because their last-received military order had been to stay there to harass the enemy.

This short list of soldierly virtues carries the risk of feeding stereotypes, especially the notion, exploited by American propaganda during the war, that every Japanese citizen was a product of the same cultural "mold," stamped into conformity with the mass of others, without initiative and ready always to obey any order of a superior. The official propaganda line in the American military, for example, "was that every Japanese serviceman died with the Emperor's name on his lips. In fact, like the G.I., he was more likely to cry 'Mother!'" And, especially among officers and university-educated soldiers, questioning of orders occasionally did occur, as when one major, facing military disaster on the Burma front in 1944, "called the whole disciplinary edifice into question by saying: 'The Emperor couldn't possibly give orders as stupid as these.'" Merion and Susie Harries put these exceptions to the rule of obedience, basic to the effectiveness of all armies, in cultural perspective when they comment:

In a society with so profound a respect for hierarchy, so intense a dislike of internal controversy, where for over a thousand years obedience has been the most highly rated virtue, insubordination of this sort, however sporadic, must have been significant. At the very least it suggests that discipline within the army was less than watertight.[24]

The discipline was certainly tighter than that of the Americans, who were pictured by Japanese leaders as a bunch of undisciplined individuals. One military report on the issue of brutal treatment of their own soldiers by Japanese officers warned against too much of it, lest the soldier "act like those who have received an education embodying ideals of liberty and popular rights."[25]

If one wants to build a stereotype of a fanatical enemy, of course, one looks for the most convincing examples and ignores the unconvincing. There was, for example, General Renya Mutaguchi who aspired to the "liberation" of India and led his armies to disaster in the battles around Imphal. As that defeat deepened, he issued an order that became famous as an extreme expression of the Japanese fighting spirit:

> The struggle has developed into a fight between the material strength of the enemy and our spiritual strength. Continue in the task till all your ammunition is expended. If your hands are broken fight with your feet. If your hands and feet are broken use your teeth. If there is no breath left in your body, fight with your spirit. Lack of weapons is no excuse for defeat.

But there were counterexamples. Faced with the same perils of devastation, one of Mutaguchi's generals, Kotoku Sato, said to his troops: "We have fought for two months with the utmost courage and have reached the limits of human fortitude. Our strength is exhausted [lit. our swords are broken and our arrows gone]. Shedding bitter tears, I now leave Kohima. The very thought is enough to break a general's heart."

When he finally retreated against Mutaguchi's orders, Sato's "men were unrecognizable as soldiers—staggering, half-naked, eating grass and slugs."[26] Equally a contrast to Mutaguchi was Kiyotake Kawaguchi, whose career in the Imperial Army was ruined because he refused to sanction the vengeful killings of Philippine officials in May 1942. "He had worked in a prisoner-of-war camp during World War I and been proud of Japan's humanitarian treatment of the German inmates. To shoot defeated opponents in cold blood, he argued, was a violation of the true Bushido," the ancient military code of the Samurai warrior. Kawaguchi had a reputation of care for his men that many an American general might have envied. On Guadalcanal in 1942, he sent a scout on a dangerous mission and "pressed into his hands a tin of sardines, the only food he had brought personally from Japan, and a gift of incredible value at a moment when hundreds of men were starving every day on the island." On the whole, say these British authors, the "social gulf" between enlisted men and officers in the British armies was far wider than that among the Japanese.[27]

Americans of my generation who are willing to have their wartime, propagandized stereotypes of the Japanese people corrected will read books like the two being quoted here; but Americans of subsequent generations should read them too, because there is such a thing as a Japanese, a German, and an American "character" expressed in these traumatic events of the 1940s. These national characters have persisted as well as changed in the past fifty years. They *need* to change in certain ways in the 21st century if that century is to be one in which cultural pluralism abounds in the midst of the competitions, the alliances, the clashes of interests, and the collaborations of a global human society. Books like *War Without Mercy* and *Soldiers of the Sun* stir in any reader awe and rage at what humans did to each other in the Pacific war. But they also stir empathies which international relations can neither dispense with nor ever have enough of. War always promotes systematic shortages of empathy between enemies. Indeed, because both Japanese and Americans failed to understand certain truths about each other, they made some great wartime mistakes, both military and political. Pearl Harbor was an example of a military success that proved to be a political mistake; the dropping of the atomic bombs was arguably another.

Empathetic understanding coupled with moral horror, however, is still a difficult intellectual-emotional achievement. For the moment, speaking from the American side of these memories, how are we to understand, while not ceasing to condemn, the rape of Nanjing, the Bataan death march, the prison-camp executions, the medical experiments on prisoners matching anything that the Nazis perpetrated, the hundred thousand dead in the evacuation of Manila, and the apparent willingness of so many Japanese military and political leaders to consider enduring the annihilation not only of an army but of the entire Japanese people as the last sacrifice demanded by true faith in their destiny?

If Americans are to pose the question seriously, they must repair to their own history for a humbling start toward an answer. Hypothesizing that the Japanese are as human as ourselves, what have we or our ancestors done that might qualify, in some human eyes at least, as atrocious? John Dower provides a model answer to this painful question:

> Allied propagandists were not distorting the history of Japan when they pointed to much that was cruel in the Japanese past. They had to romanticize or simply forget their own history, however, to turn such behavior into something uniquely Japanese— to ignore, for example, the long history of torture and casual capital punishment in the West, the genocide of the Indian population in the Western Hemisphere by the sixteenth-century conquistadors, the "hell ships" of the Western slave trade, the death march of American Indians forcibly removed from the eastern United States in the 1830s, the ten thousand or more Union prisoners of war who died at Andersonville during the U.S. Civil War, the introduction of "modern" strategies of annihilation and terrorization of civilians by Napoleon and Lee and Grant and Sherman, and the death marches and massacres of native peoples by the European colonialists in Africa and Asia right up to 1941. In their genuine shock at the death rituals which the Japanese engaged in, moreover, the Westerners tended to forget not only their own "epics of defeat" (immortalized in such names as Roland, Thermopylae, the Alamo, and Custer), but also the self-sacrifice against hopeless odds of thousands of Allied fighting men. To give but one example, the number of United Kingdom airmen who gave their lives in World War Two was ten times greater than the number of Japanese who died as kamikaze pilots. The acceptance of certain death by the latter did indeed set them apart, but the difference can be exaggerated.[28]

The natural tendency of many Americans to celebrate some of these events as heroic, even if regrettable, had its mirror match in the eyes of the enemy. But that is the uncomfortable point: it is easier to pin the label *atrocity* on the excesses of the enemy while finding excuse for the excesses of the people one counts one's own. "Our atrocities" are episodic, committed in the heat of human extremity; "their atrocities" are unceasing, despicable, bestial. My Lai is our exception; Nanjing is their rule. Further, amplified and falsified in cloaks of propaganda, an enemy's atrocities turn atrocity itself into one's own norm for war. Japanese propaganda might fantasize that to qualify for the Marines a young American had to murder his parents and that America intended to turn all of Japan into a depopulated park at the end of the war, but enough true stories lay behind these vicious fictions to make them sound plausible: American soldiers did cut off Japanese soldiers' ears and heads as souvenirs, the Navy did sink some Japanese hospital ships, the Army did exterminate wounded

Japanese soldiers when there was no reason to fear booby traps, and some prisoners were executed in defiance of the Geneva convention. Dower's pages fill with gruesome illustrations ad nauseam. Among the more palatable: "*Life* published a full-page photograph of an attractive blonde posing with a Japanese skull she had been sent by her fiance in the Pacific. *Life* treated this as a human-interest story, while Japanese propagandists gave it wide publicity as a revelation of the American national character."[29]

The limits of empathy can soon be reached by anyone who attempts exercises such as this: not only is it difficult to understand how one's fellow humans act in the midst of circumstances that one has never encountered personally; but the mind does not, at some point, *want* to understand. Moral consciousness continues its warning: "Others did it, but you do not have to." When others do it to one's own comrades, however, instincts for self-preservation and rage for revenge attack that consciousness and may for a time kill it. Thus it was on the Russian front, in Auschwitz, and at Iwo Jima. That it could happen to any human whatsoever is the frightening thought that seeps upward in any mind daring to look at this history. Rage and projection onto the other are the most comforting ways to protect oneself from such a thought; fear, trembling, and tears are morally better, for they suggest that somewhere in the self can still survive the whisper: "They did not have to do it, nor do you."

To attribute moral responsibility to humans faced with even the most horrible circumstances of war is to construct a basis for identifying "crimes against humanity." In war, all humans commit or condone atrocious acts, but even in hell, we are told, there are low, lower, and lowest depths. The Pacific war entered those last depths in ways that remain opaque to those of us who did not personally endure the combat. The great numbing fact remains that, as the war progressed, the two sides treated each other less and less as humans worth anything but death. Put side by side, illustrations like these two ought never to be lost to the memories of both sides, for the respective *concepts* of the enemy are grimly parallel. Racism finally comes to this:

General [Thomas] Blamey gave an emotional speech to his exhausted Australian troops, who were just beginning to turn the tide against the Japanese on [New Guinea]. "You have taught the world that you are infinitely superior to this inhuman foe against whom you were pitted," he said. "Your enemy is a curious race—a cross between the human being and the ape. And like the ape, when he is cornered he knows how to die. But he is inferior to you, and you know it, and that knowledge will help you to victory. . . . You know that we have to exterminate these vermin if we and our families are to live," he concluded. "We must go to the end if civilization is to survive. We must exterminate the Japanese." In an interview around the same time that was quoted on page 1 of the *New York Times*, Blamey, visiting the Buna battlefield, was quoted in much the same terms. "The Jap is a little barbarian. . . . We are not dealing with humans as we know them. We are dealing with something primitive. Our troops have the right view of Japs. They regard them as vermin." The general even went on to refer to the enemy as simply "those things."[30]

What distinguished Japan's bacteriological warfare program was not the tactics proposed, but the grotesque cruelty of the experiments on which the program was founded. The story of Unit 731, the Manchurian center of the Japanese army's researches into the potential of biological weapons, is a story of hideous suffering inflicted on thousands of victims, most of them Chinese, labeled and treated by their captors as *maruta*, "blocks of wood." . . . the Kwantung Army's scientists took advantage of the moral scruples which made similar experiments by the Allies unlikely. [Prime Minister] Tojo is said to have shared these scruples to the extent that he declined after a while to watch the films that the scientists made of the experiments. . . .

"You couldn't say I want to do this or that in war, however good or bad," recalled the printer of Unit 731 scientific treatises, Uezono Naoji, of what he saw in the human experimental unit. "The Japanese way is to obey a superior. It was the same as if the order came from the Emperor. Sometimes there were no anaesthetics. They screamed and screamed. But we didn't regard the maruta as human beings. They were lumps of meat on a chopping block."[31]

Pearl Harbor and Hiroshima: Undigested Memories

Whatever the provocation of a war, antagonists always accuse the enemy while excusing themselves. Whether they should therefore be judged simply as moral (or immoral) equals will never be easy for their successors to say. Patriotism aside, self-critical Americans and Japanese have a lot of painful history to recollect as they form their own opinions about the behavior of their ancestors in this or any other war. That both sides committed atrocities of mind and deed is undebatable. Whether the two sides were equally atrocious must remain an open question. How open it might have to remain can be suggested in the following wartime newspaper editorial. (If school-teachers in the two countries were to devise a quiz about their students' knowledge of World War II, they could well ask, first, "Which side wrote this?" and, second, "When?")

[They are] utterly lacking in any ability to understand the principles of humanity. Whatever may be the state of their material civilization, they are nothing but lawless savages in spirit who are ruled by fiendish passions and unrestrained lust for blood. Against such enemies of decency and humanity, the civilized world must rise in protest and back up that protest with punitive force. Only through the complete chastisement of such barbarians can the world be made safe for civilization.

The answers are (1) *The Nippon Times* of Tokyo and (2) March 29, 1945.[32] The occasion was the fire bombing of that city in which eighty to a hundred thousand civilians died on the night of March 9–10. By the end of the war, American planes had bombed sixty-six[33] Japanese cities, killing an estimated four hundred thousand civilians. Not more than half of these perished in Hiroshima and Nagasaki. Tokyo became another Hamburg and Dresden: "The heat from the conflagration was so intense that in some places canals boiled, metal melted, and buildings and humans burst spontaneously into flames. It took twenty-five days to remove all the dead from the ruins."[34] A survivor of this terrible night, age fifteen, looked out on the ruins of his city and was one day to find a phrase from the Hebrew Bible for describing it: *tohu wa-bohu.*

Familiar landmarks were gone; rice shops, schools, post-offices, beancake shops, temples and shrines at which people had prayed for victory—even railway stations

had disappeared. And the *oikoumene*, the inhabited world, was changed into a deso-
late world. A threatening silence enveloped the place which had been called Tokyo,
City of the East. I saw the *tohu wa-bohu*, "darkened desolation," not a mythological
one, but an historical one in 1945 produced by the thousands of B-29s manufactured
in Wichita, Kansas.[35]

This vivid description could stand for either Tokyo in March or Hiroshima in
August of 1945, which is to say that the real, additional horrors in Hiroshima should
not obliterate memory of the U.S. Air Force's ability to "scorch, boil, and bake to
death" masses of urban civilians months before the completion of its exotic new
nuclear weapon. (Those were the verbs used by Air Force General Curtis LeMay.)

Yet nothing so epitomizes the conflicting long-term memories of the two sides of
the Pacific war as their ceremonial-symbolic ways of remembering the pair of events
bracketing the entire conflict: Pearl Harbor and Hiroshima. In part, the enduring moral
standoff between the two nations into the 1990s stems from their clashing assessments of the two events. The standoff was profiled in the commemoration of the fiftieth anniversary of Pearl Harbor in the United States in December 1991.

The Pearl Harbor Anniversary. Under the spell that the number 50 casts over western culture, surviving American veterans of the war and their political leaders prepared several years in advance for the December 7 ceremonies, especially for the
mandatory one in Hawaii. Three months prior to the date, Frank F. Fasi, mayor of
Honolulu (now the capital of a state 23 percent of whose citizens are of Japanese
descent), stated publicly that in his opinion the Japanese government should now
apologize for the attack and then be invited to participate in the December commemoration at Pearl Harbor.[36] During the ensuing weeks, Japanese politicians had many
occasions to consider such an apology; leaders of both the Socialist and Liberal
Democratic parties had apparently agreed to promote such a resolution. Then conservatives in the parliament balked, and passage was decisively crippled when, asked
on December 1 in a television interview if he would apologize for the dropping of
two atomic bombs on Japan, President George Bush replied: "War is hell, and it's a
terrible thing, but there should be no apology requested," adding that he agreed with
President Harry Truman that the bombing of Hiroshima and Nagasaki saved "millions" of Japanese and American lives. Within minutes, word of this remark reached
Japan, prompting the immediate reply of a senior government official: "What is the
meaning of issuing a resolution when Bush has said that use of the atom bomb was
justified to end the war?"[37]

Like the Bitburg Cemetery ceremony six years before, an international dialogue
preceding a mere ceremony was to reveal continuities and clashes, along with a few
signs of change, in the cultures of these former enemies. In a rare display of high-
level political argument over the meaning of words in two radically different languages, the leading politicians of Japan and the United States jousted with each other
over what each was to *say*, come December 7. Some days before the date, reporters
asked Prime Minister Kiichi Miyazawa if he personally intended to apologize for
Pearl Harbor. "I cannot answer that question," he replied stiffly. His assistants hastened to say to the reporters, "Remove that question from the record."[38] Just before

the anniversary day, however, Miyazawa finally conceded that Japan did have "responsibility" for beginning the hostilities; President Bush was to respond, in Honolulu on the seventh, that this was a "thoughtful gesture . . . much appreciated by the people of the United States of America."[39]

The struggle over the political words acceptable to the constituents of each leader, however, was longer and more complex than this summation can suggest. The 1991 debate over "apology" went back at least to the ambiguous language of Japanese political leaders at the end of the war, beginning with the historic Imperial Rescript of August 15, 1945, in which Emperor Hirohito spoke painfully to his people about "ending war" rather than "defeat," about his "sense of regret" about the war rather than any sense of wrong in Japanese war aims, and about "the cruel bomb" rather than any other cruelty in more than a decade of Japanese invasions of their Asian neighbors. Fifteen days later a new prime minister, Prince Higashikuni, in a press conference, did use the word *defeat* and did speak ambiguously (to western ears) of the need for all hundred million of the Japanese people to "repent"—but there was no hint here of "the need to offer an apology to the nations Japan had brutalized."[40] Indeed, the United States could hardly claim a moral right to head the list of nations who deserved an apology from the Japanese. Nearby Asians had a much stronger claim—Korea, for example. Four years after the end of the war, in a confidential letter to General Douglas MacArthur, Prime Minister Shigeru Yoshida stated bluntly that Koreans now in Japan (some of them transported from Korea for forced labor) should be sent back to Korea, "that Japan had not enough food to feed them, that they did not contribute to the building up of Japan, and that they bred criminals. Nothing could have been further from his mind than the thought of offering an apology for the great injustice Japan had perpetrated upon Korea and its people." Even sixteen years later in 1965, in "the Japan-Korea Joint Statement issued by the foreign ministers of Japan and Korea there appeared twenty vague words of Japanese apology for 36 years of colonial brutality."[41]

This excursus on Japan's ongoing struggle for the right words to say to its modern Asian neighbors is important for Americans to hear, because it underlines the cultural continuities and changes at stake in the whole matter of official and unofficial language of "responsibility, apology, and repentance" as they apply to both personal and political understanding in these clashes of cultures. As late as 1984, the octogenarian Emperor Hirohito welcomed a president of the Republic of Korea to Japan for the first time and formally greeted him in a public reception with the words: "It is regrettable that there was an unfortunate past between us for a period of this century and I believe that it should not be repeated." The language was strictly parallel to that inscribed on the memorial monument in the Hiroshima Peace Park, language, says Kosuke Koyama, that "suggests that something inexorably happened, quite apart from any human action or responsibility."[42]

The language of historic, politically enacted responsibility did creep into statements official and personal in all these years, however—tokens of conceptual change more difficult for the Japanese than moralistic Americans are likely to suppose. A political culture that has long been accustomed to accord unimpeachable and exclusive authority to an emperor will not generate among citizens much conversation over questions like: "Is it right or wrong? Who is responsible? What shall we do to change the course of the nation?" These questions are rare enough in the conversational culture of the West, and they can virtually disappear in wartime. But they do have roots in western angles of vision. Not so in Japan: in 1972 Prime Minister Kakuei Tanaka made a rare concession to visiting Chou En-lai, "Japan realizes [with a sense of repentance] her heavy responsibility in causing enormous damage to the Chinese people in the past through the war."[43] But such official language was rare up to 1991. In the wake of the Emperor's death in 1989, Prime Minister Noboru Takeshita remarked publicly that future generations would have to determine if in fact Japan was an invader in World War Two![44]

Episodically over this whole period, however, notable clusters of Japanese citizens, many of them distinguished scholars, sought to break through the apology barrier in their culture; and signs of cultural change gleam in many of these efforts. In 1967 the United Church of Christ in Japan (Kyodan) issued a "confession" not far in spirit from that of Darmstadt twenty years earlier, stating on behalf of Japan's tiny minority of Christians that they had "neglected to perform our mission as a 'watchman'" over the life of their nation during the war, and sought forgiveness from the churches and other "brothers and sisters of the world, and in particular of Asian countries, and from the people of our own country."[45] Some courageous Japanese academics in this debate have concentrated on the importance of rectifying the history books studied in high schools and universities of the land so that the facts about the huge human costs of the "Greater East Asia Co-Prosperity Sphere" will no longer be disguised under phrases like "the Korea incident," the "advance into China," "comfort women" from Korea, and the "contributions to Asian development" of Japanese occupation.[46] In 1982, for example:

> When the eminent historian Professor Saburo Ienaga tried, as he wrote in the preface to the English edition of his notable book *The Pacific War*, "to show the Japanese people the naked realities," he was subjected to official persecution. Japanese courts upheld the Education Ministry's censorship of Ienaga's factual account of the Japanese "rape of Nanking" in 1937. As Ienaga observed, the less the young people of Japan are taught the true history of the war, the greater the risk of a "similar danger" in years to come.[47]

In 1982 eight prominent Japanese citizens, in stinging concrete terms, called for "an official statement from the Japanese government" apologizing, in detail, for past crimes against its neighbors. "The words of criticism [concerning textbooks] from Korea and China must alarm Japanese people who so far failed to make their government apologize for the sins committed in the past."[48] Ten years later, in October, 1992, on his first visit to China the new Emperor Akihito spoke of his sadness at remembering the war but said not a word of apology. Indeed, three years earlier he had criticized Chinese President Li Peng for quoting the Emperor as referring to the "unfortunate history" of the war with China. That phrase, said Akihito, was spoken in a conversation meant to be private![49] In that same year, however, as he took up his new imperial office, Akihito defended the right of the mayor of Nagasaki, Hitoshi Motoshima, to express his opinion publicly, at the 1989 Hiroshima anniversary of the atomic bombing, that "it is time that the new emperor as well as the people of Japan took responsibility for the last war. A force which was called 'the Imperial

Army' after all engaged in atrocities all over Asia."[50] The new emperor had not learned a new moral vocabulary for remembering the war, but he had learned to accept the disciplines of democratic freedom of speech.

In politics, words can be weapons, fences, or bridges. Across cultural divides, the world human community is still learning the differences.

All of this received abundant illustration in the debates over words that swirled around the 50th Anniversary Commemoration of Pearl Harbor. On December 5, 1991, Japan's Foreign Minister, Michio Watanabe, said in an interview with the *Washington Post* that the Japanese experienced "deep remorse" over the victims of the war on both sides. The Foreign Ministry moved immediately to clarify the meaning of the Japanese words *fukaku hansei,* which the minister had used in echo of the same word used by former Prime Minister Toshiki Kaifu in a speech earlier that year in Singapore. The word, said the Foreign Ministry, means "self-reflection" and not "remorse." Under no circumstances, they said, "did it constitute an apology."[51] This exchange cloaked the prime minister's concession with ambiguity. At last some Japanese head of government had accepted "deep feelings of responsibility (*sekinin*)" for the war. But what do Japanese mean by "responsibility"? And why the resistance in Japanese culture to what westerners mean by "apology"? Little apparent in the speeches that weekend, of course, was any expression of "responsibility" for the war on the American side. The political problem for the American president on this issue was not unlike the problem of his opposite number in Japan: Americans were remembering an unprovoked attack; the Japanese, the provocations. In the standoff, leaders were playing the roles of descendants of victims, not descendants of people who inflicted mixtures of good and evil on each other.

All the more remarkable in this event, therefore, was evidence of rising support among some citizens and politicians in Japan for the apology that many Americans and more Asians had long demanded. Parliamentary debate on the matter continued into the anniversary day itself. Socialist opposition members called government to account for having "turned its back on the historical truth" by refusing to "sincerely apologize" for Japanese aggressions in the war. Failure to do that, said Makoto Tanabe, Socialist party chairman, "will erase the bright future courses of the former aggressor"—that is, Japan. Apology was due in abundance, he said, to the millions of Asians who suffered from this aggression, especially Chinese, and Koreans, and in particular women of both countries.[52] The contest over words was strenuous in these debates. Several days before, the prime minister had rejected a Socialist appeal for further reparation to individuals still living in Asian countries who had been cruelly treated during the war. Prime Minister Miyazawa replied to this that the government had already made reparations to the governments of these victims—"peoples to whom Japan had caused annoyance," using a word that well illustrates the Japanese propensity for softening the description of "regrettable" events almost to the verbal obliteration of historic fact. The rage that greeted the word *annoyance* in cities like Nanjing, Seoul, and Singapore that day is easy to imagine.[53]

At issue in all this were two diverse, culturally conditioned ways of remembering a painful, morally important past. Americans had heard moral and empirical realism in the official expressions of remorse, guilt, and commitment to change in the public statements of many Germans in the 1945–85 period. The overwhelmingly positive western reception of the von Weizsäcker speech of 1985 was strong evidence that Germans and Americans inhabited something of a common moral universe. (Indeed, the German president's university education and long-time experience as a lay leader of the Evangelical Church had prepared him with far more historical and theological awareness than could be ascribed to the great majority of modern American politicians.) Only dimly aware of the Hebrew-Christian roots of Euro-American culture as most of them may have been, Americans and Germans knew something of what it means to "repent." The Hebrew word means "to turn," and western publics are not wholly deaf to turnings from the past which are empirically candid, morally honest, and publicly explicit. A "clean break," at least in rhetoric, western publics have come to expect of political leaders, especially those whom America has defeated in a war.

Not so for the Japanese angle of vision on evils in their past. As a newswoman well acquainted with modern Japan put it:

> The overriding lesson Japanese learned is that war brought them suffering, not that war made them do reprehensible things. In six years of living in Japan, this reporter frequently heard a proverb in response to questions about the war: "Let the past flow away like the river." In pursuit of forgetfulness, Japan's Government has allowed textbooks to be increasingly sanitized—in just one infamous example, the invasion of China was called an "advance."[54]

She goes on to quote Professor Carol Gluck of Columbia University, a specialist in the recent history of Japan: "Japanese haven't faced up to the responsibility, complicity, incrimination of all of us in total war." Gluck's language here—"all of us"— matches western moral tradition: individual responsibility persisting even in the midst of coercive circumstances; citizens' share in the policies of democratic governments; and realistic distinctions between greater and lesser responsibility for greater and lesser political evils. Americans, unfortunately, tend to leave some of these distinctions to academics. As a political people, we would be better served by politicians who confessed our collective sins once in a while, even when our sins are enmeshed in the sins of others, as they certainly were in the Pacific war.

If capacity to think in terms of this dynamic—the polarities of past and present, individual and society, greater and lesser responsibility—is reflective of the western moral tradition, then the debate with westerners on these matters is likely to continue in Japan for a long time to come. The pioneers in this dialogue are likely to be those academics, journalists, and others not in public office who have experienced the clash of the two cultures in their own life experience. One example of such a person in 1991 was Professor Kiyoko Takeda Cho, professor of history at the International Christian University in Tokyo. Now retired, Professor Takeda-Cho was doing her doctoral study in New York City under the guidance of Reinhold Niebuhr at Union Theological Seminary when, in early 1942, she boarded the Swedish ship *Gripsholm* for a return to wartime Japan. Said she to a reporter in December 1991: "In general, Japanese tend to forget the past, thinking that it can be washed away" without agonized attention to its moral dimensions. "But I always tell my students that recognizing what we have done in the past is a recognition of ourselves. By conducting a dialogue with our past, we are searching how to go forward."[55] She went on to observe that most Japanese share "a profound sense of fatalism, a resignation to events encouraged by popular interpretations of Buddhism and Confucianism that stress a fixed, often predetermined, course of events."[56] A preoccupation with personal moral responsibility is hard to fit into this tradition, said sociologist Rokuro Hidaka of Seika University in Kyoto: "In Shinto, the priest can purify you and any blemish can be removed"—an interpretation of the remission of sins as individualistic and non-political as the medieval Christian sacrament of penance. It is also an interpretation quite transferable to the easy relation between Christian faith and the exigencies of war as sometimes institutionalized in the work of western military chaplains.[57]

But as the above comments from Japanese academics strongly suggest, eastern and western lenses are beginning to overlap in the 1990s, especially in the eyes of many younger Japanese. To be sure, Mieko Hiratani, 25-year-old magazine editor, was still speaking in classic cultural tones when she said to Susan Chira: "I don't feel guilty about Pearl Harbor. Wars are often full of treacheries like that, aren't they? I don't think many people of my generation think about the war anyway. It is only one piece of knowledge for the entrance examination." But Tomohiko Teramoto, age twenty-eight, was making new connections between both sides of the debate when in the week of the fiftieth anniversary he decided to visit Pearl Harbor, a brave thing for a Japanese tourist to do in that particular week. He came, he said, because he had no direct experience of war, but he knew that "it's bad to forget. Japanese should remember Pearl harbor, and Americans should remember Hiroshima."[58]

They should remember, *and they should appropriate each other's memories.* That was the lesson in empathy that could have been promulgated in both the American and the Japanese observance of the fiftieth anniversary. As the observance itself proved, the two peoples have a long way to go before they learn this lesson mutually. One official view in Japan is that it will take many more decades before historians can understand what "really" caused the war; until the historians tell the story in its complexity, there is no point to talking about the war publicly. The American view is that we do not need to know all the details to decide on Japan's major culpability. Unfortunately, the attack on Pearl Harbor rendered a moral disservice to Americans not only in the event but in the excuse it gave the American memory to cover over the complexities and mutual culpabilities of the Pacific War. Because we "remember Pearl Harbor," it is as if Americans have no need to remember anything else about that war.

Forgiveness for Pearl Harbor? As we have seen, moral judgment and repentance enter logically at the beginning of any genuine process of forgiveness. After 1945, the mending of American-Japanese political relations was rapid and pragmatic, as American leaders saw the defeated country as their trans-Pacific front against the Soviet Union and (soon after) Communist China and North Korea. The interest of the United States in the rise of a democratic, anticommunist political order in Japan cleared the way for new feelings and new policies between the two countries, in the course of which both sides had new opportunities to see each other as multidimensional human beings. The wartime propagandistic image of Americans as destroyers of other peoples dissipated quickly in postwar Japan; we were not, after all, a nation intent on the massacre of the Japanese people. Wartime images of the Japanese, in turn, began to lose much of their power in the minds of Americans, too, especially as our occupying troops began to experience the gentleness, artistry, pragmatism, social cohesiveness, and respect for authority in Japanese culture. Americans are not the only pragmatic people in the world: the Japanese quickly acknowledged that their war had not succeeded. The victors deserved respect for their success; they had earned their right to shape a new Japanese society and especially to abolish the military system that had led to such disaster. The nation now turned away from that system, accepting an Allied insistence that Japan renounce war "as an instrument of national policy" by entrenching that phrase in Article Nine of a new national constitution. These changes, solidified by the time of the Korean War in 1950, permitted Americans to see Japan as a vicious enemy turned—thanks to paternal American guidance—to a dependable political ally. Still invisible in these early decades was the potential of Japan as America's chief economic rival in a world economy.

Would it be absurd to tag this rapid transformation of a wartime into a peacetime relation as an example of forgiveness in politics? As the fiftieth anniversary events testify, the answer is difficult and necessarily ambiguous. Moral stances native to two cultures are still clashing. Americans remain perplexed and offended that any Japanese official in 1991 could continue to speak of the evils of the Pacific war as an "annoyance" to other countries, and especially that any should resist at least apologizing for the "sneak attack" on Pearl Harbor. On their side the Japanese are equally perplexed about American preoccupation with this detail of the war. Why the western attachment to Geneva conventions, especially its expectation that wars, to be "just," must be formally declared beforehand? Knowing that westerners did set store by formal declarations of war, Admiral Isoroku Yamamoto, who commanded the attack on Hawaii, had agreed with his government that Japanese diplomats would deliver a formal declaration of war to Washington a half hour before the scheduled bombardment of Honolulu. For various circumstantial reasons, the declaration was delivered after the attack had begun. Adolf Hitler had not acted much differently in invading Poland or the Soviet Union, so why make so big a point of a half hour's or a half day's notice? Surprise is an ordinary military principle; if one means to go to war, why not go with maximum chances for victory? But the moral notion of justice *in bello* in the West required due notice. Yamamoto himself knew that well enough to fear the effects of the attack on the American public. Chinese and Russian propagandists had been warning Americans for a long time that in Japan they faced a ruthless, cruel enemy. Now Americans believed it, turning overnight from their yearning for isolation to "a deep-rooted moralistic animosity against Japan that was to last throughout the war and beyond."[59] The admiral and other Japanese leaders might hope that in face of quick Japanese military successes in the Pacific, America could be persuaded to negotiate an end to the war, since (contrary to immediate American fears) no military strategist in Tokyo imagined that Japan could mount a successful invasion of California. Yamamoto had studied in the United States, and he probably knew that the "sleeping giant" awakened by Pearl Harbor would arm himself, not only with great industrial might, but also with great moral self-righteousness. The latter proved to be an awesome weapon, capable of lending its sanction to acts of defense against the Japanese which were indistinguishable, on occasion, from their acts of aggression.

Postwar learnings of both sides, perhaps, should by now have moderated these misunderstandings, teaching Americans, for example how

> Most Japanese do not share America's taste for precise judicial determinations of blame [such as was meted out in 1949 to seven Japanese "war criminals" in their execution by an Allied tribunal]. They prefer to solve disputes by seeking consensus and conciliation, sometimes relying on intentional vagueness. In their eyes, this is not a failure of morality but a positive virtue, a quest for harmony.[60]

The "quest for harmony," after its offensive disruption, is as much at the root of the idea of forgiveness as is the requirement of moral judgment, at least in western tradition. But the priorities and tonalities here are different in the two cultures, and the difference will continue to rankle the two sides for a long time to come.

In the meantime, however, there are encouraging signs that various citizens of the two countries have begun to travel the road to empathy with each other's ways of entering and recovering from violent conflict. The social psychology of George Herbert Mead will well serve this journey. Mead was sure that "intercultural learning is only possible on the basis of empathy. . . . people cannot hear their own words unless they adopt the same attitude which another person would adopt if he or she uttered the same words. Meaningful communication between people of different cultures can only take place if there is reciprocal anticipation of the expectations and perspectives of the other."[61]

The Pearl Harbor anniversary in 1991 offered some poignant reminders of this wisdom. Among the reminders were gestures of forgiveness, some personal, some on behalf of groups.

Among the latter was a moving statement by the Yokohama Association of Bereaved Families of War who, on December 7, 1991, published an open letter in American newspapers under the heading, "Dear Citizens of the United States of America." Identifying themselves as families "who lost close relatives in the Allied bombings of Yokohama," the letter begins with "the deepest apology to all the American people" for "this foul way of starting a war without any formal declaration, and for the many thousands of victims of this surprise attack." They then went on to remind Americans that "many hundreds of thousands of civilians died in the Allied air raids on more than 100 Japanese cities." (The numbers here were "generous" on both sides: 2,403 Americans died at Pearl Harbor and 1,178 were wounded. The death total of Japanese civilians from bombings of sixty-six cities has been estimated at 400,000, a figure that stands out starkly enough against some 300,000 American military deaths in all of World War II. There were 1,740,955 probable Japanese military deaths, and—who knew for sure?—10 million Chinese.[62]) "We have not forgotten our sorrow" over these personal losses, the letter adds—an implicit invitation to American readers not to forget them either.

The final paragraph of the letter is doubly remarkable for its use of terms intimately associated with the traditional theological definition of forgiveness in the West. Yokohamans had erected a peace monument in their city inscribed with the words "Love, Peace, Earth" and the names of known bombing victims, after the model of the monument in the Peace Park of modern Hiroshima.

All the citizens of the world are welcome to visit the Yokohoma Peace Monument. We particularly encourage and invite American citizens to come, as one way of demonstrating our sincere reconciliation. The bereaved families of the deceased in America and Japan can never forget the horrors of war, but we hope that they can by now pardon each other. On this occasion of the 50th anniversary of the outbreak of the war, let us truly reconcile with each other, deepen our unexpected friendship all the more, and never stop advancing toward the realization of a permanent world peace.

We pray for the health and peace of mind of all the American people.[63]

Not often in all the linguistic agony of the fiftieth anniversary did anyone on either side seem to feel comfortable with assertions of "apology," "pardon," and "reconciliation." That these Yokohama folk could do so was remarkable.

But the event was not unique. Off in Missouri John E. Basquette, the state director of the Pearl Harbor Survivors Association, remembered the satisfied smiles on the faces of close-flying Japanese pilots at Pearl Harbor and said to a reporter that he was not about to forgive or forget: "They make such a big deal each year on the anniversary of Hiroshima and Nagasaki." (Basquette was ahead of most Americans. in knowing that fact.) "But they keep saying, 'Forget Pearl Harbor.' My theory is 'If you hadn't started it, there wouldn't have been a Hiroshima.' Any time Pearl Harbor flashes on the TV screen, I get tears in my face." In his theory, Basquette was in step with most of his fellow citizens, fifty years ago and in 1991. But down in Atlanta, John J. Westerman, Jr., a fellow member of the Survivors Association who had been an ensign aboard the battleship Oklahoma and had seen his best friend die on December 8, had had the task of telling five wives that they were now widows.

> Still, Mr. Westerman, now 72, recently made an effort at reconciliation with Japanese veterans. As a member of the survivors association, he planned to meet some Japanese pilots who took part in the attack [by inviting them to visit Atlanta]. But the plan was vetoed by the national leaders of the association.
>
> "A lot of people believe that it's time for us to look to the future and put the fighting behind us," he said. "But I understand that every veteran's got to heal his wounds in a separate way."[64]

Ritual observances of the anniversary occurred all over the United States—at the Alamo in San Antonio; at naval installations in Baltimore, New York, Buffalo, Pittsburgh, Charleston, and Portland; and in front of the Liberty Bell in Philadelphia.[65] Meantime, in Hempstead, Long Island, at the Eisenhower Center, there gathered some dozens of governmental and academic professionals to reflect on the causes, results, and future of Japanese-American enmities. In the company was Akira Iriye, a Harvard history professor, who said bluntly that the people of his ancestral country had for the most part "chosen to forget" the horrors of the war, in particular those they inflicted on their fellow Asians. Historians in Germany, he said, had set an example which not many Japanese historians were yet imitating. But among the conferees was Arnold Bocksel, 78-year-old veteran of the Bataan Death March, who had spent 3½ years in a prisoner-of-war camp. It was, he said, an "entirely alien" experience of suffering; but nonetheless, "I forgive the Japanese for what they did to me. My personal religious ethic teaches me that. . . . To me it's like a serious wound I've had that's left an ugly scar."[66]

Meantime also, President George Bush was speaking of Pearl Harbor memories of his own, about courage, democracy, and promises of world peace. The words he chose, and the response they met with, in an audience composed mostly of survivors and their families, displayed the difference between personal willingness to forgive and the pressure on a political leader not to get too far ahead of the ideologies and ethics of constituents. Prime Minister Miyazawa was facing the same problem; so was John Westerman in Atlanta. Constituents have differing degrees of readiness to forgive the evils that others have committed against them. Mr. Bush knew this as he came to the end of his speech. Rather more convincingly than Ronald Reagan at Bitburg, he spoke of reconciliation and moving into the future:

> Let me tell you how I feel. I have no rancor in my heart toward Germany or Japan— not at all. And I hope, in spite of the loss, that you have none in yours. This is no time for recrimination. World War II is over. It is history. We won. We crushed totalitari- anism, and when that was done we helped our enemies give birth to democracy. We reached out, both in Europe and in Asia, and made our enemies our friends. We healed their wounds and in the process, we lifted ourselves up.

To this the reporter added the commentary, "Mr. Bush's words brought respectful applause, but it was not an easy sell for this audience.[67]

Or for almost any audience of older Americans, haunted by "Pearl Harbor ghosts" in spite of a culture that has encouraged them to skip the past and get on with the future.[68] The American president was doing what political leaders often find it hard to do: nudge the proclivities of an audience and open a window onto new ways of dealing with old hurts. In two respects he signaled the limits of his will or ability to push their limits: already he had publicly refused to concede any degree of blame on his country for having ended the war with two nuclear bombs. At an early morning gathering of the Pearl Harbor Survivors Association in Honolulu's Punchbowl Na- tional Cemetery, he also ignored certain facts about the Pacific War as he said: "Americans did not wage war against nations or races. We fought for freedom and human dignity against the nightmare of totalitarianism." It was a comforting moral thought, but the uncomfortable truth was otherwise. Racism *had* been a central po- litical force in the Pacific war, and to his moral credit, the President chose this occa- sion to pay tribute to those citizens of Japanese ancestry, buried in this cemetery, "whose love of country was put to the test unfairly by our own authorities. . . . They . . . and other natural born Americans were sent to internment camps simply because their ancestors were Japanese."[69]

Before the war was over, homeland Japanese had come to believe that their "race" was in fact the target of the U.S. Air Force's city-smashing fire bombs. Then two atomic bombs had sealed this impression. Who were Americans now to complain of atrocities? If Americans had such moral passion for an apology for Pearl Harbor, why their opaqueness to understanding Japanese passion for an apology for Hiroshima?

In sum, December 7, 1991, evoked on both sides a few strong personal expressions, a few collective voices from unofficial bodies of citizens, and a few murmured beginnings from high podiums of forgiveness in international politics. The volume of the voices was subdued. It was likely to continue so until Americans, too, came to terms, in larger numbers, with past and present facts of racism in their own and others' countries. Symbolically, to the Japanese, that meant coming to terms with Hiroshima.

Forgive Hiroshima? Certain municipal politicians with an exquisite sense of history had years ago established a "sister city" relation between Honolulu and Hiroshima. Among the other ceremonies, two pairs of Protestant and Roman Catholic church services took place concurrently on December 7. In the Roman Catholic one, a bishop of Italian ancestry in Honolulu issued a joint call with his Japanese counterpart for "reconciliation and forgiveness."[70] In all of the ceremonies, no one seemed to suggest that forgiveness was a short process. The continued standoff around the atomic bomb was one lingering reason.

By a huge majority, the Japanese people in 1991 were sure that Americans had not come to terms with Hiroshima. A *New York Times* poll in early December in the two countries found that some 40 percent of Americans thought that Japan should apologize for Pearl Harbor, and 55 percent of Japanese thought so to—a surprising and hopeful majority in Japan that apparently had yet to influence the head of government. But the discrepancy in the answers to the second question was more revealing: Should the United States apologize for dropping the atomic bombs? Yes, said 16 percent of Americans; yes, said *73 percent* of Japanese. From these results one might speculate that awareness of the importance of apologies in the realm of political conflict is even less in the United States than in Japan, but less speculative is the overwhelming difference of perception about the American initiation of nuclear war. The issue remains vivid, strong, and persistent in the Japanese public mind. For Americans it is just one of the final horrors of a horrible war. Pearl Harbor and Hiroshima are opposite ends of an hourglass; the sand flows in opposite directions depending on the tilt of the glass in favor of one or the other perspective.

On the American side, those who remember living through the final half of the war are not surprised to be told that, as the defeat of Japan became inevitable, the Pacific war descended steadily into a vortex of increasing carnage. Not only did Japanese soldiers by the thousands charge into certain death in the face of machine guns, accompanied by wounded men intent on dying before being taken prisoner, but Japanese civilians on the islands of Saipan and Okinawa died in suicides that left battle-hardened American soldiers stupefied with horror. Begun in June 1944, the Saipan battle ended in July with the deaths of two out of three civilians living there—some 22,000 of them. "There were virtually no survivors from the 30,000-strong garrison. Bulldozers had to be brought in to shovel the dead into mass graves—2,000 corpses from the last banzai charge alone. It was also the costliest battle of the war so far for the Americans: Over 14,000 were killed or wounded."[71] Killing as many enemies as necessary to end the war: that was the purpose that dominated Americans at home and abroad during this final catastrophic year, which saw firestorms sweep through Hamburg and Dresden as well as Tokyo and Yokohoma. Soldiers became convinced that in defeat the Japanese were as dangerous and as willing to die as they were in victory. The "war without mercy" therefore kept escalating.

Dower summarizes the context in which the Americans, military and civilian, celebrated the invention and use of the atomic bomb in the following narrative, whose final incident has to be profoundly embarrassing to any American who dares to believe and remember it:

> The atomic bomb . . . was in this setting but a more efficient way of killing, and its use marked the beginning of the end of the long, unnecessary death agony. . . .
>
> On August 10, the day after the Nagasaki bomb (and two days after the Soviet Union declared war on Japan), the Japanese government made clear it intended to surrender, although the terms remained to be ironed out. Between then and the actual end of the war, two now-forgotten happenings took place that symbolize the war hates and race hates which had driven both sides so far, so disastrously. After the saturation bombing of Japanese cities began in March 1945, the Japanese military in the home islands commenced summarily executing the small number of U.S. airmen who fell into their hands. On August 12, eight were executed in Fukuoka; on August 15, the formal cease-fire a whisper away, eight more were killed by the military command in the same city— marking Japan's last moment of war with a final atrocity. While this was taking place, General Henry H. Arnold, one of the major planners of the U.S. bombing strategy, was desperately attempting to arrange "as big a finale as possible" to end the war. It was his dream to hit Tokyo with a final 1,000-plane air raid—and on the night of August 14 he succeeded in collecting such a force and sending it against the already devastated capital city. A total of 1,014 aircraft—828 B-29 bombers and 186 fighter escorts— bombed Tokyo without a single loss. President Truman announced Japan's unconditional surrender before all of them had returned to their bases.[72]

Anyone with the courage to empathize with the demonic *spirit* that swept over both sides in these final paroxysms of World War II will find him or herself shaken by the potential of human beings for cruelty to the utter extent of their collective abilities. Here shouts the lesson of Françoise Fenelon in the records of the Pacific war as well as in the Nazi death camps. Dower underscores the theme when he notes how "it is possible to obscure what war is all about . . . by denying enemies their humanity and seeing them as beasts, demons, or devils." The demonic spirit mobilized huge, unprecedented technical, social, and psychological resources on both sides of this war; but at the end the Americans "outproduced" the enemy on all of these fronts: pride joined with ideology, revenge with religious confidence, instruments of propaganda with technologies of weapons delivery, massive visitations of suffering with the distancing euphoria of victories headlined in daily news, fear of a lengthened war with determination to end it at any cost to the enemy. By the summer of 1945, in the minds of Americans, "the enemy became remote, monolithic, a different species, ultimately simply large numbers to tally up gleefully on one's growing list of estimated enemy dead."[73]

Aside from this overburden of horror, what then do 73 percent of the Japanese public want Americans to understand about the latter's public memory of the Hiroshima and Nagasaki bombings?

Americans will hear the answer the more clearly if they have had the chance to visit postwar Hiroshima. If one went, as did this writer, twenty-four years after

August 6, 1945, one saw an urban phoenix risen from its ashes. A first American thought at this sight is, "Cities can recover from nuclear bombing!" But a tour of Hiroshima's Peace Park and its Atomic Bomb Museum raises doubts about the human depth of that apparent recovery. Americans, who have not yet experienced a single hour of airborne bombs on the roofs of their cities, must listen to the testimonies of others to know what such an hour is like. The Atomic Bomb Museum in Hiroshima is as good a place as any on earth at which to begin listening. Here are the melted bottles, ashes of paper money that was incinerated inside a locked safe, human silhouettes burned into stone, pictures of the *Enola Gay*, diagrams of the bomb, and then the photographs: piles of bodies, corpses drifting downriver, faces burned beyond recognition, bodies with skin falling off like loosened clothes, bewildered children dying in ditches.

Out the window of the museum can be seen the now famous steel-frame skeleton of the former Industry Promotion Hall (now the Atomic Bomb Memorial Dome), and near at hand is the white marble cenotaph, in the center of the Peace Park, which in American eyes is likely to resemble the upper story of a Conestoga wagon. An inner box contains the growing list of names of persons dead or eventually to die from the atomic blast of August 6, 1945. The number is not far from 100,000.

An American's personal visit to the Hiroshima Museum is a walk into the Japanese memory of war with America. Another American visitor, Tom F. Driver, reflected on the human destruction of morality epitomized in this bomb:

> There were no limits here. Once the bomb had fallen, *anything* could happen. What atomic weapons meant, what the death camps in Europe had meant, was that nothing ever more was sacred. In our day, it had been revealed that human beings are capable of demolishing every imaginable boundary. Morality is not innate. There are times and places from which it disappears. These instances are awesome. They are the reversed image, the diabolical mirror of the holiness of God.[74]

As an American walks out of the Hiroshima museum, however, he or she is liable to be burdened with profound moral ambivalence: One is haunted and angry at a great *absence* inside its walls. Of Japanese complicity in the beginning and the course of the Pacific war there is here no sign. Here, rather, is a brush with clashing collective memories: If Americans are going to acknowledge that this "cruel and unnatural bomb" was an excess of violence, what excesses are Japanese (and their educators) ready to acknowledge in their part of this tragic past?

On the end of the cenotaph in Hiroshima there is a short inscription that embodies the Japanese way of grasping this memory: "Rest in Peace: The error will not be repeated." An alternate English translation could be, "We will not repeat the error"; but between the two translations lies the gulf that separates two cultural dispositions for thinking about the evil in human history: westerners want to insist that history does not just happen; men and women make it happen. *We*, the likes of us, do these things, and when we remember them, we are to remember the *agency* that belongs to us and our kind. There must be room for contrary choice, say all freedom-affirming western moralists who think, in their moments of calm, about what they did in their moments of fury.

The contrary Japanese disposition roots in a wisdom that values indirection, the soft approach to difficult human things, and an account of tragedy that prefers the passive to the active voice. "Responsibility" in this world view is more an adjustment to circumstance, less a struggle to overcome it or to think that it could have been overcome. Implied in this adjustability is readiness to leave evil enough alone in its past and to treat it as something now external to the present. The ancestors made a "mistake [*ayamachi*]"; they chose the wrong target, and they missed hitting it. We must move on from their mistake and not repeat it. A scholarly, bicultural Japanese Christian says of the cenotaph inscription in Hiroshima: "*Ayamachi* is a tormentingly light expression for this catastrophe in the history of humanity and of the planet. What happened there was certainly more than an *ayamachi*."[75]

In the cases of the two nuclear bombs that destroyed Hiroshima and Nagasaki, there is a second cultural ingredient at work in the displays of carnage in the museums in both cities. In their other-directed, harmony-prizing habit in human relations, the Japanese are likely to perceive that human harmony is a matter of balance between one obligation and another. This is one way of dealing with the American propensity for remembering Pearl Harbor and forgetting Hiroshima: "You want us to remember the one; we want you to remember the other. The two evils cancel each other out. We are even, and we should therefore issue to each other mutual permission to forget."

Ready on the tongues of countless Americans is the rejoinder: "Two wrongs do not make a right. Bring all wrongs to the light of day!" The founders of the Hiroshima Peace Park mean to do exactly that: "An evil thing happened here. Americans did it." It may be a half-truth, but it is still truth.

What were the particular evils of the atomic bombs in Japanese eyes? They were several, and Americans should memorize them:

> The Americans dropped this city-consuming weapon on Asians, not on Europeans with whom they were equally at war.
> They dropped it when the Japanese nation was prostrate and near to defeat.
> The weapon by its nature eliminated all distinctions, precious in western "just war" theory, between military and civilian targets; it was a weapon of terror against whole urban populations, including, in Hiroshima, a large number of Korean forced-laborers.
> The results, in the lives of those who survived the blast, were uniquely terrible: radiation burns, cancer, premature death, and lifetime ostracism.
> In their close scrutiny of these results, in their research after the war, the Americans treated the bombing as a military experiment, more cruel and more costly in lives than anything the Japanese armies did in the war.
> And finally, by their proven willingness to use such a weapon, the Americans opened the world to the Nuclear Era and its absolute threat to human existence.

The argument here, fueled by selective fifty-year-old memories, is not likely to be settled between the two countries anytime soon. Americans are likely to reply that, had the scientists readied the bomb early enough, it surely would have been dropped on the Germans, whose nuclear science had first raised the Allied fear which led directly to the Manhattan Project; that as of August 6, few outsiders could have been certain that the Japanese government was really ready to surrender; that the bomb gave the emperor himself a fateful reason to proceed to the surrender; that target discrimination had dropped out of the war long before 1945 on the part of almost every combatant including the Japanese; that the suffering of war victims can only be arranged on a relative scale; that postwar military science helped to discover just how terrible the weapon is; that the weapon held Japan's old enemy, the Soviets, at bay for forty-five years; and—the capstone American argument—by helping to end the war quickly, the bomb saved millions of Japanese as well as American lives.

The Hiroshima question is a tough, long-standing, and not-soon-ending issue of interpretation between the historians, the politicians, and the citizens of the two countries in 1994 and beyond. It is one of the questions which Japanese officials mean to keep open when they say that, after all, historians need many more decades to determine the real causes of the Pacific war—before they disentangle the strands of colonialism, economic need, political rivalry, and cultural conflict that provoked the war. Suspended judgment on this large matter again reflects the Japanese preference for treating past evils as objective happenings for which no one person, or a whole nation, should be deemed "responsible." When, on December 1, 1991, President Bush was asked if the United States should apologize for Hiroshima, he reverted to the common American assumption that the bomb "saved millions of lives." As leading Japanese politicians of all parties protested the remark, Sadao Asada, professor of history at Doshisha University, surmised: "The Bush comment has touched a nerve among the Japanese people at the worst possible time," adding that to his sure knowledge President Truman himself had estimated that the bomb saved only 500,000 American lives, with no proof that even this estimate was justified.[76]

At stake in this distressed trans-Pacific dialogue were the three issues, all of them ancient in the grudging progress of two peoples toward mutual assessment of painful past conflict: (1) What were "the" facts, and which were the most important facts? (2) How could anyone have acted differently? (3) Whose sufferings were morally justified, whose unjustified?

1. The first question is presumably for historians to answer; but if they are to answer in ways that lead to some reconciliation of memories on both sides of the Pacific war, Japanese and American historians will have to undertake more work *together*.[77] Journalists of both countries, too, will have to continue their popular education of the two publics toward some approximate appreciation of each other's recollections of what their ancestors did and did not do. Among the rather settled facts seem to be the following:

a. As early as January 1944, Japanese leaders had concluded that the war was lost, but the idea of surrender was so little considered by the political elite (until the summer of 1945) that the military proceeded systematically to prepare for an invasion of Japan by the Americans. In 1945, civilians, from the very old to the very young, were being trained to become resisters to the death, after ancient Japanese precedent.

b. Credible plans for the invasion of Japan were equally afoot among the Americans. That invasion was scheduled to begin on November 1, 1945. In the meantime, the American air force was to continue its obliteration bombing of Japanese cities. It is almost certain that deaths in those cities, in these intervening months, would have equaled the deaths in Hiroshima, and if the probable deaths in the Soviet invasion of Manchuria were added, the total would have exceeded the deaths in Hiroshima and Nagasaki. By 1945 the Japanese populace, especially in every large city, must have been painfully aware that the country was prostrate: "In the view of the people," said Kosuke Koyama, "the atomic bombs were blasted over a dead horse."[78]

c. A majority of the military, scientific, and political advisers to President Truman were strongly in favor of using the atomic bomb against a Japanese city; but a vocal minority cautioned that its *political* implications should be given far more emphasis than many around the president were willing to consider. Among the scientist-opposers were Leo Szilard and Dr. James Franck; among the political, John J. McCloy; and among the military, no lesser figures than Admiral William D. Leahy and General Dwight D. Eisenhower. Both of the latter believed that Japan was otherwise near surrender and that world opinion would turn against the United States if it used the bomb. (Subsequent historians, however, would assemble evidence that the sector of "world opinion," of most interest to American policymakers was the Soviet Union.[79])

d. Allied intelligence knew that certain high officials in Japan were seeking a way to end the war, that they had sought an intermediary for doing so in the Soviet Union, and that their major resistance to the "unconditional surrender" demand of the Potsdam conference (July, 1945) centered on their desire to retain the institution of the emperor. In fact, as a group, high officialdom in Tokyo was evenly divided on the question of surrender versus fighting on; only the decisive intervention of Emperor Hirohito himself finally broke this deadlock.

e. To almost the last moment, the chance for a military coup, to shortcut the imperial decision of surrender, was quite real. A final attempt to prevent the emperor from broadcasting the surrender was foiled by loyal palace guards.

f. In a poll taken in December 1945 by the magazine *Fortune*, 75 percent of the American public approved of the bomb's use against Hiroshima and Nagasaki; some 13.8 percent thought that a demonstration of the weapon's power should have been arranged in an unpopulated region of Japan; and only 4.5 percent thought that it should not have used at all.[80] Notable here is the fact that obliteration bombing, as the aim of air attacks on Japanese cities, began with the great March 9–10 raid on Tokyo at the initiative of American air force generals and not as a political decision in Washington. No major protest of this shift away from discrimination between military and civilian targets occurred during the spring among the media, the churches, or other groups of American citizens. The policy "just kill them" slid into effect with hardly a ripple of public awareness that "kill their military" had always been a policy for conducting a just war. By now, toward Germany and Japan, the American public conscience had been inured to the difference. Neither military nor political leadership seemed interested in awakening that conscience to what once had been its ordinary principle.[81]

All this is to say that, at the time, only a minority of Americans and their leaders saw the atomic bomb as a *qualitatively* unique weapon of destruction. It would take some years of the nuclear era for growing numbers to think otherwise.[82]

2. Historians have explored the range of alternatives to the Hiroshima and Nagasaki bombing, and on the coming fiftieth anniversary of the war's end, a careful study of "what might have been" would equip American leaders in the White House and Congress with some perspectives that could turn them away from the brusque response of President Bush in 1991: "There will be no apology." Should there be simple defense of what was done? Not if the plausible alternatives are clearly remembered:

a. That the bomb should be used to end the war seems never to have been questioned by the people to whom President Truman looked for advice in the summer of 1945. A $2 billion investment in the Manhattan Project argued for using the new weapon, not to speak of the political rage that might have erupted in an American public belatedly informed that its war deaths might thereby have quickly ended. There was in fact some discussion in the circle around Truman about ways to demonstrate the power of the weapon apart from using it to kill a city. A military target removed from an urban center was urged by a few advisers, even though it would have been easier then for Japanese military leaders to keep the facts about the weapon's effects from Tokyo political leaders.[83] But it was not a suggestion that received much attention in Washington. By July 1945 resistance to the bombing of cities had almost disappeared.

b. A few farsighted persons around the U.S. president perceived the possible political impacts of the new weapon and urged him to consider a political approach to securing a Japanese surrender. The most influential proponent of this strategy was probably John J. McCloy, Assistant Secretary of War. In mid-June, before the first bomb had been tested, McCloy attended a high-level meeting of military leaders in the White House. At the end, he asked for permission to suggest "a political solution" to the problem of getting the Japanese government to surrender.

> "I said I would tell them [the Japanese] we have the bomb and I would tell them what kind of a weapon it is. And then I would tell them the surrender terms." He thought the Japanese should also be told they could keep their emperor. What if they refused, he was asked. "Our moral position would be stronger if we gave them warning."
> Truman indicated that he would think about it.[84]

There is little evidence that Truman thought about it for long.

c. An equally political solution, eventually and promptly adopted as a postwar occupation policy by the American president and by General Douglas MacArthur, was the continuation of the institution of the emperor. Had that possibility been communicated to the Japanese government in July 1945, it would at least have added one more persuasive reason for surrender to the arguments of the peace party in Tokyo's war cabinet. Knowledgeable diplomats like Joseph Grew and Henry Stimson were already recommending this concession; had they known in advance what a key role the emperor was to play in the actual decision of the Japanese government to surrender in mid-August, their own argument for the concession would have seemed clairvoyant indeed.

d. There was at least one more alternative, and that was to bomb not more than *one* city. In a fatal delegation of power to the Pacific-based military and an equally fatal substitution of tactics for strategy and politics, President Truman authorized the two available bombs to be dropped as weather and other military conditions allowed in early August. Weather conditions decided the day of the Nagasaki bomb, scarcely three days after Hiroshima. We now know that it took the Japanese cabinet and the emperor a week to decide on surrender, not a long interval for the making of so fateful, painful, and controversial a decision. (It was two or three days, in fact, before the military was willing to tell the war cabinet the facts about the destruction of

Hiroshima.) Better one city killed than two: even that slim nod to the ethics of just warfare would have constituted a sign of restraint on the part of the war makers—a shred of humanity in the fabric of violence. For at least 40,000 people in Nagasaki, that shred meant the difference between death and life.

It is hard, these fifty years later, not to conclude that one of these alternatives should have been tried by the American government. Proponents of alternatives were always in the minority as the president considered these heavy questions in the summer of 1945. Eventually Americans may have to "remember Hiroshima" as a painful example of how the minority is sometimes right.

3. The question of whose suffering counts the most in any moral assessment of the Pacific war is probably unanswerable. When all the deaths are added up, of course, the Japanese toll far exceeds that of the Americans, who remain among the least war-scarred peoples on earth. The suffering of other Asians was so great that much of it lies buried in the untraceable graves of war victims. Soon, one hopes, Japanese leaders provide clear, public, comprehensive data on the pain which Japan imposed on its near neighbors between 1933 and 1945. Meantime, Americans will be right to ask if, in their zeal for remembering Hiroshima, a new generation of Japanese leaders and citizens will be reexamining the end of the war with attention to the question of *Japanese* alternatives for bringing on that end sooner. In late 1988 the mayor of Nagasaki publicly raised just this question: If the Emperor was capable of seeing the folly of continuing the war after the atomic bomb, why did he not see it after the March 1945 destruction of Tokyo? Having prepared their people for suicidal resistance to an inevitable land invasion, did the government not know that the Americans would do everything in their power to destroy Japan with minimal destruction to themselves?[85] Propaganda and military preparation on both sides were escalating the "war without mercy." Each side had made clear to the other that it had huge reserve potential for inflicting yet more death upon the other. Indeed, who is to say that, in this dense interchange of violence and counterviolence, the crimes of one side had no provocation in the crimes of the other? That either looked at the other through a thicker veil of ignorance? Or that either had greater wisdom or strategy available for ending war, among the most difficult endings that human collectivities ever contrive?

In sum, if and when the politicians, scholars, and ordinary citizens of Japan and the United States give serious attention to this history, they will have to retreat from easy slogans about "remembering Pearl Harbor" and "remembering Hiroshima." These two slogans obscure the vast, unjustified injuries that each side inflicted on the other, especially as the war drew to a close. If leaders or citizens of the two countries approach the fiftieth anniversary of the war's end in 1995 in anything like a mood of apology for the wrongs to be remembered from that war, they should survey together a wider range of painful fact than this pair of slogans will ever imply. Already by 1993 certain Japanese leaders had begun to specify publicly some of the excesses of their own side in the Pacific war. There is less sign of a equivalent move on the part of any American leader, though the material for such a move is now accessible in a growing abundance of scholarship on the war. If U.S. leaders, especially the president, fail to appropriate the American side of these horrors, they will miss the depths of what should be mourned and celebrated in the end of World War II. As in personal relations, so in international relations: one true apology can release another. Neither Japanese nor Americans have yet released each other into that freedom.

Crossing the Cultural Divide

A potential for such release seemed to slumber on the edges of the testy exchanges of the fifty-year anniversary of Pearl Harbor. Some president, some prime minister in the future, will have it in his or her hands to awaken that potential. Here the work of historians like John Dower, Carol Gluck, and their Japanese colleagues will be profoundly serviceable to the achievement of empathetic and moral interchange between Japanese and American politicians and publics. Gluck, for example, in a remarkable 1990 article, surveys popular Japanese images of their history since the year 1926. She describes how that period is divided sharply between its first twenty and its last forty-five years. Japanese historians traditionally periodize the national past in terms of the reigns of emperors. With the death of Emperor Hirohito in 1989, the Showa period (1926–89) ended. But, as darkness divided from light, events split the period in two. With the eager collaboration of their American occupiers, politicians and people in postwar Japan suddenly severed themselves from the disasters of the war, adopting, like many Germans, the notion that 1945 was "zero hour," the time of an utterly new national start. The name of the new start, preferred by both victors and vanquished, was *democracy*. It was, in eyes of most Americans, an incredibly quick change. Subject to the imperial authority of an American general, the vanquished quickly adopted the governmental forms of the victors, some of whom wondered: How could the Japanese people become overnight such willing political partners and imitators of the people who bombed their cities?

The answer, as Professor Gluck eloquently demonstrates, lay partly in the ease with which Japanese culture permits its people to lay to rest eras of suffering, to close their eyes to an evil past, and to envision new futures. One element in the permission is common to many another culture: "Let the dead bury their dead."[86] But another is a habit of mind in great tension with the culture that sustains democracy: delegate the blame for great catastrophe to "them" while "we" cope with it only as its victims. In empathy for this point of view, an American has to concede that an authoritarian society cultivates just this habit among its citizens, a fact abundantly clear in recent histories of Germany and Japan. If the experience of membership in some "loyal opposition" is rare in one's life, what else is politics but something that "happens," and what other voice does one have in politics but a passive voice? Hence the Japanese facility for assuming that guilt for the evils of the war could be projected on to a few leaders, if not exclusively on to the emperor himself:

> Culpability was accepted from the first [in 1945] in that "the reckless war" was confronted as unjust and catastrophic. Responsibility was sought and found in the military, who with the collusion of the bureaucracy, big business, and the landlords, laid a grid of domestic oppression and military aggression across Japan and much of Asia. In 1946 the first postwar history textbook stated that "the Japanese people suffered terribly from the long war. Military leaders suppressed the people, launched a stupid war, and caused this disaster." In 1975 a popular version read: "The Pacific war—a war of peculiar savagery which Japan could have avoided if only its armed forces

had kept away from politics." Had things been that simple, and inevitable, the burdens of Showa history would be light indeed.[87]

The great mass of the people, in this version of their history, are victims, not agents; in that history, the passive voice dominates the narrative: the China War "was caused," Pearl Harbor "was bombed," and the atomic bomb "was dropped." The war crimes of seven leaders may have deserved their hanging by the Allied occupiers, but the masses had no part in the commission of those crimes. They could turn quickly from the sufferings of the past to the promises of the future.

But the turn may be all too quick, observes Professor Gluck, in tones that echo a western perspective as native to her historical craft as to my own.

> The contemporary issue here has to do with mastering the past. The victims' history repeated in the post-Showa retrospectives omitted a painful lesson of World War II since learned around the world: that it is not possible to wage a total war with 28, 280, or even 28,000 people and that the responsibility for war lies far more broadly in society than was earlier believed, or hoped. . . . Even those who did not actively march or collaborate are now judged as participants. It takes both states and societies—which is to say the individuals who comprise them—to make a total war.
>
> By their own critics and those abroad, the Japanese are chastised for their amnesiac memory. Comparisons with Germany suggest that whereas the Germans remember Nazism, the Japanese remember the war, not the system that engendered it. The chronology of remembrance is also different. For years a quiet generation of Germans remained silent until a younger generation challenged public memory to confront the Nazi past in the 1960s. In Japan the confrontation was immediate in 1945, and the postwar reforms were deliberately constructed in the negative image of the prewar system. While this early mastery of the past had genuine institutional consequences, it also had disadvantages since it froze the condemnation of the war into orthodoxy at a stage when the division of villains and victims seemed starkly clear. Mastery remains an issue in both countries, as in others, and passivity and indifference erode the impulse to assume responsibility for history. Yet not to feel responsible for the past is not to feel responsible for the present. . . .[88]

The maxim to be drawn from all this is at once political, philosophical, and ethical: *You shall know them by their self-implication in their political memory.* You shall know the depth of their democratic habit by their willingness to assign widespread credit and blame for goods and evils in the past of their societies, and by their willingness to look for remnants of that past in their present.

Professor Gluck may exaggerate the degree to which the facts of massive human collaboration in total war have been "learned around the world." Americans, too, like to "skip the history lesson and get on with it." No large proportion of postwar-born Americans go out of their way to assert the contrary: "Let's look again at the history, or we may never get on to 'it'—a real change from the past."

The past from which change is so much needed in the modern world is *racism,* as the history of the Pacific war dismally demonstrates on both sides. Whether repentance for their traditional racism is occurring in depth in the life and culture of the Japanese people must remain an open question in the minds of many Americans and even more in the minds of many of the peoples of East and Southeast

Asia, whose suffering in the "Greater East Asian War" greatly exceeded that of the Americans.

The summer of 1993 saw some remarkable signs of groundshifts among officials and a growing number of younger Japanese, however; these shifts are promising preparation for a more honest 1995 fiftieth anniversary of the war's end in both the United States and Japan than either of us mounted for the commemoration of Pearl Harbor. In early August, about to depart from office in the wake of a revolt in the long-ruling Liberal Democratic party, Prime Minister Kiichi Miyazawa repeated his early 1992 "sincerest apology" to those Asian nations, especially Korea, hundreds of thousands of whose young women were abducted for the "comfort" of Japanese soldiers in every war zone.[89] But Mr. Miyazawa's successor, Morihiro Hosokawa, descendant of a prominent Samurai family, wrote a more radical page in the slim history of apology for the war when he said to reporters soon after taking office, "I myself believe that it was a war of aggression, a war that was wrong"—simple, direct words without precedent on the lips of any Japanese head of government.[90] A few days later, in his first official address to the Parliament, Mr. Hosokawa was more explicit yet: "I would thus like to take this opportunity to express anew our profound remorse and apologies for the fact that past Japanese actions, including aggression and colonial rule, caused unbearable suffering and sorrow for so many people."

Commented *The Economist* in early 1994: "The prime minister's apology for Japan's behavior in the second world war palpably reduced hostility in South Korea."[91] Responding cautiously to the address on American public television, James Fallows, editor of *The Atlantic* and a longtime student of Japanese culture, said that time would tell if the speech signaled an important change in that government's stance on the war. He warned that Americans have tended to overestimate the speed with which change occurs in Japan—but Ms. Ayako Doi, editor of *The Japan Digest*, pointed to the speech as emblem of generational differences in contemporary Japan:

> The people who grew up in the war and in post-war poverty are different from those who have grown up in the new Japan. . . . The older generation sees Japan as having been driven to the war. . . . The new generation should know that it is not sufficient for government alone to apologize and take responsibility for the war; the whole people should admit that they supported it.[92]

Here is new language indeed: an acknowledgement of citizen "responsibility spread thin," and a willingness of one generation to speak openly of the political sins of a previous one. Here is the start on a belated Japanese analogue to the post-1945 debates in Germany around these same concepts.

At least debate and these terms of debate have surfaced in Japan's public discourse. Chances are that a new generation of leaders does mean to "inform our children what their forefathers did in the past,"[93] as Japanese leaders perceive the benefits of even a few words of apology for their relations to their Asian neighbors. Among the channels of information will have to be school textbooks; as significant an index of change will be the $120 million war memorial museum now being planned by the government for the commemoration of the 1995 anniversary. Will it display Japan simply as victim or also as agent of wartime evils? The world can be sure that internal debate about that question will be flourishing in Japan even as the museum building goes up in 1994. One remarkable contribution to this new ferment came in August 1993 in a touring exhibition, under private sponsorship, that modeled vividly the medical experiments conducted by the Japanese military in Manchuria. The very existence of this project is astonishing.[94] As Gluck says: "[T]here is more to this moment of national memory than immediately meets the eye, just as there is more wide-ranging and contentious debate about the past in Japan today" than any viewer of its television in the eighties might conclude.[95]

While Americans watch for signs of cultural retreat from racism and historic amnesia in Japan, the Japanese have every reason to reciprocate. Which of the two societies has the most dismal record for racism and self-congratulating perception of its past? That question, in eyes looking across the Pacific from both sides, is worth long-term pursuit. Countries whose leaders mostly "bash" each other are in retreat from empathy into moralism and away from patient, repentant acknowledgement of painful political pasts. And they are generating dangerous new hostilities. In personal relations nothing works worse than self-righteousness. It works no better in politics.

Remembering Japanese Americans

What works much better is self-criticism and self-reform. And in at least one instance, consummated in the year 1988, Americans and their government demonstrated that they were capable of a degree of repentance for racism in their own national past in which observant Japanese have to be intimately interested: it is the case of American treatment of its own citizens of Japanese ancestry during the national crisis of 1941–45. The case is worth studying in detail, for it finally composed an ambiguously positive chapter in the checkered history of collective repentance and forgiveness in official America's dealing with the legacies of the Pacific war.

Exclusive Enmity and Empathy: Who Can Become American?

Like religion, the democratic philosophy of government proposes some norms for human behavior which seem to defy certain human proclivities. Though perhaps "created equal," humans affirm and exploit their inequality. Though they almost all participate in a culture, a family, and a political community of some kind, these vary enormously, and they all may provoke conflicts with other cultures, families, communities. It is not easy, in a debate on the subject, to prove that in the midst of all this variety that there persists a single "human nature." More to the practical political point, one great agony of the twentieth century centers on the ebb and flow in the scope and limits of the bonds of citizenship in particular regions and nations of the planet. In 1992 the awakening of slumbering ethnic loyalties and the shattering of various political states has become regular headline news: Yugoslavia, Somalia, the vast former Soviet Union. These phenomena should sober any moralist or political philosopher about the possibility that humans were ever intended to build a political order that excludes ethnic identity as relevant to the privileges of citizenship. Is it not one thing to dream about *e pluribus unum*, another to find an example of a country which embodies that dream politically? If racism and race-consciousness are so ordinary in the history of *homo sapiens*, why exclude them as principles of political inclusion and exclusion?

The United States of America has often laid claim to being a nation constructed on the rejection of such principles. Yet racist compromises to political equality are so notorious in American history that no observer can be blamed for concluding that few Americans really break with world patterns of preference for one's own "kind." The very Constitution of the country made peace with the principle of slavery and exclusive voting rights for men who owned land. Immediately, in the first year of the Republic, 1790, a new Congress passed an immigration law which restricted naturalized citizenship to "free white persons," thus expressing the reigning cultural expectation that the "New World" of America would be an extension of the European *white* world. Even as the Statue of Liberty was raised, in the centenary year of the Republic, the legislators of the land were closing the "golden door" of American citizenship to "tired . . . poor . . . huddled masses" from the "teeming shore" of Africa and Asia. The first federal law barring Chinese from American citizenship came in 1878. In successive legislation in 1882, 1892, and 1902, the Chinese Exclusion Act became tighter and tighter. In 1922 it was extended to the Japanese by the Supreme Court, and in 1924—the climax of racist law in the naturalization policies of the United States—Congress excluded all "Orientals" from citizenship.

The first legal break in this history was to come in 1943, when, in deference to the American alliance with Chiang Kai-shek, a Chinese person could at last become a U.S. citizen. Three years later, Filipinos made the list; finally, in 1952, the Japanese were accepted with passage of the McCarran-Walter Act. Soon afterwards a crowd of thousands of long-time Japanese-American residents stood in the Hollywood Bowl to recite their pledge of allegiance to the world's oldest constitutional democracy just as one of the world's youngest, Japan, was coming to be.

How these Japanese Americans finally arrived there with right hands upraised was a long story, but it is now a well-documented story likely to become standard in the nation's history books. Prodded by historians and the steady vocal demands of two Japanese American congressmen from California, the federal government in 1980 appointed its Commission on Wartime Relocation and Internment of Civilians, chaired by Joan Z. Bernstein and composed of eight other distinguished Americans.[96] Their report, delivered two years later and based on exhaustive archival research and interviews with 750 witnesses, was published in 1983 under the title *Personal Justice Denied*.[97]

Amid the deluge of government reports that flow from Washington into the libraries of Americans citizens, this one deserves a special place on the shelves. Written in studied historical detail, moral passion, and a spirit of collective repentance, it is a document which all Americans should celebrate. Herein are the reasons why a government must sometimes ask its citizens to face the wrongs it did in the past to some of their fellows, to repudiate the views of a one-time majority of citizens, and to accede to measures of restitution to victims of that majority's misguided patriotism. Before any critic of the democratic dream, as it has been compromised in the United States, dismisses that dream cynically, he or she would do well to read *Personal Justice Denied*. It is the story of how, belatedly but finally, a part of the American dream underwent national rehabilitation, proving that on occasion *governments* can repent.

"Racial Prejudice, War Hysteria, and Failure of Political Leadership"

Japanese Americans have memories of World War II not much shared by the majority of us, their contemporary neighbors. For example:

> On December 30, 1944, Sgt. Frank Hachiya parachuted behind enemy lines in the Philippines on an intelligence mission. As he was returning to the American lines, he was mistaken for a Japanese soldier and shot. He delivered the maps of the Japanese defenses he had captured. He died three days later.
>
> In the meantime, the American Legion post of his home town, Hood River, Oregon, had the names of 14 Japanese Americans, including Hachiya's, removed from the town's honor roll.
>
> When the Army announced that Hachiya was awarded the Distinguished Service Cross posthumously, it was an embarrassed town that restored the names.[98]

Just two weeks before his death, over 100,000 ethnic kin of Sergeant Hachiya had finally been officially released from three years of imprisonment as aliens dangerous to the American war cause. Without rehearsing here the whole history of their wartime ordeal, it is important for other native-born Americans like myself to dwell on certain details of the narrative if only to demonstrate the first rule of forgiveness in politics or any other human relation: face the facts of wrong before presuming to move beyond them. Face the complex of human decisions that produced the wrong, too.

Behind it, said the commission in 1982, lay three categories of error: war hysteria, racial prejudice, and failure of political leadership.[99] For those who have never been vulnerable to it, "wartime hysteria" may sound odd and exotic, but to Americans in 1942, hysteria had a certain plausibility. If "the Japs" could attack Honolulu, they could attack California—a view that some military leaders shared during the first six months of 1942. When that six months ended with the Battle of Midway, however, no sane military strategist still entertained the possibility that Japanese planes could reach San Francisco, not to speak of Japanese armies.

Behind the initial (and speedily discredited) military argument for excluding Japanese citizens from the West Coast, however,[100] lay the more influential forces of popular racial prejudices. In turn, those prejudices found reinforcement in political leadership, some of it at very high levels of the federal government. If anything is clear from the beginning of this tortured history, it is that democratic populaces exert real influence on democratic leaders. Less clear is how much those leaders reciprocate, especially by calling the attention of constituents to the fact that democracy consists of minority rights as well as majority power.

For many decades, political pressure for most of the nation's anti-Asian racist legislation had originated in the western states. To build railroads and to cut forests in the West, Chinese and Japanese workers might be admitted temporarily to the country, but the dominant white settlers of that region were clear that they should never become "real" Americans. By 1907 Californian economic interests had induced the U.S. Congress to ban the importation of Japanese laborers. In 1913, the state passed its Alien Land Law, forbidding Asians to own property in the state. (By an ironic coincidence, 1913 was the year in which British-ruled South Africa passed the first law in a series of laws that would allocate 88 percent of its most fertile farmlands exclusively to white ownership.)

Added to this long preparation of a majority of West Coast whites for rejecting the idea that Japanese immigrants or their children could ever become true Americans, Pearl Harbor solidified this prejudice with additives of patriotism and morality. Having long tried to exclude Asians from economic and political privilege, the organized promoters of racist legislation in the coastal states now had all the reason they needed to tell the public and its elected leaders: "We told you so." Hysteria, prejudice, and political power now combined to move a majority of 130 million Americans to promote, support, or passively consent to the removal of 120,000 persons—two-thirds of them native-born citizens[101]—into some ten internment camps scattered in remote areas of seven interior western states.

A prime promoter of this movement was Lt. General John L. DeWitt of the Western Defense Command, in whom the three arguments for internment coalesced in exquisite combination. He had the prejudice, the hysteria, and the power, and he used all of them in the first months of the war to persuade public and politician alike that people of Japanese ancestry should be removed immediately from his command— that is, from all three coastal states of the Union. In his considered recommendation to the Department of War (and thence to President Roosevelt) he stated the case for internment in blunt terms:

> In the war in which we are now engaged racial affinities are not severed by migration. The Japanese race is an enemy race and while many second and third generation Japanese born on United States soil, possessed of United States citizenship, have become "Americanized," the racial strains are undiluted. . . . That Japan is allied with Germany and Italy in this struggle is no ground for assuming that any Japanese, barred from assimilation by convention as he is, though born and raised in the United States, will not turn against this nation when the final test of loyalty comes. It, therefore, follows that along the vital Pacific Coast over 112,000 potential enemies, of Japanese extraction, are at large today. There are indications that these were organized and ready for concerted action at a favorable opportunity. The very fact that no sabotage has taken place to date is a disturbing and confirming indication that such action will be taken.[102]

Had the success of the general's recommendation been less prompt, its deductive, speculative, and paranoid character might have been grist for popular humor. But there was little humor in the wartime atmosphere of American society at the moment. The president of the United States soon followed with Executive Order 9066, which gave to General DeWitt the authority to remove from his command aliens of any nationality deemed dangerous to the national defense. The objects of the order were the West Coast Japanese, however, not Germans or Italians living there. Later historians would reflect on the case that could easily have been made for interning them, too: over a million aliens from those two enemy countries resided in the United States in 1942. First- and second-generation German Americans, all citizens, numbered about 8 million. Their numbers posed a great obstacle to sending *them* to camps, of course. The logistics would be formidable. More important, most of them were voters. Many had great influence in Washington, and some noncitizen refugee Ger-

mans and Italians were scholars, scientists, and other professionals of great distinction. Among them were the people whose theories would lead to the making of the
atomic bomb. Added to all this power was their membership in the white race.

Popular support for the proposal came massively from newspapers, citizens associations, and West Coast political leaders, perfecting their argument for Japanese
detention with the paternally benign, self-reinforcing prophecy that, if these dangerous aliens were not taken into "protective" custody, their lives and limbs would be
in danger from hostile white neighbors. Indeed, local and state politicians pushed
for the issuing of Executive Order 9066 over against a significant number of high-
level federal officials who knew from the first that the military, legal, and constitutional bases for the measure were weak or nonexistent. Among the early critics were
J. Edgar Hoover (it was, said he, a move from "public and political pressure rather
than factual data") and the attorney general of the United States, Francis Biddle (who
advised the president and others that the war notwithstanding the laws and the Constitution protected citizens against unprovoked arrest).[103] Among the early supporters of the policy were prominent Americans who within a decade would become more
prominent yet and who would live to confess their collaboration in a large injustice:
Secretary of War Henry L. Stimson ("this forced evacuation was a personal injustice"), Supreme Court Justice William O. Douglas (the evacuation "was ever on my
conscience," for he had joined a majority ruling of the high court in deeming the act
constitutional), and future Chief Justice Earl Warren (who in 1942 was on the verge
of running for governor of California. "I have since deeply regretted the removal
order and my own testimony advocating it, because it was not in keeping with our
American concept of freedom and the rights of citizens"[104]).

Responsibility—guilt—for the collective wrong about to be done was thus widely
shared. The morally important point for late-century Americans to remember is that
not only did high officials fail to obey laws 1½ centuries old in the republic but masses
of citizens furnished the "democratic" political fuel for this official failure. Right up
into late 1944, Executive Order 9066 went its unjust way, imposing extra months of
virtual imprisonment on Japanese citizens because an American president, advised
since the springtime that the exclusion orders were no longer justified, wanted to be
sure of votes in California in the presidential election of November. Roosevelt accompanied this latter use of his power with the suggestion that "for the sake of internal quiet" of the country the current camp residents might be distributed throughout
the United States, "one or two families to each county as a start"![105] To the credit of
the military profession, the successor to General DeWitt in the Western Defense
Command, C. H. Bonesteel, communicated to the president his opinion that there
was no realism and little law on the side of the "distribution" plan. People tend to
like to return *home,* he said; and in fact "if they are not returned a very large number
of them will bring legal action to accomplish it."[106] It was a nice display of elementary, ordinary empathy for fellow humans: they will want to go home. Unfortunately,
in the heat of the affair, such empathy was not ordinary but rare.

There is much to be learned here about how democracy works in America
and how it may fail to work; but the chief lesson is that the "power elite" is not
solely responsible for the failures. Ordinary voters had their large part in concocting
the injustice. If, as would one day happen, the U.S. government were to repent

of the whole incident, it would have to do so in the name of many a nameless citizen.

That other side of practical democratic protection from prejudice and its demagoguery—organized citizen counterprotest—was not wholly absent in those early 1942 months, but it was sporadic and slow to achieve public voice. The president of the University of California, the Federal Council of Churches, a number of other church bodies, and a few labor leaders protested and would continue to do so in the next three years. The single largest public demonstration of opposition came on February 19, 1942, when a thousand members of the United Citizens Federation gathered in Los Angeles to protest the exclusion. Earlier that very day the president had signed Executive Order 9066. The wheels were rolling toward "the first instance in American history when ethnicity alone defined a group of Americans who were to be incarcerated behind barbed wire."[107]

"We Departed for an Unknown Destination"

The story of the three-year ordeal of the camps endured by 120,000 people of Japanese ancestry has finally been told at length in books and other documents that came to prominence in the wake of the 1982 Commission Report. Books like this one have every reason to defer to this documentation: "See, for details. . . ." But the details, however redundant for some scholars of the subject, are worth repeating far and wide by others. Certain human sufferings will always be too deep even for the most careful reports from persons who endured them; a fortiori, those who merely read the reports can hardly pretend that they fully understand the experiences behind them. But these sufferings are too important—especially if they are not to recur—not to be remembered repeatedly. What Japanese Americans suffered as evacuees in World War II may not have been as terrible as the experiences of other thousands of people in the war, but accurate memory of their particular experience requires that some of the details survive in the consciousness of their contemporary American neighbors if the latter are to be better neighbors than were their predecessors. Empathy for real enemies requires as much; empathy for unreal, falsely accused "enemies" requires even more.

A sample of the details might include the following excerpts from the commission's interviews of 750 survivors of the camps and their descendants:

> What I remember most was my father who had just purchased a Fordson Tractor for about $750 a few months prior to the notice.
> Imagine his delight, after a lifetime of farming with nothing but a horse, plow, shovel, and his bare hands, to finally be able to use such a device. He finally had begun to achieve some success. A dream was really coming true.
> He had much to look forward to. Then came the notice, and his prize tractor was sold for a measly $75.

> *   *   *

> By the middle of May, when the valley folks were sent to the assembly center, the telephone peas were waist high and strung, the pole beans were staked, early radishes and green onions were ready for the market, strawberries were starting to ripen and the lettuce had been transplanted.

Not much is known about how the crops fared in the harvest nor what prices were obtained, but the Issei farmers went into camp with their heads held high, knowing that they had done everything that was possible to help our nation face its first summer of World War II.[108]

*   *   *

It is difficult to describe the feeling of despair and humiliation experienced by all of us as we watched the Caucasians coming to look over our possessions and offering such nominal amounts knowing we had no recourse but to accept whatever they were offering because we did not know what the future held for us.

People who were like vultures swooped down on us going through our belongings offering us a fraction of their value. When we complained to them of the low price they would respond by saying, "you can't take it with you so take it or leave it. . . ."

*   *   *

I went for my last look at our hard work. . . . Why did this thing happen to me now? I went to the storage shed to get the gasoline tank and pour the gasoline on my house, but my wife. . . . said don't do it, maybe somebody can use this house; we are civilized people, not savages.[109]

*   *   *

On May 16, 1942, my mother, two sisters, niece, nephew, and I left . . . by train. . . . We took whatever we could carry. So much we left behind, but the most valuable thing I lost was my freedom.

*   *   *

Henry went to the Control Station to register the family. He came home with twenty tags, all numbered 10710, tags to be attached to each piece of baggage, and one to hang from our coat lapels. From then on, we were known as Family #10710.

*   *   *

On May 16, 1942 at 9:30 a.m., we departed . . . for an unknown destination. To this day I can remember vividly the plight of the elderly, some on stretchers, orphans herded onto the train by caretakers, and especially a young couple with 4 pre-school children. The mother had two frightened toddlers hanging on to her coat. In her arms she carried two crying babies. The father had diapers and other baby paraphernalia strapped to his back. In his hands he struggled with duffle bag and suitcase. The shades were drawn on the train for our entire trip. Military police patrolled the aisles.

*   *   *

At the entrance [of the camp] . . . stood two lines of troops with rifles and fixed bayonets pointed at the evacuees as they walked between the soldiers to the prison compound. Overwhelmed with bitterness and blind with rage, I screamed every obscenity I knew at the armed guards daring them to shoot me.[110]

The last witness, William Kochiyama, was one of those Japanese evacuees for whom some U.S. government officials had a certain ready empathy: it was to be expected, was it not, that after long ostracism and now internment most of these people would want to reject U.S. citizenship and return to Japan one of these days? Try, as some of them had, to demonstrate that deep down they wanted to be Americans, surely they would now revert to being just what General DeWitt said they were: "A Jap is a Jap." They would go home, all right—to Japan.

The statistics tell another, amazing story of how few among 120,000 residents of the internment camps fulfilled the general's tautology. Not only was no Japanese American of the first or second generation ever convicted of espionage, but, before December 1944, 5,000 had accepted the chance to work on farms, 4,300 had become students at American colleges, and 1,208 had become members of the U.S. Army along with 33,000 other Nisei (principally from Hawaii, which had a large Japanese population and no camps). In the first year of camp life, only 2,255 of the 120,000 had requested repatriation to Japan. The next two years of camp experience, however, did produce a large increase in the number who expressed a desire to return to Japan— 16 percent of the total, some 20,000. Again, this was rage and alienation which aggressive Americans could understand. Not so easy for them to understand was the eventual retreat of the majority of these disaffected camp dwellers from their expressed wish to become citizens of Japan. After the war, most tried to withdraw their renunciation and were permitted by U.S. courts to do so in 1948. Eventually only 8,000, or less than 7 percent, of the 120,000 would return to Japan. "They just threw back their citizenship at us," said Edward Ennis, head of the Alien Enemy Control Unit. "This was a perfectly honest expression of what they felt."[111] The astonishing question was why did they not throw it back in much larger numbers? After three-quarters of a century of being told legally and now violently that they were not wanted in America among its citizens, why did they still covet the privilege? Some Americans, especially those untroubled by the experience of racial persecution, may look at the 7 percent figure with no sense of surprise, but this requires a kind of arrogance that assumes, "Sure, everyone wants to be an American." That some want to be in spite of what they have experienced from so-called "real" Americans remains one of the mysteries of a kind of patriotism in which many Japanese Americans obviously excelled. What hurt him the most, said one first-generation father, "is the fact that my children's loyalty to their own country is questioned!"[112] Internees like this man were mustering continued devotion to a country that was grossly mistreating them. By a large majority, they exhibited a capacity for loyalty that survived suffering at the hands of those who oppressed them in the name of that very same loyalty. This is the truth that must be put in sober counterbalance to the sad reflection of the commissioners that the deprivations and indignities of the camps left 16 percent of the evacuees bitter toward the United States.

> No other statistics chronicle so clearly as these the decline of evacuees' faith in the United States. In the assembly and relocation centers, applications to go to Japan had been one of the few nonviolent ways to protest degrading treatment. During three years of rising humiliation, 20,000 people chose this means to express their pain, outrage and alienation, in one of the saddest testaments to the injustice of exclusion and detention. The cold statistics fail, even so, to convey the scars of mind and soul many carried with them from the camps.[113]

And they carried these scars for the rest of their lives.

The Road to Apology and Restitution: A Government Can Repent

The internment of Japanese Americans stemmed from failure of all levels of the system to protect a minority from colossal injustice. The legislatures, the Congress, the governors, the president, the courts, the political parties, the ordinary voters, and the constitutional writs of the land—by active or passive collusion—all failed here as democratic institutions.

The internment "incident" tells us much about how human societies behave at war. Ignored or superseded by alleged overriding necessity were those democratic values for which the war was supposedly being fought. Among the ironies of the event was a proposal in October 1942 to President Roosevelt, from Elmer Davis, director of the Office of War Information, that loyal Nisei citizens be permitted to volunteer for the military in order to counter current Japanese propaganda in Southeast Asia "that this is a racial war." In early 1943 government adopted the proposal, and in announcing it Roosevelt took high democratic ground:

> No loyal citizen of the United States should be denied the democratic right to exercise the responsibilities of his citizenship, regardless of his ancestry. The principle on which this country was founded and by which it has always been governed is that Americanism is a matter of the mind and heart; Americanism is not, and never was, a matter of race or ancestry.[114]

Where had this presidential rhetoric been one year before? How might it have stemmed the racist flood that was to carry 120,000 Americans of Japanese ancestry, loyal almost to the person, off to desert camps? In early 1942, the president should have listened more carefully to voices like those in his own administration who, as this second year of war came, were recalling government to the task of leading and not just following the majority of its citizens. John J. McCloy, assistant secretary of war, urged this stance when in April 1943 he wrote to General DeWitt that it was time to consider how to return the majority of evacuees to their homes:

> That there is serious animosity on the West Coast against all evacuated Japanese I do not doubt, but that does not necessarily mean that we should trim our sails accordingly. The longer California luxuriates in the total absence of the Japanese the more difficult it will be to restore them to the economy of California. They have a place in California as well as in any other state as long as military considerations do not intervene. I cannot help but feel that social considerations rather than military ones determine the total exclusion policy.[115]

This was leadership. But it was not to prevail. Forgotten now were those precedents in the history of the republic when democratic institutions did pass the acid test of their staying power—the exigency of war. Toward the end of their moving report, the commission quotes such a precedent in the refusal of the Supreme Court to grant a victorious Union army the right to impose martial law on loyal border-state territory during the Civil War:

> When peace prevails, and the authority of the government is undisputed, there is no difficulty in preserving the safeguards of liberty; . . . but if society is disturbed by

civil commotion—if the passions of men are aroused and the restraints of law are weakened, if not disregarded—these safeguards need, and should receive, the watchful care of those entrusted with the guardianship of the Constitution and laws. In no other way can we transmit to posterity unimpaired the blessings of liberty.[116]

Institutions that fail to live up to their principles are fortunate if the principles nonetheless persist. Then, like the Prodigal Son, they can "come to themselves"[117] in suitable forms of repentance. Like *forgiveness*, the word *repentance* falls from most western lips in reference to the crimes and the reformation of individuals. Rare as it may be in politics, however, there is such a thing as the repentance of institutions. With a pride that may counter some of the shame which most Americans should experience in recollecting the history sketched here, we can gratefully remember just such a rarity: what the United States government finally did to rectify some of the damage it had inflicted on Japanese-Americans during World War II.

The process took over forty years. Even as the war was coming to its terrible finish, tributes to the fighting abilities of Japanese American combat infantry in Italy and France multiplied; as he presented the Presidential Unit banner to the 442nd Regimental Combat Team, President Harry S. Truman saluted the fact that these remarkable Nisei soldiers "fought not only the enemy, but prejudice."[118]

The fight for restorative justice was just beginning for this much abused group of Americans. By 1948 those who had suffered large property losses from their internment put forward conservative claims for $148 million in reparations, only to be granted a stingy $37 million by the Congress.[119] Next came presidential pardons for internees who had refused the draft or renounced American citizenship; then, the McCarran-Walter Act of 1952, which rectified a century-old racist immigration law, although not abolishing quota preferences for Europeans. The latter change would finally pass Congress in 1965.

In the meantime, thousands of internees were reestablishing their family, economic, and community lives in various parts of the country. Some among them followed a traditional Japanese inclination to let the most painful parts of the past remain unspoken, even in family conversation. In their hearings in 1981, reported the commission, "It became obvious that a forty-year silence did not mean that bitter memories had dissipated; they had only been buried in a shallow grave." As the third-generation son of one interned family testified: "When I first learned of the internment as a youth, I found that it was a difficult matter to discuss with my parents. . . . My feeling was that there was much more to their experience than they wanted to reveal. Their words said one thing, while their hearts were holding something else deep inside." It was, said Dr. Tetsuden Kashima of the University of Washington, a matter of "social amnesia . . . a conscious effort . . . to cover up less than pleasant memories."[120]

But many of the internees and their midcentury-born children were not about to forget their wartime internment. Organized into the Japanese American Citizens League (JACL) and helping to elect representatives and a senator to Congress, some began to press a new generation of politicians toward acts of public apology, compensation, and symbolic forms of restitution. American government has been little used to such measures although it could confidently urge them upon its defeated opponents Germany and Japan. In a stroke of high symbolism, these efforts first bore fruit in the Bicentennial Year of the Declaration of Independence in the proclamation "The American Promise," by President Gerald R. Ford, officially revoking Executive Order 9066, which no American court had yet declared illegal. The language of the president must have brought tears of satisfaction to some now elderly former evacuees: the date of the proclamation was February 19, 1976.

> In this Bicentennial Year, we are commemorating the anniversary dates of many of the great events in American history. An honest reckoning, however, must include a recognition of our national mistakes as well as our national achievements. Learning from our mistakes is not pleasant, but as a great philosopher once admonished, we must do so if we want to avoid repeating them.
>
> February 19th is the anniversary of a sad day in American history. . . .
>
> We now know what we should have known then—not only was that evacuation wrong, but Japanese-Americans were and are loyal Americans. . . .
>
> . . . Because there was no formal statement of its [Executive Order 9066's] termination, however, there is concern among many Japanese-Americans that there may yet be some life in that obsolete document. I think it appropriate, in this our Bicentennial Year, to remove all doubt on that matter, and to make clear our commitment in the future.
>
> NOW, THEREFORE, I GERALD R. FORD . . . do hereby proclaim that all the authority conferred by Executive Order No. 9066 terminated upon the issuance of Proclamation No. 2714, which formally proclaimed the cessation of the hostilities of World War II on December 31, 1946.
>
> I call upon the American people to affirm with me this American Promise—that we have learned from the tragedy of that long-ago experience forever to treasure liberty and justice for each individual American, and resolve that this kind of action shall never again be repeated.[121]

It was an official apology. It added impetus to the move of the Congress, four years later, to appoint a commission to review the history of the internment and make recommendations for further reparation that might be due, symbolically and materially, to the survivors and their immediate descendants. In September 1987, against threat of veto by a president who had been governor of California, the House of Representatives passed the bill that, with Senate approval, was to become the Civil Liberties Act of 1988. The bill contained a formal congressional apology for the internments, authorized a fund of $1.2 billion for payments of $20,000 each to the 60,000 or more internees still alive in 1988, and established a foundation of $50 million for the promotion of the cultural and historical concerns of Japanese Americans. Soon after, the Civil Rights Division of the Department of Justice set up an Office of Redress Administration to begin the process of locating survivors of the camps.

It was an example of "special-interest legislation" that was special indeed. Two Japanese American congressmen from California, Norman Y. Mineta and Robert T. Matsui, who with the JACL had lobbied for the bill, had been interned with their families as children. House Speaker James Wright lauded the measure, passed on September 17, bicentennial of the day in 1787 when final draft of the U.S. Constitution was signed in Philadelphia: "I can think of no finer way to celebrate the signing of the Constitution than to rectify this wrong." White House staff, in saying why President Reagan opposed the bill (which he eventually signed), pointed out that an apology to the evacuees was already on the record (through President Ford) and that Congress had long ago made its restitution payments of 1948. In the debates on the House floor, a California Republican congressman, Dan Lungren, urged that the bill consist only of the apology and the education fund. Restitution, he said, suggests "the misguided notion that the dollar sign is the only sign of contrition." (Two California counties, Los Angeles and San Francisco, had already disagreed with Mr. Lungren by providing payments of $5,000 to evacuees who had lost their civil service jobs during their internment.[122]) In reply, supporters said that $20,000 was itself only token compensation for losses of property, income, career, and other suffering for which no amount of money could ever compensate.[123] Apology and reparation needed each other if neither was to be cheap. Together both served political "contrition." In October 1990 President George Bush sent a letter with each $20,000 check that combined the apology side of the affair with a sense of tragedy and an assertion of American ideals:

> A monetary sum and words alone cannot restore lost years or erase painful memories; neither can they fully convey our Nation's resolve to rectify injustice and to uphold the rights of individuals. We can never fully right the wrongs of the past. But we can take a clear stand for justice and recognize that serious injustices were done to Japanese Americans during World War II.
>
> In enacting a law calling for restitution and offering a sincere apology, your fellow Americans have, in a very real sense, renewed their traditional commitment to the ideals of freedom, equality, and justice. You and your family have our best wishes for the future.[124]

The response of the Japanese American community was quiet triumph. As Mamoru Maji of Hood River, Oregon, had said on the publication of the *Commission Report* in 1983, "It is a gratifying feeling that we have that some of the wrongs are recognized." Who could know or recognize all of them? Nothing in human affairs embodies perfection; public repentances are always flawed. But Grace Uyehara, president of the JACL, saluted H.R. 442 with words ancient in the American political creed: "Their votes show that civil rights violations are taken seriously, and that amends go beyond mere apology. . . . H.R. 442 affects all Americans."[125] In his published account of his youthful experience of the internment, Joseph Kitagawa echoed the same view: by this act of official apology and restitution, "America redeemed equality and freedom, which were robbed not only from persons of Japanese ancestry, but also from all Americans."[126]

Not all Americans were happy with this belated governmental repentance. Representing the unhappy, in a letter published in parallel with Ms. Uyehara's by the *New York Times*, were the bitter words of a resident of the borough of Queens in New York City, who repeated the old justifying arguments for the internment—the crimes of the Japanese armies, the "close ties to Japan" of many of the evacuees, and the principle "that a country does what it must in war to survive and win—there is no second chance."[127] Two years later, in August 1990, California Assemblyman Gil Ferguson introduced a resolution in the state legislature calling for a revision of public school textbooks claims that the 1942–45 internments were motivated by "race prejudice," not by military necessity. The resolution also called for the use of the term *relocation centers* rather than *concentration camps*. The happy news was that the Ferguson resolution failed by a vote of 60 to 4; the unhappy news was the belief of eminent Japanese Americans like Kitagawa that "similar attempts will no doubt be repeated in the future" of American political history.[128]

"Errors not to be repeated": every national history is full of them. Will the United States ever repeat this one? In spite of law, court decisions, and public ritual, no one can say for sure. All barriers to the repetition are fragile; they hold at bay forces too perennial in human affairs to be considered permanently under lock and key. The Furies of revenge still slumber somewhere, and the demons of racism too. Humane politics is about keeping awake "the better angels of our nature," as Lincoln said. But such wakefulness requires that "slow boring of hard boards" by which Max Weber described politics as a vocation. In that vocation, every citizen of a democracy has a role to play.

Destroy democracy in war, and it may be hard to revive in peace: Americans had a brush with that sober truth in the 1940s. But American government did revive democratic justice in relation to Japanese Americans in the 1980s. Imperfect as the repentance was, it was a great improvement on the political temptations of "social amnesia." Neither in personal nor political contexts is any human repentance ever quite complete. That is one of the gaps which forgiveness fills, especially the forgiveness that consists in the willingness of offended people to resume neighborly relations with the offenders.

The Still Waiting Occasions

At the end of World War II, as they returned to their California and other neighborhoods, Isseis, Niseis, and Sanseis of the camps were coming back to neighborhoods densely infected with continuing racial prejudice. The process of repentance among some of those neighbors must have been slow and sometimes invisible. But war had quickened the process. Mitsuo Usui testified to this fact to the commission at its meeting in Los Angeles in 1981:

> Coming home, I was boarding a bus on Olympic boulevard. A lady sitting in the front row of the bus, saw me and said, "Damn Jap." Here I was a proud American soldier, just coming back with my new uniform and new paratrooper boots, with all my campaign medals and awards, proudly displayed on my chest, and this? The bus driver upon hearing this remark, stopped the bus and said, "Lady apologize to this American soldier or get off my bus." She got off the bus.
> Embarrassed by the situation, I turned around to thank the bus driver. He said that's okay, buddy, everything is going to be okay from now on out. Encouraged by his comment, I thanked him and as I was turning away, I noticed a discharge pin on his lapel.[129]

It is easy to prove that "everything" was not going to be "okay" with Japanese Americans in any of the years following 1945, not to speak—yet—of other minorities in the country who emerged from the war cynically sure that "liberty and justice for all" was an American myth. As Mr. Usui took off his uniform, restrictive housing covenants were still preventing him from moving into various Los Angeles neigh-

borhoods. The sufferings of the war had overwhelmed many of those same neighbors with their own bitter anti-Japanese memories, and still ahead was a revival of
the economic and political power of Japan itself, which was to face Americans right
into the 1990s with strong temptation to arouse their old racism from its slumbers.

At the end of his study of the Pacific war, Dower notes that the temptation afflicts
both sides again in the 1990s. As they flex their new economic muscle on the world
stage, "Many Japanese . . . attribute their impressive accomplishments to the unique
and ineffable spirit of the Yamato race." In response, in the competition-beset western democracies, old stereotypes rise publicly from whisper to mutter to open insult.
"In a poll conducted among Australian executives in October 1984 . . . a remarkable
89 percent stated that the Japanese were untrustworthy and unethical." Adds Dower:
"It is natural for the language of war to be applied to the battlefields of commerce."
Here the rhetoric is again that of World War II. In 1985, Ronald Reagan, beginning
to campaign for his second term, sought to clarify "two facts: First, we're still at war
with Japan. Second, we're losing." A U.S. senator called a Japanese decision to ex-
port more automobiles to the U.S. "an economic Pearl Harbor." Meanwhile, on the
thirty-eighth anniversary of the Hiroshima bomb, a prime minister of Japan made
the undiplomatic remark that "the Japanese have been doing well for as long as 2,000
years because there are no foreign races" in the country; and a paper of its defense
agency spoke of Japan's strength in its "one race, one state, and one language."[130]

Most certainly there are, in both the United States and Japan, more than enough
remnants of racism to worry citizens who yearn to move beyond the old horrible
history of wars without mercy. No easy moving on seems possible, and a distinc-
tively modern requirement for doing so is that the citizens of the two countries seek
each other's help. Japanese Americans won a significant fight with racial prejudice
inside the United States with the passage of the Civil Liberties Act of 1988. In the
future the people of Japan itself may have a role to play in helping Americans to dig
deeper yet into the roots of racial prejudice in the grounds of our own history. Americans may have a reciprocal role in Japan. As Carol Gluck wisely notes, "When it
comes to war, national history is clearly an international affair. Revising one's history is one thing; revising another country's history is something else altogether."
But that something else may now belong to the ongoing responsibility of citizens for
each other's understanding of how their mutual pasts should and should not shape
their mutual futures. We will better understand ourselves, says Gluck, if we look
together at the histories that have bound us together. "There are elements of international remembrance, such as imperialism and the holocaust, which by now belong
both within and across the narratives of a single country's past." The Germans and
the Poles are apparently learning that. The Americans and Japanese can learn similarly. We have similar choices: whether we will confront our pasts "with sober remembrance or resist with a forgetting born of arrogance and power." And we have
similar reasons to pay heed to words enshrined at the behest of the war victor in the
1947 constitution of Japan: "We believe that no nation is responsible to itself alone,
but that laws of political morality are universal."[131]

The most sober—and hopeful—form of international remembrance is forgiveness,
that long, many-sided, seldom-completed process of rehabilitating broken human
relationships. The evidence in this chapter suggests that the process has begun be-

tween the Japanese and the Americans, that it has a long journey ahead in both countries, that it is the opposite of forgetting, that it requires strong increases of intercultural empathy, and that it is still the power of recalling the reality of the past which delivers the present from the tyranny of the past. Trickles of forgiveness in the relations of the two countries have been fitful and often swallowed up by recurring tides of bitter memory. But the trickles are worth nourishing; they could become the benign wave of our mutual future.

Unknowingly, perhaps, certain participants in the fiftieth anniversary of Pearl Harbor brought the elements of forgiveness—judgment, forbearance, empathy, and renewed community—into a focus that punctuated the memory of a dark day with signs of change. Three months before the memorial event of December 7, 1991, Takashi Hiroaka, Mayor of Hiroshima, came to Honolulu to lay a wreath at the Arizona Memorial. A month before that, Robert I. Fiske, now a Honolulu resident who had been a Marine bugler aboard the battleship *West Virginia* on December 7, 1941, was on hand to guide visitors to the memorial. In the crowd was a Japanese tourist of his own generation who put his hand on Fiske's shoulder and said "in halting English, 'I am so sorry,' and broke into tears."

Said Fiske to a reporter: "The war's over now. Besides, my daughter married a Japanese boy, so what can I do?"[132]

Three forgiving citizens and one interethnic marriage do not a new international order make. But they signal some healing of huge, old hurts. The twenty-first century will need every bit of such healing if it is to recover from the sins of the twentieth.

6

Justice and Forgiveness: The Long Road to Equal Citizenship for African Americans

When I was told, it takes time, when I was young, I was being told it will take time before a black person can be treated as a human being here, but it will happen. We will help to make it happen. We promise you.[1]

James Baldwin

People, I just want to say, you know, can we all get along? . . . I mean, we're all stuck here for a while. Let's try to work it out.[2]

Rodney King

Either we learn a new language of empathy and compassion, or the fire this time will consume us all.[3]

Cornel West

On a streetcorner in Los Angeles at the height of the riots that rocked the city for three days in April 1992, a line of peaceful sidewalk protesters passed a young white man kneeling in the street. His hands were wrapped around a basketball, his face was creased with pain. Another young man, black, left the line of protesters, put his hands, too, on the basketball, and sought for a moment "to console him."[4] It was a gesture of empathy remarkable in the midst of any human conflict.

A long time would have to pass before Los Angeles and the United States were "consoled" for the deaths, the billion-dollar property destruction, and the wounded-wounding rage which this event deposited on the pages of recent American history.

Among other things, Los Angeles demonstrated that in modern urban America a majority of rioters are not necessarily black, nor do all of them come from the poorest of the poor. As for protests against injustice, Hispanic and Asian Americans can mount them, too. As for reason to despise one's neighbors, middle-class white Americans can find that, too, whether they indulge in looting or in contempt for looters.

We are a nation heading toward new levels of pluralism in our politics, our economy, and our culture. We are the world's largest immigrant nation. Traditionally we assume that immigrants start at the bottom of the social status hierarchy. We like to believe that, no sooner does some ethnic group establish itself as truly American, than another puts in its claim: Irish, Italians, and Jews in their turn; now Hispanics, then Asians. Ethnic pluralism means for us an unending, difficult exploration of the hypothesis that it is possible to build a nation from the nations and to do so through a porous class system in which many are ascending while few are descending in status. Demographers tell us that, by the middle of the twenty-first century, a majority of the population of the United States will no longer be descendants of white European ancestors. In this and many other countries of the future, contradictions to particularistic ethnic bases of political "belonging" will deepen. In newly urgent ways, humans will be asking themselves an old question: "Who is my neighbor?"[5]

This book has concerned *political* neighborhood, mutualities of citizenship. Who is my fellow citizen with whom I must deal, even if antagonistically?—also an old question. Rodney King, believed by many Americans to have been maltreated by the police and the courts of his city, had his own tenuous answer to this question. "We're all stuck here a while. Let's try to work it out." There is politics in this "we"— and tenuous hope for the American future.

The Oldest American Civic Injustice

The hopes and behaviors associated with shared civic membership are the ingredients of political culture. Nothing is more crucial in that culture than its open and hidden answers to the question: "Who can belong, who cannot, to this political order?" Various qualifications to the simple answer—"anyone"—have littered the political history of the United States: you must be male, of age, a property owner, literate in English, native-born, healthy, professionally skilled, employable, quota-eligible, innocent of crime, a refugee from political persecution, a resident for five years, able to answer a hundred questions about American history and government—all these have functioned historically to restrict the number of people on whom the rights of U.S. citizenship could legally be conferred. Left out of this list, however, is its most notorious item: *race*, the oldest, most intransigent functioning bar to citizenship in the history of the country.

One should remember that the truly original issue of multiethnic political relation came with the meeting on these shores of Europeans with Native Americans. The latter were the first to face the new, modern issue of whether immigrants can or should become members of an earlier established society. Many Native Americans today ruefully tell stories of the tradition of hospitality in their cultures on grounds of which their ancestors welcomed the first Europeans to set foot in this, a "New World" to them. Whether more isolated human tribes are models of hospitality to foreigners, anthropologists will have to tell us. For the moment it is critical to any humanistic perspective on modern politics to remember that the United States from 1789 on had in its midst 2 million descendants of *unwilling* immigrants. Their residence on the continent was as old as that of most of the ancestors of the authors of the Constitution.

Their presence was long-established; the definition of their civic status was older yet. Long ago human societies invented the notion of "slave," a notion that Columbus and others imported into their New World. As the Anglo-Saxon victors of the American Revolution began to shape the constitution of their new political order, however, the concept "slave" had acquired an intransigent, particularistic adjective: "black." The equations, "slave=black" and "black=noncitizen" were to become the greatest of all the corrupters of the new democratic order of the United States of America.

Sociologist Orlando Patterson has documented the intellectual-institutional nature of slavery exhaustively in his book *Slavery as Social Death*.[6] Not only the West but every continent has a history of this institution, a fact that excuses neither slave-selling African chiefs nor European captains of slave ships waiting off the coast of Ghana. Defined as a sheer instrument of another's will, a slave is a thing to be manipulated in the interest of "its" owner. Essential to this definition, says Patterson, is a polar political opposite—citizenship, acceptance into a status of membership in the society in which some "honor" can be ascribed or achieved in the company of one's fellows. Slavery is a status which, even after its occupant has been legally freed, often clings to his or her reputation and descendants. Coming "up from slavery" is no simple matter in any historical society. Its prejudices feed on the pasts of its members, burdening them with the status of their ancestors.[7]

The preposition *up* is right for the postliberation social journey of a slave, for humans have never invented a more rock-bottom status for their fellows than slavery. Says Patterson:

> To the aristocrats who controlled the rules of the honor game, [even] elite slaves were always contemptible and inassimilable isolates and outsiders. True honor is possible only where one is fully accepted and included, where one is considered by one's potential peers as wholly belonging. This the elite slave never achieved—even, astonishingly, when he himself was a monarch. . . . His marginality made it possible for him to be used in ways that were not possible with a person who truly belonged.[8]

"Truly to belong": that is what *citizenship* means in a root sense. It is what Martin Luther King, Jr., summarized as the overall purpose of the civil rights movement on the day of the 1963 March on Washington: "a quest to get into the mainstream of American society."[9] It is what the United States early denied to humans who were not "free white men" in the first naturalization law of the Congress in 1790 under a Constitution which had just installed slavery as a legal institution. So, not just black immigrants, but the nation itself had a long way to go "up from slavery." Many others were also excluded from full rights of citizenship in this 1790 America—the landless and, in particular, all women. But the two adjectives *free white* formed a unique double lock on the door to citizenship for one group of residents in the new country: they excluded *slave black*—terms that applied to some 17 percent of the human beings living in the young United States.

Perhaps nothing illustrates the power of socially enforced *definitions* of human being so critically as does the history of slavery: here the *idea* is everything, even when it is overlaid by various pragmatic, customary softenings of its exclusionary hard core of meaning. Already, from the Declaration of Independence to the doubts of a Jefferson about its compatibility with slavery to the troubled moral conscience of some southern planters, there were forces for the softening. But the core was always there, a "place" for black Americans uniquely subordinate to the place of other Americans present and future:

> As Genovese and others have shown, as long as black Americans "knew their place" they were paternalistically, sometimes even lovingly, accepted as "our people" by the master class and their associates. But even while knowing their place, they were ruthlessly excluded from what European sociologists of the twenties, and more recently Daniel Bell, have called "the public household"—all those areas of society where power is competed for and status and honor are claimed, conferred, and accepted.[10]

In his most striking theory, Patterson believes that the institution of slavery was the backdrop, the thesis that brought to human awareness—in slaves and in their owners—the concept of its antithesis: *freedom*. To be free is to be an agent of one's own life and a participant in give-and-take relations with other human beings. To be enslaved is to be denied both self-definitions.

Modern Americans of every ethnic background are likely to wonder how slavery could have been tolerated intellectually or institutionally on these shores. An account of how and why it was tolerated hardly belongs here; suffice it to note that the contradiction between slavery and the liberal democratic rhetoric of the Constitution writers cannot be remembered too often, because the legacy of that contradiction still haunts the relations of modern African Americans to other Americans, even to those of us who are overtly eager to count ourselves as fellow human beings and fellow citizens.

It is easy to demonstrate that slavery was a tap root of the greatest political tragedy of our history—the Civil War—-and that its legacy lingers in the continuing injustices which many African Americans experience in their daily existence in the 1990s. Not so easy to demonstrate is that, even as they suffer from this legacy, African Americans have made and are making their own contributions to the political culture of this land—still becoming democratic. The extrapolitical contributions, of course, are many—the average white American will think first of music and athletics. Less likely to be singled out by most whites is the note struck by Rodney King when he asked yearningly if Americans everywhere could just "get along." Two neighbors imaged the same yearning that week in April 1992 when one turned aside from his march for justice to console a grieving white holding a basketball. The contribution glimmering here is a persistent claim to humanity and citizenship alongside people who have long tried to deny them both. That contribution has much to do with an ethic for enemies: *the willingness to count oneself as neighbor and fellow citizen with enemies in spite of the latter's continuing resistance to reciprocating.* In the most practical sense this *is* forgiveness in politics: "We will be neighbors to you even while you are busy being unneighborly to us. We belong together, and one day you too will know it. We will persist until you do."

To the promising and astonishing evidence for thinking that this is the gift of their African American neighbors to the community of all Americans, let us turn.

An Early Civil Rights Movement: 1865

When they emerged from the Civil War legally free, 4 million former black slaves, with their forebears, had been physically a part of our society for almost 2½ centuries. During these centuries, English common law had defined them as disposable property, and as recently as 1857, the Dred Scott decision of the U.S. Supreme Court had confirmed the substance and the effects of that definition. Blacks experienced white people's politics from the margins, and many must have known that they were a bone of contention but not the central issue in the decision of two governments to go to war in 1861. As that war began, few prominent white officials on either side spoke openly about a future United States in which former slaves could enjoy the privileges of citizenship. Indeed, many had long been skeptical about such a future. In the 1840s, in a letter to Edward Everett, minister to Great Britain, U.S. Secretary of State Abel P. Upshur had speculated that, if equality between whites and blacks ever came in the States, one of the groups would have to move to another country "or be exterminated. This would be the slaves, because they are the weaker party." John C. Calhoun, the leading southern politician of the day, thoroughly agreed: "It is impossible for them to exist together in the community," he said, thus accurately implying a minimalist definition of true political existence.[11] Even Abraham Lincoln never affirmed a belief in the "social equality" of black and white Americans, but by the end of the Civil War he had concluded that legal equality must be instituted for former slaves.

In 1865, in short, everywhere in America black people faced "Not Wanted" signs, and thus they had few ordinary human reasons to anticipate citizenship as a consummation devoutly—or realistically—to be wished. Understandably, they might consent to staying in the country as long as they had no power to go anywhere else. But as for citizenship, who, as a slave, could be other than suspicious and resistant? Whites might assume that American citizenship was a privilege coveted by anyone worthy of being called human, but such an assumption would have been naive, obtuse, arrogant, and evidence of little empathy with the experience of oppression. A modern analogue of this is the difficulty that most American whites have in empathizing with separatist movements among Native Americans. If one's life experience of a white-majority society is full of bitter injustice, why should participation in that society be counted a pleasure or a privilege?

But there is another side to this lack of empathy for separatism, prefigured in the classic paranoid intuitions of slaveowners in the antebellum South. In spite of paternalistic "love" of masters for slaves, must it not be supposed that slaves everywhere were seething with rebellion drawn from endless reservoirs of hostility for centuries of suffering? Having lived closer to slavery than other whites, southern slaveowners exhibited here a level of human understanding that escapes some modern residents of suburban America who have never set foot in a black urban ghetto. As Vincent Harding notes, in his passionate history of the black civil rights movement, whites both northern and southern assumed this readiness to rebel right through to the Civil War. At war's end, rumors spread throughout the white South that the newly freed were on the verge of armed revolt. In South Carolina in the late fall of 1865, whites spread the word that "the negroes have an organized military force in all sections of the State, and are almost certain to rise and massacre the whites about Christmas time."[12] To label such fears as paranoid does little justice to the human psychology imaged in the myth of Cain. What is a more human response to violence than counterviolence? And what act in American history was more violent than slavery?

Such expectations among southern whites flew in the face of most of the prewar and wartime evidence. Armed revolts enough there had been to demonstrate that slaves yearned desperately to be free and could summon the courage to risk death for freedom, but overt vengefulness against white people had been rare. One might say, superficially, that the military odds did not favor the success of slave revolts. Why then did whites fantasize that the revolts would come? That guns and knives would soon appear in millions of black hands? Harding has his own answer: Deep down, whites knew that wild justice applied to them, too.

> Hidden among the fantasies and dreams, was there some fierce yearning for scourging, for unmediated justice to be raked across their lives and burned into the marrow of their beings by the black men and women whom they had so often, so carelessly, at times so harshly abused and destroyed? Would bloody resurrection against themselves have satisfied some necessity deeper than words and consciousness, something in them that searched frantically for the pathway back toward humanity and community?[13]

Much empirical evidence already pointed down a different pathway. That evidence should have occasioned surprise. The newly freed were apparently thinking about "a common destiny more hopeful, though more difficult, than mutual extermination. The persistent invitations were everywhere," invitations to a new political community by black people who expected to become citizens of a victorious Union, even though on their side most whites dreaded the new experience of sharing citizenship with former slaves.

Soon and unmistakably, in November 1865, that invitation sounded in Charleston, South Carolina. In the Zion Presbyterian Church, in the city where secession had been born, there met a "Colored People's Convention," some two thousand former slaves celebrating their new freedom in public opposition to a state legislature already at work imposing new legal inequalities on them. The document written at this convention was as astonishing for its political scope as it was tragic in its eventual massive rejection by the majority of white Americans, southern and northern. The declaration bore the title, "Address to the White Inhabitants of the State of South Carolina." One paragraph had the stamp of a Jeffersonian devotion to human rights, applied now to "millions of oppressed" worldwide.

> It is some consolation to know, and it inspires us with hope when we reflect, that our cause is not alone the cause of four millions of black men in this country, but we are intensely alive to the fact that it is also the cause of millions of oppressed men in other "parts of God's beautiful earth," who are now struggling to be free in the fullest sense of the word, and God and nature are pledged to their triumph.

But the most astonishing single note struck by this address was its claim to American identity "in the fullest sense of the word":

We are Americans by birth, and we assure you that we are Americans in feeling; and in spite of all the wrongs which we have so long and *silently* endured in this country, we can exclaim, with a full heart, "O America, with all thy faults we love thee still."

. . . We would address you—not as Rebels and enemies, but as friends and fellow-countrymen, who desire to dwell among you in peace, and whose destinies are interwoven and linked with those of the whole American people, and hence must be fulfilled in this country.[14]

Contemporary Americans of all races who do not resonate with astonishment at these words are historically unmusical. A blasé response, "Of course they wanted to be American citizens," does no justice to all the reasons they might not want to be, regardless of all the reasons they might not be permitted to be. Right down to 1993 an African American theologian spoke for many a colleague when he exclaimed, "If there is a black American who has never had the thought, 'I want out of this [country],' he grew up somewhere else!"[15] In Harding, as African American historian and analyzer of the politics of civil rights, the astonishment runs deep: "One can easily imagine the inner struggles which the black delegates had to wage in order to approve a document calling their former masters 'friends and fellow-countrymen.'" Here was a vision of the American civil community that transcended the vision of the Jeffersonians. Now the United States was to be a more inclusive national community than the majority of the Constitution makers assumed when they left Philadelphia in 1787.

It was a fearful dialectic, especially as the emerging Afro-Americans realised that if their vision prevailed, they must ultimately do the work of rebuilding in concert with the people who had been their legal owners, who had been the despoilers of their women, the breakers of their men, exploiters of their labour, murderers of their children, or a host of guilty bystanders. Still, at great inner cost they were calling for a new beginning—not forgetting the past, never forgetting it, but seeking to overcome it, to transform its meaning through the creation of a new future.

No more accurate description of forgiveness in politics is likely to be coined than this: "never forgetting the past, but seeking to overcome it, to transform its meaning through the creation of a new future" of civic relationship between wrong-sufferers and wrongdoers. At the end of the Charleston Colored People's Convention, after "animated debate," a special resolution passed making the reality of forgiveness in the document plain in every way but in use of the word:

As American chattel Slavery has now passed forever away, we would cherish in our hearts no malice nor hatred toward those who were implicated in the crime of slaveholding; but we would extend the right hand of fellowship to all; and would make it our special aim to establish unity, peace, and brotherhood among all men.

Harding's amazement again is boundless:

What manner of men and women were these? Refusing to flinch in the face of the past, attacking the criminal system which had bound them, they extended the "right hand of fellowship"—a distinctly Christian phrasing—to the former criminals, offering to build together a new society. . . . Whoever they were, however they managed to control the memories, fears, and anguish of the past, they were not fools, for among the rights they demanded was the right to "keep and bear arms."[16]

That right was classic among Americans, too.

Arms—and wars—settle a limited number of political questions. The leaders of that great hopeful Charleston meeting published their hopes rather than their fears that day, knowing very well that their future incorporation into the American body politic might be cruelly postponed. The process of the postponement—as it proceeded through the nineteenth into the twentieth century—cannot be traced here, but to be noted and underscored is a point often lost in discussions of human rights among libertarian and other Americans who have never been victims of gross social injustices: these recently freed men and women inserted into their ideology of freedom a facilitating virtue of forgiveness rare in the political rhetoric to which they were now heir. They countered the paranoia of their white neighbors with public foreswearing of revenge and public affirmation of intent to join the political community that had enslaved them, turning its own ideological tradition to their cause *and expanding its scope to include the likes of former slaves.* In this they were themselves the pioneers of a new, larger democracy than most of their historic neighbors had ever intended on this continent.

Is there, in the culture of a significant segment of African Americans a predisposition toward, an ingrained *gift* for, injecting forgiveness into their political relations with the white majority of this country? The Charleston Convention suggests that hypothesis. A century later other evidence accumulated in the work of the black-led civil rights movement of the period 1955–70. To that latter evidence I want to turn, but with a disclaimer: The idealization of any subgroup of humans always runs the risk not only of naivete and selective sifting of evidence but also of practicing sophisticated racism. Whom we degrade we may also idealize, and in both gestures we may deprive others of their true humanity. Among the "rights" that ought to be ascribed to any of our neighbors on earth ought to be the right to be as wrong, as imperfect, and occasionally as villainous as we may expect ourselves to be. In the movie *In the Heat of Night*, set in Mississippi, the black detective Tibbs patiently endures racist slurs from Sheriff Gillespie. One day a member of the local white elite slaps Tibbs for "insolence," and the detective slaps him back. The sheriff reacts with genuine surprise: "Why, you're just like us!" In effect, he is saying "You are tough, retaliatory, and ready to fight back, when all the while we thought you and 'your people' were models of forbearance." Ironically, the sheriff's remark betrays both ambivalence and contradiction: he is relieved to find out that a black man fights back, but he intuits something in African American culture that is different and not "like us." That difference found poignant expression in a 1985 essay by black writer Stanton Wormley, Jr., "Fighting Back." Once in 1970, he reported, he had refrained from fighting when provoked by a drunken white soldier. Again, in 1983, similarly provoked in a restaurant, he did fight back, instantly cowing his verbal assaulter. Later, the incident troubled him: "I had retaliated, and it felt good. But later, my exaltation passed, leaving a strange sensation of hollowness. . . . I realized that there was a trace of sadness in my knowledge that I, too, had learned to fight back."

Very striking in this essay is Wormley's generalization of his experience to world politics:

> I can't help feeling . . . that when one gains the ability to fight back one loses something as well. What that something is, I can't easily define: a degree of compassion, perhaps, or tolerance or empathy. It is a quality I hope is possessed by the men in Washington and Moscow who have the power to dispense the ultimate retribution.[17]

My surmise is that both of these incidents touch upon something real in the culture of African Americans that is discernibly different from the culture of large numbers of white Americans. To be sure, one can dismiss the singularity or importance of a certain conciliatory spirit among many black Americans by saying that it is a survival tactic to which all minorities resort. One can dismiss it as an instance of the "Stockholm effect" wherein political prisoners come to "love" their oppressors. One can even deplore it as simply one of the reasons why African Americans have been slow to inherit their democratic rights: they have substituted patience and neighborliness for aggression and separatism as pathways to power in this society. This last claim will get attention some pages hence, but for now my hypothesis and disclaimer come down to this: history equips every particular people with experience which, unwittingly perhaps, becomes their gift to host cultures. That is one reason why the "melting pot" image of the American dream is not only insulting to unique cultural traditions but is likewise a superficial dismissal of a major modern political problem. How does a nation open itself to the civic inclusion of people from other nations? How do its longer resident people learn to become neighbors to new peoples? The answer may be *not by pretending that all are destined to dissolve in a stew of anonymity but by discerning and preserving the gifts which each may bring to a new democratic mix.*[18] African Americans have had long centuries of learning to be Americans, but the legacies of slavery, segregation, and continued hampered opportunity have equipped many of them to speak in the American "public household" from some unique points of view.[19] Among the questions to which their American experience may have equipped them to speak is: What makes it possible for the politically excluded to include excluders in their own political vision and then to proceed politically to weaken the powers of exclusion? How do they relate now to their political enemies in ways that hold out the possibility that the latter may yet become their civic, political friends? In the mid–nineteen eighties the African American bishops of the American Roman Catholic church stated very clearly their belief that, partly out of their ancient roots in Africa and partly out of the legacies of slavery and segregation, the black Christians of America had such a gift to offer to America as a whole:

> Our contribution to the building up of the Church in America and in the world is to be an agent of change for both. . . .
>   Let us, who are the children of pain, be now a bridge of reconciliation. Let us, who are the offspring of violence, become the channels of compassion. Let us, the sons and daughters of bondage, be the bringers of peace. . . .[20]

White Americans, pondering words like these, may not at once grasp the implicit corollary. In white America's future the question is not, When in all respects will "they" become like "us"? But rather, How, in some respects, might "we" do well to become like "them"? The issue is what the terms *pluralism* and *multiculturalism* should mean in a democratic society if they do not mean merely "every culture for itself." Perhaps the really challenging, really threatening meaning is, "All have something to learn from the 'other.'"

What do other Americans have to learn from African Americans about an ethic for enemies? The civil rights movement of 1955–68 offers some instructive answers. So also does the history of the black power movement, which overlapped and complemented it. Compared with these, little in American history is as instructive about the scope and limits of forgiveness in politics.

Wholly Belonging: The Civil Rights Movement, 1955–68

The road to full membership in American society was to be longer, bloodier, and littered with more broken black lives than any participants in the Charleston Colored People's Convention could have anticipated. By a vast array of formal and informal exercises of majority power, white-dominated governments and other organizations were to assign African Americans to an inferior social status burdened with the legacy of slavery. This ongoing oppression is only too familiar to almost all Americans of the twentieth century. Legal segregation of public facilities, educational discrimination, economic intimidation, political disenfranchisement, lynchings, residential segregation, and media stereotypes so abounded in the post-1865 era that the children of the society, black and white, had much reason from birth to internalize the principle "Black is inferior." The damage done human beings by this conviction can probably never be calculated. One contribution of the civil rights movement of 1955–68 was its assault on the cultural power of this principle in political terms. If white Americans could not soon be delivered from this prejudice in their personal emotions and ideologies, the public props to it could at least be kicked down. Even that was to prove a long road, down which twenty-first-century Americans will still find themselves traveling. But thanks to the civil rights movement of the fifties and sixties, many a prop did fall, leaving racism with fewer visible means of support in the politics of the country.

Basic to this struggle was the remarkable ability of many African Americans through four generations to uphold a vision of full American citizenship while pursuing small changes in the systems of injustice that plagued their lives. Pushed back into political impotence in the post-Reconstruction era, especially in the South, the newly freed maintained for themselves the one institution that the society could not directly control—the church, where for generations they could teach each other and their children that "God is no respecter of persons" and that in Jesus all humans could obtain "power to become children of God."[21] James Cone's testimony about his childhood experience in the Macedonia A.M.E. Church in Bearden, Arkansas, in the nineteen-forties, echoed the experience of millions of African American Christians across two centuries:

> After being treated as things for six days of the week, black folk went to church on Sunday in order to affirm and experience another definition of their humanity. In the eyes of the Almighty, they were children of the God whose future was not defined by

the white structures that humiliated them. . . . The last became first in that the janitor became the chairman of the Steward Board and the maid became the president of Stewardess Board Number One. Everybody became somebody, and there were no second-class people at Macedonia.[22]

Implicitly and invisibly to many white people, for ninety years after the Emancipation Proclamation, the black church by its very existence was already in revolt against the racism of the surrounding society. But open protest against racist social institutions by churches tended to be rare, and even the vitality of their inner life could be viewed by the leaders of white society as a sign that segregation applied to the things of the spirit as well as to the things of secular society—education, residence, political power. In fact, the event that became known as the beginning of the movement—the Montgomery bus boycott in December 1955—was not at first an attack on segregation as such but merely a demand for polite treatment of blacks by bus drivers, a new rule that blacks did not have to give up seats to whites, and the hiring of black drivers on bus routes serving mostly black passengers.[23] For years local black leaders had been looking for a way to challenge segregationist institutions legally, and in Mrs. Rosa Parks's defiance of bus-seating law, they saw their opportunity.

Montgomery

From the first of the boycott movement, leaders realized that even the small cracks in the system embodied in their three modest demands would be seen by whites as the opening wedge for pulling down the system itself. Like slavery, segregation was an interconnection of laws, customs, economic interests, and political controls that stood or fell together; to remove one beam in the structure was to shake the whole— or so most enemies of civil rights for black Americans quickly assumed at the end of the Reconstruction era in the South. A whole array of white interests, material and ideal, were at stake in this system for keeping black people "in their place." To protect those interests, whites had long used the tools of official and unofficial violence, and leaders of the black community in Montgomery kept this threat in mind from the first of the bus boycott. The person who soon articulated a strategy for dealing with the threat was twenty-six-year-old Martin Luther King, Jr., pastor of the Dexter Avenue Baptist Church for the previous fifteen months.

> In the weekly mass meetings that developed as a series of increasingly politicised, religious revival sessions, King set out to put forward his evolving philosophy of Christian non-violence. At first, it was defined primarily as a refusal to act violently to the violence of whites, as a willingness to return love for hatred, and a conviction that their action was not only constitutional but within the will of God—therefore within the onward, righteous flow of history. . . .

But over the weeks to come King was to broaden his interpretation of what black people in this capital city of Alabama were beginning to do; the "soul" of the entire country, he said, needed redeeming from its failures to live up to its ancient democratic creed. Moreover, echoing the worldview of leaders of the Colored People's Convention of 1865, King asserted that the liberation of black Americans was one wave in an ocean surge of colonized people around the world against their colonizers. The continuing struggle was not for free choice of a bus seat but for society's recognition of the humanity of all its members.[24] And precisely because God was on the side of this movement, it had to be pursued by the godly means of nonviolence in the face of violence.

Over the next twelve years, until his assassination, Martin Luther King, Jr., persisted in his call for a nonretaliatory struggle for justice against laws and antagonists often backed up by one or another form of retaliatory violence. First tagging this the response of "passive resistance" and later as Gandhian "nonviolence," King called his church followers to a moral protest fortified by other forms of pressure which, while short of violence, constituted real power. From one point of view, nonviolence was simply the tactic of choice for a minority challenge to a large majority with its access to multiple defenses of systematic injustice. King knew that the official custodians of violence in America—the police and the military—could quash the movement if it ever became one of organized violence. Further, he understood the capacity of unofficial custodians of violence—the Ku Klux Klan and its kin—for fighting fire with fire. King saw that controlling the instinct for retaliation within the movement was a pragmatic as well as a moral priority—a combination that ought to carry weight in any political ethic. He and his associates were sure that the success of the movement depended on its ability to model a form of public behavior eminently democratic: the exercise of free speech, voluntary organization, free-market choice (i.e., boycotts), public communication, legislative lobbying, and appeals to duly constituted authority. Some of these activities might include civil disobedience to laws deemed morally unjust, but along with civil disobedience all of them were well within the legal traditions of American democracy. As even the Charleston Colored People's Convention had implied, resort to violence for political purposes was also an American tradition, and King's eventual refusal to permit weapons in the movement even for self-defense was, from this perspective, "un-American," just as the murders to come in the history of the movement were regrettably American. The next twelve years would be full of violence, mostly the violence of *white* people, and the movement would be frequently accused of "stirring it up"—i.e., nonviolently stirring up violence in whites. Eight years after 1955, King himself conceded to one audience that violent responses to nonviolence seemed an unavoidable fact about social change: "You make people inflict violence on you, so you precipitate violence."[25] Had he wanted to exploit the tradition of armed protest, of course, King could have done so, probably with grim consequences. When black leaders of other strategic persuasions proposed that African Americans could only overcome violence with their own counterviolence, King was the first to note that few of these leaders "had the nerve" to practice what they preached.[26]

To the pragmatic reasons for the nonviolent principle, however, one has to add the political wisdom that forms of protest anticipate themselves, preenacting behavior which their agents will probably continue once they achieve political power. Revolutions face this problem classically: What will prevent them from violently "consuming their own children"? King was well aware of this problem. He regularly decried Marxists who seemed ready to justify any unjust political means in the name of just political ends. The pragmatic means, the political ends, and the moral disciplines of non-violence were densely mixed in this philosophy; it was one sign of King's genius as a political leader that he understood the mixture and could articulate it. Violence can be very *impractical* indeed when, as Gandhi said, its eye-for-eye retaliations end up "making the whole world blind." It can be very *unpolitical* as it destroys old coalitions and makes impossible new ones. And it can be deeply *immoral*, not only in its effect on its objects but for its subjects as well. At its moral heights, nonviolent response to violence, said King, "will cause the oppressors to become ashamed of their own methods and we will be able to transform enemies into friends." But even when that does not happen—it happened too seldom to sustain this hope in King himself as the years went on—nonviolence ennobles those who practice it against their enemies. "It gives them new self-respect. It calls on resources of strength and courage that they did not know they had." Comments James Cone:

> King emphasized that violence never creates the conditions for reconciliation; it only breeds more of the same. The American dream is possible only if Negroes struggle for justice with a method that has reconciling power built into it. Non-violence [said King] "helps you to work for something that is morally right, namely integration and the brotherhood of men, with methods that are morally right." King deeply believed that "in the long run of history, destructive methods cannot bring about constructive ends." Why? Because "ends are pre-existent in the means."[27]

As Cone himself has written elsewhere: "Revenge may be understandable in view of the enormity of the violence that oppressors commit against their victims; but it cannot be condoned because it destroys the humanity that we claim to be defending. Revolutions are made because of love, not hate."[28]

King's political ethics here assumed a complex combination of remembering past evil and "forgetting" it—"in the sense that the evil deed is no longer a mental block impeding a new relationship." In quoting this sentence from King's book *Strength to Love*, Richard H. King makes the judgment:

> From this point of view, King's ultimate significance, one which has yet to be fully appreciated or absorbed, lies in his effort to incorporate the complex dialectic of forgiving and forgetting in (American) politics. Through that effort King suggested a way of beginning things anew, of taking action to rectify yet transcend the history of vengeance, and of transforming the compulsion to repeat into the capacity to act.[29]

Close to King in Montgomery, Bayard Rustin later testified to the effect of this philosophy in mobilizing blacks into a disciplined body of political actors. In this method of protest they lost their fear and gained new public stature as citizens.

> What King delivered to blacks there, far more important than whether they got to ride on the bus, was the absence of fear . . . [He] had this tremendous facility for giving people the feeling that they could be bigger and stronger and more courageous and more loving than they thought they could be.
>   In fact, when the Ku Klux Klan marched into Montgomery and we knew they were coming, Dr. King and I sat down and thought it over. And we said, "Ah! Tell every-

body to put on their Sunday clothes, stand on their steps, and when the Ku Kluxers come, applaud 'em." Well, they came, marched three blocks, and unharassed, they left. They could not comprehend the new thing. They were no longer able to engender fear.[30]

The Montgomery bus boycott proved that large numbers of black citizens of a southern city could publicly unite for social change in their own interest. This was a major political achievement in a society whose white leaders had long exercised control of blacks by strategies of threat, force, and divide and conquer. The triumph of the movement over the latter ploy demonstrated a certain ordinary relevance of forgiveness to domestic party politics often overlooked in theories of power conflict. People who are shut out of power in most of their society are understandably hungry for those badges of leadership which even a small organization can bestow. Cone's reflection on the experience of a black "nobody" in Bearden who became a "somebody" by being elected to an office in the church is eloquent testimony to this. But this very fact complicates the requirement of collaboration in any political movement: Who will get the most prominent places of leadership? Who will have to serve as the movement's anonymous "foot soldiers"? In Montgomery these questions surfaced early among veterans of politics inside the black community who rightly worried that "many individual leaders . . . would be unable to put aside their rivalries and desires for self-advancement long enough to agree on a unified community effort."[31] As an elderly black woman said to Bayard Rustin early in the boycott: "I've been around a long time. These Negroes in Montgomery are never going to stick together. They're going to run downtown and tell the white folks everything we're doing."[32]

But they did stick together, and in doing so they would craft one of the great political achievements of voluntary organization in the history of American politics. In future campaigns, they would not always stick together, and that inevitability of human politics would weaken the movement on occasion. But they were well aware of what King called "the cancerous disease of disunity" that plagues all political parties[33]; and often enough they argued and composed their differences in private in order to make the movement powerful in public. Especially as the movement became a national coalition of diverse civil rights groups, divisions between leaders would run deep, as organizational pride mingled with ordinary egotism. The director of education of the Southern Christian Leadership Conference (SCLC), Dorothy Cotton, however, described the bond between many of her peers even in the thick of internal conflicts related to the leadership of Hosea Williams: "If we live to eighty and not see each other from now to then, I think that bond will be there. . . . Even those of us who don't see eye-to-eye on a lot of things. . . . I've gotten really mad at Hosea, really wanna put him in a trunk and shut the door and sit on it sometimes, but there is a bond. . . . We love each other, and I think we always will. It was my family."[34]

Like families, many in the movement learned to stick together in part because they understood the functional importance of that combination of judgment, forbearance, empathy and will to renewed community that I have called political forgiveness. One can call it mere pragmatism, but when put to the service of high causes, forgiveness acquires a political value—in any political party—at once practical and profound. One witness to SCLC staff meetings described this phenomenon as follows:

> Looking back on it, it was a very strange organization. . . . You had an executive staff of fourteen highly egotistical, stubborn arrogant people, who were strongly convicted, but willing to lay aside their strong convictions for *a* unity. . . . There was kind of a commitment to a broader something than any of us had been involved in. . . . [For example, Andrew Young] had, and possesses even now, the unique capacity to find the avenue to reconcile divergent points of view when the moment comes that all that can be gotten out of a situation has been gotten. The idea was to reconcile and wait for another day.[35]

His gifts for reconciling and waiting marked King, too, as a politician of great skill. He knew how to keep fractious followers focused enough on a goal to soften their animosities towards leaders and each other.[36]

Class conflict, ordinary in grass-roots politics, was not absent from these tensions. In every city where the movement recruited supporters in the black community, the poor and middle class found themselves in unfamiliar contact with each other in church pews, lines of march, and prison cells. Some new sense of each other's humanity emerged in many of these new settings, as middle-class and poor blacks endured common suffering. Implicit in the stories here are new experiences of empathy and forbearance for resentments of the past. Harding describes an incident in the 1961–62 campaign in Albany, Georgia, in terms reminiscent of the history of the early Christian movement as it endured persecution:

> . . . the invidious class distinctions that had plagued Albany and so many other similar black communities were momentarily forgotten as people from every level of life and experience were jammed into cells. One woman, Norma Anderson, the wife of the osteopath who led the movement, told me that she had never known an experience of communion in a church which equaled the deep unity that she felt one night as she and eight other tired, thirsty, frightened, but courageous women in a cell built for two persons, passed around an old canning jar of water, sharing so much more than the lukewarm liquid that they drank.[37]

Someone has said that "the parliamentary system depends upon the forgiveness of sin." It does so in the sense that opponents in struggle over one issue may find themselves needing each other in struggle over another. Politics is often about conflicts of power, but political power itself springs from collaborations, without which fractious groups of people are readily at the mercy of their collaborating enemies. The case for the relevance of forgiveness to conflict between real enemies may always be hard to make, especially in the heat of conflict itself. But neither side will long be powerful against the other without those quiet, private layings aside of the resentments and grudges which afflict every human relation sooner or later. The ability of black people to mount a civil rights movement in the years 1955–68 is remarkable in just this respect. They proved themselves capable of political power in circumstances that could easily have shattered that power. The first show of that capability came in Montgomery. Supporters would sustain it for at least twelve years to

come. They would do so in part because, internally as well as externally in the movement, they knew something about political forms of the forgiveness of sins.

Greensboro and Nashville

On February 1, 1960, in Greensboro, Franklin McCain, a freshman at the traditionally all-black North Carolina Agricultural and Technical College, with three of his
classmates, began the first lunch-counter sit-ins, a tactic for desegregating public
accommodations that was to spread across many parts of the country. Said McCain:

> The movement started out as a movement of nonviolence and as a Christian move-
> ment, and we wanted to make that very clear to everybody, that it was a movement
> that was seeking justice more than anything else and not a movement to start a war.
> . . . We knew that probably the most powerful and potent weapon that people have
> literally no defense for is love, kindness. That is, whip the enemy with something
> that he doesn't understand.[38]

The sit-ins were a signal that young blacks, many of them students born during World
War II, were ready to challenge segregation in all of its local expressions. One of the
architects of the sit-in movement was John Lewis, native of Martin King's home city
of Atlanta, in 1960 a theological student.

> It was my responsibility to draw up some do's and don't's on the sit-in movement.
> . . . It was some simple rules, and the whole idea, matter of fact, came from the Mont-
> gomery Bus Boycott. . . . Don't talk back. Sit straight up. Don't laugh out. Don't
> curse. And at the end of the rules it said something like, "Remember the teachings of
> Jesus, Gandhi, Martin Luther King. God bless you all."

Asked about the reaction of management when the students sat down at a lunch
counter, Lewis recollected:

> Well, they said something like "We cannot serve you here." They closed the counter,
> put up a sign saying Closed, and we just sat there. I remember once we went to the
> Trailways Bus Station in Nashville and we stayed all night sitting there. [They] just
> closed down the counter and closed the restaurant. And we got very sleepy and we
> would put our heads down and this waitress would walk about with this big knife,
> hatchet-like, and she said, "This is not a hotel. There will be no sleeping here."
> [Laughs] And little things came out of that whole effort. Somebody said, "We can't
> serve you. We don't serve niggers," and somebody said, "Well, we don't eat them."[39]

"The greatest enemy of authority . . . is contempt, and the surest way to undermine it is laughter."[40] Humor under stress marked the spiritual resiliency of many
people in all sorts of demonstrations in which the movement would achieve its greatest
political gains. Politeness in the face of vulgarity, kindness in face of cruelty, calm
in the face of threat were qualities that movement leaders counted on to shame their
enemies into compliance with their aims if not into imitation of their methods. Especially in the early years of the civil rights movement, King himself believed strongly

that the "good people" of the American South would eventually rally to the side of a justice that was promoted with such "calm and loving dignity."[41] Later King would read his experience of white violence and intransigent legal institutions as teaching the lesson that various other forms of power, not bare humane example alone, would have to be mobilized to effect basic change in American society. But to the last King believed that pressure and power must not include violence, for violence damages or prevents the very political relationship it aims at achieving. In 1963, in his annual report to the convention of the SCLC, King summarized the strategy behind all the demonstrations that had multiplied across the country in these years:

> In the past our demonstrations against public accommodations have been highly suc-
> cessful precisely because they were unique in doing three things: first, they called
> attention to the evil; second, they aroused the conscience of the community; third,
> they eliminated the evil *itself* when men, women, and children stood firm and ac-
> cepted what came.

In this same report King went on to say that the Movement would soon "have to shift from protest to politics," national politics, and that in the shift new coalitions with white Americans would be vital. "Each day it becomes clearer that the solution to our full citizenship, political and economic, cannot be achieved by the Negro or civil rights forces alone."[42] Aroused consciences among some segments of the white citizenry prepared the way from some of the long-delayed change, but the more truly political elimination of the "evil *itself*" came in the very *civility* of the nonviolent face with which the Movement preenacted the public mores of a democratic political order, modeling authentic forms of citizenship in the very act of challenging defective ones. When disobedient to segregationist norms, they would be civilly so— they would go quietly to jail in hopes of getting laws changed. And even if many white critics did not take note of the "civil" in the disobedience, some did to their embarrassment. James McBride Dabbs of South Carolina, for example, challenged his upper-class white peers with the observation that politeness was a traditional virtue of Southern culture. The polite people in the sit-in furor were those at the counter; the ugly folk tended to be behind the counters and out on the streets.[43] Virginia archconservative James J. Kilpatrick responded similarly to the lunch-counter sit-in scene with irony that became famous:

> Here were the colored students, in coats, white shirts, ties and one of them was read-
> ing Goethe and one was taking notes from a biology text. And here on the sidewalk
> outside, was a gang of white boys come to heckle, a ragtail rabble, slack-jawed, black-
> jacketed, grinning fit to kill, and some of them, God save the mark, were waving the
> proud and honored flag of the Southern States in the last war fought by gentlemen.
> Eheu! It gives one pause.[44]

The high-culture snobbery of Virginians and South Carolinians toward their own and deeper-South "rednecks" had fomented its own class prejudice for centuries in the region. Observant southern blacks knew that this prejudice was their enemy, too, especially in its potential for excluding them from votes, jobs, decent houses, and other signs of full citizenship in American society. In their defiance of upper- and middle-class contempt for them, did the black ghetto gang member and the rural Ku Klux Klan member have a certain justification for *their* contempt for "civil" protest? It is a critical question for anyone who, in the midst of political struggle, wonders if moral judgment against diverse enemies can or should combine with empathy and hope for new civic bonding among them all.

But here, too, the middle-class leaders of the movement had an empathetic advantage over many members of a secure white establishment: they were closer to poverty in their own lives and among their own neighbors, and on occasion they had shown shrewd appreciation for the ways in which powerful white people could serve their own interests through the manipulation of the "ragtag rabble" of their own race. When they presented their demands to city councils and governors of the south, movement leaders were critically aware of this dynamic. That is why they could lay before these high officials the argument: "You call on violent people to oppose us when it is in your interest to do so. Now call on them to respect us, for our peaceful demonstrations are in your interest. You should see in demonstrations a display of democratic civility."

Birmingham

In the history of the civil rights movement, two events will always be remembered as the high points of its moral, political, and legislative successes: the campaigns in Birmingham (1963) and Selma (1965). The one prepared the way for the passage of the federal Civil Rights Act of 1964, which mandated the desegregation of public accommodations throughout the country; the other hastened the passage of the Voting Rights Act of 1965, which facilitated federal enforcement of voting rights denied to many black southerners since the 1870s. In each case, *police* violence proved to be the great political "friend" of the movement's goals, for the age of national television and newspaper photography had fully arrived. The covert violence of racial segregation became nationally visible in images of overt violence in two Alabama cities.

At issue in Birmingham was equal access of black citizens to the parks, restaurants, swimming pools, motels, and other public facilities of the city as well as jobs in downtown stores. The pervasive strategic issue of the protest, however, was "negotiation." In a meeting with several white ministers on April 25, Martin King heard them complain that local black protesters "were not interested in negotiation" but only in stirring up public tension. To this King replied with words that echoed his recently written *Letter from Birmingham City Jail:* "The purpose of . . . direct action is to create a situation so crisis-packed that it will inevitably open the door to negotiation. . . . We who engage in nonviolent direct action are not the creators of tension. We merely bring to the surface the hidden tension that is already alive. We bring it out into the open where it can be seen and dealt with."[45] Most of the political structures of Birmingham had long been arranged to prevent "negotiation" between white and black leaders of the city. One of the principal aims of the Birmingham campaign, and the one longest resisted by the city government, was the appointment of a biracial committee whose business it would be to bring to the surface "hidden tensions" and deal with them in public deliberation. Here was a demand for the most primi-

tive, basic form of civil participation: the right to speak to and work with the powerful in pursuit of one's neglected interests. *Open public talk* may be an elementary
form of politics, but it is a prerequisite to any process even remotely promising public forgiveness for public sins. How can injustice be understood, corrected, or finally
forgiven if it cannot be accurately identified? Who is going to identify it if not the
people who suffer from it? And what can citizenship mean to them if they have no
freedom to speak up in the public household?

Unlike the rural world of the Deep South, Birmingham was a city born of post-
Civil War industrialism. Its steel mills fed on the adjacent coal fields of Appalachia,
and its discriminatory employment opportunities reflected the "whites mostly" principle on which post-1865 southern industry had been conceived. Local blacks experienced Birmingham as a city where violence lurked beneath the surface of every
social crisis, and local black leaders, as they invited King and the SCLC to a nonviolent
campaign in the city, were unsure of their ability to control counterviolence inside
the black community. As they began to organize for the coming protest in the spring
of 1963, leaders of the SCLC observed how

> Certain powerful contradictions began to surface. On the one hand, the "Command-
> ments" handed out to demonstrators began, "Meditate daily on the teachings and life
> of Jesus," and included such additional admonitions as "walk and talk in the manner
> of love for God is love. . . . Refrain from violence of fist, tongue, or heart." But at the
> same time, Jim Bevel [of the SCLC] and other staff members were confiscating a
> good number of knives and other weapons from some of the brothers who had come
> prepared for other ways of walking and talking. . . . In many ways the black commu-
> nity of Birmingham in 1963 was a long way from the praying and singing folks of
> Montgomery in 1955. Still the leaders moved from a religious base. On Good Fri-
> day, when King and Ralph Abernathy led their first march, Martin quoted from Jesus:
> "Peace I leave with you. . . . let not your heart be troubled, neither let it be afraid."
> Ralph said, "You may call it city jail, but I call it Calvary. . . . where he leads I'll
> follow." And Reverend Lindsey, one of the many courageous local leaders, perhaps
> caught the dilemma of the situation best of all, when just before marching out to meet
> Bull Connor's police and dogs and high-powered fire hoses, he said, "We are going
> to set this city on fire with the Holy Ghost."[46]

For arousing national awareness of intransigence in the segregationist structures
of the South, movement leaders were counting on Police Commissioner Connor's
troops to display all the viciousness that local blacks had long experienced in the
city. With dogs and fire hoses, he did not disappoint them. Unlike his shrewd counterpart in Albany, Georgia, Chief Laurie Pritchett,[47] Connor had little concern for
what the national media could do to shape the conflict in Birmingham. He was unaware that "so long as the Laurie Pritchetts of the South succeed in maintaining segregation in a fashion that eschewed violence and brutality, it seemed that [President
John F. Kennedy and Attorney General Robert F. Kennedy] would be content to leave
civil rights on the back burner" of the federal government's attention.[48]

But Connor's violence could only impress the nation if he were met with the discipline of nonviolence among the demonstrators. That contrast would make evening
news with moral impact. The SCLC leaders had learned that lesson well in Albany.

J. T. Johnson, a native of that city, though long since a resident of New Jersey, credited Martin King personally with teaching him this moral-tactical lesson:

> . . . whenever we was in crisis, you would feel somethin' when Dr. King was on the scene. . . . it was a strange feelin' you would get, motivated in a sense to go on regardless. I don't care what was out there or who was out there. The nonviolent would come to you and you would march. . . . Even if they had guns it didn't bother us. . . . It was amazin' because I kinda came up through poolrooms. . . . so I have been through the streets and everything else, and the way to survive out there was to fight. But when I got involved in the Civil Rights Movement, nonviolence became kinda a way of life more or less with me.[49]

Johnson differed not only from Malcolm X and other advocates of self-defending violence among northern urban African Americans but as well from many southern black descendants of the 1865 Charleston Convention with its "right to bear arms." Hartman Turnbow, a black farmer in the Mississippi Delta, on occasion debated Dr. King himself on the point: "I said, 'This nonviolent stuff ain't too good. It'll get ya killed.' . . . It ain't but one thing that is good. . . . Every what the Mississippi white man pose with, he got to be met with."[50] Andrew Marrisett, recruited off the streets of Birmingham to be a staff member of the SCLC, believed that the Birmingham campaign was the great eventful arbiter between the two sides of this critical moral-political debate. He reflected to Howell Raines on his growing up in the tense, violence-prone culture of the city: ". . . Where I came from I had to fight my way through. You know, I had to be mean or else I wouldn't survive." Birmingham and Selma, he believed, were the most powerful successes of the movement in keeping its demonstrators nonviolent. As they met in churches to prepare for the streets, he said, "We used to have to run people home, because they would bring their guns." When guns appeared in the lines of march, the leaders would say, "Hey, man, lookie here, you know, if you want to kill cops, you go on over there and form your own little group, but don't kill them in this nonviolent line here." For the further education of such a weapons carrier, leaders then "would try to get him to the mass meeting and get him involved. We would sit beside him . . . and get him involved in spirit, and we would sing the songs and do the chants and the freedom-now things, and then we'd hear Dr. King speak, and that would quiet down the angriest lion. . . ."[51]

Without necessarily arguing a case for principled pacifism, any student of forgiveness in politics should recognize that nonviolence in movements for political justice fits the purpose of challenging violence-enforced social injustice. Governments and political philosophers have often assumed the dogma that justice in a society must always, as a final resort, be enforced with violence. The notion of "legitimate" violence hangs on this claim. But the weakness of the claim comes when new legitimacies are at stake and all sides claim the privileges of violence. Basic to the movement was its aim of achieving a new *mutuality* in the relations of minority citizens and the majority, including the government which the latter dominated. It pursued this aim implicitly by restricting its strategies to forms of pressure short of harming other people's lives and limbs, however many of their own lives and limbs might be sacrificed in the process. It forecast, in its means of protest, a more just, future civil society. It also asserted nonretaliation as a prelude to setting up those structures of

negotiation in which *debate* about justice could continue with a new mix of participants at the table. As Hannah Arendt and other observers of processes worthy of the
name "political" have insisted, violence is marginal to that process in that it quashes
debate and substitutes, for war with words, war itself.[52] Through nonviolence in the
civil rights movement, people previously excluded from public conversation claimed
their place in it by making it difficult for their enemies to claim that they, the protesters,
knew little about that kind of conversation.

As noted early in this book, even if violence must be granted its role in the protection of justice and social order in all societies, it does not have to be retaliatory, or
mere response in kind. If the decision against retaliation in kind is the very beginning of the forgiveness process, whether we view it through the eyes of Aeschylus
or Martin Luther King, Jr., then the movement's successes in Birmingham and Selma
must be counted as among the great historic displays of a start on forgiveness in
politics. It can be so counted because of its companion success in building a new
network of communication and action among white and black leaders, especially in
Birmingham.

The great central issue in Albany had been the consistent refusal of the city commissioners to put themselves into "face-to-face contact" with the leaders of the protest. Upsets of local peace and boycotts of businesses had moved the mayor finally
to criticize his own colleagues for "condemning responsible business and religious
leaders for discussing problems now facing this community." Recalcitrant commissioners in both Albany and Birmingham, however, knew the ways of political power;
not to sit down with opponents is to keep them on the fringes of change. As in personal relations, so in political: bent on protecting oneself from the influence of others,
one should refuse so much as to meet them. In the midst of the Albany struggle, President Kennedy had put the issue in an international frame:

> I find it wholly inexplicable why the city council of Albany will not sit down with
> the citizens of Albany, who may be Negroes, and attempt to secure them, in a peace-
> ful way, their rights. The U.S. government is involved in sitting down at Geneva with
> the Soviet Union. I can't understand why the government of Albany . . . cannot do
> the same for American citizens.[53]

Of course the president did understand: by not sitting down with certain "citizens of
Albany," its government could keep on denying that they *were* citizens.

The movement encountered the same resistance in Birmingham. There the political situation was complicated by the fact that by virtue of a recent referendum, local
government was in the midst of a constitutional change that left current accountability structures rather ambiguous while leaving Police Commissioner Connor with
enough legitimate power to meet demonstrators with hoses, dogs, billy clubs, and an
armored car. By his use of these methods, Connor ensured worldwide fame for Birmingham in the media and a wave of popular national sentiment in favor of federal
action to protect the rights of black southerners.

Meantime, given that local government was partially in a power vacuum, that a
major target of the demonstrations was new job opportunities for blacks, and that
merchants in particular were now suffering from the black boycott of their stores,

business leaders in Birmingham initiated their own quiet negotiations with leaders of the movement. Thus began the building of new structures of inclusion in the economic and political life of the city—a network of relations between leaders of the black community and business leaders who had the power to effect equal job opportunity for blacks. Whites in these secret meetings represented 80 percent of the "hiring power" in the city. In advance of any formal agreements with local government about public accommodation laws, in secret meetings early in the morning or late at night, in homes and churches and deserted office buildings, leaders of the two sides began to treat each other as equals for the first time in their lives. The meetings began, on the white side, largely our of fear of what continued boycotts and disruptive demonstrations would do to the economy of the city.

In retrospect, leaders of the movement were sure that the mass demonstration of hundreds of black high school students on May 7 was the event that finally persuaded this elite to negotiate seriously. Weaponless the teenagers may have been, but their defiance of dogs and hoses carried a message of worse, perhaps violent resistance to come if leaders of the two communities did not strike up a new public bargain. "Masses of unrestrained black teenagers had convinced the downtown businessmen in a way that peaceful picketing or sit-ins never had that segregation was not worth the price they would have to pay."[54]

But the inner dynamics that enabled black and white leaders of the city to stumble toward some new levels of political and economic justice are worth remembering here, especially for answering the question of why some mass demonstrations ushered in change and others did not. Vincent Harding, who was present for most of the Birmingham campaign, gave four reasons for the success of these behind-the-scenes talks: (1) White business leaders expressed their intentions to push for public desegregation of accommodations and new job opportunity, and black leaders came to trust those intentions. (2) In turn, whites learned new trust of these black leaders in their first face-to-face contact. The achievement of this mutuality of trust was at first slow, said Harding. "At first [the whites] wanted to be the one to decide who would and who would not be accepted as a Negro leader, but soon found they had to take seriously the young minister who explained that 'Negro leadership is now largely determined by the willingness of a man to suffer for the people.' They had to learn to deal with activists and 'jailbirds,' as well as Negro businessmen and educators, and among them all they found men who cared deeply about the city of Birmingham, men who sought the things that make for peace." (3) The sheer power of the white business elite meant that it could effect many changes in the city's economy. Allied to this openness to change was the perception of business executives that the city government, in its zeal for protecting segregation law, was ignoring the city's industrial prosperity. Ordinarily uncomfortable about assuming the responsibilities of government, in the current power vacuum many executives found themselves ready to act politically. (4) Harding credits the success of the secret talks finally to the integrity of the strong-willed local leader of the movement, Rev. Fred Shuttlesworth. "He prides himself on his ability to keep his word. It is worth noting that on May 14, when he called for the removal of state troopers from Birmingham, Shuttlesworth said: '. . . we want the city police, whom we respect, to take charge.'"[55]

Experienced local blacks had their reasons for trusting local rather than state police—reasons that would multiply in the coming year in Selma. With a segregation-ist governor (George Wallace) in power in Montgomery and a state police chief (Al Lingo) notorious for violence, the state had been responsible for some of the worst abuses of brutality in the local demonstrations. Some local police had even walked off the job in protest against the tactics of their state colleagues. All told, Shuttlesworth's "respect" for the local police stands out as a testimony to his own integrity as a leader intent on restoring a new civility to his city. Who but a leader with a very steady focus on the future of Birmingham could confess respect for its local police on *May 14*, 1963? The statement was kindly, forbearing, accenting some-thing positive in the midst of many an experienced negative. In particular, it was a hopeful salute to the possibility of a new day of police-community relations in Bir-mingham. Ten years later, Shuttlesworth reflected on the event and used his custom-ary theological language to describe it:

> I think the idea of facing "Bull" Connor was the thing. . . . we knew that we would have the spotlight, I think that. To me, it was a matter of life and death, not only to face "Bull" Connor, but to see if it is true—and it *is* true; I don't think I should say it like that—to really *prove* that where sin did abound, grace did much more abound, where darkness is, then light can overcome it.[56]

The counterpoint and echo of Shuttlesworth's hope for change, precisely in the role of the local police in a future Birmingham, appeared in the early 1970s in Howell Raines's interview with Captain Glenn V. Evans, whose division had transported hundreds of demonstrators to jail in 1963. He said to Raines that the demonstrations and "various other things" in these months had caused him to change his attitude, "not exclusively the attitude of a police officer, but also as a human being." He told the story of how one night on a bus he saw a frustrated young black mother yank her child to the back of a bus from a front seat in which the child had chosen to sit. Evans broke into tears as he described the incident. "How do you explain [this] to a child? . . . I came to the conclusion that there wasn't any way to explain it. . . . You see, I had this experience prior to our demonstrations. . . . But I was still under the control of my chief of police and my commissioner of public safety [Connor] and the other political leaders of the community, and I was still under the influence of the commu-nity to maintain the status quo."[57]

The story of how some white Americans in this era came to *repent* of their racist attitudes may never be fully told, but such repentance was the other side of the will-ingness of many blacks to forgive the past on condition that whites would collabo-rate in the building of a new political future for Americans of all ethnic origins. Whether on a bus or in a once segregated park or behind closed doors, some whites in Birmingham learned in this period to *see* their black neighbors with unprecedented empathy. They began to stumble into new relationships on many levels including the political.

The immediate postscripts to the great Birmingham demonstrations were full of mixed hope and despair, however. On the weekend after the first formal agreements on the dismantling of local segregation law, the Gaston Motel, headquarters of the SCLC, was bombed in an attempt on the life of Martin King. The home of his brother in a nearby community suffered the same. A riot ensued, uncontrollable by local movement leaders, persuading John F. Kennedy to federalize the Alabama National Guard. This was to be the summer when Governor Wallace would try to block the integration of the University of Alabama, when Kennedy would seek passage by Congress of a civil rights bill on public accommodations, when Medgar Evers would be murdered in Mississippi, and when the March on Washington would bring together a quarter-million people, a fourth of whom would be white. During all of these months Birmingham continued its uneasy search for new justice and peace. Both were shattered again on September 15 by the murder of four black children with a bomb planted in the Sixteenth Street Baptist Church in Birmingham. "It was the greatest human tragedy that had befallen the movement," says Garrow, and the tragedy was the deeper for all the apparent "progress" that the city had made in drawing up a modicum of new power and new opportunity for its black citizens. Almost every knowledgeable Birmingham leader knew that the journey toward just civil community would be a long one; racism had roots in history, institutions, laws, customs, and feelings that no society uproots overnight. A lot of new justice would have to come before a lot of new forgiving could come, too.

No one in the white community in Birmingham understood this better than Charles Morgan, an attorney, who on September 16 delivered a biting, bitter speech to the all-white Young Men's Business Club of the city. The speech earned him much national publicity and an eventual accumulation of local pressures to move to another city. It shared little of Shuttlesworth's confidence in the victory of "light" over darkness in Birmingham, but it asserted another inclusiveness missing in the city's popular culture: the inclusiveness of guilt. Who killed four little girls yesterday? Morgan asked this audience.

> The "who" is every little individual who talks about "niggers" and spreads the seeds of his hate to his neighbor and son. The jokester, the crude oaf whose racial jokes rock the party with laughter. The "who" is every governor who ever shouted for lawlessness and became a law violator. . . .
>   Who is really guilty? Each of us. Each citizen who has not consciously attempted to bring about peaceful compliance with the decisions of the Supreme Court; each citizen who has ever said, "They ought to kill that nigger." Every person in this community who has in any way contributed to the popularity of hatred is at least as guilty, or more so, as the demented fool who threw that bomb.[58]

The unrelieved judgment of this speech contrasted with the mingled judgment and hope of many a contemporary speech by the Shuttlesworths and the Kings of the movement. Such a speech, rare from white lips, reminded pained hearers that judgment against evil is as basic to the ethics of forgiveness as forbearance from revenge in kind. The anger that greeted these words was understandable, but it signaled the truth that white defenders of racist institutions were less ready to *accept* forgiveness for these long-standing sins than were black protesters to *offer* that forgiveness. The offer had never been unconditional: it asked for repentance and new justice in return. Morgan's hard moralism assaulted a local culture that, with the aid of churches, had so individualized the notion of sin as to sever most whites' consciences from any sense of implication in the origin and maintenance of social evil. When Martin King wrote his *Letter from Birmingham Jail* five months earlier and said "I Have a Dream" to the great March on Washington only nineteen days before Morgan's speech, he had voiced a blend of judgment and hope akin to that of the religion of the black church, reflecting as well a democratic pragmatism which sees humanly initiated evil as humanly curable. In this tortured summer of 1963 King was closer than Morgan to the pragmatism of forgiveness in politics, but had a white populace heard more of Morgan's language in the public rhetoric of politicians and church leaders, such words would not have sounded so outrageous in white ears.[59] No one, and no society, is ready for forgiveness without being ready for repentance.

Selma and Mississippi, 1964–65

For many active politicians in American society, power, not truth or right, is the chief goal of all who engage seriously in political competition. A proper, empirical, historical identification of truth in public affairs is indispensable, however, to the forgiveness and the new covenants that Hannah Arendt identified as the twin requirements of genuine social change. Silence about the evils of the past is a great fortifier of injustice in the present, including the injustice of good law on the books that is ignored in public practice. Publicity for truth can be the first, essential round in the fight for just change.

In two local movement campaigns political power—the vote—was the focus of the struggle. But weaving through the effort was the theme of breaking silence, the liberation of whites and blacks in American society to *talk* about conditions that many were not yet "brave enough to try to cure."[60] In its public demonstrations, the movement was freeing whites like Charles Morgan to say to fellow whites what had not been said before.

From other platforms—such as the churches and the newspapers—the same freedom began to ring episodically but influentially. One example was Ralph McGill, editor of the *Atlanta Constitution*. As one of his associates said of him, his achievement was "to start a conversation," like those black southerners had already started in places like Montgomery.

> To know that period of the South is to know that it was frozen in silence. . . . Neighbor and neighbor were afraid of each other. . . . And for a man to sit down with his neighbor and say, "Hey, I'm not sure we're right" could have ruined the man in most southern states. . . . Only the politicians, who aggravated emotions, were discussing it. McGill suddenly and boldly on the front page of the *Constitution* began to talk openly about the rights and wrongs of segregation, and this led people to be emboldened to talk about it even if all they did was cuss McGill.[61]

In Selma, local black leaders had decided by 1964 that it was time to claim that form of public talk embodied in the vote. The adoption of the 1964 Civil Rights Act, brought to the national agenda by the Birmingham campaign, was not yet changing ways of public life in little towns like Selma. Locals knew that equal access to motel accommodations promised less to the black community than equal access to voting and economic opportunity. To leaders of the national movement, "it seemed possible that Selma might become the voting rights symbol that the movement needed." With confidence in that possibility, Martin King joined some dozens of Selma black citizens waiting in the rain at the registration office of the Dallas County Courthouse in Selma and said to them, "We are going to bring a voting bill into being in the streets of Selma." And they did[62]—in this centenary of the end of the Civil War.

As all movement historians agree, the Selma campaign was its high point of success if measured by national political result and attraction of a large national interracial group of supporters to the cause. Few comparable illustrations of local impact for national change can be found in American history: frequent marches from Brown Chapel to the courthouse; clubbings by local and state police; long legal appeals in courts for permission to march to a state capital 51 miles away; hundreds of imprisonments; three murders; memorial services for these dead; some two thousand marchers representing all regions of the United States, with a national labor union leader, a Greek Orthodox Archbishop, and the world's youngest Nobel Peace Prize laureate locking arms in the lead—all of this came to political climax on March 15, 1965, when Lyndon B. Johnson, Texas-born American president, bluntly told Congress and 70 million listening Americans that "it is wrong—deadly wrong—to deny any of your fellow Americans the right to vote in this country." For the first time in the nine years of the movement, an American president put his own unambiguous stamp of approval on demonstrations that had so often been accused of being lawless. Johnson compared the struggle to the Battle of Lexington; then, in a touch symbolically as momentous, he vowed to Congress that in this cause "we *shall* overcome."[63]

A President's public use of the great Freedom Song evoked tears from Martin Luther King, Jr., as he listened to the speech in the home of the parents of the murdered Jimmie Lee Jackson. Few historians would doubt Garrow's judgment: "Never before in nine years time, had the movement received the breadth of national support, and the strength of federal endorsement, that this week had witnessed. It was an emotional peak unmatched by anything that had come before, nor by anything that would come later."[64] One of King's closest advisers, Stanley Levinson, expanded on this judgment in a long letter to King soon after the Selma victory:

> Selma was bigger than Birmingham, though it was smaller in scope, because for the first time whites and Negroes from all over the nation physically joined the struggle in a pilgrimage to the deep south. This was a new level of commitment because it entailed danger and continuity. But more important, the elements who responded were for the first time a true cross-section of America. . . .

Levinson went on to say that King himself was "one of the exceptional figures who attained the heights of popular confidence and trust without having obligations to any political party or other dominant interests. Seldom has anyone in American history come up by this path, fully retaining his independence and freedom of action." The civil rights movement "is the single movement in the nation at this time which arouses the finer democratic instincts of the nation." Levinson saw some of those instincts at work even on the side of angry whites in Selma: "Considerable restraint was exercised by the authorities there" in contrast to Birmingham.[65] Opinions would differ about the last judgment, but the fact remained that, thanks to Selma, a majority of Americans were now ready for the federal government to enforce voting rights in the South.

What did this success have to do with ethics between political enemies in the United States of America? It was pertinent in at least two respects: One, it underscored the integrity of a transition from one form of nonviolent protest—demonstrations—to another—voting. The public demonstrations of 1955–65 were extraordinary exercises of power by a people who had been largely denied its ordinary exercise in electoral politics and officeholding. As such, the demonstrations were consistent with the always precarious achievement of democracy in moving conflicts of interests out of the sphere of violence into a system of rule by a majority bound to respect for the rights and interests of minorities. Movement leaders knew what all students of politics know: without power to protect it, hardly any human interest is safe—a theme about which the leaders of the fifties, including King, did not need the black power movement, still to come, to instruct them. With votes, minorities may not be able to overcome majority power, but they are safer than when they must depend wholly on the kindness of the majority. Voting power meant that more than ever black citizens of the country were politically *here to stay*, as the Charleston Colored People's Convention had affirmed one century before.

There was a second, more immediate shift, pertinent to an ethic for enemies and visible in the direct negotiations of movement leaders with their governmental opponents. Assured that they could now count on more political clout with elected politicians than ever before, movement leaders showed up in the offices of presidents, governors, and mayors with unprecedented frequency. In those offices they could speak some truths that they had never had opportunity to speak there before. One conversation of this sort is worth quoting, for it illustrates that blend of candor and warmth which black ministers in the South have long exhibited as leaders of their churches.

Two weeks after the highly publicized march from Selma to Montgomery (March 21–25, 1965), SCLC leaders, most of them ministers, sat in the office of their arch enemy Governor George Wallace. The visit resembled a pastoral call. Joseph Lowery, the spokesperson, reported the conversation as follows:

> . . . We met with him for ninety minutes. . . . I said to him that, "I am speaking to you as a Methodist preacher to a Methodist layman," which he is, and I said, "God has given you great gifts, great gifts of leadership, powers of persuasion, and he will call you to account for how you use them."
>
> And he said, "Well, I don't advocate violence." I said, "You don't in so many words, but you do. You get on television, you rave against people taking the rights of little people and the government coming in and stirring up trouble, and you get your emotions released on TV. But the fella in the dark street, he doesn't have that forum, so he gets a lead pipe to identify with you, and he cracks somebody's skull. . . . You are responsible for dividing us, and you are responsible for the violence. . . ."
>
> . . . he probably for the first time got to see face to face how the black community felt about him and his leadership. And we weren't bitter, we didn't attack him in any vicious manner, but I did try to impress him with the moral responsibility that was his.[66]

The substitution of the politics of the vote for the pseudopolitics of the lead pipe was at work in this unprecedented conversation. Also at work was that notable combination of hard truth with soft-speaking, which is mightily akin to the amalgam of judgment, forbearance, empathy, and will to community of which genuine forgiveness consists. Among the governor's constituents that day, none would have surpassed these clergy visitors in their practice of this combination.

Lowery believed that from 1965 George Wallace stopped blaming Alabama's problems on local and national black protesters and began blaming "big government" in Washington instead. Much to the astonishment of people outside Alabama and in one of the ironic political turnabouts of American politics, black Alabaman voters could take credit (or blame) in 1982 for reelecting Wallace to a fourth term as governor. The issues of repentance and forgiveness became publicly prominent in this event. Civil rights leaders urged the nomination of a Democratic "New South progressive" from Birmingham in the September primary, and two-thirds of black voters statewide supported Wallace's primary opponent. Even in the primary, however, he won 30 percent of black votes and almost every predominantly black county "by preaching a populist litany of jobs, forgiveness and a return to better times."[67] In November, an estimated 70 percent of black voters were in the Wallace column, many of them having decided that his Republican opponent was less trustworthy. Black rural voters, enfranchised only since the late sixties, thus joined Wallace's traditional base of white rural and urban blue-collar voters in a true populist coalition to elect the man who, now in a wheelchair, convinced them that he was no longer a racist. Jobs were the central issue in this election, and poor people of both races seemed to agree with Dr. Robert Galliard, school board member and president of the Mobile County chapter of the NAACP, that, between the two party candidates in November, "the Republican had nothing to offer so far as employment is concerned but to fill up the jails—that was his solution to unemployment."[68] And he added: "Forgiveness has nothing to do with it."

On the second point, numerous Alabama blacks disagreed. After the election, Delores Pickett, who had organized the Wallace appeal to black voters in the primary, said, "forgiveness is in our Christian upbringing. It is something Martin Luther King taught us. Wallace said he made mistakes, and people have started to believe him." Many were still believing in 1991, when a long-time observer of the civil rights movement could say of an aging, ailing Wallace: "Those who know him say that above all he regrets using the racial issue for political gain."[69]

King, too, had dreamed of a populist coalition such as Wallace assembled in 1982, though we may be reasonably sure that even his devotion to forgiveness in politics would not have extended unambiguously to support for the reelection of that old enemy. Indeed, Wallace himself seldom used the language of repentance and forgiveness in his public retreats from his segregationist past. But apparently he was not shy about using it as, prior to the election, he wooed black rural preachers "by staying on the telephone late at night and calling them individually asking for their forgiveness for past racial transgressions and their support from the pulpit."[70] Publicly Wallace preferred the word—echo of Hiroshima—*mistake*: "I have seen the mistakes all of us have made in years past," he said from the pulpit of a black Baptist church in September. But soon afterward he exclaimed to a reporter:

I'm not apologizing for anything. . . . Some of my attitudes were mistaken, but I haven't been an evil man. I never intentionally hurt anybody. I never advocated anything for the devil. But every man has sinned and come short of the glory of God. Now I can see it was wrong, but it was honest. But it's been a long time. It's ancient history. We've got to move forward. My door is always open to black and white.[71]

Apology glimmered in his "Now I can see it was wrong," and restitution, too. In fact he had brought jobs, community colleges, and trade schools to many parts of the state for members of both races. Said young Eddie Reeves, an unemployed black 19-year-old of Lowndes County (immediately south of Selma), "I can forget all that civil rights stuff ever happened if George Wallace can get me a decent job."[72] And said Arthur Gillis, 64-year-old "undecided" black farmer living near Montgomery, "Folks won't hold his old self against him. . . . I don't know what he meant back then, but it don't bother me none."[73] It was as if Gillis was able to consign the old Wallace to what the Bible calls "the mystery of iniquity." *Time* editor Lance Morrow found another sort of mystery brewing in all this:

> George Wallace's gubernatorial campaign this year is exploring a few deeper mysteries of the human character or, at any rate, of the human memory: questions that involve the capacity of the politician's heart to change, the mind to forget, and the Alabama black to forgive. The South has profound shallows. . . . The Deep South is supposed to be the one American region where the past means something.[74]

But Morrow's view from midtown Manhattan did not take account of other deep currents in Deep South culture and its options for dealing with the past beyond mere intransigent remembering. Andrew Young, now mayor of Atlanta, understood the paradox of black support for Wallace in Alabama even if (along with almost all civil rights leaders) he urged the nomination of a liberal Democrat.

> "I don't have any qualms about his racial position if he's a changed individual. There's an age-old notion that nobody is better for blacks than a converted southerner. . . . To see an old hard-shell like Wallace come into the fold is every preacher's dream," Young grinned. "Whether it's really happening or a farce, we won't know for a while. But there is a sense of forgiveness, a feeling that because of his own suffering, Wallace has a new understanding for the suffering of others. I don't know if that translates into votes, but there's no bitterness over the past. . . . The irony is that we never would have made the kind of progress [we did] without a Wallace, although he may not understand that."[75]

Perhaps no one could quite understand it: without newly enfranchised black voters, Mayor Young would not be mayor, nor Governor Wallace governor. However one assessed the number of personal white "conversions," the power of votes to change the dynamics of racial politics could not be doubted by any of these observers. The tonality of talk about sin and repentance in politics here was rich with many dimensions of black people's culture, religion, self-interest, and historical experience. Black rural Alabamians seemed to know something about how a society changes for the better: by a certain balance between realism and hope, trust and mistrust of power, justice and compassion, remembering and forgiving. Northern journalists might call it an instance of a "tribal ethic,"[76] but it seemed closer to truth to say that it was an instance of people determined to live together as neighbors in one political community in spite of all the pulls of history to the contrary. No one put this mixture of dimensions more simply or eloquently than did John Lewis, veteran of the Selma and Mississippi voting rights campaign and (in 1990) a member of Congress from Atlanta. Reflecting on the Selma campaign, the "old" George Wallace, and his old allies, Lewis said in 1992:

> I don't feel bitterness towards George Wallace and Sheriff Jim Clark and the KKK. I see them as victims of the system, and we were out to change that system. We weren't out to destroy America; we were out to change America to be at peace with itself. . . . We are one people, one family, one house—the American house.[77]

But the *votes* were basic. And basic to the votes had been a change in law and law enforcement which had cost the suffering of thousands of people in the movement. No one had to tell a John Lewis or an Andrew Young that southern politics, however full of irony and paradox, had changed for the better in 1982 because of blood and tears shed in Selma in 1965 and—even more—in Mississippi in the years 1963–66. No summary of the impact of the movement on the political culture of the South can be complete without a return to some account of that latter struggle.

Mississippi Summers

In the early sixties, slowly and sometimes painfully, the civil rights movement was reintroducing its followers and its enemies to an old arrow in the quiver of principles necessary for the pursuit of self-interest in a democracy: the opportunity to speak truth to power, whether by a vote, a petition for grievance, or a public display of justified anger. In a society which, especially in the South, had often covered up racial and other conflict as too dangerous to bring into the open, this was in itself a considerable contribution to a reformed and renewed political culture. No matter that inside the civil rights movement as well as on the frontiers of its outside struggle with white intransigence, outbursts of hostility and actual violence sometimes led to tragic disruptions of unity among the oppressed and new alienations from the oppressor. Such conflicts are old in politics, and sometimes it takes the composure of a Martin King to mend the fences that break under these blows, to continue negotiations that both sides seem bent on shattering. In the wake of that determination to keep fences mended and dialogue going, surprising new reconciliations sometimes occur in the public square—as when on March 17, 1965, after renewed police violence in Montgomery had exacerbated tensions in the movement, threatening to obscure the victory now in the making, the local sheriff issued a rare public apology for the violence of his deputies the day before.[78]

To demonstrate that one can confront and oppose enemies without attempting to annihilate them is a political gain in any civic culture. To educate the enemy in the justice of one's cause and to persuade that enemy to consent to that justice is a still greater gain. In that gain a certain measure of forgiveness comes to birth along with beginnings of new social covenants. Such gain is fragile among fractious humans, and in America it seems always vulnerable to new onslaughts of racism fortified with renewed violence. Above all, the civil rights movement affirmed that public democratic dialogue can and must include every citizen. To the extent that it did so for African Americans, it was doing so for every person and group to whom a majority might turn a deaf ear into the far future of the country. The lesson and benefit of what Japanese Americans achieved between 1942 and 1988 were exactly the same.

In the South, at least, movement leaders knew that Mississippi would be the ultimate test case of its ability to pry open civic society for black people. In 1962, in all eleven southern states, 26.8 percent of blacks eligible to vote were actually registered. In Alabama the figure sank to 13.4 percent, but in Mississippi it was a minuscule 5.3 percent.[79]

By 1993, changes in voting participation, number of black elected officials, and open rejection of racist politics by officeholding whites in Mississippi would be so dramatic that it must now be difficult for young people there to remember the costs of this change paid by thousands of people from inside and outside the state in the early 1960s. The Voting Rights Act of 1965, crafted out of Selma and enforced finally with federal registration supervisors, became the watershed event in this phase of the struggle. The cost of the enforcement of these first black inroads into electoral participation since Reconstruction would include murders, mental breakdowns, numerous imprisonments, and vast white anger fueled by racist rhetoric of state and local politicians.

Without surveying the whole history of several "Mississippi summers" here, anyone thinking back to this chapter of American history can see in the biography of one heroine of the movement in this state an embodiment of that chapter. She embodies not only the courage but also the astonishing forgiving spirit of untold numbers of black Mississippians. Further, responses to her story among many white people down to her death in 1977 hold some promise for their conversion, too, from old racist politics to the politics of inclusive democracy. At the same time, the failures of many liberal whites in a national political party to translate the moral power of that story into political recognition would dim that promise with the compromises that await every moral hero or heroine who ventures into democratic coalitions.

The heroine was Fannie Lou Hamer. A person of remarkable native intelligence and even more remarkable courage, Mrs. Hamer studied the Mississippi state constitution closely enough to pass a devious official voter registration "test," on her second try, in her hometown of Ruleville on January 10, 1963. Some of her white neighbors had no intention of celebrating her success.

> I passed that second test, but it made us become like criminals. We would have to have our lights out before dark. It was cars passing that house all times of the night, driving real slow with guns, and pickups with white mens in it, and they'd pass that house just as slow as they could pass it . . . three guns lined up in the back. All of that. This was the kind of stuff. [My husband] Pap couldn't [find work]. . . .
>
>   So I started teachin' citizenship class [in the Voter Education Project of the SCLC] . . . and later on I became a field secretary for SNCC—I guess being about one of the oldest people at that time that was a field secretary, 'cause they was real young. . . .

That summer of 1963 she was arrested, with six other black women and men, in Winona, Mississippi, for entering the "white" washroom in a bus station, where town officials had not yet bowed to the ruling of the Interstate Commerce Commission desegregating transportation facilities. The old brutal rituals of police intimidation were reenacted that day in the county jail.

"Cain't you say yessir, nigger? Cain't you say yessir, bitch?"
And I could understand Miss [Annelle] Ponder's voice. She said, "Yes, I can say yessir." He said, "Well, say it." She said, "I don't know you well enough." She never would say yessir, and I could hear, when she would hit the flo', and then I could hear them licks just soundin'. [Softly] That was somethin'. That's an experience—that's an experience that I wouldn't want to go through again. But anyway, she kept screamin', and they kept beatin' on her, and finally she started prayin' for 'em, and she asked God to have mercy on 'em, because they didn't know what they was doin'.[80]

The police beating which Fannie Lou Hamer herself then endured in the Winona jail was soon to become a politically powerful story, especially as she told it to the 1964 convention of the Democratic party in Atlantic City, where she was a leader of the Mississippi Freedom Democratic party (MFDP), whose delegation challenged the legitimacy of the all-white "regular" delegation from the state. Despite little success in Atlantic City, the televised testimony of Mrs. Hamer to the credentials committee proved yet another media triumph of the movement.[81] Members of her delegation left Atlantic City frustrated and angry at what powerful national Democrats thought they had to do to win an election in 1964, but the president thus elected would in a few months finally spend some of his prestige among southern whites by backing a voting rights bill. Out of that legislation would come new balances of electoral power throughout the Deep South. When he signed the 1965 Voting Rights Act, Johnson would remark to his adviser Bill Moyers, "We [the Democratic party] can say good-bye to our majority in the South for the next generation,"[82] a prediction that fell short only in the case of Jimmy Carter, elected president in 1976 by margins of votes cast by black southerners, many of them enfranchised through the effects of the 1965 act.

In 1966, three years after her time in the Winona jail, *Mississippi Magazine* named Fannie Lou Hamer one of the state's six "women of influence" and printed her picture alongside that of an aristocratic white neighbor also from the Delta. In 1973, her home town of Ruleville held Fannie Lou Hamer Day, and the white mayor, who had once jailed her husband for an overdue water bill, said that "she would go down in history as a champion of her people."[83] In his long interview with her in 1975, Howell Raines asked: "Do you think through all the years leading up to the Movement days, did white people in Mississippi know they were wrong?"

She replied: "Some of 'em really didn't, 'cause I don't think they really saw us as human beings. . . . I always believed some cared and some I don't think saw us as people." It was at once a moral and a political reply, for in the voting campaign of the movement politics and morality touched each other. Citizen rights both express and promote moral dignity, a circular relation eloquently illustrated in the interconnection of the new power and the new respect which came to black people in many corners of the South once they entered the electoral process. Now they had a public presence, making it yet more difficult for racists to pretend that they were not really "people."

Fannie Lou Hamer died two years after the Raines interview, on March 15, 1977, the exact twelfth anniversary of Lyndon Johnson's memorable speech to Congress on behalf of the Voting Rights Act. In the months preceding, in spite of illness, she was working to unite the black and white factions of the Mississippi Democratic party in anticipation of the 1976 Democratic convention in New York City. That fall before her death, she must have had the satisfaction of knowing that, thanks to the margin of Democratic votes cast by southern blacks for Jimmy Carter, he was elected as the first Deep South-born president since Reconstruction. Fannie Lou Hamer knew that she had a role in the election of this American president, who, among other open acknowledgments of his debts to the likes of her, would appoint a close associate of Martin Luther King, Jr., Andrew Young, as United States ambassador to the United Nations. A few weeks after March 15, 1977, the Mississippi state legislature unanimously passed a resolution praising Hamer's service to the state.

Thousands of anonymous others, however, also deserved such resolutions; no account of the civil rights movement should neglect to note the personal price that some of them paid for their devotion to the political dream of a Fannie Lou Hamer and a Martin Luther King, Jr. Many of these unsung heroes and heroines were ordinary southern black people, some sixty-three of whom were murdered for their political activity in the years just prior to the 1964 Mississippi campaign. More subtly devastating was the psychological strain that unnumbered workers in the movement suffered in their adherence to nonviolence over against constant hostility from local white residents. David Dennis, codirector with Robert Moses of the Mississippi Summer Project, described the interior toll on one worker, George Raymer, who died of a heart attack in the early seventies. "He dropped out of high school and came into Mississippi with me and wanted to stay, and he worked day and night, worked hard. . . . According to the doctors he had a heart of a seventy-year-old man. . . . George wasn't even thirty. . . ."[84] Mental hospitals, jail, and alcohol claimed a share of workers. Said David Dennis in 1993, "When the movement moved on these people were left behind, like the M.I.A.'s from the Vietnam War."[85]

If in the 1990s racism is far from absent in the customs, cultures, and institutions of political life in Mississippi or anywhere else in America, the ways in which it has diminished ought not to be overlooked in any remembering of this history. Writing in 1984, Aldon D. Morris, African American sociologist, summarized his assessment of the "new south" as follows:

> Prior to the movement the system of segregation forced blacks to live in a separate and limited world characterized by poverty, racial discrimination, powerlessness, symbolic subordination, and imperative acts of deference to white supremacy. The South is a different place today. Most of the "white" schools, washrooms, theaters, swimming pools, parks, bus seats and other facilities are either integrated or at least not segregated by law. This does not mean that the races are thoroughly integrated in the South, because economic and residential segregation, which lead to segregation in other spheres of life, is widespread nationally. Nevertheless, with many symbols of white supremacy dismantled and many facilities formally desegregated, Southern

blacks now live in a world where they can function with fewer restrictions and one that does not automatically strip them of human dignity. In a recent speech Stokely Carmichael [chairman of SNCC in 1966 and an originator of the "black power" movement] told a young questioner who doubted that the civil rights movement had made a difference that "blacks in Montgomery will never go to the back of the bus again." That is the essence of the change. The battles of the movement, culminating in the passage of the 1964 Civil Rights Act, made this significant change possible.[86]

In the middle seventies, even the militant Hartman Turnbow (whom Martin King never convinced to adopt nonviolence) stated that he considered Mississippi the best place to live in the entire country. Here, he said, "you can just enjoy yourself better. It's just a better living. A better way of life And I'm goin' finish it right here. I'm just sayin' for a poor person, it's just gittin' right." Interviewer Raines believes that "the South, by getting right, had at last allowed Hartman Turnbow to be the gentle man it was always his nature to be."[87] The terms which both of these men use to describe the changes are quiet indexes to the intimate relation in all this history between anyone's ability to "enjoy oneself" and what a surrounding society "allows."

A society that tags any of its members as inferior diminishes their ability to enjoy who they are. But there is a complementary diminishment on all sides of a human relation afflicted by racism. A self that stands up against such diminishment needs others to stand with; both the means and the end of personal worth require a society, a social means of support. The means and the ends of racism require the same. They both require society, citizenship, and politics. "Strangely enough," said Martin King in 1961, "I can never be what I ought to be until you are what you ought to be."[88] In individualistic, Lockean America, it did sound strange. It was a truth that Americans all needed to learn, but which the culture of African Americans apparently taught them long centuries ago. If culture critics want to see demonstrations of what "the social self" looks like in practice, they should look first at the history of African Americans.

The struggle for the dignity and participation of all Americans in their society has miles to go before its 1994 prophets can sleep in peace, but they are further down their road now than ever they could have been without the successes of the civil rights movement in the fifties and sixties. Even the limited gains of the movement convinced many other Americans of the era that if blacks could make such gains, so could any group of citizens with valid complaints about the society: hence the emergence, in the late 1960s, of movements for peace in Vietnam, the rights of women, the social responsibility of corporations, the protection of the world's ailing natural environment, and the rights of gay and lesbian people. For all of these citizen initiatives in the post-1968 era, the civil rights movement could claim to have put in place a powerful precedent and hope.

But the most powerful precedent and hope lay in the movement's achievement of voting rights for African Americans. Political representation in local, state, and national legislatures would not, even in 1993, fulfill their need for transformed systems of economic, social, and educational opportunity. After 1965, however, real power for meeting that need began to accrue in the hands of black politicians, especially in the once all-white legislatures and city councils of the South. By 1991, Alabama had 706 black elected officials, Mississippi 690, and Louisiana 551. In mid-

1992, by dint of court-mandated redistricting, blacks would compose almost a fourth of the Mississippi legislature in a state with 36 percent black population. By 1992, seventeen out of forty black members of the U.S. Congress were from the South. About 70 percent of the country's 7,552 black elected officials in 1993 were from seventeen southern states and the District of Columbia. Nationally, the number of congressional and state legislative representatives went from 182 to 484 in 1970–91 period; the number of elected city and county officials from 715 to 4,508 in the same period; and the number of elected law enforcement officers from 213 to 847. In August of 1993, among the most impressive symbols of justice delayed and justice finally achieved would appear in Selma, Alabama, its black population now at 58 percent. There, where support for the Voting Rights Act of 1965 had been most decisively mobilized, thanks again to a redistricting order, five out of nine city council seats went to black leaders.[89]

Ironically, these achievements of real political power were too far in the future or too irrelevant to the gnawing needs of many African Americans to persuade some of them that the dream of Martin King was both right and realistic. And the place of nonviolence as a path to the achievement of power was to come under growing black criticism as the movement celebrated its tenth anniversary in the midst of all it had to celebrate. A new movement seemed about to supplant and contradict King and all his political works: it called itself black power. Is there anything to learn from that successor movement about the place of forgiveness in the ongoing political relations of white and black Americans? That neglected question deserves some attention here.

Black Power and Political Forgiveness?

The word *power* fell from the lips of Martin Luther King, Jr. early and late in his public career, more frequently than many of his white admirers tend to remember. In the spring of 1956 he said to a mass meeting of black supporters of the Montgomery bus boycott that "until we as a race learn to develop our power, we will get nowhere. We've got to get political power and economic power for our race," and we can begin to do so now in the voting booth and by setting up our own bank here in Montgomery.[90]

As his experience and national leadership grew, King came to understand more and more the varieties and uses of power for social change in America. In 1961, in a heated telephone exchange with Attorney General Robert Kennedy, he said flatly, "You must understand that we've made no gains without pressure and I hope that pressure will always be moral, legal, and peaceful." In early 1963, as he met with SCLC leaders to reflect on the mistakes of the Albany campaign and to plan for Birmingham, he acknowledged that the movement had to choose the targets of its demonstrations carefully, since in some communities the path to influencing the political elite lay through the economic elite. "You can march on City Hall" if you have votes, but you had better march on the department stores if you have only your buying power.

Especially in the last three years of his life, as the movement spread to northern cities, King developed yet more respect for the power of credible threats to the economic and political interests of the policymakers. By the spring of 1967 he had begun to see a new, just American society chiefly as new power balances between the powerful and the powerless. "[I]ntegration," he said to the SCLC staff, "must be seen not merely in aesthetic or romantic terms; it must be seen in political terms. Integration in its true dimensions is shared power." He then went on to words that echoed Reinhold Niebuhr: "One past shortcoming [of the movement] was that 'all too many people have seen power and love as polar opposites,' when in fact 'the two fulfill each other. . . . power without love is reckless, and love without power is sentimental.'" Just ten days before his death, in late March 1968, he uttered virtually the same words to an annual convention of the Rabbinical Assembly in upstate New York.[91]

But there were two principles in King's philosophy of power that, in the mid-sixties, brought him into collision with movement leaders attracted to the slogan, "black power:" (1) nonviolence and (2) "black and white together." The moral and religious roots of these principles were always clear to him, but he frequently pointed out that sheer political pragmatics made them mandatory, too. Nonviolence was consistent with many forms of pressure against injustice, but violence to life and limb merely repeated the crimes that had long been committed against African Americans. Moreover, pragmatically, the violence commanded by a white majority could overwhelm any violence that a minority could muster. As he came to the end of his life, King saw much hypocrisy among white Americans in the matter of "legitimate" violence— that is, violence in war and against the nonviolent protests of the poor. But he was sure that, if the movement ever turned to violence, it would worsen the plight of minorities. Similarly, he was sure that under modern conditions of life no minority in America could survive without constructively relating to people outside their own community. Neither in moral nor in practical terms was any human an island. Like Rodney King twenty-five years later, Martin King was sure that black separatism held no future for African Americans. Whatever the solution to their continued sufferings, "[i]t had to be a solution based on the assumption that the black minority and white majority must learn how to live together as brothers and sisters *in America*."[92]

Both principles came under public attack on June 16, 1966, when Stokely Carmichael, chairman of SNCC, stood on the back of a truck and shouted the slogan "black power" to a crowd of marchers in Greenwood, Mississippi. The marchers were continuing the walk to Jackson begun by James Meredith, who had been shot from ambush on June 6.[93] The phrase rang with the realities of political justice on the day when Carmichael uttered it in range of the media. He knew about the counties in the Deep South in which black people composed a majority, in which none of them could vote, and whose white law enforcers regularly ignored the violence of whites against blacks. The powerlessness and passivity of black people—even their reputation for returning love for hate—seemed to *invite* their continued exploitation by the powerful, or so Malcolm X had claimed right up to his own death from violence in 1965. Was it not time for black people to acquire power to protect their own lives and interests? When in American history had whites disdained power for that purpose?

In the midst of all the tensions which the "black power" chant continued to stir between the Jackson marchers, King made his "most passionate speech" of the march in defense of his two unshakable principles. The murder of black people may be a "popular pastime" in Mississippi, said King to the marchers, but countermurder was no true political response. Further: "I'm not interested in power for power's sake" but in power that is moral and effective for the interests of black Americans. "We are ten percent of the population of this nation," and we cannot "get our freedom by ourselves. There's going to have to be a coalition of conscience, and we aren't going to be free here in Mississippi and anywhere in the United States until there is a committed empathy on the part of the white man. . . . We can't win violently."[94]

In these same years, the most powerful voice of scorn for the notion of "committed empathy" from white Americans, and the most articulate public antagonist of Martin King, was the Nation of Islam leader Malcolm X. Up to the last year of his life, Malcolm poured out contempt for the integrationist ideal. Instead he called African Americans to self-respect, primary loyalty to each other, and pride in their African heritage as the only way back to the humanity that white America had so long denied them. Malcolm had equal contempt for nonviolence, telling his followers to defend themselves against the violence which once had enslaved their ancestors and now confined them to the poverty of inner-city ghettos. He hurled the badge of collective guilt into the face of every white American: "You cannot find *one* black man . . . who has not been personally damaged in some way by the devilish acts of the collective white man!"[95] The only "solution" to this bedevilment, said Malcolm up to almost the end of his career, was separation.

But in the months after the Birmingham campaign, as James Cone has documented in his careful study of the two leaders, Martin and Malcolm drew closer to each other's political philosophies than contemporary journalism permitted the public to perceive. As he too faced the realities of black life in the city ghettos of the North, King understood better the profound alienation of young black men and women from all sense of belonging to a society that was rich, democratic, and the "defender of freedom" across the Pacific. Their experience in the ghetto was one of poverty, powerlessness, and oppression. Their occasional resort to crimes of violence was the fruit of despair and want of self-respect. They learned violence, often enough, from the local police; when drafted into an army now fighting in Vietnam, they learned anew that in some circumstances the American government saw *massive* violence as the legitimate *servant* of "liberty and justice for all."

Middle class in origin, Martin King had long ago demonstrated his own remarkable capacity for "committed empathy" with the black poor of the South, and increasingly he came to express it for the black poor of northern cities. Increasingly, too, he came to believe that good will and empathy from white Americans were rarities and that the majority of whites would have to be pressured into accepting political equality and economic justice for their black neighbors. In spite of this shift in stress in his philosophy of change, however, King's "dream" of an America inclusive of all races and his certainty that nonviolence was the only right, practical path to that new America did not waver.

In the last year of his life, Malcolm underwent changes in his outlook that were to bring him closer to King on the matters of both nonviolence and integration. During his first visit with Islamic leaders in the Middle East in 1964, Malcolm learned that orthodox Islam taught interracial unity, especially among its adherents. In Mecca, he said, "I witnessed such . . . overwhelming spirit of true brotherhood as it is practiced by people . . . here in this ancient holy land." There were even white people in those crowds around the Khabela: "They were of all colors, from blue-eyed blonds to black-skinned Africans. But we were all participating in the same ritual, displaying a spirit of unity and brotherhood that my experiences in America had led me to believe could never exist between the white and the non-white."[96]

Malcolm was a man with an acute appreciation of fact, including facts new to him. His Middle East experience led to his decisive break with the leadership of Elijah Mohammed in 1964. In the next year, he began to applaud the politics of the civil rights movement. Tolerance began to replace his scorn for the idea that blacks could ever be the willing political partners of white people, especially in the United States. "Now that I have more independence-of-action I intend to use a more flexible approach toward working with others to get a solution"—to the problem of his own alienation from large numbers of ordinary African Americans and from leaders of the movement in particular. His language became conciliatory toward them; more remarkably, it became repentant. For the concrete achievements of food, clothing, housing, education, and jobs for all African Americans, their leaders must cooperate, he now said. He himself must now do so: "I am not out to fight other Negro leaders or organizations. We must find a common approach, a common solution, to a common problem. As of this minute, I've forgotten everything bad that the other leaders have said about me, and I pray they can also forget the many bad things I've said about them."[97] Against the background of all the rancor which Malcolm's rhetoric had stirred in the minds and emotions of his critics, black and white, this was an astonishing public plea. It was a gesture toward mutual forgiveness among black leaders themselves, fractured as they often were in these months over matters of political philosophy, strategy, and mutual personal respect. In the last months of his life, Malcolm had even begun to retract some of his hostile remarks about white people.[98]

That white and black Americans might both learn something about political repentance and forgiveness from *Malcolm X* was a radically new thought in the public consciousness of 1964. It is still in 1994, for most, a new thought. "Self-criticism and humility," comments Cone, "are rare traits among leaders in the government, churches, and freedom movements. . . . The leaders of the poor cannot represent their constituency well unless they remain humble and self-critical."[99] *A fortiori*, neither can leaders of the rich.

In a word, Malcolm was finally ready to be political in ways that Martin had long ago exemplified in his rightly celebrated capacity to bring fractured, hostile people into practical cooperation for the sake of high political causes. As Cone comments, "Martin's prestige in the black community was primarily the result of his ability to transcend many petty differences among civil rights leaders and effectively speak to the everyday needs of black people."[100] In this Martin was in every sense a skilled politician, while Malcolm was chiefly a brilliant ideologue.

There are many illustrations of King's political skills scattered throughout his biography.[101] He regularly distinguished between the compromisable means and ends of politics and the uncompromisable; he overlooked personal slights if that was the price of continued cooperation; even in moments of triumph over enemies of the movement, he took care to make them feel that they were not being handed a defeat but the chance to live now on new levels of justice and reconciliation. Late in the Albany campaign, he said to Mayor Asa Kelley that the movement wanted, not "victory" but "reconciliation." And in Chicago four years later he concluded a long round of tense negotiations with Mayor Richard Daley and city real estate leaders with the words:

> I speak to everyone on my [movement] side of the table now, and I say that this must be interpreted, this agreement, as a victory for justice and not a victory over the Chicago Real Estate Board or the city of Chicago. I am as grateful to Mayor Daley as to anyone else for his work. I think now we can go on to make Chicago a beautiful city, a city of brotherhood.

At this, spontaneous applause broke out "from all sides of the table."[102]

King knew when to speak words of political healing. He knew that moral politicians will not want to speak them too soon—or too late: too soon, and justice may get short-changed; too late, and unity may never return. The dialogue of justice and unity is what politics—and forgiveness in politics—ought to be about.

Affluent Americans in the 1990s, especially those who can afford to ignore the grass-roots conflicts of ordinary politics—precinct caucuses, back-room compromises, and settings aside of personal ego for the sake of large public achievement— may be tempted to underestimate the crucial importance of that fragile unity in the civil rights movement which enabled it to make an impact on American law and political culture. In fact it was no small achievement, especially among a people so pushed out of the political mainstream that they had to learn politics in churches and lodges rather than in political parties and legislatures. Their modest political experience and the gnawing realities of poverty and discrimination gave them every reason to hunger after power, prestige, and recognition in ways that can stir up rivalries in any political movement and destroy it in its beginning. At times the civil rights movement seemed in danger of such self-destruction, but along with many other persons of political skill and strong personal character, the likes of Martin King held ordinary people together for the accomplishment of some extraordinary political goals. The divisions in the movement did not really grow out of disputes over black power so much as out of ordinary interpersonal and inter-organizational competition over choices of leadership, strategy, and allocations of money.

Above all, the political-ethical question that hovered over the movement and haunted Martin King to the end of his days came down to this question: What *breadth* of political community do Americans really mean to constitute among themselves? Without intending to do so, the black leaders of the civil rights movement prepared the way in the 1980s for the American government to acknowledge at last that it had ignored its own founding principles when it interned Americans of Japanese ancestry. They prepared diverse other groups similarly, as we have noted. At the same time, they exemplified to many an anxious neighbor, descendant of white Europeans, the uncomfortable side of Martin Luther King's "dream": a *new* United States in which no one's inherited culture was superior to another's and to which people of every culture on earth might conceivably belong. The poignant plea that Rodney King uttered in 1992 ("We're all stuck here for a while. Let's try to work it out.") was an echo of what another King had said twenty-five years before: "For better or worse we are all on this particular land together at the same time, and we have to work it out together."[103]

In words like these, Martin Luther King, Jr. was publishing a new, revised edition of the theory of a multinational nation which was implicitly planted on the shores of Virginia the moment in 1619 that black slaves were unloaded on the Jamestown wharf. The theory did not come even to full literary expression among those enlightened rationalist white American men who wrote the Declaration of Independence and the U.S. Constitution a century and a half later. As we have seen many times in these pages, political behavior often enough lags behind political ideals; the moral-political achievement of Martin King's final years was his dream of multicultural democratic humanism, brought at last out of the shadows of its ambiguity in the most hallowed documents of American history. It was time, King said on hundreds of occasions, to translate the moral dignity of all humans into terms of the rights and duties of citizenship in a country whose preeminent founding philosopher had written that "all men are created equal." All *humans*, King kept saying, even though his women hearers had reason to wonder if even *he* had learned to include them in the practical implications of his humanistic dream for America.[104]

In short, as in this late twentieth century white Americans celebrate his birthday as a national holiday, they should acknowledge that in Martin Luther King, Jr. a greater political moralist than Thomas Jefferson had arrived in America, for more clearly and radically than that celebrated predecessor, King saw that both the ideals and the structures of American democracy had to be reformed and revolutionized to become *really* humanistic.[105] "Martin really believed that the people of the world are one," says James Cone. The implication of that belief, if it is not to degenerate into bland aphoristic liberalism, is the radical humane mutuality of plurality of cultures in a single political order.

> If African-Americans or any other people define their freedom struggle in terms of the superiority of their culture over others, they will develop . . . [an] arrogant and condescending attitude toward others. Martin King was right: We are bound to each other—not just blacks with blacks nor whites with whites or Koreans with Koreans, but all races of people in the United States and throughout the world are one human family, made to live together in freedom.

The rainbow and not the melting pot really is the better image for this version of the democratic dream, and Americans-all can begin to remember Martin Luther King, Jr., as a person who, more clearly than Jefferson or Lincoln, discerned the possibility that a truly "new nation" might be built on grounds of the "proposition that all humans are created equal" in value. Therefore they equally deserve the privileges of citizenship. It is a truly radical idea, especially in late-twentieth-century global politics, in which numerous nations are celebrating their right to form themselves politically on the basis of some uniform ethnic tradition. Not for them the idea that a nation might aspire to a citizenry that is "the world in miniature."[106]

The idea of a nation whose residents affirm each other's humanity in all its variety was far removed, too, from the American horizon on the day that a morally stunted, politically ignorant white American snuffed out the life of Martin King with a single bullet. The urban riots that followed this assassination, right down to 1994, pushed the dream of an inclusive, humanistic America further yet into the future, leaving in history yet another racist atrocity to be remembered, mourned, and repented of in the lives of every honest American. The remnants of racism die hard everywhere on earth. Could there be enough repentance, enough forgiveness, to clear the way for such a truly new future for this or any other nation on earth? Malcolm X and his kin showed us how heavy the question is; Martin and his, how the hope in the question must not go away.

"That Old and Still Unpaid Debt"

In politics as in every other human relation, the two sides of forgiveness must never be lost to sight: forgiveness is interdependent with repentance. Absent the latter, the former remains incomplete, conditional, in a posture of waiting. So, if in the culture of African America there resides a unique reservoir of willingness to forgive the rest of America for its crimes against black people, there resides there also a waiting for degrees of political-social repentance not yet visible to many black people in the America of 1994. What they most wait for is a new measure of *economic* justice. A celebration of the contribution of the civil rights movement to the hope of a genuinely humanistic version of democracy in America would be incomplete without recognition of this still looming national agenda.

On the day of his assassination in Memphis, Martin King was in that city to support a garbage workers' strike. All of them knew that the achievement of civil rights in American politics had less daily meaning to most African Americans than the achievement of economic justice in their world of work. In his final speeches, writings, and programs, King focused ever more steadily on the economic "strides toward freedom" that America would have to take in relation to its poorest citizens—black and white—if they were to become citizens in every sense of the word. The poor for him included the "people left behind"[107] of every race; but proportionate to their share in the national population, African Americans had, by far, more than their share of poverty.

Had he lived to 1994, he would still be working on this economic side of injustice and pain in this national society. As Lawrence Mamiya wrote in 1992: "It is a hard lesson of recent history that the Civil Rights movement took its most devastating hits and crashed on the shoals of the economic issues of the poor in American society. . . . The new cross of American society is also an old one, the cross of the poor. Who will pick it up and carry it?"

Quoting from a recent comprehensive study of the National Research Council,[108] Mamiya points to the growing polarization between the incomes of a rising African American middle class and the neighbors they probably left behind in an urban ghetto. Some 22 percent of white families in 1986 had incomes over $50,000, as did 8.8 percent of African American families, an increase from 4.7 percent in 1970, accompanied by a similar increase from 15.7 percent to 21.2 percent of African American families with incomes over $35,000. But in these years the proportion of black families with incomes of less than $10,000 a year grew from 26.8 to 30.2 percent, and this was a trend due to continue into the 1990s. Median black family income has climbed slowly in comparison with white family income—it is now about 60 percent of the latter. An equally telling statistic, says Mamiya, is the fact that white people overall in this country "have an intergenerational wealth base of ten times as much family wealth as African Americans." Among other things, this means that those African Americans who achieve middle-class status have very little economic cushion for maintaining that status or for helping their families and friends to achieve it too.[109]

The Los Angeles riots of April 1992 were still ahead when this Vassar sociologist, a Japanese American born in Hawaii, summarized his response to these and other statistics of poverty in the United States in a moral judgment: "The United States as a society has neglected the poor in its midst for too long and is now beginning to pay for its stubborn dereliction in rising crime rates, the collapse of urban infrastructures and services, and educational and economic vulnerabilities."

The language was close to that of Martin King twenty-five years earlier. But rational economic perceptions were now different: in the late sixties American citizens and politicians were riding the crest of economic prosperity that convinced many that they could simultaneously win a foreign war in Vietnam and a domestic war against poverty. In retrospect we all know that it was an impossible goal. But King knew the same in prospect. Writing in 1967, he said that the federal government's 1964 War on Poverty had "seemed to herald a new day of compassion" in a nation that "would no longer stand complacently by while millions of its citizens smothered in poverty in the midst of opulence." When he looked at the figures, however, he could only conclude that, compared to its budget for military war, the budget for the poverty war "could not launch a good skirmish against poverty."[110]

In that economically optimistic year of 1966, some members of the Johnson administration actually began to calculate what a real war on poverty might cost the people of the United States. King quoted one of them, Hyman Bookbinder, assistant director of the Office of Economic Opportunity, in his last published book: the project, said Bookbinder, would come to about a trillion dollars.

> [Bookbinder] was not awed or dismayed by this prospect but instead pointed out that the growth of the gross national product during the same period makes this expenditure comfortably possible. It is, he said, as simple as this: "The poor can stop being poor if the rich are willing to become even richer at a slower rate." Furthermore, he predicted that unless a "substantial sacrifice is made by the American people," the nation can expect further deterioration of the cities, increased antagonism between races and continued disorder in the streets. He asserted that people are not informed enough to give adequate support to anti-poverty programs, and he leveled a share of the blame at the government because it "must do more to get people to understand the size of the problem.[111]

Remembering the next twenty years of economic change in the life of Americans makes these opinions painful reading: The GNP stopped growing at its 1960–70 rate; wage-earner income from 1973 was to stagnate and even decline; middle-class Americans found two jobs per family necessary for maintaining their economic status; tax revolts would multiply; international competition would throw thousands of Americans out of their jobs; a "secure" job now seemed improbable for wage and salary earners alike; in the 1980s, the very rich got richer at a faster pace than anybody else; and, as the national debt soared, a Republican administration convinced the U.S. Congress to divert $2 trillion of the federal budget out of human service programs into the largest military buildup in the nation's history. A "comfortably possible" war on poverty, in 1993, had begun to look fantastic to many Americans and their elected politicians. Who could win a national election in 1992 with a promise to construct Bookbinder's trillion-dollar antipoverty program, now increased by inflation to $3 trillion? Who had the political nerve to call for "a substantial sacrifice of the American people" to conduct an assault, serious this time, upon poverty?

Some would say that amid the current economic anxieties of many Americans there is simply no resonance for the economic desperation of that minority of their neighbors who are poor, getting poorer, and disproportionately African American. What *does* seem to add at least a flicker of understanding of the size of the problem, in our public as a whole, is an event like the Los Angeles riot of 1992. The grim predictions of a King, a Bookbinder, a Mamiya, and a host of other surveyors of the facts seem only too realistic in the wake of such events.

The potential of urban violence as public education for empathy for the poor seems very limited. After the Watts riots in 1965, Martin King heard young men there boast of the "success" of the conflagration: "We made them pay attention to us."[112] After the South Central Los Angeles riots of 1992, a journalist, visiting that community one year later, reported that her conversations with residents uncovered little jubilation: "Indeed, there is deep frustration that the riots got so much more attention than the unemployment, poverty, crime, isolation and racism that many believe set the scene for the turmoil." It was an old story. As Dr. Medria Williams, a black clinical psychologist at work in the area put it: "What matters is what led to the rebellion in the first place, and none of that has been addressed" by any responsible national political leader. "The country has learned nothing from this, and this is the tragedy."[113]

There are many things to learn from eruptions of violence in the contemporary American city, and it is not the task of this book to catalogue or speculate about all of them. But the interpretations of two residents of the city and one other Californian are worth noting here, for they underscore the complex message of the event to persons like myself concerned, in particular, with the future of African Americans.

The first is Madison T. Shockley, II, a young black pastor, whose congregation is at an the intersection of four communities in South Central Los Angeles. He observes that very few noncommercial buildings were damaged in the melee. The destructive hostility and the plundering had a common root, he says: frustrated response to a culture that celebrates daily the joys of owning things while tolerating levels of poverty that make ownership out of reach.

> Many poor people have been convinced that life means owning things. Being locked out of participation in consumer capitalism is for them their biggest problem. But access to consumption must be balanced—for all of us—with a change in this ideology. "How do I get what they've got?" is the wrong question for poor and rich alike. ... Race lit the fuse of the South Central riots, but class fueled the explosion.[114]

Then there was a dark psychosocial underside to this "multicultural uprising," he adds, an underside that former Sacramento resident Cornel West describes as "the murky water of despair and dread that now flood the streets of black America."[115] In 1970, says West, blacks had the lowest suicide rate in America; now young blacks have the highest rate. A name for this spreading ghetto despair is nihilism, "*the lived experience of coping with a life of horrifying meaninglessness, hopelessness, and (most important) lovelessness.*"[116] Underneath both the passive despair and the wild hostility of many poor people in the city was just this radical deficit of personal meaning, Shockley testifies. Many who heard the verdict of police innocence in the Rodney King case understood this syndrome only too well. On the one hand some "simply went into a depression and submitted, and said, 'The quality of my life has been compromised for the rest of my life. There's not a jury in the land . . . that would convict an officer of beating me half to death, and that is my life.'" But the complementary reaction was: "I will not go down quietly. . . . If I cannot be comfortable, then you cannot either." Cornel West summarizes both of these roots of black despair: "The fundamental crisis in black America is twofold: too much poverty and too little self-love."[117] The two are intimately connected.

But there was at least a third dimension to the Los Angeles tragedy: the looters and burners were multicultural; hostility flowed in many directions, especially between blacks, Latinos, and Asians. At root this dimension was suffused with perceived economic competition.

An astute, passionate account of this side of the event came six months later from Jack Miles, a white editor at the *Los Angeles Times* and a resident of the city since 1978.[118] Since the Watts conflagration of 1965, South Central has changed: for every black resident of South Central L.A. there is now a Latino resident. Miles finds a cameo version of the economic competition between the two groups in the fact that in the previous five years downtown hotel workers have shifted from being "almost 100 percent black and organized [in a union] to 100 percent immigrant, and non-union." Multiply this experience across the local economy, and one has the basis for the surmise:

> Whatever measure of power and influence [blacks] had pried loose from the White power structure, they now see as being in danger of being transferred to the Latino community. Not only are they losing influence, public offices, and control of the major civil rights mechanisms, they now see themselves being replaced in the pecking order by the Asian community, in this case the Koreans.

Told from this angle, the story defies the orthodox version of how economic America came to be: penniless, newly arrived immigrants are supposed take their places at the bottom of the escalator to be replaced by later arrivals. Such orthodoxy obscures the racist bar that kept African Americans far away from any "melting pot." They have to tell the story differently: slavery, segregation, and a uniquely strong white prejudice against black-skinned people weighted down their climb upward; no escalator for them, just the bottom of a ladder. And for at least one-third of African Americans in 1994, the inertias of that weight may well keep them at the bottom—while immigrants from Mexico and Asia climb over them, as for centuries white

Europeans climbed over them with the help of clear-cut long-time "affirmative action" consisting of employment preference for white people. Further, some new immigrants, especially Asians, may not be the penniless "tired and poor" but people with substantial financial and back-home family support. They are equipped for some quick jumps up the traditional ladder.

Against the background of the history of the civil rights movement, the irony here is that in the same year, 1965, when voting rights acquired real legal clout from the federal government for African Americans, that same government passed a long overdue immigration law that corrected the ancient white American preference for Europeans and opened up immigration quotas to all continents. Irony upon irony, says Miles, prejudice against black people in American culture gets expressed among Los Angeles white residents who will hire a newly arrived Latino immigrant from Mexico before they will hire "a fifteenth-generation" black resident of the United States. "They trust Latinos. They fear or disdain blacks. The result is unofficial but widespread preferential hiring of Latinos—the largest affirmative-action program in the nation, and one paid for, in effect, by blacks. . . . Latinos, even when they are foreign, seem native and safe, while blacks, who are native, seem foreign and dangerous." It is an embarrassing admission, confesses Miles. And the basic explanation for him lies not merely in the tangled economics of interethnic competition, but in the most damaging of all the facts of American history: "This is what slavery has done to us as a people, and I can scarcely think of it without tears."

Jack Miles offers no shrewd new way to untie this knot of old racism, rising poverty, and despair among many residents of the urban ghetto. In unprecedented volume, capital and labor now crisscross national boundaries around the globe. Perplexed, as many liberals and conservatives have to be in the 1990s by the apparent inability of this country to sustain a free market of immigrants and jobs without further damaging its already most damaged subgroup of citizens, they are likely to be at a loss for wisdom about how we might construct a new war against poverty in competition beset, debt burdened America. Perplexing, too, is the new phenomenon that many of the growing number of Asian and Latino immigrants across the land are still citizens of their home countries, whose political leaders consider them constituents with interests to be protected, even if they work in the United States.[119] "In short," concludes Miles ruefully, "America is no longer quite free to address the needs of is own underclass in isolation from similar needs elsewhere in the world."

We *are* free, however, to adopt from Miles the *moral* clarity that ends his article on the recent Los Angeles tragedy: its roots, for African Americans, in a far older tragedy: "My deepest, least argued or arguable hunch is that everything in America begins with that old and still unpaid debt."

There are some easy ways for both liberal and conservative white Americans to avoid thinking that the country has, hanging over its history, a national debt to African Americans. Conservatives can say, with some discomfort, that the passivity of the nonworking poor justifies the fall of some into despair, that for some people in American society there is simply no hope of economic salvation. Liberals can admit, with much discomfort, that opportunity for work should open to all the world's poor, that we cannot keep faith with the old American dream if we deny economic opportunity to legal immigrants, including those whose culture enables them to take quick advantage of enterprise in America. But these traditional ways of thinking do not address the plight of that one-third of African Americans who continue to be our worst case of poverty, sustained by the double burden of historic slavery and persisting antiblack racist prejudice. To this prejudice even Latinos and Asians are susceptible, especially after they arrive in San Francisco or New York. "It goes without saying," says Cornel West, "that a profound hatred of African people . . . sits at the center of American civilization."[120] Unfortunately, especially for white Americans, this fact does *not* go without saying. It ought to be said long enough and urgently enough to keep high in the rhetoric of our national discourse a public focus on *this* unpaid debt. If we keep it there rhetorically, we might, if only from embarrassment, finally do something to pay it in fact as well as in principle.

Like other payments, this one will cost money, more than this country has ever "thrown at" the problems of intergenerational poverty. That money alone will not "solve" the poverty problem in America does go without saying. Poverty is a multi-leveled reality. The very stringency of our new economic time calls for new, astute collaboration between government, voluntary sectors, religious congregations, business corporations, and local community leadership for a major assault on all the conditions that make for despair and self-hatred among one sector of African America. For this we may even have to modify our liberal immigration policies, as Jack Miles gingerly suggests in his essay. But like Martin King, those most conscious of America's debt to its black poor will not ask the nation for less than an inclusive focus on the needs of all the poor. Any genuine national attack on poverty will necessarily focus on poor blacks in great numbers. It is the greatness of that number, all out of proportion to their share in the population, which remains the statistic that advertises this as the great continuing moral scandal of American life.[121] Conservatives in the 1980s scored a great propaganda triumph when they coined the phrase "throwing money at a problem." That was a screen behind which national budget makers could throw money away from human services into an unprecedented military buildup. All told, the United States has spent some *twelve trillion dollars* since 1945 protecting itself militarily from the external threat of Communism, enough money, we are told, to replace every human structure erected on the land between Maine and California. Personally and collectively, we spend money on our priorities. The nation may find itself economically exhausted by its success in the Cold War, but remaining as we are the wealthiest country in the world, we have no morally plausible case for claiming that we cannot afford to subsidize useful jobs for the poor, greatly increased rehabilitative help for damaged ghetto youth, and new resources for reconstruction of our equally damaged inner-city communities.

A moralist like myself, of course, can be readily accused of taking his own easy way out for writing about this matter, when like many of the Americans quoted in this chapter, I too lack a program for solving the problem of poverty in America. But moral conviction combined with empirical realism could contribute at least two improvements in the quality of our public discourse here: first, it might first reaffirm the humanistic American dream that assumes, with an ancient scripture, that human beings really do not "live by bread alone" but by a personal worth that transcends the worth of their wealth and power. We Americans tend to be hypocritical here: we like to agree with this reply of Jesus to the Devil and to affirm that our humanity really does not "consist of the abundance of things one possesses."[122] But competitive markets and the pleasures of discretionary income seduce us into acting and thinking otherwise, so that we fall easily into the belief that one can never make too much money or accumulate too many possessions. Many an impoverished ghetto resident shares this belief, if Madison Shockley is right. Tax resistance roots in this seduction, and moral protest against it begins to sound old-fashioned in modern America, but if the protest ever disappears from our consciences or our public forum, we will lose one of the bedrock assumptions that makes democracy possible: humans have inherent value, inherent rights, and inherent obligations to each other.

A second gain from such moral clarity might be that it might move the majority of us to confess that *the* problem of poverty resides not alone in the poor but in the minds, the policies, and the budget priorities that link the rest of us to the life and death of the poor. Many of *us* are *the* problem; and in nothing do so many Americans participate more in that problem than in the ease with which we exempt ourselves from the accusation of racism just because we celebrate the civil rights movement and its very real political improvements in the lives of African Americans. The minds, the customs, and the institutions of the country are still enough laced with the scars and inertias of racism to keep even the most liberal and moral American in a posture of humility and repentance. That, of course, is the complementary side of forgiveness in politics, but it is time that we set out for ourselves an agenda of repentance in economics, one not to be accomplished overnight but one no longer subject to indefinite delay. Until we make the sacrifices as a nation and organize ourselves for that agenda, we can anticipate more despair and violence in our cities and greater threat to our dream of becoming a nation composed of nations.

Perhaps that is the real promise of national moral clarity which we owe to the poor of the land and especially to the black poor: that we will not have to wait until social chaos is so near our front doors that we have to resort to collective self-defenses so violent and so repressive that democracy itself is sacrificed in our desperate attempts to save it. The United States of America has been blessed by the leadership of a black community that has often expressed its willingness to forgive a nation for its crimes against black people on the condition that the nation acknowledge the crimes and make specific restitutions for their damages. Because those damages persist in the lives of so many African Americans, because those who have substantially recovered from the legacies of slavery are a minority, the agenda of restorative justice has to be heavy for this and the upcoming generation of Americans. Whether we call it justice or rehabilitation or reparation is less important than that we call it the first order of our domestic national business.

Until we make it that, African Americans have every right and obligation to reserve a certain portion of forgiveness in themselves for the day when that business has at last been tended to, that debt at last paid. Then the promise of words written forty years ago by James Baldwin will become a truth about American history that enters into the experience of every old and every new resident living between these shores:

> The time has come to realize that the interracial drama acted out on the American continent has not only created a new black man, it has created a new white man, too.

No road whatever will lead Americans back to the simplicity of [a] European village where white men still have the luxury of looking on me as a stranger. I am not, really, a stranger any longer for any American alive. One of the things that distinguishes Americans from other people is that no other people has ever been so deeply involved in the lives of black men, and vice versa. This fact faced, with all its implications, it can be seen that the history of the American Negro problem is not merely shameful, it is also something of an achievement. For even when the worst has been said, it must also be added that the perpetual challenge posed by this problem was always, somehow, perpetually met. It is precisely this black-white experience which may prove of indispensable value to us in the world we face today. This world is white no longer, and it will never be white again.[123]

In one of his accounts of the civil rights movement Vincent Harding says that, as he approached the end of his life, Martin Luther King, Jr., was "groping his way toward a new integration" among Americans.[124] No "new integration" will ever be possible between enemies in a struggle over social justice without their mutual achievement of a new memory of the past, a new justice in the present, and in a new hope for community in the still-to-be-achieved future. In every one of these dimensions of social renewal forgiveness has a powerful place. In its judging, empathizing, revenge-refusing, and reconciling work, it makes new society possible. African Americans, early and later, have been the most credible of our witnesses to this complex truth. They ask nothing less now than that other Americans will accept and act on that truth with them.

7

Whither Forgiveness in American Politics?

Whence did I acquire the power to love and forgive except from the
world, from life itself, which has bestowed it on me, ready for my
use when I was ready to use it?[1]

                                                        Petru Dumitriu

The spotlight we flash into the darkness of the past is guided by
our own concerns in the present. When new preoccupations arise in
our own times, the spotlight shifts, throwing into sharp relief
things that were always there but that earlier historians had
casually excised from the collective memory. In this sense, the
present may be said to re-create the past.[2]

                                                Arthur M. Schlesinger, Jr.

Midway in the writing of this book, in early 1992, I had the opportunity to test its
major themes in three months of conversation with a cross section of citizens of South
Africa. At first, many of them took occasion to warn me against my becoming "another American writing a book about South Africa." To this warning I always replied that my book centered on my own country but that a good reason for foreign
travel is to understand one's own more clearly through the perspectives of another.

In fact Americans can achieve impressive new clarity about the reality and costs
of racism in their own United States by observing the same in modern South Africa.
The *apartheid* regime of forty years has inflicted upon that society a stark version of
racist exploitation that mightily resembles slavery. South African whites may resent
the analogy, but not many black South Africans will. All wise people in both countries are likely to agree that recovery from structured, coercive racism in any society
is a long process. Estimates vary widely as to how long it will take a new government in South Africa to repair the damages done its majority during centuries of exclusion from land ownership, first-rate education, modern health care, decent housing, the best jobs, political power, and public recognition of human dignity. But
Americans who know the post-1865 history of freed black slaves and their contemporary descendants have every reason to wonder if a society so damaged can recover
in only a few decades.

Conversation with South Africans these days will alert any visitor to certain common political tasks that, in their various forms, face the upcoming generation of citizens in many countries of the world. In my own visits to fifty countries during my lifetime, in none has the subject of forgiveness in politics commanded the careful, immediate attention of my conversational partners as it did with those in South Africa in 1992. A British friend commented recently, "No one in Britain is interested in forgiveness, for no one believes in sin anymore." However much that may be so in western countries, in their flirtations with the ethical relativism discussed in Chapter 3, it is impossible *not* to believe in "sin" either in South Africa or in the United States as regards the evils of racism. A white South African, descendant of the English, commented to me in January 1992: "In his historic speech ending the official *apartheid* era two years ago, President F. W. de Klerk said, '*Apartheid* was a well-intentioned system that failed.' The opposite was the truth: it was a system born of evil intention, and it succeeded all too well." Clarity about this point is the beginning of political wisdom in South Africa. Americans owe it to each other to achieve analogous clarity about the roots and fruits of racism in our own history.

South Africans, especially black South Africans, can help us toward such clarity if, conscious of the great differences between our two countries, we attend to the similarities. Notable for the theme of this book is what South Africans say about the pertinence of all sides of a forgiving-forgiven transaction in their present and future politics: the white government and the white citizens of their country, they say, must make public apology for the sins of racism; there must soon be some tangible restitution for its deep damage to millions of human lives; the country must begin to fashion for itself a pluralistic political culture that sustains both difference and connection between diverse groups in its population; and it must do so with all due haste—it does not have forever to recover from its collective misdeeds if it is to save its collective humanity. Above all, a new South Africa must heed the ancient wisdom of an African culture built around

> . . . the importance, the worth, of human beings in any society. This value is best expressed by a fundamental African concept, *ubuntu.* Although not readily translatable into any European language, it shares much common ground with many religious and humanistic movements around the world. . . . A quality of interaction, *ubuntu* is a thread which runs through people's relationships with family members, neighbors, and strangers. The African proverb, *Umntu ungumntu ngabanye abantu* (A person is a person by means of other people), suggests that one's own humanness depends upon recognizing the humanity of others and their recognizing yours.[3]

In concluding this study, let us consider similar requirements as they bear upon the present and near-future responsibilities of leaders and citizens of the United States. To address this agenda is to explore concretely the future import of forgiveness in the domestic and external politics of my own country. Not to address this agenda will be to risk captivity to inertias in our past that, unchecked, could undermine the American political experiment and destroy the bonds of our nationhood. In 1994 we witness a vast array of new breakups and new peace between and within nation states around the world. Politicians everywhere know how fragile even an old peace can be. New or old, the forging of bonds between enemies is a prime political achievement, dramatized in late 1993 by new agreements between the Israelis and the Palestinians. To that event, Ambassador Abba Eban paid a pair of hopeful and cautious tributes: "They have achieved an irreversible revolt against the inertia of history.... We are like two climbers tied together with a rope. Either both or neither will survive."[4]

The hope and the caution belong to both the internal and external peace of nations. In at least four respects, America's leaders and citizens have work to do for achieving that "revolt against the inertia of history" that is forgiveness in politics.

The Place of Apology

In the spring of 1993, Leslie Gelb, writing in the *New York Times*, speculated on what American policy towards Vietnam might now be if we were to discover in "old Soviet archives" new evidence that Vietnam had murdered all those American prisoners of war still listed in our records as missing in action. The list of countries that have killed and otherwise harmed our citizens since the end of World War II is very long, he went on to say: Iraq, Iran, Cuba, Libya, Syria, and—above all—the Soviet Union. Yet, especially in the wake of vast changes in the world of Communism since 1989, commercial interests are urging the U.S. government toward a policy of "forgiving and forgetting and getting on with the business of making money" in new trade relations with these former national enemies. In early 1994, President Clinton finally yielded to this urging as regards Vietnam. What prevents American political leaders from promptly doing so? One answer, said Gelb, is the tendency of the American public to assess the crimes of nations *morally*, and to expect leaders of enemy nations to "admit their misdeeds" before strategic U.S. interests mandate a resumption of contact and commerce with them. "[F]ew politicians will risk moving counter to these feelings," so characteristic of American political culture. To outsiders it sometimes appears as an odd characteristic.

> Public confession sounds silly to foreigners. But it isn't, especially not to Americans. It's very hard to trust anyone tomorrow who denies yesterday's proven sins. Confession isn't everything—and maybe Washington needs to do a little of its own. But honesty can start the process of reconciliation.[5]

Washington does need to "do a little of its own." That little may be prerequisite to the little that our enemies might begin to do, too. As Nicholas Tavuchis points out in his fine book on the sociology of apology, there is something mysterious about the power of a mere "speech act" to transform a hostile human relationship.[6] A compelling political example of this mystery occurred during the visit of President Harry Truman to Mexico in March 1947. At his own initiative, Truman made an unscheduled stop at Chapultepec Castle in Mexico City at the graves of six teenage cadets who killed themselves rather than surrender to the American army that invaded Mexico almost exactly one hundred years before. Truman placed a wreath on the monument and bowed his head for a few minutes, in much the same gesture as Willy Brandt was one day to make in Warsaw. The public effect of these few minutes of symbolic action by an American president was astonishing. David McCullough describes it:

> The story created an immediate sensation in the city, filling the papers with eight-column, banner headlines. "Rendering Homage to the Heroes of '47, Truman Heals an Old National Wound Forever," read one. "Friendship Began Today," said another. A cab driver told an American reporter, "To think that the most powerful man in the world would come and apologize." He wanted to cry himself, the driver said. A prominent Mexican engineer was quoted: "One hundred years of misunderstanding and bitterness wiped out by one man in one minute. This is the best neighbor policy. . . ."
>
> Asked by American reporters why he had gone to the monument, Truman said simply, "Brave men don't belong to any one country. I respect bravery wherever I see it."[7]

—words from a World War I veteran and a diligent reader of history, the most diligent to occupy the White House since Woodrow Wilson.

Tavuchis concludes his description of the forms of apology in human affairs with the most difficult one—the collective, which has been the focus of this book. An apology "from the Many to the Many" has a number of distinctive features, he notes: only "an authoritative deputy" can utter it, a person representing the collectivity.[8] Such apology is "quintessentially public" and not the private opinion of the deputy. It is always a matter for *public record*; as a private communication it is trivial. It is likely to be formal in tone, "indirect, allusive, and . . . addressed to a wider audience as much as it is to the offended. . . . it speaks to interested third parties, the wider society, its own institutional history, and posterity." It seldom attempts to enumerate all the evils for which the apology is made, usually an impossibility in light of the large number of people involved in the wrong suffered and wrong done. In its rhetoric subjective sorrow for the past is subdued in deference to a clear practical collective aim of documenting "a prelude to reconciliation." But finally and at the same time,

> . . . a collective *mea culpa*, publicly uttered in response to its own call, simultaneously bespeaks recognition and commitment to a normative domain beyond that of immediate self-interest and effectively shifts the moral burden onto the offended party by focusing upon the issue of forgiveness.[9]

Missing from this elegant description is the suggestion that an official apologizer (especially the political leader) may allude to the sins of the enemy but must do so without turning the apology into covert counteraccusation.[10] Given such complex specifications, Tavuchis is surely right to observe: "All told, the consummate collective apology is a diplomatic accomplishment of no mean order."[11]

Within months of the publication of this book, the world will commemorate the fiftieth anniversary of the end of World War II. It will be a time for just such a diplomatic accomplishment—"of no mean order." We have seen, in the case of the fortieth anniversary, that it is possible, even likely, that political leaders in Germany, Japan, and the United States will bungle the event by inviting their respective publics to forget the war or to indulge in various forms of national self-congratulation. The real difficulties of the American observance in 1995 will center on Japan. We know from the histories reviewed here that Americans and Germans are far down the road to postwar reconciliation partly because of the latter's numerous public turns away from their Nazi past and because at least some German leaders have done more than "a little" public confession of the evils of the Nazi era.

In 1995, Americans will have an opportunity to decide if we are ready for what John C. Bennett once called "the next step that our generation needs to take"[12] in relation to our former enemy, Japan. Will we be moral enough and historically realistic enough to give our national political leaders room to remember the Pacific war on our behalf in some new public acknowledgment of America's sins in that war? Or will we expect them to cloak our public recollection of the war with the simplicities of "Remember Pearl Harbor"? As we have seen, the beginnings of realistic remembering of the war have already begun on the Japanese side. But the corollary to this beginning is growing Japanese impatience with a former American enemy whose leaders, by their silences and their focus on Pearl Harbor, act as though Americans have nothing to apologize for in their conduct of that war.

Due regard to the ambiguities of violent international conflict should restrain later generations from claiming too much moral clarity about this or that event in any war. Seen in its context past and future, the Hiroshima bomb was very questionable— militarily, politically, and morally. But it was the latest stage in a vortex of indiscriminate cruelty into which both sides had steadily descended, and *this* should occupy the moral rhetoric of politicians on both sides at the fiftieth anniversary commemoration.

The "authoritative deputy" to utter this rhetoric, on the American side in August 1995, will have to be the president of the United States. As the date approaches, I hope that it is not an affront to democratic decorum for this American citizen to suggest that his president summon the intellectual, moral, and political courage to frame a speech along these lines:

> Americans will always remember Pearl Harbor as the beginning of a horrible war with a powerful enemy. Both sides experienced horror. Both suffered greatly, but the Japanese finally suffered more than did Americans.
>
> Both had reasons to think that its side was justified in going to war. Americans can understand how some Japanese leaders of that time saw their country threatened by economic pressures that tempted them into the politics of war. We can understand, too, that many people in both our countries want to forget that long-ago war and to get on with the business of the future.
>
> But we cannot build a new world future together if together we cover up the wrongs we committed against each other in the Pacific war. As Americans we gratefully welcome the recent public admissions of public leaders in Japan that the war of 1931–45 was an unjustified aggression, beginning with aggression against Japan's near national neighbors and then against the United States.
>
> War in our century teaches us that there are no innocent combatants. Today we should honor the courage and sacrifice of men and women on each side. Let us hope that our memory and our consciences will enable us to admit that World War Two consisted at times in excesses of horror. No side can be proud of those excesses.
>
> We know that much Japanese resentment of American conduct of the war centers on the war's end—the atomic bombing of Hiroshima and Nagasaki. Our own historians disagree over the military and political wisdom of that bombing. In retrospect,

we have much reason to wonder if the mass-killing of people in *any* city on earth is compatible with the "just war" tradition in western civilization. Techniques for killing whole cities from the air were developed by Germans, British, and Americans during this war. American raids on the cities of Japan in 1945 killed as many people by "conventional" air raids as we did with atomic bombs at the end of the war. As the war drew to an end, on both sides the life of an enemy became increasingly cheap. This somber lesson of modern war we all should take to heart. The evil an enemy does tempts us to evils of our own. This fact does not excuse evildoing. It should move the doers, if only in retrospect, to confession and apology.

It is not enough, therefore, at this half-century mark after the Pacific war, to remember Pearl Harbor or to remember Hiroshima. We must remember the war itself, the unjustified devastations and cruelties that all sides perpetrated. We know that wars lure combatants into cycles of revenge and counter-revenge. There are enough examples of this cycle around the globe in 1995 to warn us all against them. The Pacific war is a like warning. In this August of 1995 the Japanese and American people must pay due honor to the courage of their forbears, but we must not pay them undue honor. We cannot honor everything they did for the destruction of each other. We cannot honor wanton cruelty, nor the racism that empowered that cruelty on both sides of the conflict.

For at the core of the evils of the Pacific war was the scourge of racism. Each side dehumanized the other with stereotypes, degrading images, and propaganda that made killing morally easier. After the war, American and Japanese people began anew to recognize each other as human. We should have recognized that during the war. The United States is still struggling with the scourge of racism in its own life. In 1942 we failed to protect ourselves against it in the case of a group of our own citizens, Japanese Americans. We have officially repented of that injustice; we want to repent of any traces of racism in our relations with the Japanese people as a whole, in the past and in the present.

War calls forth great heroism on all sides; the Pacific war did so. But it calls out the worst in us as well. Let us, in 1995, do everything we can, as an American and a Japanese people, to help each other to direct our capacities for heroism to the building up of our neighbors rather than toward destroying them.

Let us honor our own countries and each other on this day; but let us clear the way for our future together by acknowledging the evils in our past in the hope that they will never again be repeated. Let us learn from this tragic past to endure our current economic competition, our cultural differences, and our misunderstandings of each other without resort to the curse of violence. Let us move into the world's future committed to helping each other enjoy the blessing of dialogue, patience, and peace.

May God bless America. May God bless Japan, too.

The moral spirit and historical realism of such a speech are rare in the politics of nations. This rhetoric will lose some votes to the politician who uses it. But it will gain new respect among the citizens and leaders of a former enemy nation. The diplomacy of such a speech would be well served by some consultation between heads of the two states beforehand, so that each has some awareness of what the other is likely to say. Political apologies, of course, are directed to home constituents as well as to the foreign. They are moments in the responsibility of democratic politicians for the moral education of their own publics. A speech in a similar spirit might be crafted by the American president for May 8, 1995, as the publics of Germany and the former Allies remember the end of the European war. On that occasion it would probably behoove Americans to remember, not only the excessive violence wreaked on a Dresden or a Hamburg, but also to reflect on how little this country did to save Jews and others from the jaws of the Nazis while there was still time to do so.

The Japanese case, however, will be the real test of Americans' ability to entertain some modicum of genuine apology for the sins of their ancestors. The 1980–88 rectification of the record of treatment of Japanese Americans should encourage our current national leaders to use their bully pulpits, audible worldwide through television, to demonstrate that "the spirit of liberty is the spirit that is not too sure it is right," that this democratic spirit is not dead in America in 1995.

Restitution and Domestic Tranquillity

In his 1858 debate with Stephen Douglas, Abraham Lincoln exclaimed: "If slavery is not wrong, nothing is wrong." When for the time being political leaders may not know how to remove some evil from the past or the present of the body politic, they serve the future of its culture by imitating the Lincoln example: at least nail a principle to some public masthead. Apologies accomplish that.

But when politically sourced evil still lingers in its social effects collective apologies will ring hollow if unaccompanied by collective tangible attempts to remedy those effects. For over a century now, Americans by a huge majority have come to confess that slavery was wrong; a lesser majority that segregation was wrong; and a smaller majority, perhaps only a minority, that many African Americans still deserve compensatory helps to enable all of them to become true participants in, and true contributors to, this country's "domestic tranquillity." Again a comparison with contemporary South Africa is instructive: there too a body of white people and their leaders has gradually come to understand the injustices which their political, economic, and ideological systems have imposed on black people (in their case a majority of the national population). Whites have even begun to speak publicly about the wrong of *apartheid*. One hears the word *apology* sometimes on white lips and frequently on black: "If *apartheid* was not wrong," black South Africans say, "nothing is wrong. Whites must *say* so, if we are to get on with a new South Africa."

But the saying must open the door to doing. As Archbishop Desmond Tutu put it in conversations with leaders of the Dutch Reformed Church, "If you steal my pen and say 'I'm sorry' without returning the pen, your apology means nothing." Apologies set the record straight; restitution sets out to make a new record. Unfortunately what whites stole from their black neighbors in South Africa is far more difficult to restore than pens. As one black South African put it: "They killed the laughter of our children."[13]

In opposition to my argument for reparations to African Americans, offered at the end of the last chapter, white Americans might reply that our society has already offered a variety of restitutions to descendants of African slaves, and that over the thirteen decades since the end of the Civil War a significant number of the descendants have "made it" in the society. In time, whites may say, all might make it. But in fact a large number have not made it, and the diverse burdens of racism, beginning with slavery, account for this fact more than does anything else. Here the impatient, pragmatic, self-helping American should remember a warning of Martin Luther King, Jr., in his "Letter from Birmingham City Jail." In reply to a letter assuring him that "the colored people will receive equal rights eventually," King warned against "the myth of time. . . . It is the strangely irrational notion that there is something in the very flow of time that will inevitably cure all ills. Actually time is neutral."[14]

Some may further reply that other minority groups have made their way into the mainstream of American society in the past century, that if "the Irish and the Koreans can make it," so should African Americans after all these years. Here again moral arguments founder on different readings of history and the social forces that shape individual human lives. In a discussion of "ancient wrongs and modern rights," philosopher George Sher asserts that "persons may deserve compensation for the effects of wrong acts performed before they were born" but that over time they can be blamed for not responding to opportunities for freeing themselves from those effects. He is clear, however, that both property and psychic losses can have effects over many generations, especially when to original injustices are added new continuing forms of the same. Such, surely, has been the case with African—and some other—Americans. Says Sher, ". . . if slavery or the appropriation of Indian lands have made it specially difficult for their victims to recoup their lost entitlements, then these wrongs may call for far more compensation than others of similar vintage."[15]

We are a long way in America from the time when Reconstruction politicians could mouth the slogan, "Forty acres and a mule." Had that promise been fulfilled, there would be more African American landowners today than there are. The jobs, the income supplements, the education, the attention to small children required for the health and welfare of at least a third of the descendants of these ancient residents in America have yet to materialize. If by virtue of an African or a Christian culture, they have contributed to our national politics a demonstration of the power of forgiveness to knit up bonds of citizenship torn by ancient wrong, they nonetheless are right to withhold some measure of that forgiveness until they are dealt a fuller measure of just reparation by this society.

Political leaders white and black may try to persuade us that pragmatism alone argues for reparation: rehabilitated citizens mean less public money for law enforcement, jails, drug control, and welfare programs, not to speak of restoring a city after a billion-dollar riot. Here, however, an ethic of principle had better fortify an ethic of consequence in the politics of justice. Grudging pragmatic political thinking about the needs of America's most damaged citizens will have no staying power if it remains uninformed by a sense of intolerable past wrong and by eyes open to the legacies of that wrong on many a corner of the land. Economically "useless" people require moral defenders. In the 1980s the defenders seemed fewer and fewer. In the 1990s their number must grow if the United States is not to diminish as a democracy.

Forgiveness Too Soon, Too Late

Published in the year when *apartheid* officially began, and widely read around the world, Alan Paton's novel *Cry the Beloved Country* draws to an end in the grief of Stephen Kumalo, whose son is about to be executed for murder. He thinks about his fellow black South African Msimangu, "who had no hate for any man" and who once said, "I have one great fear in my heart, that one day when they turn to loving they will find we are turned to hating."[16] This line has been widely quoted, perhaps because twentieth-century readers know that a deep impatience with racism surges everywhere in our time, that its victims in many places will not wait forever to be counted by others as fully human beings. Across the earth, those who promote or fight racism with guns are locked in many a contest with those who promote or fight it with legal reform and coalition politics. In both South Africa and the United States, the contest is not over.

In 1994 many civically and economically excluded people in both countries are suspicious of too much and too early talk about forgiveness in politics. In a candid discussion with young American blacks, they are likely to say, "Martin Luther King, Jr., talked that way, and where has it gotten us so far?" The deep religious roots of the forgiving disposition in ancient African culture and modern American black churches, they say, is fading; among young blacks in ghetto gangs, it has disappeared completely. Annelle Ponder and Fannie Lou Hamer may have practiced forgiveness in that Winona, Mississippi, jail; but those days are passing among African Americans, say these skeptics. Many may decry the use of violence as an outlet for outrage, as many did decry it after the Los Angeles riot of 1992, but they sympathized with the emotional explosion behind the event.[17]

Once again, contemporary South Africa should be a warning sign and a sign of hope for Americans. Patience and readiness to reconcile with enemies seem still strong in that country, moving white journalist Alistair Sparks to exclaim, "The astonishing thing about most black South Africans is that there isn't more of a spirit of retribution among them."[18] White America has every reason to remain similarly astonished at the history of forgiveness in the politics of black America from 1865 until now. But the circumstances of economic stress among Americans generally in the nineties, the constraints on national budgets and individual pocketbooks, and weariness with the persistence of poverty now afflict the moods of both the impoverished and the well off among us all. African Americans may think ruefully that their patient ancestors forgave their enemies too soon and expected more justice from the latter than they were willing to institute. White middle class Americans may deceive themselves into thinking that there is no longer anything to forgive; the statute of limitation on forgiveness has run out, and now all Americans are responsible for what happens to them. As one white suburban woman put it in 1992, "It's up to them to paddle their own canoe. Don't always think about the fact that they were slaves."[19]

Of the two views, the second is nearer to dangerous blindness. As Americans we are pressed now on every side, internally and externally, by varieties of human neighbors whose enmities multiply in step with their interests. The oldest of these enmities—the racist hostility that white Americans have exhibited toward African Americans—continues to feed on an ignorance of "the other" perpetuated by structures of segregation, especially in our large cities. In her 1992 account of two adjacent Chicago suburbs, Isabel Wilkerson describes, in chilling terms, the twenty-year migration of whites from Roseland to Mount Greenwood, 2 miles away, as middle-class Chicago blacks were moving into Roseland.

> "Wherever you go you see hatred," said Clemmie Raggs, a forklift operator who lives in Roseland. "You never know where racism is going to stick its head up."

"The institutions, the media, the politicians—the whole system keeps the races divided," said Robert Scott, a Roseland resident who is a sewer maintenance worker. "We got the opportunity to move out to white areas, but they don't want us there."

Despite frequent negative experiences with whites, most Roseland residents said they would still welcome a person of the other race into their home and would like to live in an integrated neighborhood.

The same question drew either blank looks or impassioned diatribes about welfare and affirmative action from most whites in Mount Greenwood. Many said they would not want a black to live next door. And while many described the few blacks they knew from work as decent, they still harbored an almost instinctive animosity toward black people in general.[20]

What makes this account especially troubling is its evidence of increasing segregation in America's cities, where 86 percent of white suburban Americans live in communities that are less than 1 percent black. Blatant in such accounts is the truth that racism thrives on the absence of personal experience of "people unlike me." For centuries, racial segregation in America has been the self-reinforcing perpetuator of racist feelings. If it is true that the fences separating the races are taller than they were thirty years ago, the buildup of resentments on both sides is inevitable, and the Los Angeles riot of 1992 is the pattern of our common urban future.

Three generations ago, southern black farm workers migrated to northern cities in search of better jobs, bringing with them a culture that, unknown to them, was the gift that pluralist urban America would desperately need if it was not to dissolve into a battlefield between warring racial interest groups. "This culture," says Robert Franklin, "was itself the result of a transformed, evolving system of traditional African religious belief, which maintained the sovereignty of a monotheistic God, the kinship of human beings, the sacredness of family and community networks, and the significance of oral culture." The churches formed out of these beliefs nurtured a consciousness that promised through these new urban residents "a mutually transforming relationship with the city. This consciousness includes a commitment to creating a nonracist church and a just society, no matter what obstacles are posed by the cultural status quo."[21]

Will they persist against the obstacles forever? Probably not: that is the threat lying alongside the promise of the American future in 1994. Of this we can be sure, however; for the tranquillity and wholeness of America in the coming century, the days for patience and forgiveness as builders of civic community are not over. These remain as main beams for the building, and Americans of all races will have an unprecedented opportunity to practice these virtues as the country marches toward new experiences of cultural pluralism. That new pluralistic day deserves some attention here. While attending to it, we have every reason to hope that those chief practitioners of the art of combining demands for political justice with forbearance and empathy—African Americans—will not weary of that practice in a time when their country needs it the most.

Pluralism: Our Coming Trial by Diversity

Like citizens of many another modern country, Americans now encounter the varieties of human experience on the street corners of our cities and towns in people, economic forces, and political dangers which may originate almost anywhere on the planet. There is one difference between this modern American experience, however, and that of most other countries: from our very beginning we knew ourselves to be a nation of immigrants. Given the racist superiority imported to America in many a white northern European mind, our clamps on definitions of "permissible" immigration have been numerous. Yet from the beginning, the lines between Scots and English, Germans and French, Italians and Greeks, have been subject to erosion. It is hard, even genetically, to be sure that your American ancestors belonged to some single racial, national, or cultural line. The likelihood for most of us is quite opposite: the roots of our family trees spread out indistinguishably into an international forest. The metaphors we should coin for imaging this dense set of historical roots may be debatable, but we must not abandon our exploration of the meaning of the concept: *democratic pluralism*.

Numerous observers are telling us now that the *pluribus* in our national motto is now putting so much stress on the *unum* that the American experiment in nationality formed from nationalities is on the brink of failure. Robert B. Reich, for one, has recently written:

> The question is whether the habits of citizenship are sufficiently strong to withstand the centrifugal forces of the new global economy. Is there enough of simple loyalty to place—of civic obligation, even when unadorned by enlightened self-interest—to elicit sacrifice nonetheless? We are, after all, citizens as well as economic actors; we may work in markets but we live in societies. How tight is the social and political bond when the economic bond unravels?[22]

Arthur M. Schlesinger has written about these same contemporary stresses in his book *The Disuniting of America*. Alarmed that the growing cultural diversity of our populace has the potential to split the nation apart politically and socially, Schlesinger is nonetheless firm in his belief that the democratic procedures and the democratic creed of liberty-for-difference and equality-in-civic-worth can accommodate this new pluralism and prove, in fact, to be its best political friend. There is, he says, an American political culture that permits, encourages, and undergirds this diversity.

> . . . When we talk of the American democratic faith, we must understand it in its true dimensions. It is not an impervious, final, and complacent orthodoxy, intolerant of deviation and dissent, fulfilled in flag salutes, oaths of allegiance, and hands over the heart. It is an ever-evolving philosophy, fulfilling its ideals through debate, self-criticism, protest, disrespect, and irreverence; a tradition in which all have rights of heterodoxy and opportunities for self-assertion. The Creed has been the means by which Americans have haltingly but persistently narrowed the gap between performance and principle. It is what all Americans should learn, because it is what binds all Americans together.[23]

Critics may fault Schlesinger's liberal optimistic reading of our national history: Have the people and institutions of American society been all that persistent in gap-narrowing? The economy of the eighties argues for the opposite. But he is surely right in saying that over centuries Americans have never been very successful in insulating themselves from the waves of new immigrants who brought the phenomenon of *difference* into our social and political encounters in numerous unavoidable ways. The Korean-Latino-black-white conflicts of Los Angeles in 1992 advertised this phenomenon on behalf of us all: no perceptive resident of any metropolitan area in the country perceived the L.A. riot as only a local event. It was, rather, a sign of the escalation of an old national crisis. Precisely because it has been with us for a long time, we have reason to *own* it as an urgent contemporary chapter of the unfinished American story.

The occasion is new enough, however, to teach us new duties. What might those duties be? And what might forgiveness as a political act have to do with discerning and performing those duties? In several institutional sectors of this national society, we could work harder at some answers, especially if we believe that our galloping pluralism is not likely to slow down anytime soon.

The first area is the study of history—not only in the formalities of schools but in the daily communications mounted between citizens by government, mass media, and voluntary associations. Nations must find ways of educating their citizens to their guilty as well as their proud pasts. When in 1987 the Japanese Ministry of Education finally allowed the phrases "invasion of China" and "rape of Nanjing" to enter the textbooks of the nation's public schools, it was a significant if belated educational event.[24] One wonders if the perspectives of Dower's history of the Pacific War have equally found their way into the textbooks of America's schools.

We have a long way to go before school texts around the world reflect the many sides of the human experience of traumatic social conflict. During the fracas surrounding the Bitburg event, Charles William Maynes noted how little students in 110 surveyed American high schools knew about the World War II era. "In the 1930s and the 1940s, Western civilization broke down. It almost disappeared. Ignorance of that period . . . can pose a much greater threat to this country's survival than similar ignorance about any other period in modern history."[25] The popular success of Ken Burns's documentary series *The Civil War* took many critics and American viewers themselves by surprise. Who could have guessed that this war, above all others in our history, is still an example of the "present past"? What twentieth-century immigrants into the United States can understand the political culture of their new home without reckoning with the significance of that war?

But there is a complementary truth: popular ignorance of the different histories that immigrants bring with them has always been a threat to the survival of the United States as a nation of nationalities. Now more than ever, black studies belong in the education of all Americans, as do Native American studies, Hispanic studies, Asian studies, European studies, and so on across the multicultural spectrum of histories that in fact have been composing the rainbow of this national culture for centuries. In this respect, Schlesinger may not do justice to his own reading of that culture when he says that there is an "American culture" distinct from its multicultural components. How can that distinction hold? The diverse components are the cultural mix; by definition they make it up. We are a people different from any European nation, and one of the profoundest of our differences has been our national experience of "otherness," beginning especially with the otherness of black chattel slavery. James Baldwin was saying that in his ironic tribute to the "American achievement" in black-white relations. Who could encounter *American* music without acknowledging the ubiquitous presence in it of African American feeling and artistry? Indeed, as Cornel West has observed, if our politics were a fraction as rich as our music, America would be a more democratic society.[26]

The moral-educational point is that the study of another culture's history, art, and family tradition is one of the exposures that make possible multicultural politics. Latino, black, Asian, and white Americans must appropriate each other's histories; otherwise conflicts between Korean grocery store owners and their neighbors will continue to thrive on mutual ignorance. Listening to the stories of one's new neighbors is a way of welcoming them into the neighborhood. Without some such welcome, democratic argument may never take place, except through the remoteness of a ballot box. Even there, if blocs of citizens do not understand why they diverge in their voting preferences, they will not image each other in understandable human terms. More: they will not be able to fulfill one of G. H. Mead's conditions for the functioning of democracy—that voters be capable, when they step into the booth, of voting someone else's real interests along with their own interests. Diverse bodies of people cohere, not only around Schlesinger's "protest, disrespect, and irreverence" toward each other. Those negative relations are only tolerable when they are sustained by respect for the humanity of the "others" and a reverence for their very lives. One does not argue long with people whom one deems of no real importance. American democracy is at its best when people of clashing points of view argue far into the night, because they know that next day they are going to count and encounter each other as residents of the neighborhood. Palaver in an African village grows from the same social root. Americans must nourish each other in their own political version of *ubuntu.*

This democratic dynamic is basic to forgiveness in politics. People who take the trouble to listen to each other are vulnerable to empathy, and the path to empathy lies through forbearance. For the moment none of us may know what truths or principles we should learn to applaud in the brew of our cultural diversity. We may not yet grasp with confidence the moral judgments that we will eventually make about our past and present relations with each other. We may lack the empathetic knowledge of others necessary for making settled judgments about them. Meantime, the forbearance that says "let us not leap into retaliating against each other" and empathy that says "we are beginning to understand why each of us feels the way we do" is a solid prelude to real politics. For politics is the struggle of diverse groups and interests to fashion common action on some common agenda. Without the time and patience for discovering that agenda, we leap to inept conclusions, and the day of realistic politics never comes. Education in the broadest sense assumes human resources of time and patience for understanding some facet of our world. A long period of mutual education awaits those of us in America who are willing to take our emerging pluralism with democratic seriousness.

There is another area in which the new diversity of America could become the gateway to a far more humane national culture than ever we have enjoyed on these shores: we could construct institutions for sharing the achievements, and the achievers, of our separate pasts; we could learn to celebrate each other's heroes and heroines.

In an article published St. Patrick's Day in 1993, Nerys and Orlando Patterson protest against the notion that Martin Luther King, Jr. "belongs" to African Americans and that St. Patrick belongs to the Irish. Greatness in any culture belongs to all cultures.[27] Every American "has the right to delight in, criticize and even claim the heritage of every group that interests him or her." Indeed, the specific celebratable power of western culture, they contend, is its "openness to the outsider's world." Isolated cultures tend toward the static; even in unexpected and unwanted collision, cultures begin to influence each other.

The case of St. Patrick, the Pattersons go on to conclude, underscores a place for forgiveness in the turning of mere cultural clash towards mutuality. In his youth Patrick was an Irish slave. He escaped to England. There he embraced the Christian faith, accepted forgiveness for youthful sins, and embarked on a mission in Ireland not only to convert his former owners to Christianity but also to turn them away from their exploitation of slaves, especially the women among them. Told in this detail, Patrick's story commends him as a transcultural hero.

> The same story, and the same parallels, could be drawn with other groups—Jews, women, homosexuals—who in overcoming their particular tragedies remade the common heritage. True stories, as opposed to mythical ones, compel comparison, empathy, and compassion.
>
> But the historical St. Patrick also has an equally important lesson for African-Americans and other minorities who feel they have been ill used. Violent abduction, slavery, hardship and terror did not lead him into ethnocentric hatred of the Irish nor to a cultural relativism which complacently justified avoidance. . . .
>
> . . . This Patrick, who helped to bring the Irish into the mainstream of Western history, who forgave and was forgiven, who suffered enslavement and overcame it, who epitomized the West's central drama—the outsider who stayed to transform the culture of his conqueror—belongs to all of us.[28]

Dietrich Bonhoeffer, Richard von Weizsäcker, Shusako Endo, Grace Uyehara, Bartolomé de Las Casas, Elie Wiesel, Martin Luther King, Jr., Malcolm X, and Fannie Lou Hamer belong to all of us Americans. We may have to struggle with our justified resentments against what some of their kin and associates have done to harm us personally and collectively. In acknowledging them as the gifted people who enhance the humanity of us all, however, we take a step away from our chauvinisms and onto a highway where strangers can meet each other on a common journey, where they can begin to find out what *benefits* come from *difference* among human beings.

The moral view of this book has been that not all human differences are to be celebrated. Some will be, once we have come to appreciate them; others we have to put on hold while we learn; and yet others we have to see as incompatible with politics based on universal human worth. Civic diversity is not the same as infinite tolerance. Well does the current German government ban neo-Nazi political parties; human beings cannot remain neighbors in a society of unlimited liberal "freedom for the thought we hate," especially when that thought takes the form of denying to others their claims to justice as well as freedom. Nonetheless, hatred of what others think or do is not the same as hating them, or banning them from a potential place in our human neighborhood. It is an old Christian principle that one must seek always to "hate the sin and love the sinner," which might have suggested to more theologians that we are called to forgive sinners more fundamentally than their sins. A potential new relation to offenders, in continuing recognition of their offenses, is the moral hope of forgiveness. Sometimes the will to forgive shrinks to a slim hope that a relation may be retrieved, a human being counted fellow human again. When we are not yet well acquainted with the human reality of strangers, we have no right to banish them from our political company. Americans, now and in the foreseeable future, must find ways of learning enough about each other to discover the benefits of difference— as well as the bonds of commonality. Democracies thrive on both.

The processes of that mutual educating, mutual adoption of heroic achievement, and mutual hope for civic relation belong to the tasks of all the institutions of a democracy. Public schools and governments have their part; so do political parties, journalists, book publishers, and families. Among all these institutions in American society, however, none is freer to contribute to the weaving of a new tapestry of intercultural affirmation than the churches, the synagogues, and the mosques of the land. Religious institutions could become a third institutional arena for the cultivation of new dialogue between the cultures in American culture. Religion can be a great divider of people; one strain of American political thought entertains a deep suspicion of religion's potential for nourishing absolutisms that destroy democratic tolerance. But the potentials are twofold: the version of Islamic faith that impelled Malcolm X to reject collaboration with white people finally opened a door to a more universalistic version, although he had to travel to Mecca to find it. For many of the world's peoples, religion has long been their chief trans-national association.

Even when its adherents use religion for retreat from politics and the troubles of their society, they are still vulnerable to turnarounds not unlike Malcolm's. The tangible connections of every American suburb to the crises of the inner city should be enough to convince comfortable suburbanites that there really is no retreat from their metropolitan neighborhood. Religion, at its best, promotes similar convictions, and on a world scale. When and if they attend congregational worship, congregants are likely to be in touch with a worldwide organization that may include humans from every continent and humans from every social and cultural stratum of the metropolis. Congregations can be doorways to the world, as many have discovered as they cope with the diverse languages, immigrant needs, and culture-rooted misunderstandings of people coming to live in suburbs, too. Some of these immigrants knock on church doors as though their faith entitled them to the company of fellow believers in any country. Of course, it does so entitle them.

Larry L. Rasmussen has defined "modernity's very trademark" as "life together as interdependent strangers." Interdependence through markets, international political relations, and mass global communications are not capable, he warns, of nourishing the needs of humans for intimacy, places to feel at home, associations in which every person becomes a person in the eyes of every other. Churches, synagogues, and mosques can become such associations for the sake of our larger-scale global association, says Rasmussen. A society that connects billions of humans together in its global networks cannot by itself nourish that intimate interdependence. Lacking enriching, personal experience of how strangers can be gifts instead of threats, the society itself

. . . has lost the wellsprings of the moral character it depends on for its own existence. It has lost its own incubator, laboratory, and training ground. It needs what only certain kinds of community can provide, but it destroys them. And the truth be known, society-without-community is as confining and uninhabitable as community-without-society is constraining and oppressive.[29]

Sheer ignorance, as well as malice, accounts for much of the harm that strangers inflict on each other on the city streets, in the national politics, and in the international relations of the United States of America. We will have less crime, less insult, less war to forgive in a future world if strangers will embrace and persist in the faith that strangeness is more gift than harm to our humanity. And once we have learned the discipline of forgiveness for the harms we do inflict, we will experience, with our enemies, a new increment of hope that neither strangeness nor enmity is forever.

Notes

Introduction

1. *Life Magazine*, June, 1992.
2. Langston Hughes, "Let America Be America Again," in Walter Lowenfels, ed., *The Writing on the Wall* (Garden City, N.Y.: Doubleday and Company, 1969), pp. 24–26.
3. James M. McPherson, *Battle Cry of Freedom: The Civil War Era* (New York: Ballantine Books, 1988), pp. 849–850.
4. Martin Luther King, Jr., *The Trumpet of Conscience* (San Francisco: Harper & Row, 1968), p. 68. The quotation is from a sermon delivered at the Ebenezer Baptist Church in Atlanta on Christmas Eve, 1967.
5. David J. Garrow, *Bearing the Cross: Martin Luther King, Jr. and the Southern Christian Leadership Conference* (New York: William Morrow, 1986), p. 561. The incident took place on May 10, 1967.
6. McPherson, op. cit., pp. 849–50.
7. Jeffrie G. Murphy and Jean Hampton, *Forgiveness and Mercy* (Cambridge: Cambridge University Press, 1988), p. 150. Murphy and Hampton discuss the concept of "moral hatred," in which the ancient Christian distinction between the sin and the sinner is taken seriously: moral condemnation of the one, empathy for the other.
8. Ibid., p. 37.

Chapter 1

1. Barbara Tuchman, *The Guns of August* (New York: Bantam Books, 1976), pp. 487–88.
2. Edwin Muir, "The Wheel," *Collected Poems* (New York and London: Oxford University Press and Faber and Faber Ltd., 1960, copyright by Willa Muir), p. 105.
3. Draco's "draconian" reputation is a false one. His legal work on the destructive potentials of revenge took the form, for example, of distinguishing between accidental and intentional homicide, and one of his laws protected a killer from the vengeance of the victim's kin. Wallace E. Caldwell, *The Ancient World* (New York: Rinehart & Co., 1949), p. 161.
4. Werner Jaeger, *Paideia: The Ideals of Greek Culture,* trans. Gilbert Highet (3 vols.; New York: Oxford University Press, 1945), vol. 1, pp. 140–41. Jaeger goes on to call this diagnosis "the first objective statement of the universal truth that the violation of justice means the disruption of the life of the community." This opinion is quite Eurocentric, ignoring as it

does the earlier literature of the Hebrew Bible, as illustrated below, not to speak of some very old tribal wisdom to be found in the cultures of Africa.

5. Jaeger, vol. I, pp. 144–45, quoting from Solon, *Fragments,* lines 17–32.

6. A. J. Podlecki, "Aeschylus," in *Encyclopedia Britannica*, 15th ed. (Chicago: 1976), vol. I, p. 147.

7. Ibid., p. 148. Cf. A. J. Podlecki, *The Political Background of Aeschylaean Tragedy* (Ann Arbor, Mich.: University of Michigan Press, 1966).

8. This is the contrast which Susan Jacoby makes in *Wild Justice* (New York: Harper & Row, 1982) p. 32. See pp. 22–34 for her claim that Euripides, not Aeschylus, is the one concerned for the empirical impacts of vengeance in human affairs. While not wanting to dwell on a contrast between these two classic writers or to pose as one equipped to make fine judgments between them, I think that it is obvious that either Jacoby or Podlecki must be wrong about the basic issues in the Aeschylus trilogy, especially in *Eumenides,* where Aeschylus is enacting a myth about the founding of the Athenian city-state. For him the beginning and the continuation of the city as a community of citizens is very much a matter of empirical "human consequences." I find Podlecki's reading the fairer, on this point, by far. Further on Jacoby's valuable work, see the end of this chapter.

9. Quotations from the play here are all taken from the E. D. A. Morshead translation in *The Complete Greek Drama,* ed. Whitney J. Oates and Eugene O'Neill, Jr. (New York: Random House, 1938), vol. I. Here, p. 272.

10. E. D. A. Morshead, "Introduction to the Trilogy *Oresteia,*" ibid., p. 164.

11. Ibid., *The Choephori*, trans. Morshead, p. 245.

12. Ibid., p. 277. The monotheistic theology to which Aeschylus eventually will appeal will seek to transform the Furies into a form in which they can be "tended," i.e. subjugated to the divine will. For now, says Apollo, "No god there is to tend to such herd as you."

13. The Furies, Apollo, and Athena all draw on the distinction between the blood kinship of children to parents and the (mere) marital kinship of a wife to a husband. Before the play is over, Aeschylus adds the additional mythic tribute to male superiority in Athens by having Apollo say that fathers are more important for the parenting of children than mothers, calling the "virgin birth" of Athena from the head of Zeus as precedent! Therefore, the murder of fathers and husbands is a more serious crime than the murder of mothers and wives. This and similar arguments aim at diminishing Orestes' guilt in some degree, "not for very logically convincing reasons," as Morshead comments mildly ("Introduction," ibid., pp. 165–66). This murky, casuistic denial of women's full and equal humanity marks the play as "unconvincing" indeed to many a modern mind. But the argument from civil peace did not require this bizarre logic to carry weight then or now.

14. Ibid., p. 284.

15. Ibid., p. 285.

16. Ibid., p. 288.

17. Ibid., p. 293.

18. Ibid., p. 298.

19. Ibid., p. 299.

20. Ibid., p. 301.

21. Ibid., p. 290.

22. Ibid., p. 302.

23. Ibid., p. 304.

24. Ibid., p. 305.

25. Wallace Everett Caldwell, *The Ancient World* (New York: Rinehart and Company, 1949), p. 254.

26. Cf. Jaeger, vol. I, p. 386.

27. As quoted on the occasion of Golding's award of the 1983 Nobel Prize for Literature, *New York Times,* October 7, 1983. Some critics blamed Golding for "apparent eagerness to think poorly of their species," especially in his most famous novel, *Lord of the Flies*; not "anthropologically satisfying," said the critics. One could imagine that Thucydides' account of Corcyraean Revolt could have been subject to the same criticism, and that both writers could only say to the critics: "This is what we have seen."

28. Thucydides, *History of the Peloponnesian War*, trans. Richard Crawley (Everyman's Library; New York: E. P. Dutton and Co., no date.) The translation itself is dated 1876. The Corcyra incident occurred in 427 B.C.E.

29. Jaeger, *Paideia,* vol. I, p. 399.

30. Thucydides, *History,* p. 223.

31. Ibid., pp. 224–25.

32. Ibid., p. 226.

33. Ibid., pp. 226–27.

34. Cf. Jaeger, vol. I, p. 402.

35. The meaning of *original sin* has commonly been interpreted by twentieth-century theologians in terms of contradictory personal experience rather than any sort of natural or historical cause. Cf., for example, Paul Tillich's claim that the "moral and tragic elements of the human situation" are intertwined. "Sin is a universal fact before it becomes an individual act, or, more precisely, sin as an individual act actualises the universal fact of estrangement" from "our true being." [*Systematic Theology*, vol. 2 (London: Nisbet & Co., 1957), pp. 44, 64.] Borrowing from Kierkegaard, Reinhold Niebuhr coined the crisp formula: "Man could not be tempted if he had not already sinned." [*The Nature and Destiny of Man,* vols. I–II (New York: Charles Scribner's Sons, 1949), p. 251.]

36. Niebuhr frequently pointed out that "original sin" is a fact of human institutions as well as individuals. He quotes "one of the great documents of social protest in Egypt, 'The Eloquent Peasant,'" who declares to a court about to condemn him: "Thou hast been set as a dam to save the poor man from drowning, but behold thou art thyself the flood." (Niebuhr, ibid., p. 258, note 8, quoting from J. H. Breasted, *The Dawn of Conscience, p.* 190.)

37. Genesis 4:17. This is an early token of the suspicion that the writers of the Hebrew Bible entertained toward human life in cities, especially the imperial cities whose armies inflicted such damage on the Hebrew people for over a millennium. See Genesis 11:1–9, Psalm 137, and the Book of Nahum. In the fifth century C.E., St. Augustine in *The City of God* pointed out that in building a city, Cain was signaling his guilt, while Abel, a herdsman and a "sojourner, built none. For the city of the saints is above." (Book XV, 1, p. 479 in Marcus Dods, trans., *The City of God* (Modern Library; New York: Random House, 1950.) In this view, cities are centers of idolatry, human exploitation, and alienation of human from human—Cain, in short, has put his mark on cities.

38. Quotations from the English Bible throughout this book, unless otherwise noted, are taken from the Revised Standard Version (copyright 1946 and 1952 by the Division of Christian Education of the National Council of the Churches of Christ in the U.S.A.)

39. See especially Hosea 11:1–9, where, in terms of human emotion associated with parenthood, a Hebrew prophet, like Aeschylus, attributes to the Divine the power to change.

40. George W. Coats, *From Canaan to Egypt: Structural and Theological Context for the Joseph Story*, The Catholic Biblical Quarterly Monograph Series, #4 (Washington, D.C.: The Catholic Biblical Association of America, 1976), p. 9.

41. Only in chapter 39 is "the Lord" (YHWH) credited with Joseph's rising good fortune in Egypt. The word *God (Elohim)* appears later only in the speech of the human characters until, in 46:2–4, God speaks directly to Jacob, assuring him that it is safe to move to Egypt.

42. Coats quotes D.B. Redford, *A Study of the Biblical Story of Joseph* (V[estus] T[estamentum] (VTsup20; Leiden: Brill 1970): ". . . the writer eschews the tedious, moralizing commentary which clutters so much of holy writ . . . he lets the story convey his message without trying to ram it down the readers' throats at every turn of the plot." (pp. 86, 247, in Coats, p. 4.)

43. Cf. chapters 12, 13, 27, 29–31, 33–35.

44. The law codes of Israel would one day make the selling of a member of one's own family into slavery a capital offense: cf. Exodus 21:16, Deuteronomy 24:7.

45. Coats, p. 32.

46. Some scholars, seeking to preserve the hero image of Joseph, have suggested that his stretched-out manipulations of the brothers are designed to test their capacity for repentance and to winnow their old jealousies from their characters. But the interpretation of Coats (p. 38) and others comports better with the realistic humanism of the story. Joseph is taking revenge. As Charles T. Fritsch comments: ". . . one can still sense the feeling of unbridled, ruthless power in the actions of Joseph as he lords it over his cowering, fearful brethren, and plays with them as a cat plays with a mouse. They are entirely at his mercy, and he can do anything he wants to them." "'God Was With Him': A Theological Study of the Joseph Narrative," *Interpretation,* vol. IX, no. 1 (January 1955), pp. 27–28.

47. Coats, pp. 43–44.

48. Scriptural Hebrew words for forgiveness are several: *kipper*, "to cover"; *nasa*, "to lift up, carry away"; and *salach*, "to let go"—actions towards sin attributed regularly in the Hebrew Bible to God. The major New Testament Greek word is *aphiemi*, variously used for "let go, send away, remit, or liberate." Cf. Alan Richardson, *A Theological Wordbook of the Bible* (New York: Macmillan and Co., 1950) and Murphy and Hampton, *Forgiveness and Mercy*, p. 37.

49. Joseph's rhetorical question, "Am I in the place of God?" may suggest the theme, already noted, that will dominate the rest of the Hebrew Bible: that only God can forgive. But the brothers, at last daring to use the word, plainly are taking the risk of asking Joseph for human forgiveness.

50. Coats, p. 46.

51. Coats, p. 89.

52. One striking exception to the generalization here is that set of regulations in the law codes of ancient Israel governing the remission of *debts*. One of these regulations calls for debt-remission every seven years, especially from debt-slavery. (Cf. Exodus 21:2–6, Deuteronomy 15:12–18 and 31:10, Isaiah 61:1–2, and Jeremiah 34:8–22.) The return of mortgaged *land* figures prominently in these laws, in both a seven-year and a forty-nine-year cycle. (Cf. Deuteronomy 15:1–11 and 31:10, Second Kings 8:1–6, and Leviticus 25.) Loans and mortgages were not to be pressed by creditors to the point that debtors had their very survival jeopardized. The most dramatic requirement here was that richer kinspeople should "redeem" their poorer relatives from various forms of helpless obligation (cf. Ruth 4:1–12 and Jeremiah 32). Resistance to this form of forgiveness in the political-economic life of Israel must have been pervasive; but it furnishes a powerful concrete social-economic precedent that may lie behind one version of Jesus' prayer, "Forgive us our debts as we forgive our debtors" (Matthew 6:12).

53. Susan Jacoby, *Wild Justice: The Evolution of Revenge* (New York: Harper & Row, 1983), pp. 361–62.

54. Flora Lewis, "The Fate of Revolution," *New York Times,* January 7, 1983.

55. The Honorable Pretlowe Winborne, in an address delivered May 16, 1964, in Raleigh, North Carolina.

Chapter 2

1. Robert M. Cover, "The Supreme Court, 1982 Term, Forward: *Nomos* and Narrative," *Harvard Law Review* 97 (November 1983), p. 33.
2. Cf. Matthew 5:17–20, 15:1–9 (Mark 7:1–13), and Luke 4:16–21.
3. Hannah Arendt, *The Human Condition: A Study of the Central Conditions Facing Modern Man* (Doubleday Anchor Books; Garden City, N.Y.: Doubleday and Company, 1959), pp. 212–13.
4. Arendt, pp. 214–15.
5. Careful readers of the Bible have every reason to surmise, with Arendt, that forgiveness came into new ethical prominence in the teachings of Jesus and in the life of the early church. But it seems historically dubious to claim, with her, that Jesus "discovered" the horizontal indispensability of forgiveness in human society. One might suppose that the nameless author of the Joseph story sensed this truth a long time before, not to speak of the wrestle in many cultures—we have looked at the Greeks—with the utter social necessity of taming the wild justice of limitless revenge. But Arendt rightly observes, probably with a majority of moderns, that "forgiveness" is a word deeply and permanently embedded in the Christian tradition, which translates into the modern prejudice (which Arendt was trying to counter) that forgiveness is a religious, not an empirical, matter. In taking this view of the new prominence of forgiveness in the teachings of Jesus, one must be careful to note that *rabbinic* Judaism of the ensuing centuries affirmed the interconnectedness of divine and human forgiveness in ways quite parallel to the language of Jesus. Ethraim Urbach concludes that for the rabbis divine compassion is contingent upon compassion between humans, making the exercise of this divine attribute "subject to man's conduct." [*The Sages: Their Concepts and Beliefs*, trans. Israel Abrahams (Jerusalem: The Magnes Press, The Hebrew University, 1979), p. 457.] Louis E. Newman documents the same conclusion: according to the rabbis, "So long as Israel is merciful it will merit God's mercy." ["The quality of mercy on the duty to forgive in the Judaic tradition," *The Journal of Religious Ethics*, vol. 15, no. 2 (Fall, 1987), p. 167.] In modern Jewish practice the rituals of Yom Kippur embody this same view. There an early prayer for divine forgiveness begins, "I hereby forgive all who have hurt me." So, eventually, the Christian and the Jewish traditions here become virtually identical, but the difference in the prominence of human forgiveness between the Hebrew Bible and the New Testament remains.
6. Marcus J. Borg, *Jesus: A New Vision* (San Francisco: Harper & Row, 1987), p. 127. Cf. Matthew 10:5–6 and 15:24.
7. Richard Horsley, *Jesus and the Spiral of Violence* (San Francisco: Harper and Row, 1987), pp. 197–98. Cf. Luke 10:13–15, Matthew 11:21–23.
8. Cf. Borg, p. 142, and Walter Brueggemann, *The Prophetic Imagination* (Philadelphia: Fortress Press, 1978), pp. 80, 96. In his recent book *Engaging the Powers* (Philadelphia: Fortress Press, 1992) Walter Wink suggests this translation of the conventional "Kingdom of God" as a better way of expressing the dynamic, current activity of the Divine in the world.
9. The early church, which saw its survival as dependent upon an accommodation with the Roman Empire that would at least vitiate its known readiness for slaughter, may have toned down the challenges of Jesus to the political powers of his day, especially the challenge to Roman power which had induced a Roman official, Pilate, to order his execution. One of the four Gospels, Luke, takes care at many points to stress the positive side of the Roman occupier and to shift responsibility for Jesus' death onto the Jewish authorities. Recent assessment of the political "turmoil" of Palestine during this era has compelled some scholars to conclude that, from the standpoint of the Roman imperialists, Jesus really did

"subvert the nation . . . causing disaffection among the people all through Judaea . . . from Galilee . . . as far as this city" (Luke 23:1–5). Luke goes out of his way to portray Pilate as dubious about all this. But the fact remained that he ordered the crucifixion, and his reason for doing so had to be that he had plenty of political agitation to deal with. Just to be on the safe side, he could go along with the charges. An image of Pilate as soft and wishy-washy is not altogether convincing: in his time he crucified thousands. It is hard to see why he would worry about one more Galilean on a cross. Concludes W. D. Davies: "That the Gospel tradition has undergone a process of depoliticization has to be recognized." *The Gospel and the Land* (Berkeley, Calif.: University of California Press, 1974), p. 344, as quoted by Richard Horsley, p. 344, note 19.

10. Horsley, p. 319.

11. John Howard Yoder, *The Politics of Jesus* (Grand Rapids: Wm. B. Eerdmans Publishing Co., 1972), pp. 112–13.

12. Rudolf Schnackenburg, *Die Bergpredigt: Utopische Vision oder Handlungsanweisung* (Dusseldorf: Patmos Verlag, 1982), pp. 55–56, as translated by Glen H. Stassen, *Just Peacemaking: Transforming Initiatives for Justice and Peace* (Louisville, Ky.: Westminster/John Knox Press, 1992), p. 39.

13. Yoder, *The Politics of Jesus*, p. 41, note 20.

14. Yoder, pp. 62–63. In his book *The Use of the Bible in Christian Ethics* (Philadelphia: Fortress Press, 1983), Thomas W. Olgetree argues impressively that the Synoptic Gospels, and especially Matthew, "reflect matrices of experience which generated ideas and understandings capable of development into original social thought" (p. 127). He believes that "the conditions of communal life" set forth in Matthew come close to matching Hannah Arendt's "account of a republic. . . . a form of political life where open discourse replaces tradition, language, custom, race, the struggle for survival, and especially violence, as the founding principle of social order" (p. 121). Olgetree is ambiguous about accepting Arendt's view of the New Testament chiefly because she ignores the eschatological, future-oriented horizons of the early Christian world view.

15. Mark 2:11. See the parallels in Luke 5:17–26 and Matthew 9:1–8.

16. Horsley, p. 184.

17. "There is . . . a terrible irony in that conjunction of sickness and sin, especially in first-century Palestine. Excessive taxation could leave poor people physically malnourished or hysterically disabled. But since the religiopolitical ascendancy could not blame excessive taxation, it blamed sick people themselves by claiming that their sins had led to their illnesses. And the cure for sinful sickness was, ultimately, in the Temple. And that meant more fees, in a perfect circle of victimization. When, therefore, John the Baptist with a magical rite or Jesus with a magical touch cured people of their sicknesses, they implicitly declared their sins forgiven or nonexistent. They challenged not the medical monopoly of the doctors but the religious monopoly of the priests. All of this was religiopolitically subversive." John D. Crossan, *The Historical Jesus* (San Francisco: Harper & Row, 1991), p. 324.

18. See especially John 9.

19. The alternate translations in the New English Bible:

"Forgive us the wrong we have done, as we have forgiven those who have wronged us" (Matt. 6:12).

"And forgive us our sins, for we too forgive all who have done us wrong" (Luke 11:4). Quotations from the New English Bible (NEB) are taken from that version published by the Cambridge University Press (New York, 1971).

20. In Matthew 5:23–24 (The Sermon on the Mount) this same priority governs the instruction that, if in the midst of a formal religious offering in the synagogue or Temple, you remember that "your brother has a grievance against you," you are to leave the ceremony at

once and "make your peace with your brother." Then come back to the altar. To live inside the circle of the divine kindness is to live there with neighbors. Ignore your relation to them, even temporarily, and you exclude yourself from that circle. It would be uncharacteristic of either Jewish or Christian prayer of that or any future time, however, to suppose that human forgiveness will induce or "cause" God to forgive. The words assume that there is a "horizontal" condition that God expects to be in place before divine forgiveness can rightly—and readily—occur. Cf. Donald W. Shriver, Jr., *The Lord's Prayer: A Way of Life* (Atlanta: John Knox Press, 1983), pp. 72–76.

21. Peter Farb and George Armelagos, *Consuming Passions: The Anthropology of Eating* (Boston: Houghton Mifflin, 1980), pp. 4, 211, as quoted by Crossan, p. 403.

22. Lee Edward Klosinski, *The Meals in Mark* (Ann Arbor, Mich.: University Microfilms International, 1988), p. 58, as quoted by Crossan, p. 341.

23. Along with many other form critics, Richard Horsley (pp. 209–28) discounts these memories as constructs of the later Christian community as it sought to retroject the opposition of their contemporary Jewish critics back into the career of Jesus. Horsley believes that Jesus made no point at all of inviting the weakest, most marginal people of the society to enjoy his company. His invitation was simply to everybody—especially to everybody living in the local village. In order to take this view, many of the texts have simply to be dismissed as apologetic fabrications of a later church trying to defend the diversity of its membership or to underscore the "everyone" by calling attention to Jesus' regard for the outcast as the test case of "*really* everyone." The church, in this view, knew that all of its members were sinners and that all were forgiven. The incidents of "tax collectors and sinners" were strictly defensive against Jewish disparagement of the young Christian movement. Crossan's insistence on the boundary-redefining potential of eating habits as at the heart of Jesus' ministry loses much of its force if one adopts Horsley's view, which I regard as strained, speculative, and almost arbitrary, like only too much form criticism.

24. Cf. the parallel, Matthew 9:10–13. The form critics see this saying as authentic and original with Jesus but the surrounding story as an invention for illustrating the saying.

25. Cf. Crossan, p. 263: The "open commensality" of these teachings would have offended the ritual laws of "*any* civilized society." Peasant communities seem often to invent such leveling social vision, says Crossan. *Minjung* theology in contemporary Korea would be a good illustration.

26. Or whether any such meal took place at all. Crossan is sure that there was no such occasion. Even if the Last Supper, too, is an invention of the church's imagination, the fact remains that the choice of a "meal" as symbolic of the heart of the message remains very significant indeed.

27. Some scholars conclude that the writer of Matthew invented this parable to drive home in dramatic fashion the radicality of that previous teaching. "It is properly a homiletic midrash on the instruction of Matthew 6:12, 14, 15, probably composed by the evangelist himself to make part of the Lord's Prayer vivid to his people." *The New Jerome Biblical Commentary*, ed. Raymond E. Brown, Joseph A. Fitzmeyer, and Roland E. Murphy (Englewood Cliffs, N.J.: Prentice-Hall, 1990), p. 662.

28. Like the sins, the references are numerous (i.e., I Cor. 1:12 ff., 3:5, 4:6, ll:2, 12:1–31, 5:1 ff., all of chapters 8 and 9, ll:21–22, and cf. II Cor. 10:7–9). On the social characteristics of the Corinthian congregation, cf. Wayne A. Meeks, *The First Urban Christians* (New Haven, Conn.: Yale University Press, 1983) and Olgetree, *The Use of the Bible in Christian Ethics*. Meeks argues that few if any voluntary associations in first-century Roman society could match early Christian congregations in their norms calling simultaneously for exclusive religious loyalty, inclusive membership, and extralocal connections with the Christian movement as a whole. In contrast to the Roman clubs and *collegia*, "it was precisely the het-

erogeneity of status that characterized the Pauline Christian groups" (pp. 78–79). Olgetree (p. 121) underscores the special importance of the norm of forgiveness in such communities: "communities transcending family, language, culture, and national identity could only sustain themselves through continual acts of forgiveness, and through a readiness to bear hurt without reprisal."

29. The Greek word *koinonia,* often translated weakly in the English *fellowship,* is probably best understood as *participation.* It is one of those multidimensional words in the New Testament that can mean the participation of congregation members in each other's lives, their participation in the power of the Spirit, and the Spirit's participation in the common life. Cf. Lionel S. Thornton, *The Common Life in the Body of Christ,* 3rd ed. (London: Dacre Press, 1950). The word appears in the benediction that concludes II Corinthians (13:14).

30. Crossan, pp. 422–23. Empirically it seems virtually impossible for groups and individuals to avoid two-way influences in almost any social relationship. Robert Cover, commenting on changing concepts of law, could have been speaking of ethics, theology, and cultural change in general: "Neither religious churches, however small and dedicated, nor utopian communities, however isolated, nor cadres of judges, however independent, can ever manage a total break from other groups with other understandings of law." (Cover, p. 33. See note 1 above.)

31. Many recent New Testament scholars have observed that these responses to attack, superficially passive, are in fact active assertions of the victim's irreducible dignity—surprising responses meant to throw the opponent off guard. Also worth observing is that these and kindred responses constitute refusals to abandon the relationship as one potentially between equals. Offers of forgiveness announce, in effect, the same refusal.

32. These quotations from Julian's *Caesars* are from Charles N. Cochrane, *Christianity and Classical Culture* [Galaxy Books; New York: Oxford University Press, 1957 (orig. pub. 1940)], p. 264.

33. *The City of God,* II, 21, trans. Marcus Dods (New York: Modern Library, 1950), p. 63.

34. For example, in one of his letters, Augustine asks: "Did not Sallust praise the Romans for having chosen to forget injuries rather than punish the offender? Did not Cicero praise Caesar because he was wont to forget nothing but the wrongs done to him?" Letter 138, 3.17, as quoted by Etienne Gilson, Foreword to *The City of God: An Abridged Version,* trans. by Gerald G. Walsh et al. and ed. Vernon J. Bourke (Image Books; Garden City, N.Y.: Doubleday and Company, 1958), pp. 17–20.

35. Cf. Gilson, ibid.

36. Gilson, ibid., p. 33.

37. *City of God,* 19.27 (Dods trans., p. 708).

38. *A History of the Christian Church,* by Williston Walker as revised by Richard A. Norris, David W. Lotz, and Robert Handy, 4th ed. (New York: Charles Scribner's Sons, 1985), p. 201. Hereafter referred to as Walker.

39. *The City of God,* XIV, 28, in Dods trans., p. 477. In a personal communication, my colleague Professor Richard Norris points out that resort to the police and other powers of the Roman Empire was inherent in the Constantinian settlement of 312 C.E. Ironically, in 314 C.E., Bishop Donatus the Great himself made one of the one of the earliest attempts to invoke imperial authority for a church cause. "By Augustine's time," says Norris, "bishops of all stripes were quite accustomed to lobbying for support at the imperial court." Both they and the emperor doubtless understood themselves as serving God together now, with little sense that one was "the state" and the other "the church." That distinction would take a long time to develop in western Europe, and it was to develop hardly at all in the eastern Empire.

40. Walker, p. 95.

41. Cf. Walker, pp. 112–13 and 225. Scholars believe that the first consistent practice of "private" confession came in Celtic Christianity in the seventh century.

42. James Westfall Thompson and Edgar Nathaniel Johnson, *An Introduction of Medieval Europe* (New York: W. W. Norton and Co., 1937), pp. 678–79. "Attrition" was the minimal spiritual attitude required for penance—sorrow for the consequences of sin, not the "inward sorrow" of contrition. The power of the keys—authority to give and withhold forgiveness—derived from Matthew 16:18–19, whose support of papal power is symbolized to this day by the Latin of these verses engraved above the capitals of St. Peter's basilica in Rome.

43. Ibid., p. 652. In putting it this way, Thompson and Johnson were perhaps assuming a notion of individual "conscience" that would only become prominent many centuries later in western culture. See below, chapter 3.

44. Kenneth Scott Latourette, *A History of Christianity* (New York: Harper & Row, 1953), p. 460.

45. Thompson and Johnson, p. 320.

46. Thompson and Johnson, p. 321.

47. Latourette, p. 464.

48. Latourette, pp. 555, 475.

49. Latourette, p. 555.

50. Barbara W. Tuchman, *A Distant Mirror: The Calamitous 14th Century* (New York: Ballantine Books, 1979), p. 594. Worth adding is the note that the *second* "longest war" in western history is the one that began in 1914 and which concluded—one hopes—in 1989.

51. Milos Vasic, "A Bridge Too Close, a Peace Too Far," Op Ed Page, *New York Times,* August 24, 1993. Vasic is a reporter for an opposition newspaper in Belgrade, the former Yugoslavian capital.

52. Cf. Edwin Muir, above, chapter 1.

53. Walker, p. 420.

54. Cf. Thomas N. Tentler, *Sin and Confession on the Eve of the Reformation* (Princeton, N.J.: Princeton University Press, 1977), p. 359. Luther is sometimes said to have embraced "two and a half sacraments," and penance was the "half"—consolation with discipline removed. Luther, says Tentler, "generally makes the connection between theological justification and psychological peace whenever he talks about the forgiveness of sins."

55. H. Richard Niebuhr, *Christ and Culture* (New York: Harper and Brothers, 1951), p. 175.

56. *Works of Martin Luther* (Philadelphia: 1915–1932), vol. IV, pp 265–66, as quoted by Niebuhr, pp. 171–72.

57. Niebuhr, pp. 177–78.

58. Cf. a study guide, *Theological Ethics: Ethics for Political Life,* by Nürnberger (Pretoria: University of South Africa, 1986), p. 136. Nürnberger terms Luther's political ethic as "dialectical" rather than "dualistic." The reformer's writings are so replete with polar opposites— two kingdoms, the "inward" and the "outward," the "left hand" and the "right hand" of the divine rule, justice and love—that it was easy for some followers to lapse into dualism and paradox. The latter, Nürnberger concedes, comes down to "disguised polytheism" (p. 137).

59. One partial exception to this summary, noted by Nürnberger (ibid., p. 140), was Luther's insistence that the medieval custom of private vengeance among feudal lords should be curbed by higher authority to keep at bay the threat of social chaos. This forbearance from vengeance was consistent with his view that private persons should never take law into their own hands. Individual Christians might have to resort to civil disobedience to unjust laws, but there is little suggestion in Luther that citizens should *organize* for resistance to unjust governments. Calvinists would develop a different mind on the matter.

60. John Mahoney, *The Making of Moral Theology: A Study of the Roman Catholic Tradition* (Oxford: Clarendon Press, 1987), p. 34.

61. Tentler, *Sin and Confession* , p. 367. Cf. Juan Friede and Benjamin Keen, *Bartoleme De Las Casas: Toward an Understanding of the Man and His Work* (DeKalb, Ill.: Northern Illinois University Press, 1971) and Luis N. Rivera, *A Violent Evangelism: The Political and Religious Conquest of the Americas* (Louisville, Ky.: Westminster/ John Knox Press, 1992). On the basis of his careful study of Las Casas' writings, Rivera (pp. 194–95) summarizes his selective condemnation of slavery: "As a Spaniard and man of the church . . . Las Casas felt firmly compelled to protest viva voce against indigenous [American] slavery. He questioned African slavery . . . but without the same dedication or devotion. And he avoided making direct negative judgments about the papal bulls that directly authorized the enslavement of Africans."

62. Cf. Ernst Troeltsch, *The Social Teaching of the Christian Churches*, trans. Olive Wyon (two vols.; London: George Allen and Unwin, Ltd. and New York: The Macmillan Company, 1931), vol. II, p. 652. Troeltsch's judgment was that in Calvinism, "for the first time in the history of the Christian ethic—there came into existence a Christian Church whose social influence, as far as it was possible at that period, was completely comprehensive" (Ibid.).

63. Sheldon S. Wolin, *Politics and Vision: Continuity and Innovation in Western Political Thought* (Boston: Little Brown and Company, 1960), pp. 167–68.

64. Cf. Michael Walzer, *The Revolution of the Saints: A Study in the Origins of Radical Politics* (Cambridge: Harvard University Press, 1965) and his extensive account of how the "Marian exiles" of mid-sixteenth-century England learned in Calvinist Geneva to talk church reform and state reform in one set of concepts and vocabulary, laying the groundwork of the debates and the course of the English Civil War of the 1640s. Here again the Christian movement evidenced its capacity for inventing an "alternative society"; under conditions of the American separation of church and state, it would continue to do so in some of the first stirrings of the American Revolution, the abolition movement, and the civil rights movement to come. In all of these movements, the church provided some "free space" for deliberation about collective action for change of a public order. In 1989 in East Germany, the churches contributed in the same way to the fall of the Berlin Wall.

65. Wolin, p. 434.

66. Cf. Jean Cadier, *The Man God Mastered: A Brief Biography of John Calvin*, trans. O. R. Johnson (Grand Rapids, Mich.: Wm. B. Eerdmans, 1960), p. 173, and John T. McNeill, *The History and Character of Calvinism* (New York: Oxford University Press, 1954), p. 438.

67. Wolin, pp. 191, 186. On the Calvinist-Puritan propensity for making analogies from church reform to governmental reform, cf. A. S. P. Woodhouse, *Puritanism and Liberty* (Chicago: University of Chicago Press, 1951), Introduction, pp. 60–100, *passim*.

68. Quotations here are from Carol Johnston, "Thinking Theologically About the Global Debt Crisis," unpublished paper, 1993. The quotation from Calvin ("bonds of mutual society") is from his *Commentary on Ezekial*. See Calvin's *Commentaries on the Bible*, Volume XII (Grand Rapids: Baker Book House, 1981), p. 223.

69. On the "spirit of liberty," cf. *In the Spirit of Liberty: Papers and Addresses of Learned Hand*, collected with an introduction and notes by Irving Dillard; 3rd ed., enlarged (New York: Alfred A Knopf, 1960), p. 190. Cromwell is reputed to have made his exclamation in the midst of a quarrel between two regiments of Scots.

70. Locke, *Of Civil Government*, vol. II, p. 6.

71. Ibid., XI, 135–38.

72. *A Letter Concerning Toleration,* in *Works*, vol. II, p. 254. Cf. pp. 235, 248–49.

73. W. T. Jones, in Edward McChesney Sait, ed., *Masters of Political Thought*, vol. II (Boston: Houghton Mifflin Company, 1949), p. 202.

74. *A Letter Concerning Toleration,* ed. James H. Tully (Indianapolis: Hackett Publishing Company, 1983), p. 51. (Originally published in London, 1689.)

75. Theodore M. Greene, Introduction to Kant, *Religion Within the Limits of Reason Alone,* trans. Theodore M. Greene and Hoyt H. Hudson (Harper Torchbooks; New York: Harper and Brothers, 1960), pp. lxxiv–v.

76. Ibid., p. lxxvi.

77. For a recent attempt to discern in Kant a place for forgiveness, cf. Allen W. Woods, *Kant's Moral Religion* (Ithaca and London: Cornell University Press, 1970), p. 239–43. Kant numbered "a concilatory spirit," compassion, and mercy among the human virtues, and he was clear that "only a forgiveness which is compatible with the moral law" could command respect. God forgives humans, for example, when and if they exhibit a repentant inner "disposition to holiness," even if they cannot undo the damages of their misdeeds. Kant demands a kind of moral perfection here—the perfection of a "pure" will. Not only does this treat lightly the problem of evil in the human will, but it pushes moral repentance and reformation back to the interior of the human self. Forgiveness as a process in which human social relations are mutually repaired gets little attention here. In the last analysis, it is hard to see why, having returned to mutual purity of intentions, humans need forgiveness; or, not having returned, that they can morally deserve it.

78. The phrase is from Emil Brunner, *The Divine Imperative,* trans. Olive Wyon (Philadelphia: The Westminster Press, 1947), Preface, p. 9.

79. Cf., e.g., Robert Bellah, et al., *The Good Society* (New York: Alfred A. Knopf, 1991), pp. 67–70, 141–42, 294–95. Commenting on the "Lockean world" of Thomas Jefferson, these authors go on to say: "In many ways this early-nineteenth-century world remains the self-image of 'America,' a land where essentially equal individuals can make their way unencumbered by ancient traditions or large institutions" (p. 70).

80. Unreferenced paraphrase from Alasdair MacIntyre, *After Virtue,* 2nd ed. (Notre Dame: University of Notre Dame Press, 1984), p. 119.

Chapter 3

1. *In Defense of Politics,* 2nd ed. (Chicago: University of Chicago Press, 1972), p. 159.

2. "The Holocaust Must Not Be Forgotten," *Times of London,* May 7, 1985.

3. In Simon Wiesenthal, *Sunflower* (London: W. H. Allen, 1970, and New York: Schocken Books, 1976), p. 186.

4. Cf. second introductory essay, "The Ethical Significance of Kant's *Religion,*" in Immanuel Kant, *Religion Within the Limits of Reason Alone,* trans. Theodore Greene and Hoyt H. Hudson (Harper Torchbooks; New York: Harper and Brothers, 1960), pp. cxxviii–x.

5. Fyodor Dostoyevsky, *The Brothers Karamazov,* trans. Constance Garnett (New York: The Modern Library, n.d.), pp. 290–91.

6. Such passages in Dostoyevsky are among the fertile sources of twentieth-century existentialist moral theory, with its claim that humans create their own willed morality, without the props of reason, history, or tradition.

7. I owe my knowledge of this incident to Walter Wink, *Engaging the Powers* (Philadelphia: Fortress Press, 1992), p. 233. The quotation is from *Tolstoy's Writings on Civil Disobedience and Non-Violence* (London: Peter Owen, 1968), p. 381.

8. Wink, *Engaging the Powers,* p. 221. His statistics are drawn from Ruth Leger Sivard, *World Military and Social Expenditures 1991* (World Priorities, Box 205140, Washington, DC 20007), p. 20. The italics are Wink's.

9. I agree with Wink's suggestion that just-war theory should be considered a body of

principles for "violence reduction" in prospect and in the event of war (Wink, p. 215). Unfortunately, when political and military leaders work at lowering the level of violence in war, their concern so concentrates on their own side that one just-war principle—proportionality between political goal and cost of achieving it—gets observed, at most, by half. The rule "Kill many of the enemy to save a few of our own" was followed consistently in the closing months of World War II and in the 1991 Persian Gulf War. Cf. below, chapters 4 and 5.

10. The Hebrew Bible's Ten Commandments begin with four that are clearly theological followed by six that are social and ethical. The first of the six requires respect for parents, an imperative on the border between "private" and "public" life. The next five are clearly in the public as well as private realm of sin: murder, adultery, stealing, lying, and coveting. The original sixth commandment, of course, is directed against the personal crime of murder, not warfare; only a larger biblical context can be rallied to the support of pacifism. The principle that there are "weightier demands of the Law," in contrast to the lesser, was attributed to Jesus in Matthew 23:23: ". . . justice, mercy, and good faith" (NEB).

11. "Excerpts from New Charter on Rights of South Africans," *New York Times*, November 18, 1993.

12. Crick, *In Defence of Politics*, 2nd ed. (Chicago: University of Chicago Press, 1972), p. 128. Cf. pp. 18, 134, and 147. Note that this definition combines a democratic ideal (tolerance) and empirical necessity (interdependence).

13. Quoted by James Reston, "All Quiet on the Potomac," *New York Times,* May 26, 1985 [Memorial Day]. Cf. her poem, "Remember," in *The Poetical Works*, ed. William Michael Rossetti, 1906 (New York: Adler's Foreign Books, 1970), p. 294.

14. Erich Maria Remarque, *All Quiet on the Western Front* (New York: Fawcett Crest, 1929–30), pp. 228–29, copyright by Little Brown and Company. Remarque would become one of the German authors banned and burned by the Nazis.

15. Iulia de Beausobre, *Creative Suffering* (London: Dacre Press, 1940), pp. 10ff., as quoted by John de Gruchy, *Theology and Ministry in Context and Crisis* (Philadelphia: Fortress Press, 1988), p. 100.

16. Interview with Bill Moyers, Public Broadcasting System, "Facing Hate with Elie Wiesel and Bill Moyers," November 27, 1991, as taken from Transcript #BMSP-19, International Cultural Programming, Inc., and Public Affairs Television, Inc., pp. 15–16. The broken language here is in the original.

17. Primo Levi, *The Truce*, trans. from the Italian by Stuart Woolf (London: The Bodley Head: 1965), as reprinted in *Out of the Whirlwind: A Reader of Holocaust Literature*, ed. Albert H. Friedlander (New York: Schocken Books, 1976), p. 426.

18. As quoted by Trude B. Feldman, "History's Sadat," *New York Times*, November 20, 1982, two years after Sadat's assassination by Islamic radicals opposed to his peace initiatives towards Israel.

19. For just such a careful study, cf. Brian Frost, *The Politics of Peace*, foreword by Desmond Tutu and concluding theological chapter by Donald W. Shriver, Jr. (London: Longmans, 1991), a survey of political events in some eleven countries in whose history traces of political forgiveness can be found.

Chapter 4

1. Bonhoeffer, *Ethics*, ed. Eberhard Bethge (London: SCM Press Ltd., 1955), pp. 53–54. Against the background of Bonhoeffer's own Lutheran theological roots, this passage is remarkable for its allowance of "something in the nature of forgiveness" in international relations.

2. Bauer, modern Jewish historian, as quoted in the exhibits of the United States Holocaust Memorial in Washington, D.C.

3. In Simon Wiesenthal, *The Sunflower* (London: W. H. Allen, 1970), p. 188. Vercors is the pen name of this French writer.

4. Cf. John Ardagh, *Germany and the Germans: An Anatomy of Society Today* (New York: Harper & Row, 1987), p. 451. But the migration was steady in the previous years, too. My own earliest German ancestor came to Philadelphia from the Palatinate in 1688.

5. Cf. Richard Fox, *Reinhold Niebuhr: A Biography* (New York: Pantheon Books, 1985), pp. 3, 41–81.

6. Fox, p. 46.

7. Fox, p. 53, quoting from an article, "The Present Task of the Sunday School" in *Evangelical Teacher,* July 1918. Cf. William G. Chrystal, ed., *Young Reinhold Niebuhr* (St. Louis, Mo., 1977), p. 91.

8. Fox, pp. 60–61.

9. Fox, p. 78.

10. Fox, p. 79, quoting from the *Evangelical Herald* of September 1923.

11. Cf. Wiesenthal, *The Sunflower*, p. 42.

12. Casualty totals from World War II are notoriously inexact, a fact that is itself an index to human obliteration in the event. The death toll worldwide has been variously totaled from 35 million to 60 million. The USSR lost at least 11 million combatants and 7 million civilians. In the first twelve months of the Russian invasion alone, Germany had 1,250,000 casualties. Overall, German losses in the war came to 3,500,000 combatants plus some 780,000 civilians. After the war, Clement Attlee told Parliament that Germany had suffered 3,400,000 "permanently wounded" people, and another half-million Germans were simply missing. More careful about risking lives in combat, the British suffered 500,000 military and civilian deaths; the Americans, 300,000. These latter figures, in contrast to "the irresponsible slaughter" of World War I, have led some historians to call "the second round" a "humanitarian war." [Frank P. Chambers, Christina Phelps Harris, Charles C. Bayley, *This Age of Conflict* (New York: Harcourt, Brace, and Co., 1950), p. 743.] But there was nothing humanitarian in these statistics overall—and this is not even to mention the war in the Pacific.

13. In formerly East German Dresden, for example, well-tutored by years of Communist accounts of the history, several generations of citizens remember that in their daylight raid on the city in February 1945, American bombers targeted large crowds of civilians who had fled to the great park in the middle of the city. Official Allied estimates of the dead from the two days of bombing vary wildly from 35,000 to 80,000; in one church museum, in the spring of 1993, there remained a penned-in "correction" by a visitor who, one suspects, had to be a Dresdener: "200,000."

14. Public and official tribute to the leaders of the British air war against Germany has displayed deep ambivalences over the years since 1945, especially around the question of what honors, if any, should be accorded General Arthur "Bomber" Harris, leader of Bomber Command who presided over the city-killing strategy of obliteration bombing. In 1992 a statue of him was finally erected in London. Protests from Germany were immediate. They came from places less famous than Hamburg and Dresden, whose citizens still harbor deep hostilities toward these events. Mayor Joachim Becker of Pforzheim, for example, protested this memorial to a general whose planes killed one-fourth of the 18,000 residents of the town in 22 minutes on March 17, 1945. In Pforzheim, Harris is known as "Butcher Harris." Said the mayor: "How can one talk of reconciliation in 1992 when the British do such things [as the erection of this statue]?" Forty-seven years later, the *symbol*-war was still smoldering. [*The Independent* (London), November 20, 1992, p. 18, "In A German Churchyard, the Past is Put to Rest."] On what else was happening in Pforzheim to put this past to rest, cf. the end of this chapter.

15. *Slaughterhouse Five* (New York: Dell Publishing Co., 1969). In his long subscript on the title page, Vonnegut notes that he is "a fourth-generation German-American . . . who . . . as a prisoner of war, witnessed the fire-bombing of Dresden . . . and survived to tell the tale."

16. "World Wars," by J. G. Royde-Smith, in *Encyclopedia Britannia,* vol. 19, p. 1008.

17. Ardagh, pp. 10–11.

18. Ibid., p. 326. Ardagh says that in the eight years following 1945, the Soviet "pillage" of East Germany amounted to 25 percent of its GNP. By 1953, East Germany was incorporated into the Soviet-controlled economic bloc (Comecon) and became its most productive member.

19. At Potsdam in July 1945, the Allies agreed that reparations from Germany would be limited to industrial equipment (in contrast to the money reparations demanded in the Versailles Treaty). A year later, in May 1946, the American, British, and French ceased dismantling factories in their occupation zones, mostly as a first response to the need for industrial support for remedying the severe food shortages. Cf. Henry Ashby Turner, Jr., *The Two Germanies Since 1945* (New Haven, Conn.: Yale University Press, 1987), pp. 12–14.

20. Ardagh, pp. 8–9.

21. Telford Taylor, high commissioner for the American occupied zone, wanted to try 5,000 Germans from all levels of the Nazi system. Between December 9, 1946, and April 11, 1949, the military courts at Nuremberg settled for 185 concentration camp guards, doctors, members of SS killing squads, and directors of major war supply corporations such as I. G. Farben, Krupp, and Flick. Of these 185, 25 were executed; 20 received life imprisonment; 97 got lesser terms; and 35 were acquitted. In 1951, an American commission suspended more than half of these sentences. German indictments of 816 persons in 1958 resulted in a similar pattern: 118 life imprisonments; 398 lesser sentences, many of which were later commuted; and no trial at all of the remaining 300. (Source: United States Holocaust Memorial.)

22. Ardagh, p. 391.

23. This comment on the trials of the fifties comes from Dr./Professor Helmut Reihlen, now living in Berlin, in a personal communication. The film *Shindler's List* portrays one such instance.

24. Ardagh, p. 391.

25. Ardagh, p. 415, where he relates two incidents, one of a medical doctor officially accused after many years of practice of being a former Nazi, who is warmly defended by his patients; and another, of Heinrich Böell's central character in his novel *The Lost Honour of Katherina Blum.* Her slander by a local newspaper is accepted by her neighbors without question, "*because they did not know her.*" (Italics Ardagh's.)

26. Ardagh, p. 395.

27. James M. Markham, "Facing Up to Germany's Past," *New York Times Magazine,* June 23, 1985.

28. Jürgen Moltmann, "Forty Years After the Stuttgart Declaration," trans. Susan Reynolds, in *Case Study 2*, The Forgiveness and Politics Study Project, ed. Brian Frost (London: New World Publications, 1987), pp. 41–43.

29. Werner Krusche, "Guilt and Forgiveness: The Basis of Christian Peace Negotiation," with an introduction by Edwin Robertson, in *Case Study 2*, above, pp. 11–13.

30. Ibid., p. 10.

31. The terms were Martin Niemöller's, as recorded in a 1972 article by Eberhard Bethge, "Geschichtliche Schuld der Kirche" in *Christliche Freiheit: Dienst am Menschen,* a collection of essays in honor of Niemöller's eightieth birthday, ed. Karl Herbst (Verlag Lembeck, 1972), p. 123.

32. Ibid., p. 131. Translations from this Bethge essay are my own.

33. Turner, *The Two Germanies,* p. 8.

34. Bethge, "Geschichtliche Schuld," p. 135.

35. The phrase is from Dorothee Soelle, *Politische Theologie,* 1971, S. 51, as quoted by Bethge, p. 138.

36. Bethge, p. 137, who illustrates this phenomenon with a devastating 1971 statement of Premier B. J. Vorster, who informs the South African churches to stick to "the Word of God."

37. Cf. *Creeds of the Churches,* ed. John H. Leith (Anchor Books; Garden City, N.Y.: Doubleday and Company, 1963), pp. 517–22. Barmen repudiated "the false teaching that there are areas of our life in which we belong not to Jesus Christ but another lord, areas in which we do not need justification and sanctification through him." The rival "lord," of course, was Hitler. Martin Stöhr says of this theme in Barmen: "The supremacy of Christ and his gifts also includes the supremacy of the Spirit and of God's word over the nations and political reality. The Barmen Theological Declaration of 1934 had formulated that for the first time, bindingly and publicly, as a confession of the [Evangelical] Church" in Germany. "Reconciliation Takes a Political Form: The Example of Poland and Germany." Unpublished essay, 1988, p. 8.

38. Krusche, in *Case Study 2,* p. 17, quoting from Koch, *Heinemann und die Deutschlandfrage,* 1972, pp. 119, 121.

39. In this year Konrad Adenauer, new chancellor of the Federal Republic, expressed his "profound conviction, that we all find ourselves in the midst of a struggle between materialism and Christianity, good and evil, and that every one of us must give his utmost to ensure that good, and with it God, will be victorious." Quoted from Koch, above, p. 419, by Krusche, *Case Study 2,* p. 19.

40. Turner, *The Two Germanies,* p. 10.

41. Ardagh, pp. 13–14.

42. Ardagh, p. 15.

43. Turner, p. 77.

44. Some 40 percent of this sum went to citizens of Israel, 40 percent to persons in other countries, and 20 percent to persons living in Germany. The totals quoted here come from the document *Restitution,* published in English translation by the Press and Information Office of the Federal Republic, June, 1988. The totals in dollars "express an average of the different [exchange] rates in effect over the last thirty years." The Allied-German Peace Treaty of 1952 and the further (Luxembourg) treaty between the Federal Republic and Israel required certain compensations to be made to the governments of Israel and twelve European nations; but by far the largest share of these compensations went to individuals in these countries both for property loss and for suffering under the Nazis.

45. Ibid.

46. Martin Stöhr, "Reconciliation Takes a Political Form: The Example of Poland and Germany," unpublished essay, n.d. [c. 1988], p.11.

47. Ibid., p. 12.

48. Ibid., p. 13.

49. Ibid., pp. 13–14. The contrary views of many of the exiles themselves can be gathered from an excerpt from a response to the Memorandum by one association of exiles, as quoted by Stöhr. The rhetoric breathes the air of the escalating Cold War: "'. . . the authors of this piece of writing clearly no longer have any relationship with their state or even with their fatherland, and therefore no longer know how to appreciate the duty to serve the community and its people.' While 'campaigns are still being waged against the horrors of the concentration camps of National Socialism, people apparently find it quite in order that the Bolshevist states of Eastern Europe and the Soviet zone should be like great concentration camps.' The Church 'is succumbing today to Bolshevist demands.'"

50. Krusche, *Case Study 2*, p. 26.

51. The interests of living people, he added, must take priority over "concern about the abstract notions of nation and *Volk.*" Turner, p. 148.

52. Stöhr, p. 16.

53. Stöhr, p. 16. The 1965 Memorandum had been published during the Second Vatican Council. While in Rome, the Catholic bishops of Poland and Germany exchanged letters of repentance and forgiveness concerning the historic relations of their two countries. Some Polish commentators read the exchange as implying equal guilt, equal repentance, and equal forgiveness on the two sides, a view that they considered grossly unacceptable. Brandt's *Ostpolitik* bore additional fruit in new diplomatic relations between West Germany, East Germany, and the USSR. In turn, it opened the door for the Federal Republic to enter the United Nations in 1973.

54. Henry Kamm, "Brandt, on Visit to Oder, Assures Poles on Border," *New York Times*, March 11, 1990.

55. The commentator was ABC News anchorman Peter Jennings, October 9, 1992. Cf. David Binder, obituary article, *New York Times*, same date.

56. Cf. Moltmann, "Forty Years After the Stuttgart Confession," in *Case Study 2*, above, p. 48–49. The only country whose losses may have approached those of the USSR was China, but statistics on the latter remain inexact. Cf. below, Chapter 5.

57. James E. Young, "Memory and Monument," in Geoffrey Hartmann, ed., *Bitburg in Moral and Political Perspective* (Bloomington, Ind.: Indiana University Press, 1986), p. 112. A large number of the journalistic accounts of the Bitburg event, quoted below, are collected in this book. Cf. also Edward Linenthal, *Sacred Ground* (Urbana, Ill.: University of Illinois Press, 1993), a study of battlefields and their monuments in American history.

58. "Transcript of Speech by Kohl at U.S. Air Base," *New York Times*, May 6, 1985.

59. *New York Times*, May 3, 1985.

60. This chronicle of events was recorded by the *New York Times*, April 20, 1985, after the visit of Elie Wiesel to the White House about to be described. For a collection of journalistic and other commentaries on the Bitburg incident, see Geoffrey Hartmann, *Bitburg in Moral and Political Perspective*, op. cit., above note.

61. The count of the graves varied from 47 to 49, and there was dispute as to whether all members of the Waffen SS, especially toward the end of the war, were actually volunteers.

62. *New York Times*, April 19, 1985. This same sentiment was expressed by Reagan in a state dinner the previous evening (*New York Times*, April 20, 1985).

63. *New York Times*, April 20, 1985.

64. Ibid. In an effort to contain the public scale of the occasion, at the last minute, the White House shifted its location from the East Room, with a capacity of 300, to the Roosevelt Room, capacity 40. (*New York Times*, April 20, 1985.)

65. From the full text of both speeches, *New York Times*, April 20, 1985.

66. Someone in Jerusalem suggested it, however: Meir Merhav, "Honoring Evil," *Jerusalem Post*, May 3, 1985, reprinted in Hartmann, ed., *Bitburg in Moral and Political Perspective*, pp. 194–98.

67. Report by James M. Markham, *New York Times*, April 20, 1985.

68. *New York Times*, April 22, 1985.

69. Cf. George H. Stein, *The Waffen SS: Hitler's Elite Guard at War, 1939–45* (Ithaca, N.Y.: Cornell University Press, 1984), and *New York Times*, May 3, 1985. The Nuremberg court in 1946 had declared the SS a "criminal organization" all of whose members were to be considered guilty of war crimes. "It is impossible to single out any one portion of the SS which was not involved in these criminal activities," said the court. Cf. *Trial of the Major War Criminals before the International Military Tribunal, Nuremburg, 1945–46*, Official Text, vol. 1, pp. 255–73, and reprinted in Geoffrey Hartmann, ed., *Bitburg*, pp. 273–79.

70. John Tagliabue, "SS Veterans Feel 'Rehabilitated' by Reagan Visit,"*New York Times,* May 3, 1985.

71. *New York Times,* April 22, 1985. Present at this campsite ceremony were members of Kohl's cabinet, President von Weizsäcker, foreign ambassadors, survivors of the camp, and citizens of the local communities. More than 50,000 people had been murdered here, in addition to the Russian prisoners of war.

72. Transcripts of both speeches from the *New York Times*, May 6, 1985.

73. *New York Times*, ibid.

74. *New York Times,* May 8, 1985. "Men favored the visit by 46 to 41 percent, but women opposed it by 40 to 36 percent. There was no clear differences of opinion by age. Military veterans were about equally divided, with 45 percent in favor and 42 opposed. Of the 22 Jews interviewed, 21 said he should not have gone and the other was undecided."

75. Ibid. Mark Krupnick, writing soon after the event, concluded that the polls showed that many Americans "were willing to forgive and forget because they cared so little" for the specifics of the Holocaust. Cf. "'Walking in Our Sleep': Bitburg and the Post-1939 Generation," *The Christian Century*, June 5–12, 1985, pp. 573–74, as reprinted in Geoffrey Hartman, ed., *Bitburg,* p. 189.

76. "'New' SS Wreaths, Old Anti-Semitism," *New York Times*, May 14, 1985.

77. The phrase is that of Mr. David Rosen, in 1994 a student for the rabbinate at the Jewish Theological Seminary of America.

78. Review of Eberhard Jaeckel, *Hitler in History* (Hanover, N.H.: University Press of New England, 1985), reviewed by Fritz Stern in the *New York Times Book Review,* May 12, 1985. By 1993 "willed amnesia" had turned for one group of westerners into outright historical denial that the Holocaust ever happened. Cf. Deborah E. Lipstadt, *Denying the Holocaust: The Growing Assault on Truth and Memory* (New York: The Free Press, 1993) and Pierre Vidal-Naquet, *Assassins of Memory: Essays on the Denial of the Holocaust,* trans. Jeffrey Mehlman (New York: Columbia University Press, 1993).

79. Dennis B.Klein, "The Will to Forget," Op Ed, *New York Times,* May 5, 1986.

80. As recorded by Lowis Lochner, Associated Press bureau chief in Berlin on August 22, 1939. (Source: The United States Holocaust Memorial.)

81. From "Rattlesnake Country," as quoted by William H. Prichard's review of Warren's *New and Selected Poems, 1923–1985* (New York: Random House, 1985) in *The New York Times Book Review*, May 12, 1985.

82. Flora Lewis, "History Doesn't Die," *New York Times*, April 26, 1985.

83. *New York Times*, May 6, 1985.

84. "Old Germans and the Young: the Divisions are Deep," *New York Times,* May 8, 1985. The notion that only individuals can be guilty or responsible is the long-lived legacy of Kant, which continues to nag western moralists with a theoretical inability to assign moral value to the acts of institutions and collectivities. A recent book by sociologist Philip Senznick cuts through this dualism of person and collective with pragmatic and empirical realism: "We need not choose between individual and collective accountability. Both may be appropriate. A railroad may be liable for its negligence, and individual employees may be punished as well." In sum, "The logic of moral action governs all moral actors, collectivities and persons alike." Selznick, *The Moral Commonwealth: Social Theory and the Promise of Community* (Berkeley, CA: University of California Press, 1992), pp. 242–44 and note 20.

85. Jürgen Moltmann, "Forty Years After the Stuttgart Confession," in *Case Study 2,* p. 46.

86. Max Weber, "Politics as a Vocation," in H. H. Gerth and C. Wright Mills, eds., *From Max Weber: Essays in Sociology* (New York: Oxford University Press, 1958), p. 118.

87. Ibid., pp. 126–27.

88. *New York Times*, May 12, 1985, and May 1, 1986.

89. James M. Markham, *New York Times*, May 9, 1985.

90. Quotations from the speech here and below are taken from an English translation furnished me by the Embassy of the Federal Republic of Germany in May 1985. A full text can also be found in the appendix of Geoffrey Hartmann, ed., *Bitburg*, pp. 262–73.

91. The speech makes almost no mention of the faults of the enemy. It seems tacitly to assume that there is enough mention of that in the nation's history and character since the 1920s. His refusal to speak, even in a clause, of the enemies' guilt is surely a sign of his own "conquest of self" (cf. the above quotation) which refuses to tell an enemy what sins it has to confess.

92. *New York Times*, May 9, 1985.

93. The spirit and historical accuracy of Gorbachev's May 8 speech in Moscow, however, contrasted radically with Weizsäcker's. In these early months of his administration, the new Secretary General of the Communist Party was not yet following the lines that several years later would make him popular in the West. The speech recited old Cold War themes: that World War II was fought not against Nazism but against capitalism; that Russians died in the war not for the motherland but for Communism; that Americans were enriching themselves now at Europe's expense and were an international menace. These readings of history matched rather precisely the lines long taken in East Germany regarding Nazism and its murder of the Jewish people: there the public had for decades been told by leaders that anti-Semitism was a product of an evil social-political system from which they now were free. No need in East Germany, then, to talk publicly of historical guilt and repentance.

94. Garry Wills, "The Words That Remade America: Lincoln at Gettysburg," as printed in *The Atlantic*, vol. 269, no. 6 (June 1992).

95. In a panel discussion at Union Theological Seminary, New York, on June 5, 1989.

96. The phrase used at the beginning of the recent book by Joram Graf Haber, *Forgiveness* (Savage, Maryland: Rowman and Littlefield Publishers, Inc., 1991), p. 1.

97. Ibid., p. 49.

98. Ibid., p. 46.

99. Romans 3:10, in allusion to Psalms 14:1–2 and 53:1–2.

100. In a radio broadcast on February 1, 1933, two days after Hitler's assumption of power, protesting on theological grounds any "leader who makes an idol of himself and his office, and who thus mocks God." This broadcast was cut off before the end of this address—possibly by action of the new Nazi controllers of the communication system. Cf. Eberhard Bethge, *Dietrich Bonhoeffer: Man of Courage, Man of Vision* (New York: Harper & Row, 1970), pp. 193–94.

101. Dietrich Bonhoeffer, *I Loved This People*, trans. Keith R. Crim (Richmond, Va.: John Knox Press, 1965), pp. 51–59, as reprinted in *Letters and Papers from Prison*, ed. Eberhard Bethge, enlarged ed. (New York: The Macmillan Company, 1971), pp. 353–54. Moltmann quotes from this poem in his essay, "Forty Years After the Stuttgart Confession," in *Case Study 2*, p. 43.

102. Saul Friedlander analyzes essays by Golo Mann, a historian, and Rudolf Augstein, editor in chief of *Der Spiegel,* both published in early 1985, in which both writers demonstrate the readiness of some German intellectuals in the eighties to relativize the crimes of Nazism by denying its uniqueness in either German or world history. Augstein calls German readers' attention to the atrocities of the Soviets, the other Allies in the war, and other notorious historical crimes. Concludes Friedlander: "President Richard von Weizsäcker's attitude toward the past is a far from common or typical one, even at the elite level" among Germans. Nonetheless, he adds, it is a regular phenomenon among German young people that, just as the first and second postwar generations tire of being reminded of Nazism, the third demands to know more about the same. Without doubt, "the weight of the Nazi era on the contempo-

rary German imagination remains massive. . . ." Friedlander, "Some German Struggles With Memory," in Geoffrey Hartmann, ed., *Bitburg,* p. 38.

103. *Dresdner Weltweit,* March 13–14, 1993. Translation mine. Ms. David's father was the distinguished Dresden rabbi Albert Wolf.

104. All these details come from John Eisenhammer, "In a German Churchyard, the Past Is Put to Rest," in *The Independent* (London), November 20, 1992.

Chapter 5

1. Shusaku Endo, *The Samurai,* trans. Van C. Gessel (Vintage Books; New York: Random House, 1984), p. 233.

2. Michael D. Cohen and James G. March, *Leadership and Ambiguity,* 2nd ed. (Boston: Harvard Business School Press, 1986), p. 227.

3. Roger L. Shinn, *Wars and Rumors of War* (Nashville, Tenn.: Abingdon Press, 1972), p. 205.

4. The illustrations of socially repressed memory in this study come chiefly from national and international life. But the tendency of human communities to bury public memory of traumatic pasts has very local forms, too. For an extended example from small-town America, see Donald W. Shriver, Jr. *et al., Spindles and Spires: A Re-Study of Gastonia* (Atlanta, GA.: John Knox Press, 1976), pp. 308–12 and note 19, p. 334.

5. George Friedman and Meredith LeBard, letters column, *New York Times,* December 2, 1991, in response to a column of November 17 by Leslie H. Gelb, "Infamy Is Still Infamy." Cf. Friedman and LeBard, *The Coming War with Japan* (New York: St. Martin's Press, 1992).

6. Cf. H. Richard Niebuhr, *The Responsible Self: An Essay in Christian Moral Philosophy,* introduction by James M. Gustafson (New York: Harper & Row, 1963), and Philip Selznick, *The Moral Commonwealth: Social Theory and the Promise of Community* (Berkeley, CA.: University of California Press, 1992), Chapter 8, "The Responsible Self," pp. 207–28.

7. Speech at the Bitburg Air Base, *New York Times,* May 6, 1985.

8. John W. Dower, *War Without Mercy: Race and Power in the Pacific War* (New York: Pantheon Books, 1986). Dower currently teaches history at the Massachusetts Institute of Technology. Into the tortured question of whether historians can or should write history with no recognition of their own values, including moral values, I will not further enter here. Professor Fritz Stern has offered a brief, convincing rebuttal to the moral-agnostic view of his profession's task in a review of the book *Hitler in History,* by Eberhard Jaeckel (Hanover, N.H.: The University Press of New England,1985), where that author, alleging neutrality, says that the Germans under Hitler "were not better or worse than those who lived before or after them or other people in their times, but they lived under special conditions." Stern, a refugee from Germany of the thirties, retorts: "This is a facile formulation. . . . Mr. Jaeckel himself acknowledges 'Germany's exceptional aggressiveness and brutality.' Historians can hardly avoid rendering judgment and for all his self-denying intention, Mr. Jaeckel proves no exception. Some of his judgments are implicit: by focusing on Hitler, he conveys the impression that the German people were passive, more passive than they probably were." (*New York Times Book Review,* May 12, 1985.) John W. Dower would surely agree with Stern.

9. Dower, *War Without Mercy,* p. 181.

10. My colleague Kosuke Koyama points out that Japanese culture yields few if any abstract concepts of "race," even though the resentment at western-white claims to superiority met with strong counterresentment. Japan's own wartime ranking of itself above other Asian nations apparently did not acquire the "racist" tag. "I was trained to think 'racially' after I came to the United States," says Koyama. (Personal communication.)

11. Dower, p. 37.

12. For example, in the first scene of the 1943 movie *Bataan*, which was still going the cable TV rounds in 1993, an American soldier takes a pot shot at a monkey on the chance that it is really "a Jap." The Japs are like "baboons, too," he says to his younger buddies. "They climb trees better than monkeys, and they can live for a month on what would last you guys two days."

13. Dower, p.19.

14. Dower, pp. 28–29.

15. Dower, pp. 31–32.

16. That is the word still used in 1991 by Meirion and Susie Harries in *Soldiers of the Sun* (New York: Random House, 1991), in their description of the rape of Nanjing: "Into the New Year [of 1938], the occupying troops murdered, raped, looted, and burned the city in a frenzy of evil that still stands as the icon of Imperial Army bestiality."(p. 222) In a book re-markable for both its documentation and its attempt to understand the Japanese soldier and his officers, the use of this word is unfortunate—not only because such behavior by humans is an insult to most beasts, but because the tag "animal" had lethal effect during the war in unleashing all inhibition on killing "Japs" on the Allied side. As a ten-year-old child in 1937, I became acquainted with the rape of Nanjing by the popular medium of bubble-gum "war cards," whose drawings vividly portrayed details of this grim event—with the exception of the rapes.

17. Ibid., p. 226.

18. This is not to say that the standards of "just war" did not deteriorate in the behavior of American soldiers in Europe in 1944–45. Veteran friends of mine tell stories of German women with babies being shot on sight when some were found to be harboring grenades, and of small groups of captured German soldiers being routinely killed. "You had to belong to a large group of surrendering Germans to be treated as prisoners of war."

19. Dower, pp. 12–13. The image of "palimpsest" here is especially apt—an ancient manuscript which has been overlaid, sometimes by many layers, with various texts, token of a time when writing materials were expensive and carefully recycled.

20. Dower's volume seeks to apportion blame for escalations of violence on both sides as the war progressed, but he is clear that the Imperial Army treated prisoners and civilians, on occasion, in ways not imitated on any large scale by the Americans. The Harries's vol-ume, noted above, is full of accounts of the organized and random atrocities that Japanese armies committed down to the end of the war, in numbers "impossible to catalog . . . murder on a scale amounting to genocide; rapes beyond counting; vivisection; cannibalism; torture; American prisoners of war allowed to drown in excrement in the 'hell ships' taking them back to Japan for use as forced labor; civilian prisoners used as human sandbags during air raids; Burmese coolies, dead and dying, stuffed under the sleeping platforms of other labor-ers on the Burma-Siam Railway." (Harries and Harries, pp. 475–76.)

21. Ted Morgan, "Voices from the Barbie Trial," *New York Times Magazine*, August 2, 1987.

22. Harries and Harries, *Soldiers of the Sun*, p. 476.

23. *War Department Pamphlet 21–13, Army Life* (Washington, D.C.: U.S. Government Printing Office, August 10, 1944), p. 159. I was among the last few thousand eighteen-year-old Americans to be drafted in the spring of 1946.

24. Harries and Harries, pp. 420–21.

25. Ibid., p. 421.

26. Ibid., pp. 412–13.

27. Ibid., pp. 337–38, 344.

28. Dower, p. 73.

29. Dower, p. 65.

30. Dower, p. 71.

31. Harries and Harries, pp. 360–61. The terms are strictly parallel to those used in the Nazi death camps by guards who referred to prisoners as "pieces" (*Stücke*).

32. Dower, p. 72.

33. This is Dower's number; others, including Yokohama families in their December 7, 1991, open letter to Americans (quoted below), put the number at a hundred.

34. Dower, pp. 40–41.

35. Kosuke Koyama, "Ritual of Limping Dance: A Botanical Observation," [Inaugural Lecture as John D. Rockefeller, Jr., Professor of Ecumenics and World Christianity], *Union Seminary Quarterly Review*, vol. XXXVI, supplementary issue, 1981.

36. Robert Reinhold, "As Pearl Harbor Day Looms, Sting of Old Wounds Revives," *New York Times*, September 1, 1991.

37. Steven R. Weisman, "Japanese Apology Over War Unlikely After Bush's Stand," *New York Times*, December 6, 1991.

38. As reported by ABC Television, "Pearl Harbor: Two Hours That Changed the World," December 5, 1991.

39. Maureen Dowd, "His Voice Breaking, Bush Remembers a Time of 'Infamy,'" *New York Times*, December 8, 1991.

40. Kosuke Koyama, "Forgiveness and Politics: Japanese Experience," in *Festschrift for Samuel Ragan, S. J.* (Gujurat: Sahipya Prakash, 1991), p. 149. Quotations here from Koyama, a scholar who exemplifies the disciplined empathy required for a "two-culture" perspective on twentieth-century international conflict.

41. Koyama, ibid., pp. 155–56.

42. Koyama, ibid., p. 157. See also below.

43. Koyama, ibid., pp. 158–59. Koyama adds the interpretative bracket—this is the connotation of the Japanese verb *realizes*.

44. A Seoul newspaper immediately protested and challenged the Japanese people editorially to accept the fact that the war was fought in the Emperor's name. *Dongwa Daily News*, February 22, 1989. (I am indebted to Ms. Eunja Lee for this reference.)

45. Published by the Kyodan, Easter Sunday, March 26, 1967.

46. The Korean "comfort women"—forced to become prostitutes for Japanese soldiers—finally became an issue of official apology and some reparations to the Japanese government in the early 1990s.

47. As quoted by Arthur M. Schlesinger, Jr., *The Disuniting of America: Reflections on a Multicultural Society* (New York: W. W. Norton and Company, 1993), pp. 50–51. Cf. Saburo Ienaga, *The Pacific War: World War II and the Japanese, 1931–1945* (New York: 1978), p. xi and Steven R. Weisman, "Japan and the War: Debate on Censors is Renewed," *The New York Times*, October 8. 1989.

48. Cf. the journal *Sekai, Iwanami Shoten*, Tokyo, October 1982, pp. 84 ff., as quoted by Koyama in a longer version of the essay quoted above, privately shared with me. The number of "comfort women" (from Korea and other Asian countries), for example, will never be known, says Koyama, "due to extraordinary care the Japanese authority took to destroy the relevant papers."

49. "Japanese Emperor Treads Warily on the War-Guilt Issue," by Andrew Horvat, *The Independent* (London), August 5, 1989.

50. Ibid. The remark by Mayor Motoshima prompted a public furor in Japan, and he was soon the target of an assassination attempt.

51. Weisman, *New York Times*, December 6, 1991.

52. Weisman, "Japan's Socialists Reproach Rulers for Refusal to Apologize for War," *New York Times*, December 9, 1991.

53. Weisman, "Japanese Apology Over War Unlikely After Bush's Stand," *New York Times*, December 6, 1991.

54. Susan Chira, "Pearl Harbor's Smoke, Hiroshima's Fallout," *New York Times,* December 8, 1991. Kosuke Koyama points out that "the primary interest of the Japanese people is continuity and growth," summarized by the historian Masao Maruyama in the expression, *tsugi-tsugi-ni-nariyuku-ikioi* or "next-next-continuously-becoming-by-momentum." Crisis, dialectic, radical breaks between cultural eras is the opposite of this mindset, imaged, notes Koyama, in the opening phrases of the Japanese constitution of 1889: "Having, by virtue of the glories of Our Ancestors, ascended the Throne of a lineal success unbroken for ages eternal. . . ." Floating on the currents of an ever-flowing stream of time, of course, is also the opposite of images of human *agency*. Koyama, "Ritual of Limping Dance," p. 99.

55. Susan Chira, "For Most Japanese, Pearl Harbor Is Just a Footnote,"*New York Times*, December 7, 1991.

56. Ibid., paraphrase by Susan Chira.

57. Koyama quotes the surviving text of a prayer by a U.S. Air Force chaplain, uttered just before the takeoff of the crew that was to deliver the atomic bomb to Nagasaki. With phrases like, "'trusting in Thee and knowing we are in thy presence now and forever,'" observes Koyama, "this prayer fails to express the transcendence and universality of God that challenges all human plans and thoughts (Acts 5:29). A slight variation of this prayer could have been said by a Shinto priest as Japanese squadrons took off to attack Pearl Harbor." Footnote 11, "Forgiveness and Politics," unpublished version.

58. Ibid.

59. Harries and Harries, p. 298.

60. David C. Unger, "1941, As Seen From Tokyo,"*New York Times*, December 8, 1991.

61. Summary of Mead by Jörg Becker of Germany, "Empathy for Islamic Culture Is Vital to Changing Age-old Stereotypes," in *Media Development* (London: World Association for Christian Communication, 3/1992), p. 34. Joerg is appropriating the views of Mead as found in an essay of Norbert Ropers, "Vom anderen her denken. Empathie als paradigmatischer Beitrag zur Völkerverständigung," in Steinweg and Wellmann, eds., *Die vergessene Dimension internationaler Konflikte: Subjektivität,* Frankfurt, pp. 114–50.

62. Cf. Dower, pp. 295–99 for a comprehensive list of these estimates worldwide. The conventional figure for military and civilian deaths in World War II is 55 million, but there are good reasons to think that the total was even larger. The point of inserting the parenthesis here is that in terms of numbers of deaths, almost every other party to the Pacific and the European conflicts suffered drastically more than did the Americans.

63. *New York Times,* December 7, 1991. By coincidence this was the very day in which the *Times* could report on Associated Press reporter Terry Anderson's release from seven years of captivity in Lebanon at the hands of an Islamic terrorist group. One page away from the Yokohoma letter appeared Anderson's statement: "I don't hate anybody. I'm a Christian and a Catholic, and it's really required of me that I forgive, no matter how hard that may be, and I intend to do that. I'm certainly not grateful. I believe they were very wrong, and did great wrong to me and my family."

64. Robert Reingold, "In Hawaii, Survivors Tell Tales of Dec. 7," *New York Times*, December 6, 1991. Concerning dates, one should note that the day of the attack in Pearl Harbor was December 8, while it was still December 7 in the United States.

65. See the Epilogue of Edward T. Linenthal, *Sacred Ground* (Urbana, Ill.: University of Illinois Press, 1993), p. 241.

66. John T. McQuiston, "Veterans Talk of Horror of War and Forgiveness," *New York Times*, December 8, 1991. A similar gathering, little covered by the media, in Honolulu on December 9–11, brought together an array of historians and war veterans from both sides

who shared their diverse war memories and research. At the end of this conference, reported Edward Linenthal, the two veteran groups "walked slowly—some with canes—to the stage area to stand together and exchange farewells as the audience joined the choir in singing 'God Bless America.'" (*Sacred Ground*, p. 243.) One wonders if the audience would have tolerated an exchange of the word *America* for the phrase, *our native lands*, which would have fitted the meter and better fitted the occasion.

67. Maureen Dowd, "His Voice Breaking, Bush Remembers a Time of 'Infamy,'" *New York Times*, December 8, 1991.

68. Cf. Thurston Clarke, *Pearl Harbor Ghosts: A Journey to Hawaii Then and Now* (New York: William Morrow and Co., 1991.)

69. As quoted by Linenthal, *Sacred Ground*, p. 240. On the internment, see below, this chapter.

70. Linenthal, *Sacred Ground*, p. 241.

71. Cf. Harries and Harries, pp. 432–33. "All over the island, civilians followed the army to their deaths—partly from fear of inhuman treatment by the enemy, partly because the army impelled them to do so, perhaps out of the samurai tradition that when the warrior lord died, his vassals and their families accompanied him. Some fell on grenades, others waded out to sea; most threw themselves off the cliffs, mothers clutching their babies, fathers pushing their children over the ledge before rushing to meet their own deaths. Horrified marines coming ashore in small craft could not steer a clear course through waters choked with corpses." On Okinawa the story was the same: 110,000 out of 120,000 Japanese soldiers killed with only 10,600 prisoners taken by the Americans and perhaps as many as 150,000 civilians killed by combat or suicide. Cf. Robert Bathchelder, *The Irreversible Decision* (Boston: Houghton Mifflin, 1962), p. 149, and David McCullough, *Truman* (New York: Simon & Schuster, 1992), p. 395.

72. Dower, pp. 300–01.

73. Dower, p. 294. Worth noting are the pair of culture-specific facts: Americans shaped their slurs of Japanese after images of "beasts;" for Americans, the Japanese preferred images of "demons" and "devils."

74. Tom F. Driver, *The Magic of Ritual* (San Francisco: Harper Collins, 1991), pp. 43–44. Driver visited Hiroshima in 1983, at the height of the Reagan Administration's demand for a United States buildup of its nuclear weapons.

75. Koyama, "Forgiveness and Politics," p. 162. The Hebrew and Christian scriptural vocabularies have four or five words for "sin," ranging from the mildest—"missing the mark"—to the most self-willed and atrocious—"high-handed sin." Japanese culture does not much support this wide range of words for describing humanly devised evil.

76. Steven R. Weisman, "Japanese Apology Over War Unlikely After Bush's Stand," *New York Times*, December 6, 1991. For a country that had expended "only" 300,000 lives of its own to help win World War II, another 500,000 was a huge number. Americans in 1945, one regrets to recall, would have countenanced the death of 5 million Japanese civilians if that were the cost of saving half a million Americans. As one group of scientists put it, urging President Truman to resist the caution of other scientists about using the bomb, "No! If we can save even a handful of American lives, then let us use this weapon—now!" Cf. David McCullough, *Truman* (New York: Simon & Schuster, 1992), pp. 439–41. McCollough's research concludes that, with General George Marshall, Truman thought in terms of 250,000 American casualties in an invasion of Japan. A few months after August 6, he remarked "that a quarter of a million of the flower of our young manhood were worth a couple of Japanese cities." Other advisers to Truman apparently estimated the probable American casualties at only 30,000 to 45,000. Cf. Gar Alperovitz, "To Drop the Atom Bomb," in *Christianity and Crisis*, February 3, 1992, p. 14.

77. Two examples of such joint work are the following: Dorothy Borg and Shumpei Okamoto, eds., *Pearl Harbor as History: Japanese-American Relations 1931–1941* (New York: Columbia University Press, 1973), and the Summer 1990 issue of the Journal of the American Academy of Arts and Sciences, *Daedalus* (vol. 119, no. 3), "Showa: The Japan of Hirohito," authored by teams of historians from both countries. The latter has been published in book form under the same title. Carol Gluck and Stephen R. Graubard, editors. (New York: W. W. Norton Company, 1992).

78. Batchelder, *The Irreversible Decision*, p. 147–50. When probable deaths by starvation, bombing, suicide, and the Russian invasion of Manchuria are added up, says Batchelder, the total would have been double the deaths inflicted on Hiroshima and Nagasaki together. Koyama's comment comes from an address, "Father, forgive . . . Who me?", delivered at the Kanuga Conference Center in North Carolina, March 2, 1994.

79. Alperovitz, "To Drop the Atom Bomb," p. 14. In his book, *Atomic Diplomacy: Hiroshima and Potsdam* (New York: Simon and Schuster, 1965), historian Alperovitz makes a strong argument for the view that political considerations were indeed uppermost in the decision for the dropping of the bomb: that the political object was not Japan but the Soviet Union. "[A] combat demonstration was needed to convince the Russians to accept the American plan for a stable peace," especially in Central and Eastern Europe (p. 240). An America overwhelmingly strong with the atomic bomb would be an America that the Russians could not intimidate into conceding total Russian hegemony in Europe after the war, ran this view. A similar motive, some scholars have suggested, may have motivated the display of Allied air power in the destruction of Dresden. (Cf. D. Irving, *The Destruction of Dresden*.) One scientific opponent of the use of the bomb against Japan, Leo Szilard, quoted Secretary of State Jimmy Byrnes as saying, in May 1945, that the overriding purpose of using it was to "make Russia more manageable in Europe." (Alperovitz, p. 242.) Alperovitz's list of military leaders who, before and after the use of the bomb, believed it to be *militarily* unnecessary, is impressive: Besides Eisenhower and Leahy, there were Admiral King, General Arnold, General LeMay, General Ismay (of the United Kingdom), Winston Churchill, Douglas McArthur, and the authors of the U.S. Strategic Bombing Survey (pp. 237–39). (At Potsdam, however, Leahy and Arnold apparently said "yes" to the bomb and Churchill certainly did. Cf. McCollough, *Truman*, pp. 437, 442). That the Soviets could in turn be intimidated into concessions on eastern Europe and international control of atomic energy turned out to be itself a profound political error, as events of the 1945–50 era were to demonstrate. As to whether impressing the Soviets was the uppermost policy-reason for using the bomb, however, Alperovitz concedes that "no final conclusion can be reached. . . ." (p. 241).

80. Batchelder, *The Irreversible Decision*, pp. 111–12.

81. Ibid., p. 184. To their credit, in the year after the dropping of the two bombs, leaders of the Federal Council of Churches (predecessor to the National Council of Churches) issued a statement condemning the action as "morally indefensible":

> We would begin with an act of contrition. As American Christians, we are deeply penitent for the irresponsible use already made of the atomic bomb. We are agreed that, whatever be one's judgment of the ethics of war in principle, the surprise bombings of Hiroshima and Nagasaki are morally indefensible." As quoted by Edward L. Long, Jr., *The Christian Response to the Atomic Crisis* (Philadelphia: The Westminster Press, 1950), p. 14, from the supplementary report of the "Calhoun Commission," *Atomic Warfare and the Christian Faith*, p. 11. The earlier main report of this commission was published under the title, *The Relation of the Church to the War in the Light of Christian Faith* (New York: Federal Council of Churches, 1944).

The note, "surprise bombings," could be nicely balanced against the typical American's resentment of Pearl Harbor. But the adjective has never gotten much public attention in any of the years since 1946.

82. Even President Harry Truman eventually changed his mind and came to see that the bomb was not a military weapon. In a meeting on July 21, 1948, devoted to the issue of which agency in the government should have custody of atomic bombs, Truman was exceptionally somber. "You have got to understand that this isn't a military weapon. It is used to wipe out women and children and unarmed people. . . . So we have got to treat it differently from rifles and cannons. . . ." But in the past he had referred to the bomb as just another weapon and to Hiroshima as just another military target. (McCullough, *Truman*, pp. 649–50.)

83. Cf. Batchelder, p. 157–58.

84. McCullough, *Truman*, p. 401.

85. Mayor Motoshima had already been threatened with assassination by monarchists when he said, in December 1988, that "Hirohito could have avoided the sufferings of thousands of Japanese . . . if he had taken action to end the war earlier." Cf. Horvat, *The Independent*, note 49 above.

86. Luke 9:60.

87. Carol Gluck, "The Showa Era (1926–1989)," in the Summer 1990 issue of *Daedalus*, p. 12.

88. Ibid., p. 13. Gluck later observes: "In Germany the generation of 1968, most of them postwar born, condemned their parents for the war they had made. In so doing, the younger generation created a further chapter in the public memory of the war, not on the basis of experience but on that of historical judgment. In Japan the war and the earlier parts of Showa history cling to the older generation, who experienced them, while the later Showa of the younger generations is not linked except by hearsay to the earlier one. During the flood of documentaries [in the 1980s], young people found it easy to turn off the set; it was a question of how much of someone else's history one could be expected to endure." (p. 21.) Any Japanese observer of recent indexes to the knowledge of, and interest in, history among American high school students will wonder if for them, too, the question is similar.

89. Between 60,000 and 100,000 Korean women were thus exploited—a fact that "recently . . . came to light," said Miyazawa in 1992. It came to light in the work of a Japanese historian and through the filing of a class action suit by Korean women survivors of this atrocity. In January of that year, on a first visit of a Japanese prime minister to Korea, Miyazawa acknowledged this new "light" to the Korean National Assembly and added: "I cannot help feeling acutely distressed over this, and I express my sincerest apology. . . . I am determined to nurture in the Japanese people, especially our youth, the courage to face squarely the past facts, understanding for the feelings of the victims, and a sense of admonition that these deeds should never be repeated." As an editorial in *the Washington Post* says, it took a court case and a history professor to move the government to this acknowledgment of a fact that was familiar to many surviving military veterans. *Washington Post*, as reprinted in the *International Herald Tribune*, January 20, 1992.

90. James Sterngold, "Admitting Guilt for the War: An Outraged Dissent," *New York Times*, August 21, 1993. The article centers on the protesting of the prime minister's remarks by the head of the Japan War-Bereaved Families Association, Sakae Suehiro.

91. "Is Japan Unreformable?" *The Economist*, Vol. 330, No. 7848 (January 29, 1994), p. 18.

92. *The MacNeil-Lehrer NewsHour*, August 23, 1993.

93. Editorial, *New York Times*, August 8, 1993. The source of the quotation is not identified.

94. As reported by ABC News, August 17, 1993.

95. Gluck, "The Idea of Showa," p. 8.

96. These included Edward W. Brooke, Robert F. Drinan, Arthur S. Flemming, Arthur J. Goldberg, and the Japanese American William M. Marutani.

97. *Report of the Commission on Wartime Relocation and Internment of Civilians,* Washington, D.C., December 1982, 467 pp., hereafter referenced as *Commission Report.*

98. Quoted from the Japanese American Citizens League Legislative Education Committee publication *Redress! The American Promise* [no date, c. 1983], p. 15.

99. *Commission Report,* p. 18.

100. For example, from February through May 1942 the Tolan committee of the House of Representatives, among other government bodies, steadily compiled evidence against the possibility of external and internal military threat to the West Coast. *Commission Report, pp. 86–87.*

101. In an odd but admirable compromise with its racist naturalization policies, American law has usually granted citizenship to children of immigrant parents born in the United States. This included children of Asians—though not, of course, children of slaves up to 1865. Not all countries, including many democratic ones, are so liberal, as is illustrated in current debates in Germany over this issue.

102. *Commission Report,* p. 6.

103. *Commission Report,* pp. 73–74.

104. *Commission Report,* p. 18.

105. *Commission Report,* p. 229.

106. *Commission Report,* p. 230.

107. Joseph Mitsuo Kitagawa, *The Christian Tradition: Beyond Its European Captivity* (Philadelphia: Trinity Press International, 1992), p. 121, from a chapter in this posthumously published book in which Kitagawa for the first time in his life wrote at length about his internment experience as a young person. As the authors of the *Commission Report* say early in its pages, the term *concentration camp* did not acquire the grim connotation that quickly attached to it at the end of the European War, with its unveilings of the Nazi death camps. The Commission came to prefer the term *detention camps,* in deference to the tangible difference of the two sorts of "concentration," even though the latter term frequently appeared in public rhetoric during the war. Apologists for the camp system will always point out how differently the Japanese were treated there in contrast to the system of the Germans, especially as the war moved toward American victory. But this is the weakest justification of any injustice whatsoever: "it could have been worse."

108. *Commission Report,* p. 132.

109. *Commission Report,* pp. 135–36.

110. *Commission Report,* pp. 126–27. *Issei* was the ordinary Japanese designation for first-generation, noncitizen Japanese immigrants to the United States; *Nisei* for the second generation, native-born; and *Sansei* for the third. The latter two groups, all legal citizens, composed two-thirds of the 120,000 evacuees. All of them had every right to use the touching phrase of the California farmer above: "to help our nation. . . ."

111. *Commission Report,* p. 250.

112. Kitagawa, *The Christian Tradition,* p. 126. With wife and children this man had returned to Japan for a brief time before the war only to discover that his children were Americans and that local Japanese regarded them as such.

113. *Commission Report,* p. 252.

114. *Commission Report,* pp. 189, 191.

115. *Commission Report,* p. 221.

116. *Commission Report,* p. 293. (*Ex parte Milligan,* 71 U.S. 2, 123–24 [1866].)

117. Luke 15:17.

118. *Commission Report,* p. 259. The same two-front war was being fought by black Americans in uniform. Cf. the 1992 documentary, "Liberators: Fighting on Two Fronts in World War Two," the story of two all-black tank and engineering units who may have been the first Allies to break into the Buchenwald death camp (broadcast December 17, 1992, by

WNET-PBS, New York.) Doubt about this achievement was raised by WNET research in 1993, but the documentary is accurate in its portrayal of the segregation and other discriminatory military practices from which African American personnel suffered throughout World War II.

119. *Commission Report*, p. 118. Contemporary estimates of the actual worth of lost property varied from $77 to $400 million.

120. *Commission Report*, pp. 297–98.

121. As reproduced in *Redress!* Japanese American Citizens League, n.d., (c.1983), p. 2. The "great philosopher" was George Santayana.

122. *New York Times*, February 25, 1983.

123. Nathaniel C. Nash, "House Votes Payments to Japanese War Internees," *New York Times*, September 18, 1987.

124. Copy supplied me by Kosuke Koyama.

125. *New York Times*, letters, October 6, 1987.

126. Kitagawa, *Christian Tradition,* p.137.

127. Ibid. The writer was John Cabot Grampp of Woodside, Queens.

128. Kitagawa, *Christian Tradition*, p. 289, footnote 8 to chapter 6.

129. *Commission Report*, pp. 259–60.

130. Dower, *War Without Mercy*, pp. 313–15.

131. Carol Gluck, "Showa," pp. 15, 24. This line from the Japanese constitution was called to my attention by Kosuke Koyama.

132. Robert Reinhold, "As Pearl Harbor Day Looms, Sting of Old Wounds Revives," *New York Times*, September 1, 1991.

Chapter 6

1. *Notes of a Native Son*, essay, "Stranger in the Village," Introduction to 2nd ed. (Boston: Beacon Press, 1984),p. xvi. (Original edition, 1955.)

2. *Life Magazine*, June 1992.

3. *Race Matters* (Boston: The Beacon Press, 1993), p. 8.

4. *Life Magazine*, June 1992.

5. Cf. Luke 10:29.

6. Orlando Patterson, *Slavery as Social Death* (Cambridge, Mass.: Harvard University Press, 1982.)

7. My own awareness of this phenomenon—and my embarrassment at it as a residue of contempt for living persons on the basis of the knowledge that their ancestors were slaves—came in 1973 in a place where an ordinary white American would least have expected to encounter it: among a group of East African Protestant ministers, most of them Kikuyus in Kenya. Having spoken of the struggle of African Americans to achieve equality in political and other ways in our country, I was appalled to hear more than one of these ministers make the suggestion: "Well, they have a lot of problems, but their ancestors let themselves be enslaved. So it's hard to think of them as equal to other people." So much, I thought ruefully, for black solidarity against oppression. And so terrible, the power of slavery to brand a people inferior for generation after generation.

8. Patterson, p. 332.

9. He used the phrase in a television program after he and other leaders of the March had met President Kennedy in the White House on that August 28. David Garrow, *Bearing the Cross: Martin Luther King, Jr., and the Southern Christian Leadership Conference* (New York: William Morrow and Co., 1986), p. 286.

10. Patterson, p. 296.

11. Quoted in Frank Tannenbaum, *Slave and Citizen: The Negro in the Americas* (New York: Alfred A. Knopf, 1947), p. 66. Everett was to be the major speaker at the dedication of the Gettysburg Cemetery when Lincoln gave his famous address. Upshur was secretary of state under President John Tyler in 1843.

12. Vincent Harding, *There Is a River: The Black Struggle for Freedom in America* (Vintage Books; New York: Random House, 1983), p. 324.

13. Ibid.

14. Ibid., pp. 324–26.

15. Dr. John Cartwright, professor of Christian Ethics at the Boston School of Theology, at the annual meeting of the Society for Christian Ethics, Savannah, Georgia, January 10, 1993.

16. Ibid., p. 328. Almost alone among white politicians of the time, Abraham Lincoln's rhetoric had sounded the same notes—cf. the Second Inaugural Address of March 1865. Historian Garry Wills believes that Lincoln derived his sense of what Christianity was politically all about from his acquaintance with the transformation of this faith among Christian slaves. ". . . when Abraham Lincoln voiced the most profound insights into political life, he was just echoing the black religious tradition." Wills sees a direct analogy here from Lincoln to Martin Luther King, Jr. to Jesse Jackson: The current political enemy belongs to the eventual "solid community." Like the newly freed slaves themselves, "Lincoln had to treat the South as still part of the nation, misled for a time but not permanently severed from the concerns (or privileges) of other citizens." Cf. Wills, *Under God: Religion and American Politics* (Touchstone Books; New York: Simon and Schuster, 1990), pp. 198, 214, 240–42, 264–66.

17. "Fighting Back," by Stanton L. Wormley, Jr., in the feature "About Men" in *the New York Times Magazine,* March 10, 1985.

18. The question of what metaphor best expresses the hope for a new cultural pluralism in twenty-first-century America is difficult. The old popular metaphor of "melting pot" was metallurgic; some now suggest that "salad" is a better image, where all the ingredients remain distinct even while mixed. There is something to be said for a food image, with its suggestion of nourishment. I would suggest, therefore, *vegetable soup*, in which each ingredient not only remains distinct—because it is not cooked to pieces—but is a contribution to the flavor of the broth, a public culture ("public household") that is the product of all these ingredients. Every addition to this mixture (immigrants) adds new flavor.

19. Daniel Bell, "The Public Household: On 'Fiscal Sociology' and the Liberal Society," *Public Interest* 37 (1974), pp. 29–68. As quoted by Orlando Patterson, *Slavery and Social Death* (Cambridge, Mass.: Harvard University Press, 1982), p. 296.

20. As quoted in *The Catholic Worker,* October-November 1985, from *What We Have Seen and Heard: Black Bishops Pastoral on Evangelization* (Cincinnati, Ill.: St. Anthony Messenger Press, 1984).

21. Galatians 2:6, John 1:12.

22. James Cone, *My Soul Looks Back,* in the series *Journeys In Faith,* Robert A. Raines, editor (Nashville, Tenn.: Abingdon Press, 1982), p. 23. The attempt to give every member some visible organizational status is still strong in most African American church life. During a visit to Ebenezer Baptist Church in Atlanta (the home church of Martin Luther King, Sr., and Jr.), on October 4, 1992, I counted the mention of over 200 individual names in the text of that Sunday's bulletin.

23. Cf. Garrow, *Bearing the Cross,* pp. 21–22 and Vincent Harding, "So Much History, So Much Future: Martin Luther King, Jr., and the Second Coming of America," in *Have We Overcome? Race Relations Since Brown,* ed. Michael V. Namerato (Jackson, Miss.: University of Mississippi, 1979), pp. 42–43.

24. Harding, "So Much History . . . ," pp.43–45. Cf. p. 36 of this article, in which Harding,

a historian, was encouraged in the 1950s by King himself to become "both an engaged participant in the movement and at the same time a committed historian and critical analyst of its development."

25. Garrow, p. 274, in a speech delivered soon after the climax of the Birmingham campaign.

26. Ibid., p. 275–76.

27. James Cone, *Martin and Malcolm and America: A Dream or a Nightmare* (Maryknoll, N.Y.: Orbis Books, 1991), p. 78. The first quotation comes from an address delivered just as the Montgomery boycott was coming to its successful conclusion, "Desegregation and the Future," given in early December 1956 to the National Committee for Rural Schools in New York City. The second comes from an address which he frequently delivered on the subject, "The American Dream." The quotation here is dated by Cone June 12, 1961.

28. James Cone, "Violence and Vengeance," in *Grapevine,* Joint Strategy and Action Committee (a coalition of 13 Protestant church bodies), vol. 15, no. 9 (New York, April 1984), p. 2.

29. Richard H. King, *Civil Rights and the Idea of Freedom* (New York: Oxford University Press, 1992), p. 137. The Martin King quotation is from his book *Strength to Love*, p. 49. In part, R. H. King's perceptive book is "a reading . . . of the civil rights movement through Arendtian spectacles." (p. ix).

30. Interview with Rustin in Howell Raines, *My Soul Is Rested: Movement Days in the Deep South Remembered* (New York: G. P. Putnam's Sons, 1977), p. 56.

31. Garrow, *Bearing the Cross*, p. 18.

32. Raines, *My Soul Is Rested*, p. 56.

33. Ibid., p. 93.

34. Ibid., p. 434.

35. Ibid., Raines's interview with Randolph Blackwell, p. 447.

36. Rivalries and uncomposed hostilities between the several organizations in the Albany (Georgia) campaign of 1961–62 take some of the blame for the relative failure of that campaign, says Garrow. (Ibid., p. 217.) Internal movement conflicts here were both local and national.

37. Harding, "So Much History . . . ," p. 52. He goes on to describe one of the critical conflicts in leadership in the Movement between "the semi-autocratic world of the black Baptist Church" and the "sometimes anarchistic-appearing participatory democracy" of the student-led movements such as the Student Nonviolent Coordinating Committee (SNCC). Ibid., p. 53.

38. Interview with Howell Raines, *My Soul Is Rested*, p. 79.

39. Raines, pp. 99–100.

40. Hannah Arendt, *On Violence* (New York: Harcourt, Brace, and World, Inc., 1969), p. 45.

41. This was the phrase used on December 21, 1956, in instructions to the first black bus passengers at the end of the 382-day boycott in Montgomery, the day after its successful appeal to the Supreme Court gained local force. King cautioned supporters of the boycott not to flaunt their victory. "Do not deliberately sit by a white person, unless there is no other seat." It is time, he said, to "move from protest to reconciliation." Garrow, p. 82.

42. Garrow, pp. 353–54.

43. James McBride Dabbs of South Carolina—writer, historian, and critic of southern white racism—frequently pointed out that African Americans were the answer to the question posed as title of one of his books: *Who Speaks for South?* One of Dabbs' illustrations was the "manners" of the young people who demonstrated at the lunch counters. Cf. *The Southern Heritage* (New York: Alfred A. Knopf, 1958) and his address, "The Tragic Fellowship of Southerners" (Atlanta: The Southern Regional Council, 1960.) Dabbs often reminded his southern white constituents that he had first become publicly involved in South Carolina racial

issues when in 1946 the state's Democratic party sought to institute an all-white primary. In a letter to the Columbia newspaper, he protested that it was simply impolite, contrary to southern manners, to tell registered black Democrats that they were not welcome to take part in the primary.

44. Raines, footnote, p. 99.

45. Garrow, pp. 246–47. Cf. the famous *Letter* in James M. Washington's comprehensive collection *A Testament of Hope: The Essential Writings of Martin Luther King, Jr.* (San Francisco: Harper & Row, 1986), p. 295.

46. Harding, "So Much History . . . ," p. 56.

47. Cf. Garrow, p. 216. In the Albany campaign of 1961–62, the very limited success of the protesters hinged in part on the internal disunity of local and national civil rights leaders and in part on Pritchett's discipline of his police to stay within the law. Says Garrow: "There had been virtually no violence committed against demonstrators during the entire nine months of protests, either by lawmen or white toughs." On one July evening in 1961, in fact, during a sidewalk demonstration, black onlookers from the sidelines threw bottles and rocks at police, prompting Martin Luther King, Jr., the next day to declare a twenty-four-hour moratorium on demonstrations and a "day of penance" as a symbolic public apology for this show of violence. (Garrow, p. 209.)

48. Garrow, p. 217. Television images of fire hoses and dogs let loose on demonstrating teenagers made the Birmingham event instantly real to millions of viewers nationwide, especially on May 7. "On that day America cringed," remembered one *Milwaukee Journal* editor thirty years later. (Mr. Sig Gessler, in an address at Columbia University, April 6, 1994.)

49. Raines, pp. 455–56.

50. Raines, p. 266.

51. Raines, pp. 148–49.

52. Cf. Arendt, *On Violence,* especially pp. 52–53, 56, where she distinguishes between power and violence. Political power grows out of group collaboration, not "out of the barrel of a gun." The gun may temporarily protect power, but it is not the source of power. *Legitimacy,* rather, is the great source of political power that endures over time, and violence cannot create it. "Violence appears when power is in jeopardy, but left to its own course it ends in power's disappearance" (p. 56). As they act together to bring about new policies or new governments, humans have to come to consensus about what legitimates the new action. And in the process they have to deliberate together—they talk.

53. Garrow, pp. 208, 214, 212. At the heart of the power struggle here was the attempt of the city government to push the "outsiders" of the movement away from any negotiating table so that only local blacks would be there. Long ago in Montgomery, leaders of the movement had learned that "outsiders" were necessary for moving local governments to take long-time "insiders" seriously. Among the failures of the Albany movement was its inability to bring the outside power of the federal government to bear upon the local struggle. By contrast, Birmingham and Selma were singularly successful in doing so.

54. Garrow, pp. 263–64.

55. Vincent Harding, "A Beginning in Birmingham," *The Reporter Magazine,* vol. 28, no. 12 (June 6, 1963), pp. 15–18. Harding gives a young white professional, a native southerner (whose identity he protects in this article) major credit for forging the first links that made this new network possible. Garrow reports that in their later assessment of the Birmingham campaign, SCLC leaders realized that they had underestimated the problem of the constitutional split between the outgoing and incoming city governments. Local business leaders had reason to be anxious about just who would be enough in charge of government to make good on any collective agreements. Garrow, p. 263.

56. Raines, p. 155. The allusions are to Romans 5:20 and John 1:5.

57. Raines, pp. 171–72.

58. As quoted in Raines, pp. 182–83.

59. As King said so forcefully in his Birmingham *letter*, "the average community is consoled by the church's silent and often vocal sanction of things as they are," but he went on to be thankful for "some noble souls from the ranks of organized religion" who "have broken loose from the paralyzing chains of conformity. . . ." (In James M. Washington, ed., *A Testament of Hope*, p. 300.) For some contemporary illustrations of some of these "noble souls" in ordinary church pulpits of the South, cf. *The Unsilent South*, ed. Donald W. Shriver, Jr. (Richmond, Va.: John Knox Press, 1965), a collection of nineteen sermons preached in the period 1957–64. Some of these ministers lost those pulpits soon after.

60. James McBride Dabbs often quoted this phrase from William Faulkner, who has a character in one of his novels who speaks about injustices in Mississippi society: "Thank God folk have enough sense not to talk about things they are not brave enough to cure." Dabbs, a South Carolinian, frequently pointed out to his fellow southerners that the word *justice* was seldom uttered in public or private in the pre- or postwar South because a society built on slavery and then segregation was obviously built on injustice. Instead, when it came to relations between the races, southerners inside and outside the churches tended to speak of "love." Dabbs was as clear as Reinhold Niebuhr about the principle: ". . . in this world love needs justice to support it. Try [as southerners did] to express it without at the same time striving for justice, and you get sentimentality." ("Christian Response to Racial Revolution," a sermon preached in Acworth, Georgia, in April 1964, in Shriver, ed., *The Unsilent South*, p. 97. Cf. also Dabbs, *The Southern Challenge* (New York: Alfred A. Knopf, 1958).

61. Eugene Patterson in an interview with Raines, p. 368. McGill and Patterson were two of the three Atlanta leaders whom the FBI contacted in January 1965 in hopes of persuading other leaders there to cancel the banquet planned to honor the city's first Nobel Peace Prize winner—Martin Luther King, Jr. The other leader who refused the request was Catholic Archbishop Paul Halliman. (Garrow, p. 382.)

62. Garrow, pp. 381, 394.

63. Cf. Garrow, p. 408. Many who participated in the March 15 march of 2,000 to the local courthouse (the memorial service for Rev. James Reeb), including myself, remember with astonishment Johnson's use of this Freedom Song text, including his emphasis on the *shall*.

64. Garrow, p. 409.

65. Garrow, pp. 418–19.

66. Raines, p. 223.

67. *The Washington Post*, September 29, 1982. He won all of those counties but one. In the primary and in the November elections, black city voters would oppose Wallace, urged by local and national civil rights leaders like Jesse Jackson and Coretta Scott King to do so. In this year of recession, Alabama had the highest unemployment rate (14 percent) in the nation, along with Michigan. Nationally the rate was 12 percent.

68. United Press International, November 4, 1982.

69. Howell Raines, "Grady's Gift," *New York Times Magazine*, December 1, 1991, p. 102.

70. Wendell Rawls Jr., "Wallace Captures 4th Term," *New York Times*, November 3, 1982.

71. The *Washington Post*, September 1, 1982.

72. The *Washington Post*, September 26, 1982.

73. The *Washington Post*, September 1, 1982.

74. Lance Morrow, "George Wallace Overcomes," *Time*, October 11, 1982.

75. *Washington Post*, September 1, 1982. In his 1972 bid for the Democratic nomination for president, Wallace had almost been killed by a bullet that left him paralyzed from the waist down.

76. Morrow, *Time*, October 11, 1982.

77. Comment from an interview excerpted in a documentary, "Abraham Lincoln: A New Birth of Freedom," broadcast by PBS, December 8, 1992.

78. Cf. Garrow, p. 409. The police attack on the demonstrators of the Student Nonviolent Coordinating Committee that day, says Garrow, "sent SNCC's leaders into paroxysms of anger," which unfortunately overflowed in vulgarity and the advocacy of violence in church meetings. A "chagrined Martin King," says Garrow, followed his usual custom of overlooking these excesses in the name of continued internal unity. The public apology of an Alabama sheriff for the conduct of his men, however, was something new.

79. Pat Watters, *Down to Now: Reflections on the Southern Civil Rights Movement* (New York: Random House, 1971), p. 133.

80. Raines, pp. 252–53.

81. Garrow has a fine summary of the failure of the MFDP to achieve more than token influence in Atlantic City, pp. 346–51. He makes clear that Lyndon Johnson's fear of losing southern votes to Barry Goldwater in the 1964 election kept him adamant about the Democrats' self-interest in according the MFDP no more than two votes on the floor. Notes Garrow: "Mrs. Hamer's powerful testimony—a vivid account of the brutalities she had suffered as a grass-roots activist in Mississippi—shocked a nationwide television audience until coverage was suddenly shifted to a quickly called presidential press conference" (p. 346).

82. Moyers related the incident in a PBS documentary on Johnson in 1991.

83. Raines, p. 254.

84. Raines's interview of Dennis, p. 276.

85. Alexis Jetter, "Mississippi Learning," *New York Times Magazine,* February 21, 1993, an account of the Delta Algebra Project of Mississippi, headed in 1993 by Robert Moses, who after years of self-chosen exile in Africa returned to the United States and has now undertaken this effort to train local African American children in basic mathematical skills.

86. Aldon D. Morris, *The Origins of the Civil Rights Movement* (New York: The Free Press, 1984), p. 287.

87. Raines, p. 20. Another testimony of the same sort was offered in the seventies by Arthur Shores, attorney for Autherine Lucy's entry as the first black student in the University of Alabama in 1956. Shores believes that the South is on its way to being "one of the garden spots in the country." Not only did he become Birmingham's first black city council member, but in 1975 the University of Alabama awarded him an honorary doctorate—as clear an institutional rejection of the George Wallace tradition as one is likely to find in the recent history of the state.

88. In his speech "The American Dream," June 6, 1961, in Washington, *Essential Writings,* p. 210. James Baldwin put the social psychology more precisely when, in a 1967 CBS News interview, he said: "If I'm not who you say I am, then you're not who you think you are." Quoted in *Split Image: African Americans in the Mass Media,* ed. Jannette Dates and William Barlow (Washington, D.C.: 1990), p. 5.

89. These statistics are gathered from several reports of the *New York Times,* in articles of August 8, 1992, November 10, 1992, January 27, 1993, and August 27, 1993, and from the Joint Center for Political and Economic Studies, *Black Elected Officials: A National Roster* (Washington, D.C., 1991).

90. Garrow, p. 77.

91. Garrow, pp. 160, 226–27, 563–64, 608.

92. James Cone, *Martin and Malcolm: A Dream or a Nightmare* (Maryknoll, N.Y.: Orbis Books, 1991), p. 131. Italics his. Even if Malcolm X and other black nationalists could not accept King's arguments about nonviolence and love for one's enemy, King insisted that on pragmatic grounds alone separatism was a dead end for real justice in America.

93. Meredith was the first black to be admitted to the University of Mississippi in Oxford in September 1962, an event that had given rise to two murders.

94. Garrow, p. 484.

95. In Cone, *Martin and Malcolm,* p. 103, quoting from an interview of Malcolm with Alex Haley, *Essence* (November 1983), p. 54.

96. As quoted by Cone, p. 205 (see notation 65, p. 340).

97. As quoted in Cone, p. 193 (see notation 32, p. 338).

98. For example: "Although Malcolm never retracted his strong opposition to white racism in America, he regretted his blanket condemnation of all whites and some of his most intemperate statements about them. Most notably in this regard was his infamous 'I just heard some good news!' statement, referring to the plane crash, just outside of Paris, that killed 130 whites, mostly from Atlanta, Georgia. 'That's one of the things I wish I had never said,' he told Alex Haley." Cone, *Martin and Malcolm,* p. 302.

99. Cone, pp.302–03.

100. Cone, p. 200.

101. For examples, see Garrow, pp. 88, 97, 101, 152, 209, 299, 343, 409, 513, and 527.

102. Garrow, p. 523. Cf. p. 213. Others in the Movement learned and practiced the same skills. Garry Wills points especially to Andrew Young and Jesse Jackson. Both have been consistent practitioners of empathy—"recognizing the justice of other people's claims." Both have been "able to make groups look less menacing to each other," as when, in the 1984 campaign Jackson came to Young's defense over the latter's conversation with the P.L.O. In that same year, Jackson publicly apologized for using anti-semitic language about New York City. In 1988, with great eloquence, he urged all segments of the Democratic Party to "be as wise as my grandma. Pool the patches and pieces [of your particular interests] together, bound by a common thread. When we form a great quilt of unity and common ground, we'll have the power to bring about health care and housing and jobs and education and home to our nation." Cf. Wills, *Under God,* pp. 250–51, 264–67.

103. Quoted by Cone, p. 294, from David Halberstam, "The Second Coming of Martin Luther King," *Harper's Magazine* (August 1967), p. 47.

104. Cf. Cone, pp. 274–78 for his agreement with those who criticize both Malcolm and Martin for their relative neglect of the rights of women inside their organizations and in American society at large. In all of his writings and speeches, for example, King never mentioned the heroism of Fannie Lou Hamer.

105. All leaders suffer from the limitations of their time and place—including Martin King, as James Cone rightly points out at the end of his *Martin and Malcolm*—and this obvious fact should keep us aware that the best of leaders open doors to successors who glimpse meanings in that "best" of which the predecessor was unaware. Jefferson tried to list England's support of the slave trade as one of the charges to be brought against George III in the Declaration of Independence, but the Continental Congress struck out the sentence, in deference to its slaveholding members. In turn, Jefferson's idea of abolition was that slaves should be trained for self-sufficiency and returned to Africa. He did not believe that whites and blacks could live together as citizens. Cf. David K. Shipler, "Jefferson Is America—And America Is Jefferson," the *New York Times,* April 12, 1993.

106. Cone, pp. 295, 314.

107. The phrase was used as the title of a study of rural poverty, authored by Charles E. Bishop (Washington, D.C.: U.S. Department of Labor, 1969).

108. Cf. Gerald D. Jaynes and Robin M. Williams, Jr. eds., *A Common Destiny: Black Americans and American Society* (National Research Council; Washington, D.C.: National Academy Press, 1989).

109. Lawrence H. Mamiya, "The Black Church and the Poor," an address delivered at Au-

burn and Union Theological Seminaries on November 6, 1991, reproduced in *The Auburn News* (New York, Spring 1992), pp. 1–6, based on the book by Mamiya and C. Eric Lincoln, *The Black Church in the African American Experience* (Durham, N.C.: Duke University Press, 1990). The statistics here come chiefly from chapter 6 of Jaynes and Williams, eds., *A Common Destiny.*

110. Martin Luther King, Jr., *Where Do We Go From Here: Chaos or Community?* (New York: Harper & Row, 1967), p 81.

111. For the Bookbinder quotations, cf. Washington, ed., *A Testament of Hope*, p. 558, and Martin Luther King, Jr., *Where Do We Go From Here: Chaos or Community?* (New York: Harper and Row, 1967), p. 81.

112. King, *Where Do We Go From Here*, p. 6.

113. Ibid., p. 112.

114. The Rev. Madison T. Shockley II, pastor of the Congregational Church of Christian Fellowship (United Church of Christ), in an address at Union Theological Seminary, May 14, 1993.

115. *Race Matters*, p. 12.

116. Ibid., pp. 14–15. Italics his.

117. Ibid., p. 63.

118. All the following quotations are taken from Miles, "Blacks vs. Browns," *The Atlantic,* October 1992.

119. Miles illustrates this political tie of Los Angeles workers to home countries in the visit of Korean leader Kim Dae Jung (a leading candidate for president of the country in the 1980s) to Los Angeles, in the wake of the riot, "to request reparations for the burned-out merchants of Koreatown." One can easily imagine a president of Mexico paying the same sort of visit.

120. Ibid., p. 73.

121. For example, the percentage of black poor in American cities is consistently about three times the percentage of white poor in comparisons of 1980 census tracts. On average, 32 percent of blacks will typically be poor, alongside 12 percent of whites in comparable tracts. Cf. Jaynes and Williams, eds., *A Common Destiny*, p. 287. In 1985, 31 percent of black and 11 percent of white families lived below the federal poverty line. This study classifies one-fourth of black families as middle class, as over against half of white families. Ibid., p. 274–77.

122. Cf. Luke 4:4 and 12:15.

123. James Baldwin, "Stranger in the Village," in *Notes of a Native Son*, p. 175.

124. "So Much History, So Much Future: Martin Luther King, Jr., and the Second Coming of America," in *Have We Overcome? Race Relations Since Brown*, edited Michael V. Namerato (Jackson, Miss.: University of Mississippi Press, 1979), pp. 42–43.

Chapter 7

1. *Incognito* (London: Collins, 1964), p. 353, as quoted by Brian Frost, *The Politics of Peace,* foreword by Archbishop Desmond Tutu and theological reflections by Donald W. Shriver, Jr. (London: Darton, Longman and Todd, 1991), p. 22. Dumitriu is a contemporary Rumanian Marxist.

2. *The Disuniting of America: Reflections on a Multicultural Society* (New York: W. W. Norton and Company, 1992), p. 46.

3. Francis Wilson and Mamphela Ramphele, *Uprooting Poverty: The South African Challenge* (New York: W. W. Norton and Company, 1989), p. 269.

4. In an address to the Radio and Television News Directors Association, Miami, Florida, October 1, 1993.

5. Leslie H. Gelb, "When to Forgive and Forget," *New York Times,* April 15, 1993.

6. Nicholas Tavuchis, *Mea Culpa: A Sociology of Apology and Reconciliation* (Stanford, Calif.: Stanford University Press, 1991), p. 6. Charles Krauthammer of *Time* used a stronger word—"miracle"—in connection with the 1983 Soviet downing of a Korean civilian airliner. "In an almost miraculous way, [an apology] seems capable of binding wounds," even between nations. *Time,* October 10, 1983, as quoted by Tavuchis, p. 61.

7. McCullough, *Truman,* pp. 542–43.

8. For lack of representative status, an apologizer may simply be dismissed as someone who does not have to be taken seriously. Tavuchis's most poignant illustration here was the apology of Kermit Beahan, the American bombardier of the B-29 that dropped the atomic bomb on Nagasaki, to that city in July 1985. An official of the city rejected the apology: "We understand his sentiments, but there are many atomic bomb victims who are still suffering and who do not wish to meet this man." *Winnipeg Free Press,* July 21, 1985, note 2, in Tavuchis, p. 150.

9. Tavuchis, p. 113. This summary of his description of collective apologies comes from pp. 97–117.

10. Von Weizsäcker's speech of May 8, 1985, matched Tavuchis's description rather closely, but not here: he steered clear of accusing Germany's enemies; also in contrast to Tavuchnis, he went into long specific detail of the crimes of Nazism. Elected politicians are likely to heed the justice of constituents who say, "Don't treat the enemy as innocent while you are denying our innocence."

11. Tavuchis, p. 100.

12. As quoted by Charles Villa-Vicencio in *A Theology of Reconstruction* (Cambridge, England: Cambridge University Press, 1992), p. 164, from Bennett's *Christian Ethics and Social Policy* (New York: Charles Scribner's Sons, 1946), pp. 76–77.

13. From an interview with Dr. Kader Asmal, professor of constitutional law at the University of Western Cape, March 1992. Asmal is a leader of the African National Congress and spent almost thirty years in exile.

14. In *A Testament of Hope: The Essential Writings of Martin Luther King, Jr.,* ed. James M. Washington (San Francisco: Harper & Row, 1986), p. 296.

15. George Sher, "Ancient Wrongs and Modern Rights," *Philosophy and Public Affairs,* 10, no. 1 (Winter 1981), p. 17.

16. New York: Charles Scribner's Sons, 1948, p. 276.

17. In response to a recent address of mine in a church in Charlotte, N.C., in which I used this and other illustrations (from chapter 6 of the present volume) of forgiveness in the civil rights movement of the sixties, an African American professional, a member of the congregation, warned me and the white majority present that "blacks don't think that way anymore."

18. Interview on ABC News, December 28, 1992. Sparks expands on this view in his book *The Mind of South Africa: The Story of the Rise and Fall of Apartheid* (London: Mandarin, 1991), as follows: "What I do not believe is that the black African masses have an intuitive yearning for vengeance and retribution. A yearning for justice, yes, and for release from poverty and oppression, but no dream of themselves becoming the persecutors, of turning the tables of apartheid on the white South Africans. For too long black South Africans have been the victims of racism and, like Jews, they abhor it. They do not want to invert it, they want to eradicate it. . . . No blacks I have ever met envisage a future South Africa without whites . . ." (pp. 249–50).

19. Quoted by Isabel Wilkerson, "The Tallest Fence: Feelings on Race in a White Neighborhood," *New York Times,* June 21, 1992.

20. Ibid.

21. Robert H. Franklin, "Church and City: African American Christianity's Ministry," in Eleanor Scott Myers, ed., *A Reader in Urban Ministry* (Louisville, Ky.: Westminster/John Knox Press, 1992), p. 146.

22. From Robert B. Reich, *Work of Nations: Preparing Ourselves for Twenty-First-Century Capitalism* (New York: Alfred A. Knopf, 1991), as quoted in a review of the book by Dennis P. McCann, *The Christian Century* 108, 31 (1991), p. 1007. Professor Larry L. Rasmussen called my attention to this quotation.

23. Arthur M. Schlesinger, Jr., *The Disuniting of America: Reflections on a Multicultural Society* (New York: W. W. Norton and Company, 1992), p. 136.

24. Cf. *Asahi* (Tokyo), July 1, 1987. The absence of these phrases had been an overt diplomatic issue between China, Korea, and Japan since 1982. Two years later the ministry reasserted it right to control the texts by eliminating the right of authors to "negotiate" before changes were made. The ministry's Textbook Authorization Research Council was now to make the changes directly. (*Japan Times*, March 9, 1989.) At least since the early 1980s, the mass media in Japan have frequently opposed such censorship, and the three major daily newspapers (*Asahi, Yomiuri,* and *Mainichi*), with a combined circulation of 20 million, have insisted that the government should be explaining textbook changes not only to other Asian countries but to the Japanese public. (I am indebted to Mr. John Reagan, former missionary to Japan, for this information.)

25. Maynes, "Facing the Dark Side of Nationalism," *Los Angeles Times,* April 21, 1985, as reprinted in Geoffrey Hartmann, *Bitburg,* p. 220.

26. Cf. "We Must Endure Lovingly," an interview with Cornel West, in *Religion and Values in Public Life*: A forum of Harvard Divinity School, Summer 1993, p. 3.

27. A point that Schlesinger also makes forcefully, *The Disuniting of America*, p. 92.

28. Nerys Patterson and Orlando Patterson, "St. Patrick Was a Slave," Op Ed, *New York Times*, March 15, 1993.

29. *Moral Fragments and Moral Community: A Proposal for Church in Society* (Philadelphia, Pa.: Fortress Press, 1993), p. 60.

Bibliography

Aeschylus. *The Eumenides.* In Whitney J. Oates and Eugene O'Neill, Jr. (eds.). *The Complete Greek Drama.* New York: Random House, 1938.

Alperovitz, Gar. "To Drop the Atom Bomb." In *Christianity and Crisis*, February 3, 1992.

Alperovitz, Gar. *Atomic Diplomacy: Hiroshima and Potsdam.* New York: Simon & Schuster, 1965.

Ardagh, John. *Germany and the Germans: An Anatomy of Society Today.* New York: Harper & Row, 1987.

Arendt, Hannah. *The Human Condition: A Study of the Central Conditions Facing Modern Man.* (Doubleday Anchor Books.) Garden City, N.Y.: Doubleday and Company, 1959.

Arendt, Hannah. *On Violence.* New York: Harcourt, Brace and World, Inc., 1969.

Augustine. *The City of God.* Trans. Marcus Dods. (The Modern Library.) New York: Random House, 1950.

Baldwin, James. *Notes of a Native Son*, 2nd ed. Boston: Beacon Press, 1984.

Batchelder, Robert. *The Irreversible Decision: 1939–1950.* Boston: Houghton Mifflin, 1962.

Bellah, Robert, Richard Madsen, William M. Sullivan, et al. *The Good Society.* New York: Alfred A. Knopf, 1991.

Bennett, John C. *Christian Ethics and Social Policy.* New York: Charles Scribner's Sons, 1946.

Bethge, Eberhard. "Geschichtliche Schuld der Kirche." In *Christliche Freiheit: Dienst am Menschen.* Ed. Karl Herbst. Verlag Lembeck, 1972.

Bethge, Eberhard. *Dietrich Bonhoeffer: Man of Courage, Man of Vision.* New York: Harper & Row, 1970.

Bonhoeffer, Dietrich. *Letters and Papers from Prison.* Enlarged edition. Ed. Eberhard Bethge. New York: The Macmillan Co., 1971.

Bonhoeffer, Dietrich. *Ethics.* Ed. Eberhard Bethge. London: SCM Press, Ltd., 1955.

Borg, Marcus J. *Jesus: A New Vision.* San Francisco: Harper & Row, 1987.

Borg, Dorothy, and Shumpei Okamoto, eds. *Pearl Harbor as History: Japanese-American Relations 1931–1941.* New York: Columbia University Press, 1973.

Brown, Raymond E., Joseph A. Fitzmeyer, and Roland A. Murphy, eds. *The New Jerome Biblical Commentary.* Englewood Cliffs, N.J.: Prentice Hall, 1990.

Brueggemann, Walter. *The Prophetic Imagination.* Philadelphia: Fortress Press, 1978.

Brunner, Emil. *The Divine Imperative.* Trans. Olive Wyon. Philadelphia: The Westminster Press, 1947.

Cadier, Jean. *The Man God Mastered: A Brief Biography of John Calvin.* Trans. O. R. Johnson. Grand Rapids, Mich.: William B. Eerdmans, 1960.

Caldwell, Wallace E. *The Ancient World*. New York: Rinehart and Company, 1949.

Chambers, Frank P., Chistina Phelps Harris, and Charles C. Bayley. *This Age of Conflict*. New York: Harcourt, Brace and Co., 1950.

Clarke, Thurston. *Pearl Harbor Ghosts: A Journey to Hawaii Then and Now*. New York: William Morrow and Co., 1991.

Coats, George W. *From Canaan to Egypt: Structural and Theological Context for the Joseph Story*. The Catholic Biblical Quarterly Monograph Series, No. 4. Washington, D.C.: The Catholic Biblical Association of America, 1976.

Cochrane, Charles N. *Christianity and Classical Culture*. New York: Oxford University Press, 1957 [orig. pub. 1940].

Cohen, Michael D., and James G. March. *Leadership and Ambiguity*. Second edition. Boston: Harvard Business School Press, 1986.

Cone, James. *My Soul Looks Back*. ("Journeys in Faith Series", ed. Robert A. Raines.) Nashville, Tenn.: Abingdon Press, 1982.

Cone, James. *Martin and Malcolm and America: A Dream or a Nightmare*. Maryknoll, N.Y.: Orbis Books, 1991.

Cover, Robert M. "*Nomos* and Narrative." (The Supreme Court, 1982 Term, Forward.) *Harvard Law Review* 97 (November 1983).

Crick, Bernard. *In Defense of Politics*. Second edition. Chicago: University of Chicago Press, 1972.

Crossan, John D. *The Historical Jesus*. San Francisco: Harper & Row, 1991.

Dabbs, James McBride. *The Southern Heritage*. New York: Alfred A. Knopf, 1958.

Dates, Jannette, and William Barlow, eds. *Split Image: African Americans in the Mass Media*. Washington, D.C.: Howard University Press, 1990.

Davies, W. D. *The Gospel and the Land*. Berkeley, Calif.: University of California Press, 1974.

De Beausobre, Iulia. *Creative Suffering*. London: Dacre Press, 1940.

De Gruchy, John. *Theology and Ministry in Context and Crisis*. Philadelphia: Fortress Press, 1988.

Dostoyevsky, Fyodor. *The Brothers Karamazov*. Trans. Constance Garnett. New York: The Modern Library, n.d.

Dower, John W. *War Without Mercy: Race and Power in the Pacific War*. New York: Pantheon Books, 1986.

Endo, Shusaku. *The Samurai*. Trans. Van C. Gessel. (Vintage Books.) New York: Random House, 1984.

Farb, Peter, and George Armelogos. *Consuming Passions: The Anthropology of Eating*. Boston: Houghton Mifflin, 1980.

Fox, Richard. *Reinhold Niebuhr: A Biography*. New York: Pantheon Books, 1985.

Franklin, Robert H. "Church and City: African American Christianity's Ministry," in Eleanor Scott Myers, ed., *A Reader in Urban Ministry*. Louisville, Ky.: Westminster/John Knox Press, 1992.

Friede, Juan, and Benjamin Keen. *Bartolemé De Las Casas: Toward an Understanding of the Man and His Work*. DeKalb, Ill.: Northern Illinois University Press, 1971.

Friedlander, Albert H., ed. *Out of the Whirlwind: A Reader of Holocaust Literature*. New York: Schocken Books, 1976.

Friedman, George, and Meredith LeBard. *The Coming War With Japan*. New York: St. Martin's Press, 1992.

Fritsch, Charles T. "'God Was With Him': A Theological Study of the Joseph Narrative," in *Interpretation*. vol. IX, no. 1 (January 1955).

Frost, Brian. *The Politics of Peace*. Foreword by Desmond Tutu. Introduction and Conclusion by Donald W. Shriver, Jr. London: Longmans, 1991.

Garrow, David. *Bearing the Cross: Martin Luther King, Jr., and the Southern Christian Leadership Conference.* New York: William Morrow and Co., 1986.

Gerth, H. H., and C. Wright Mills, eds. *From Max Weber: Essays in Sociology.* New York: Oxford University Press, 1958.

Gilson, Etienne. Foreword. *The City of God: An Abridged Version.* Trans. Gerald G. Walsh et al. and ed. Vernon J. Bourke. (Image Books.) Garden City, N.Y.: Doubleday and Co,, 1958.

Gluck, Carol, and Stephen Graubard, eds. *Showa: The Japan of Hirohito.* New York: W. W. Norton Co., 1992.

Haber, Joram Graf. *Forgiveness.* Savage, Md.: Rowan and Littlefield Publishers, Inc., 1991.

Hand, Learned. *In the Spirit of Liberty: Papers and Addresses of Learned Hand.* Third edition. Ed. Irving Dillard. New York: Alfred A. Knopf, 1960.

Harding, Vincent. *There Is a River: The Black Struggle for Freedom in America.* (Vintage Books.) New York: Random House, 1983.

Harries, Meiron, and Susie Harries. *Soldiers of the Sun.* New York: Random House, 1991.

Hartmann, Geoffrey, ed. *Bitburg in Moral and Political Perspective.* Bloomington, Ind.: Indiana University Press, 1986.

Horsley, Richard. *Jesus and the Spiral of Violence.* San Francisco: Harper & Row, 1987.

Hughes, Langston. "Let America Be America Again." In Walter Lowenfels, ed., *The Writing on the Wall.* Garden City: N.Y.: Doubleday and Company, 1969.

Jacoby, Susan. *Wild Justice.* New York: Harper & Row, 1982.

Jäckel, Eberhard. *Hitler in History.* Hanover, N.H.: University Press of New England, 1985.

Jaeger, Werner. *Paideia: The Ideals of Greek Culture.* Trans. Gilbert Highet. Three volumes. New York: Oxford University Press, 1945.

Jaynes, Gerald D., and Robin M. Williams, Jr., eds. *A Common Destiny: Black Americans and American Society.* Washington, D.C.: National Research Council and National Academy Press, 1989.

Kant, Immanuel. *Religion Within the Limits of Reason Alone.* Trans. Theodore M. Greene and Hoyt H. Hudson. (Harper Torchbooks.) New York: Harper and Brothers, 1960.

King, Martin Luther, Jr. *Where Do We Go From Here? Chaos or Community?* New York: Harper & Row, 1967.

King, Martin Luther Jr. *The Trumpet of Conscience.* San Francisco: Harper & Row, 1968.

King, Richard H. *Civil Rights and the Idea of Freedom.* New York: Oxford Univesity Press, 1992.

Kitagawa, Joseph Mitsuo. *The Christian Tradition: Beyond Its European Captivity.* Philadelphia: Trinity Press International, 1992.

Klosinski, Lee Edward. *The Meals in Mark.* Ann Arbor, Mich.: University Microfilms International, 1988.

Koyama, Kosuke. "Ritual of Limping Dance: A Botanical Observation." Inaugural lecture as John D. Rockefeller Professor of Ecumenics and World Christianity. In *Union Seminary Quarterly Review*, vol. XXXVI, 1981.

Koyama, Kosuke. "Forgiveness and Politics: Japanese Experience." In *Bread and Breath: In Honor of Samuel Rayan, S.J.* Gujurat: Sahipya Prakash, 1991.

Krusche, Werner. "Guilt and Forgiveness: The Basis of Christian Peace Negotiation." In *Case Study Number Two.* The Forgiveness and Politics Project. Ed. Brian Frost. London: New World Publications, 1987.

Latourette, Kenneth Scott. *A History of Christianity.* New York: Harper & Row, 1953.

Leith, John H., ed. *Creeds of the Churches.* (Anchor Books). Garden City, N.Y.: Doubleday and Company, 1963.

Levi, Primo. *Survivor in Auschwitz.* New York: Collier, 1961.

Levi, Primo, *The Truce*. Trans. Stuart Woolf. The Bodley Head, 1965.

Linenthal, Edward. *Sacred Ground*. Urbana: University of Illinois Press, 1993.

Lipstadt, Deborah E. *Denying the Holocaust: The Growing Assault on Truth and Memory*. New York: The Free Press, 1993.

Locke, John. *A Letter Concerning Toleration*. Ed. James H. Tully. Indianapolis: Hackett Publishing Company, 1983.

Locke, John. *Of Civil Government*. Cambridge, England: Cambridge University Press, 1960.

Luther, Martin. *Works of Martin Luther*. Ed. H. E. Jacobs. Volume IV. Philadelphia: 1915–1932.

MacIntyre, Alasdair. *After Virtue*. Second edition. Notre Dame: University of Notre Dame Press, 1984.

Mahoney, John. *The Making of Moral Theology: A Study of the Roman Catholic Tradition*. Oxford: Clarendon Press, 1987.

Mamiya, Lawrence, and C. Eric Lincoln. *The Black Church in the African American Experience*. Durham: Duke University Press, 1990.

McCullough, David. *Truman*. New York: Simon and Schuster, 1992.

McNeill, John T. *The History and Character of Calvinism*. New York: Oxford University Press, 1954.

McPherson, James M. *Battle Cry of Freedom: The Civil War Era*. New York: Ballantine Books, 1988.

Meeks, Wayne A. *The First Urban Christians*. New Haven: Yale University Press, 1983.

Miles, Jack. "Blacks Vs. Browns." In *The Atlantic,* October 1992.

Moltmann, Jürgen. "Forty Years After the Stuttgart Declaration." Trans. Susan Reynolds. In *Case Study Number Two*. The Forgiveness and Politics Project. Ed. Brian Frost. London: New World Publications, 1987.

Morris, Aldon D. *The Origins of the Civil Rights Movement*. New York: The Free Press, 1984.

Muir, Edwin. "The Wheel." In *Collected Poems*. New York and London: Oxford University Press and Faber and Faber Ltd., 1960. Copyright by Willa Muir.

Murphy, Jeffrie G., and Jean Hampton. *Forgiveness and Mercy*. Cambridge: Cambridge University Press, 1988.

Namerato, Michael V., ed. *Have We Overcome? Race Relations Since Brown*. Jackson, Miss.: University of Mississippi Press, 1979.

Newman, Lewis E. "The quality of mercy: on the duty to forgive in the Judaic tradition." In *The Journal of Religious Ethics,* vol. 15, no. 2 (fall, 1987).

Niebuhr, Reinhold. *The Nature and Destiny of Man*. Two volumes. New York: Charles Scribner's Sons, 1949.

Niebuhr, H. Richard. *The Responsible Self: An Essay in Christian Moral Philosophy*. Introduction by James Gustafson. New York: Harper & Row, 1963.

Niebuhr, H. Richard. *Christ and Culture*. New York: Harper and Brothers, 1951.

Nürnberger, Klaus. *Theological Ethics: Ethics for Political Life*. Pretoria: University of South Africa, 1986.

Oates, Whitney J., and Eugene O'Neill Jr. (eds). *The Complete Greek Drama*. Two volumes. New York: Random House, 1938.

Ogletree, Thomas W. *The Use of the Bible in Christian Ethics*. Philadelphia: Fortress press, 1983.

Patterson, Orlando. *Slavery as Social Death*. Cambridge: Harvard University Press, 1982.

Podlecki, A. J. *The Political Background of Aeschylaean Tragedy*. Ann Arbor: Univesity of Michigan Press, 1966.

Podlecki, A. J. "Aeschylus." In *Encyclopedia Britannica*. Vol. I. Chicago: William Benton, 1976.

Raines, Howell. *My Soul Is Rested: Movement Days in the Deep South Remembered.* New York: B. P. Putnam's Sons, 1977.

Rasmussen, Larry. *Moral Fragments and Moral Community: A Proposal for Church in Society.* Minneapolis: Fortress Press, 1993.

Redford, D.B. *A Study of the Biblical Story of Joseph.* VTsup20. Leiden: Brill, 1970.

Reich, Robert B. *Work of Nations: Preparing Ourselves for Twenty-first-century Capitalism.* New York: Alfred A. Knopf, 1991.

Remarque, Erich Maria. *All Quiet on the Western Front.* New York: Fawcett Crest, 1929–1930.

Report of the Commission on Wartime Relocation and Internment of Civilians. Washington, D.C.: United States Printing Office, 1982.

Rivera, Luis N. *A Violent Evangelism: The Political and Religious Conquest of the Americas.* Louisville: Westminster/John Knox Press, 1992.

Royde-Smith, J. G. "World Wars." In *Encyclopedia Britannica,* Fifteenth Edition, vol. 19.

Schlesinger, Arthur M., Jr. *The Disuniting of America: Reflections on a Multicultural Society.* New York: W. W. Norton and Company, 1992.

Schnackenburg, Rudolf. *Die Bergpredigt: Utopische Vision oder Handlungsanweisung.* Dusseldorf: Patmos Verlag, 1982.

Selznick, Philip. *The Moral Commonwealth: Social Theory and the Promise of Community.* Berkeley, Calif.: University of California Press, 1992.

Shinn, Roger L. *Wars and Rumors of Wars.* Nashville: Abingdon Press, 1972.

Shriver, Donald W. Jr. *Forgiveness and Politics: The Case of the American Black Civil Rights Movement.* Case Study No. 1, The Forgiveness and Politics Project. London: New World Publications, 1987.

Shriver, Donald W. Jr. *The Lord's Prayer: A Way of Life.* Atlanta: John Knox Press, 1983.

Shriver, Donald W. Jr., John Earle, and Dean D. Knudsen. *Spindles and Spires: Religion and Social Change in Gastonia.* Atlanta: John Knox Press, 1976.

Shriver, Donald W. Jr., ed. *The Unsilent South: Prophetic Preaching in Racial Crisis.* Richmond: John Knox Press, 1965.

Silber, John R. "The Ethical Significance of Kant's *Religion.*" In Immanuel Kant, *Religion Within the Limits of Reason Alone.* Trans. Theodore M.Greene and Hoyt H. Hudson. ("Harper Torchbooks.") New York: Harper and Brothers, 1960.

Sivard, Ruth Leger. *World Military and Social Expenditures 1991.* Washington, D.C.: World Priorities, 1992.

Sparks, Alasdair. *The Mind of South Africa: The Story of the Rise and Fall of Apartheid.* London: Mandarin, 1991.

Stassen, Glen H. *Just Peacemaking: Transforming Initiatives for Justice and Peace.* Louisville: Westminster/John Knox Press, 1992.

Stein, George H. *The Waffen SS: Hitler's Elite Guard at War, 1939-45.* Ithaca: Cornell University Press, 1984.

Stern, Fritz. *Dreams and Delusions: National Socialism in the Drama of the German Past.* ("Vintage Books.") New York: Random House, 1989.

Stöhr, Martin. "Reconciliation Takes a Political Form: The Example of Poland and Germany." Typescript, n.d. [c. 1988].

Tannenbaum, Frank. *Slave and Citizen: The Negro in the Americas.* New York: Alfred A. Knopf, 1947.

Tavuchis, Nicholas. *Mea Culpa: A Sociology of Apology and Reconciliation.* Stanford, Calif.: Stanford University Press, 1991.

Tentler, Thomas N. *Sin and Confession on the Eve of the Reformation.* Princeton, N.J.: Princeton University Press, 1977.

Thompson, James Westfall, and Edgar Nathaniel Johnson. *An Introduction to Medieval Europe*. New York: W. W. Norton and Co., 1937.

Thornton, Lionel S. *The Common Life in the Body of Christ*. Third edition. London: Dacre Press, 1950.

Thucydides. *History of the Peloponnesian War*. Trans. Richard Crawley. (Everyman's Library.) New York: E. P. Dutton and Co., n.d.

Tillich, Paul J. *Systematic Theology*. Three volumes. London: Nisbet and Company, 1957.

Troeltsch, Ernst. *The Social Teaching of the Christian Churches*. Trans Olive Wyon. Two volumes. London: George Allen and Unwin, Ltd., and New York: The Macmillan Company, 1931.

Tuchman, Barbara. *The Guns of August*. New York: Bantam Books, 1976.

Tuchman, Barbara W. *A Distant Mirror: The Calamitous 14th Century*. New York: Ballantine Books, 1979.

Turner, Henry Ashby. *The Two Germanies Since 1945*. New Haven, Conn.: Yale University Press, 1987.

Urbach, Ephraim. *The Sages: Their Concepts and Beliefs*. Trans. Lewis E. Newman. Jerusalem: The Magnes Press of The Hebrew University, 1979.

Vidal-Naquet, Pierre. *Assassins of Memory: Essays on the Denial of the Holocaust*. Trans. Jeffrey Mehlman. New York: Columbia University Press, 1993.

Vonnegut, Kurt. *Slaugherhouse Five*. New York: Dell Publishing Co., 1969.

Walker, Williston. *A History of the Christian Church*. Fourth edition, revised and edited by Richard A. Norris, David W. Lotz, and Robert T. Handy. New York: Charles Scribner's Sons, 1985.

Walzer, Michael. *The Revolution of the Saints: A Study in the Origins of Radical Politics*. Cambridge, Mass.: Harvard University Press, 1965.

Washington, James M., ed. *A Testament of Hope: The Essential Writings of Martin Luther King, Jr.* San Francisco: Harper & Row, 1986.

Watters, Pat. *Down to Now: Reflections on the Southern Civil Rights Movement*. New York: Random House, 1971.

West, Cornel. *Race Matters*. Boston: The Beacon Press, 1993.

Wiesenthal, Simon. *Sunflower*. London: W. H. Allen, 1970, and New York: Schocken Books, 1976.

Wills, Garry. *The Words That Remade America: Lincoln at Gettysburg*. In *The Atlantic*, vol. 269, no. 6 (June 1992).

Wilson, Francis, and Mamphela Ramphele. *Uprooting Poverty: The South African Challenge*. New York: W. W. Norton and Co., 1989.

Wink, Walter. *Engaging the Powers*. Minneapolis: Fortress Press, 1992.

Wolin, Sheldon S. *Politics and Vision: Continuity and Innovation in Western Political Thought*. Boston: Little Brown and Company, 1960.

Woodhouse, A. S. P. *Puritanism and Liberty*. Chicago: University of Chicago Press, 1951.

Woods, Allen W. *Kant's Moral Religion*. Ithaca and London: Cornell University Press, 1970.

Yoder, John Howard. *The Politics of Jesus*. Grand Rapids, Mich.: William B. Eerdmans Publishing Co., 1972.

Name Index

Subject Index

A-bomb. *See* Hiroshima
African Americans, 3–4, 10, 72, 170–217, 231;
  economic status of, 211–17, 224–27, 229,
  268 *n*; in World War II, 260–61 *n*. *See also*
  Churches; Civil rights movement; King,
  Martin Luther, Jr. (Name Index); King,
  Rodney (Name Index); Slavery
Albany, civil rights campaign in, 190, 204, 208,
  263–64 *n*
American perspective, of this study, 71–72
Apartheid, 218–19, 224–25
Apology in politics, 134, 136–37, 141, 220–22
Appomattox, 5
Areopagus, 14, 17
Armenian Americans, 103
Asia, Japanese invasion of, 135–37
Austro-Hungarian Empire, 4

Barmen Declaration, 87, 114, 249 *n*
Bataan, 126, 131, 142
Berlin Wall, fall of, 92
Biological weapons, Pacific War, 132
Birmingham: civil rights campaign in, 187–94,
  204, 206, 264 *n*, 266 *n*; bombing of Sixteenth
  Street Baptist Church, 193
Bitburg Cemetery, 84, 92–107, 111–12, 122,
  128, 134, 143, 229, 250–51 *n*
Black power movement, 203–7
Bosnia, 3, 5, 10, 20, 52, 67, 155
Bundestag Speech, Richard von Weizsäcker's,
  108–16, 138
Burma, 129

Cain and Abel, myth of, 23–24, 29, 175, 237 *n*
Calvinism, 54–59, 61–62
Capital punishment, 13, 23
Casualties of war, 65. *See also* World War II,
  casualties in
Catholicism, 49–52, 55, 58
Christian Democratic Party, German, 82
Churches: Romanian, 4; Christian tradition and
  forgiveness, 10, 33–62, 239–45 *n*; German,
  World War II, 87; German, post-World War

II, 84–88, 90, 114, 138; African American,
  103–4, 178–80, 196, 226, 232, 262–63 *n*,
  265 *n*; Japanese, 136
Civil Liberties Act of 1988, 165, 168
Civil Rights Act of 1964, 187, 194, 203
Civil rights movement: Reconstruction, 174–77;
  1955–1968, 5, 172, 177, 179–97, 199–211,
  225, 263–67 *n*, 269 *n*; post-1968, 197–200,
  202–4, 208, 210–17, 225, 227
Civil War, American, 5, 8, 77, 112, 128, 131,
  173–74, 229, 262 *n*
Cold War, 5, 9, 72, 79, 90, 92, 124, 139, 220,
  249 *n*, 252 *n*, 258 *n*, 259 *n*
Collaborators: with Nazism, 83–84, 104–6,
  109–10, 114–15; with Japanese imperialism,
  138, 153
Colored People's Convention of 1865, 175–77,
  180–81, 189, 196
Columbus Quincentennial, 3–4
Comfort women, 136–37, 154, 255 *n*, 259 *n*
Commission on Wartime Relocation and Intern-
  ment of Civilians, 156–57, 160, 165–67,
  260 *n*
Community discipline, in New Testament,
  42–45
Compensation. *See* Reparations
Compensation Laws, German, 89
Confessing Church, German, 86–87
Contrition, in Christian churches, 49–52
Corcyra, 18–22
Crucifixion of Jesus, 41–42

Darmstadt Declaration, 87–88, 136
Day of Indulgence, 51
Debts, forgiveness of, 238 *n*
Declaration of Independence, American, 59, 66,
  267 *n*
Delta Algebra Project, 266 *n*
Denazification, 80–84
Disciples, the twelve, 37–38, 40
Divine forgiveness, 29–30, 41–43, 53–54,
  245 *n*
Donatists, 48–49